מסורה

ArtScroll Halachah Series®

Rabbi Nosson Scherman / Rabbi Meir Zlotowitz
General Editors

The Laws of

Published by

Mesorah Publications, ltd

פתחי הלכה

KASHRUS

A comprehensive exposition of their underlying concepts and applications

by **Rabbi Binyomin Forst**

FIRST EDITION
First Impression . . . June, 1993

Published and Distributed by
MESORAH PUBLICATIONS, Ltd.
Brooklyn, New York 11232

Distributed in Israel by
MESORAH MAFITZIM / J. GROSSMAN
Rechov Harav Uziel 117
Jerusalem, Israel

Distributed in Europe by
J. LEHMANN HEBREW BOOKSELLERS
20 Cambridge Terrace
Gateshead, Tyne and Wear
England NE8 1RP

Distributed in Australia & New Zealand by
GOLD'S BOOK & GIFT CO.
36 William Street
Balaclava 3183, Vic., Australia

Distributed in South Africa by
KOLLEL BOOKSHOP
22 Muller Street
Yeoville 2198
Johannesburg, South Africa

ARTSCROLL HALACHAH SERIES®
THE LAWS OF KASHRUS

ISBN
0-89906-103-6 (hard cover)
0-89906-104-4 (paperback)

Please address any questions
or comments regarding the
contents of this volume to the author:

Rabbi Binyomin Forst
566 Oak Drive
Far Rockaway N.Y. 11691

Typography by Compuscribe at ArtScroll Studios, Ltd.

Printed in the United States of America by Noble Book Press
Bound by Sefercraft, Quality Bookbinders, Ltd. Brooklyn, N.Y.

This volume is dedicated to the memory of

מיכאל בן צבי הירש ז"ל

נפטר י"א כסלו תשנ"ב

Milton Schulman ז"ל

He was an "Ish Tamim" — a complete person.
He related to all generations and all sorts of people equally —
with selfless generosity, a caring manner and good humor.

He loved Torah — he embraced learning with an earnest enthusiasm
that inspired all who knew him.

He loved *avodah* — he was always
at morning *minyan,* never missing a day.

He embodied *gemilas chassadim* — we will never
know of the myriad of quiet kindnesses he did
for countless people — friends and strangers alike.

He was full of vitality — he lived long and accomplished much.

He was alway happy and eternally grateful to *Hashem* for his lot in life.

He gave so much of himself in every way to all who touched him
that his passing has caused a sudden vacuum in each of our lives.

He has left us a lustrous legacy of strength and compassion,
of caring and commitment, of service and faith.

He was an unassuming model of a loving father and grandfather,
loving spouse, and loving friend. And we all try to emulate him
and to live up to his legacy.

תנצב"ה

Dedicated lovingly and reverently
by his wife,

Mrs. Milton Schulman

and children,

Robert and Susan Schulman

Howard and Tzila Schulman

Fred and Cindy Schulman

and families

ב״ה

שמעון שוואב
אב״ד דק״ק
קהל עדת ישרון
נוא־יארק, נ.י.

RAV SIMON SCHWAB
736 WEST 186TH STREET
NEW YORK, N. Y. 10033

RES: 927-0498
OFFICE: 923-5936

ערב ר״ח ניסן תשנ״ב

הנה ידידי הדגול מרבבה בתורה ובי״ש אוצר כל כלי חמדה הרה״ג מהור״ר בנימין עובדי׳ פארסט שליט״א, חובר חברים מחוכם, וכבר נודע בשערים בספריו המצוינים בהלכות כשרות ובהל׳ ברכות, ואשר כבר הסכימו עליהם גדולי תורה וגדולי הוראה — וכע״ע מוציא לאור ספר חדש על הרבה עניני מאכלות-אסורות ודיני טבילת-כלים עם כמה הוספות בפרטי דינים ומראי-מקומות — והכל כתוב ללועזים בלעז בשפת-המדינה שילמדו ממנו גם פשוטי עם איך לעשות שאלת-חכם מפוסקי הלכה-למעשה. והכל נעשה בסדר יפה ובשפה ברורה, דבר דבור על אופניו — ולא באתי אלא לברכו מקרב ולב שיזכה בס״ד ויצליח מאד. וימצא חן ושכל טוב בעיני ה׳ ואדם. וכל ספריו בכלל וספר זה בפרט יהיו לתועלת לכל מבקשי-השם, וזכות הרבים תהיה תלוי׳ בו — כעתירת אוהבו ומוקירו בלב ונפש

שמעון שוואב

אברהם פאם
RABBI ABRAHAM PAM
582 EAST SEVENTH STREET
BROOKLYN, NEW YORK, N. Y.
11218

בס"ד כ"ז ניסן, י"ב למטמונים, תשנ"ג

הנה ידידי הרה"ג מוהר"ר בנימין עובדיה הלוי פארסט שליט"א המציא לי תבורו על הלכות בב"ח ותערובות, שבו מבאר יסודות ההלכה, הכללים והמושגים שההוראה תלויה בהם, וכל עקרי הדינים לפרטיהם סובבים עליהם.

המחבר כבר נודע לתהלה בחבוריו בהלכה הקודמים שהסכימו עליהם גדולי ישראל ונתקבלו בתשואות חן אצל לומדי תורה ודבר ה' זו הלכה. והנה עיינתי קצת בחיבור הנוכחי וראיתי שכולו יפה אף נעים, מבואר היטב ומסודר בטוב טעם ודעת, ומובטחני שיהי' לעזר ללומדי יו"ד ורבים יאותו לאורו.

והנני מברכו מקרב לב שיצליח בעבודתו הקודש וילך מחיל אל חיל להפיץ מעינותיו חוצה להגדיל תורה ולהאדירה, מתוך בריאות הגוף ומנוחת הנפש ושמחת לב.

אברהם יעקב הכהן פאם

אברהם יעקב הכהן פאם

ישיבה שער התורה-גרודנה
Yeshiva Shaar Hatorah-Grodno

בס"ד

Rabbi Zelik Epstein
Rosh Hayeshiva

אהרן זליג הלוי עפשטיין
ראש הישיבה

כבוד הרה"ג הנעלה מוה"ר בנימין עובדי' פארסט שליט"א שלום וברכה

עברתי על הקונטרסים ששלח לי כת"ר בעניני תערובות שהם חלק מחיבורו בהלכות או"ה שכת"ר עומד להוציא לאור בשפת המדינה. גדולי דורנו כבר סמכו ידיהם על כת"ר ועל חיבוריו שהדפיס מכבר בשם פתחי הלכה והעידו על טיב המחבר והחיבורים. וכמעשהו בקודמים כך מעשהו בזה, הצעת הענינים וניסוחם הוא מדויק זך ונקי. והשפה נקיה וברורה ובטח יהי' לברכה לאלה הצמאים לדבר ה', זו הלכה ברורה. והנני בזה בברכה שיזכה להמשיך בעבודת הקודש ולהפיץ מעינותיו חוצה לזכות בהם את הרבים ולהגדיל כבוד התורה והיראה.

בהוקרה ובידידות

אהרן זליג הלוי עפשטיין

אהרן זליג הלוי עפשטיין

ברוקלין כ"ג אייר ה' תשנ"ג

117-06 84th Avenue Kew Gardens, N.Y. 11418
(718) 846-1940

HASKAMOS GIVEN TO THE ORIGINAL HEBREW VERSION OF "HILCHOS KASHRUS" PUBLISHED BY THE AUTHOR IN 1984*

משה פיינשטיין
ר"מ תפארת ירושלים
בנוא יארק

בע"ה

בשמחה ראיתי כמה קונטרסים מהספר החשוב שהרה"ג מוהר"ר בנימין פארסט שליט"א מכוין להוציא לאור הדפוס, ואף שמחמת טרדותי המרובות וחולשת בריאותי ל"ע, קשה היה לפני לעיין הרבה בהם, וגם כידוע אני נזהר מליתן הסכמה אמיתי על ספר הלכה מאחר שבלי לעיין בכל הספר ולהגיד שההחלטות מוצדקים, מה שייך ליתן הסכמה על הדינים שיש בו, מ"מ מאד נהנתי מהמקצת שראיתי.

ובאתי בזה גם ליתן ברכתי להמחבר הנ"ל שיצליחהו השי"ת בהפרצת ספרו זה, להגדיל תורה ולהאדירה, ושיהיה באמת לתועלת הרבים, לזכות בידיעות ההלכות הנחוצות לאלו שקשה להם לעיין במקורי הדינים, ושח"ו לא יצא שום תקלה מספרו זה, שכידוע, יש חשש של מכשול על כל ספר של ליקוטי הלכות, כדביארתי בתשובותי.

ובזכות ידיעת התורה נזכה הוא וכל שאר ישראל ביחד בקרוב לגדר של "ומלאה הארץ דעה" בביאת הגואל צדק.

ועל זה באתי על החתום בז' אייר תשמ"ג בנוא יארק.

משה פיינשטיין

יעקב קמנצקי
מאנסי, נוא יארק

בע"ה

כבוד ידידי הרב הנעלה מוה"ר בנימין עובדיה הלוי פארסט נ"י שלום וברכת כ"ט.

ראיתי את חיבורו על הלכות כשרות ונוכחתי כי ב"ה עשה מלאכת שמים חשובה מאד כי הוא מסודר וכתוב בלשון ברור וטוב ומתבררים בתוכו כמה הלכות הנחוצות בענינים אלו. ואף שלא עלה בידי לעיין בכל דבריו סמכתי על חזקת חבר שלא יוציא מתחת ידו דבר שאינו מתוקן. ותקותי כי חיבורו יביא תועלת מרובה ויוסיף זהירות בהלכות איסורי מאכלות ויתן ד' שיעלה בידו להוציאו לאור ויתרבה כבוד שמים על ידו.

וע"ז בעה"ח כ"ו ימים לחדש אדר א' פה ברוקלין נוא יארק.

יעקב קמנצקי

*The current English edition is greatly expanded and contains materials not included in the Hebrew version.

Table of Contents

CHARTS

Preface

אוֹדֶה ה׳ מְאֹד בְּפִי וּבְתוֹךְ רַבִּים אֲהַלְלֶנּוּ

It is with deep gratitude to the *Ribono Shel Olam* that I present this, my second *sefer*, to the English speaking public. *Hashem* has granted me the undeserved privilege of having the first volume on *Hilchos B'rachos* printed three times and of seeing it attain widespread acceptance among the public. However, my feeling of joy is tempered with trepidation. The responsibility of authoring a *sefer* on *Hilchos Kashrus* is enormous. While writing on *Hilchos B'rachos* is a matter of mastering the *halachos* relating to *b'rachos* and applying them to current problems, writing on *Hilchos Kashrus* presents several major problems: Firstly, the subject matter is among the most involved and difficult in *Shulchan Aruch*. Secondly, placing a *halachic* handbook in the hands of the layman may tempt him to resolve *halachic* questions on his own. This should not be done. All problems regarding *kashrus* must be presented to a trained *moreh hora'ah* (a *halachic* decisor) who will weigh all of the particulars of the given circumstances and render a decision. The layman, even if learned, is usually not proficient enough in *halachah* to deal with most problems that arise. Thirdly, there are many opinions and numerous customs regarding what may or may not be done. In addition, each housewife has her tradition as to what is or is not proper. Hence, while some may feel that this work presents positions which seem too lenient, others may contend that it is too exacting and strict. Some may feel that the *halachos* are explained in too great detail, thus leading people to erroneously believe that they need not ask a *moreh hora'ah*. Others may feel that the work unfairly leaves some questions unresolved. It is for these reasons that, at several junctures during the years of preparation of this *sefer*, we considered abandoning the project. However, due to the encouragement of others and the firm belief in the necessity of this work, the project was continued. It was felt that the benefit of an awareness of the many possible problems regarding *Hilchos Kashrus* far outweighs the concern that the *sefer* will be misused. We believe that anyone reading this volume will gain an understanding of and improve his observance of the *halachos*. At the same time, the recognition of their complexity will serve as an encouragement to present any problem to a *moreh hora'ah*. Thus, with gratitude to *Hashem*, together with a fervent prayer that He enabled me to present these *halachos* correctly and competently, I offer this *sefer* to the reader.

☙ This work

This *sefer* is **not,** and should not be used as, a *halachic* manual or an authoritative collection of *halachic* decisions. The purpose of this book is to *teach*, not to resolve; to *inform*, not to decide. For this reason we have chosen to present the material in its unique form. The *sefer* teaches and explains thoroughly and gives practical guidance. The reader will find this work an invaluable aid in understanding the concepts of *Hilchos Kashrus*. Each of the principles is analyzed and explained, and its sources and logic are clearly set forth. It is only after the fundamental concepts have been fully explored that the practical applications of the *halachos* are presented. The purpose is to acquaint the reader with the underlying principles so that he may recognize a problem and present it intelligently to a *moreh hora'ah*. We have given practical guidance relating to situations in which the *halachah* is straightforward; however we avoided rendering decisions in a case that is subject to differing opinions or conditions. Rather, the reader is advised to consult a *halachic* authority. We also, provided the more advanced reader with additional source material in the footnotes so that he may research the question further. If, in the course of studying this book, any variance becomes apparent between this work and one's custom, a *moreh hora'ah* should be consulted and his ruling should be followed.

Each *halachah* is footnoted with its source in *halachic* literature or its logical basis. The reader is encouraged to refer to these footnotes since they include considerable additional information and points of interest which will broaden the scope of his understanding. In order to facilitate the learning process, each chapter or section is followed by a summary so that the reader may quickly review the principles discussed. The reader is cautioned, however, not to rely upon these reviews alone, since they cannot contain all the pertinent information. Numerous charts are included throughout the work to clarify many of the complex topics discussed. The charts, too, should be used only to understand the text, but never to render a *halachic* decision. Chapter Thirteen is unique in that it does not explain the *halachah* but rather presents an alphabetical listing of most utensils found in the modern kitchen and advises how they may be used without causing *kashrus* problems. Chapter Fourteen offers an alphabetical listing of most of the concepts used in *Hilchos Kashrus* and elaborates upon their principles and applications. The *sefer* is fully indexed so that the reader may easily find any *halachah* noted herein. Furthermore, we added an index following the order of *Shulchan Aruch, Taz, Shach* and *Issur V'heter* so that one studying these texts will be able to find practical applications of their rulings.

ACKNOWLEDGMENTS

There are many individuals to whom I owe a debt of gratitude for their assistance in producing this volume.

The SCHULMAN family: MRS. MOLLY SCHULMAN and her children, DRS. ROBERT and SUSAN, HOWARD and TZILA, FRED and CINDY and their families have dedicated this *sefer* in loving memory of their husband and father, MR. MILTON SCHULMAN ז״ל. May this *sefer* and those who study it bring merit to his memory. I was personally acquainted with Mr. Schulman and knew him as a warm person, deeply committed to *yiddishkeit*. His children reflect his love for Torah and they dedicate time from their busy schedules for *limud haTorah*. Howard, or Howie as we affectionately call him, has attended our weekly *shiur* with diligence for over a decade. May the grandchildren continue in their path and bring much true *nachas* to their parents and grandmother.

MRS. YOCHEVED NISSAN reviewed and edited the entire manuscript. Her grammatical knowledge and literary skills were most instrumental in enriching the quality and clarity of this volume.

MR. JONATHAN RIKOON took time from his busy schedule to edit the entire volume. His comments and corrections contributed greatly to enhance the readability of this book.

RABBI JOSHUA SCHWAB, my dear brother-in-law, reviewed most of the manuscript for *halachic* accuracy. His learned and concise comments led me to revise the text on many occasions. In addition he served as my vehicle to transmit questions to HAGAON R' YOSEF SHOLOM ELIASHIV and seek his advice. Nevertheless, final responsibility for the *halachos* presented herein rests upon the author alone.

REB AVROHOM YEHUDAH, my dear son, also reviewed sections of the manuscript and offered many thoughful and useful *halachic* comments.

I am also greatly indebted to the following individuals who were most helpful with *halachic* comments; RABBI AVROHOM KLEINKAUFMAN, RABBI FEIVEL COHEN, RABBI MOSHE BROWN, RABBI SHMUEL FELDER and RABBI YAAKOV FORCHHEIMER.

RABBI MOSHE WEINBERGER, kindly edited and contributed to the introduction and MR. MARK SALAMON helped me with some of the technical aspects involving kitchen appliances.

I am grateful to the Torah Academy for Girls, Bais Yaakov High School of Long Island and to its *menahel*, my dear friend RABBI MOSHE WEITMAN. My years of association with the school as its *Halachah* teacher was the major stimulus to author *seforim* in practical *halachah*. I also extend my sincerest thanks to RABBI MEIR ZLOTOWITZ and RABBI NOSSON SCHERMAN for undertaking to publish this work and for their many helpful suggestions; to RABBI MOSHE LIEBER who supervised the entire project in general and contributed substantially to the overview; to RABBI SHEAH BRANDER for enhancing the beauty of this volume with his graphic skills; to the ArtScroll editorial and typesetting staff: MRS. ETHEL GOTTLIEB, CHAYA GITTY ZAIDMAN, ELI KROEN, MRS. BASSIE GUTMAN, NICHIE FENDRICH, and MINDY KOHEN.

Above all, my deepest feelings of gratitude are extended to my dear parents MR. and MRS. SIEGMUND FORST and my parents-in-law RABBI and REBETZIN MORDECHAI SCHWAB. Their years of self-sacrifice, devotion, inspiration and encouragement have guided and inspired me in all my endeavors. I pray to *Hashem* that He grant them many healthy years to derive true *nachas* from their children, grandchildren and great-grandchildren.

I could never adequately express my gratitude to my wife MILKA. This work would not have been possible without her sacrifice and encouragement. May it be *Hashem's* will that we merit much *nachas* from our children: AVROHOM YEHUDAH and CHAVIE, DEVORAH and YOEL WEINBERGER, RIVKY and MESHULEM EPSTEIN, CHANY, YISROEL, NECHAMA and YONA, and our grandchildren: MIRIAM and ROCHEL FORST, DOVID WEINBERGER and YONI EPSTEIN. May He grant our sincerest desire that they follow in the path of their forebears — one of dedication to Torah and *yiras shomayim*.

Sivan 5753 / June 1993
Far Rockaway, New York

Binyomin Forst

Overview

רָאוּי לָאָדָם לְהִתְבּוֹנֵן בְּמִשְׁפְּטֵי הַתּוֹרָה הַקְּדוֹשָׁה וְלֵידַע סוֹף עִנְיָנָם כְּפִי כּוֹחוֹ . . .

It is appropriate that one meditate, according to his intellectual capacity, regarding the laws of the Torah to understand their deeper meaning. Those laws for which he finds no reason and knows no purpose should nevertheless not be treated lightly.

(*Rambam Hilchos Me'ilah* 8:8)

⧼ Reason or Faith

Throughout the ages Torah observant Jews followed the dictates of Torah as a matter of basic faith. That is as it should be. Our adherence to the Torah and its laws cannot be dependent upon our finding them satisfactory. This is the principle of *naaseh v'nishma* ("we accept to do and we will hear") the declaration of commitment which preceded the receiving of the Torah itself. Acceptance of this principle, unconditional commitment to the will of Hashem, is the prerequisite to acceptance of the Torah (See *Shaarei Teshuvah* 2:10). One who puts the commandments of Hashem under scrutiny before unreservedly assuming their fulfillment is essentially not accepting the dictates of Hashem but rather those of his own intellect. He recognizes no higher authority than that of his judgment. As Rabbeinu Yonah so poignantly states "For if a servant says to his master, 'I will do all that you tell me except one thing,' he has shed the yoke of his master and does what is fitting in his own eyes" (*Shaarei Teshuvah* 1:6). Acceptance of the Torah entails subordination to its laws regardless of whether or not we can intellectually comprehend their logic or emotionally identify with them.

This being so, any examination of the meaning of *mitzvos* seems superfluous. Why bother explaining something that requires no rationalization. The fact that Hashem commands us to perform a *mitzvah* is reason enough, indeed the only reason, that the *mitzvah* must be carried out. Nevertheless, *Rambam's* ruling clearly states that not only is one permitted to meditate upon the meaning of the *mitzvos*, it is appropriate to do so.

Herein lies a dilemma. Granted that we should ponder the *mitzvos*, but isn't this ultimately an exercise in futility? Can the finite mind of man actually grasp the infinite wisdom hidden within each *mitzvah*? Surely, any interpretation that we may offer is a product of human understanding. Can our limited faculties comprehend and encapsulate the true meaning of the Divine *mitzvah*? Perhaps we need to re-examine the purpose of attempting to understand *mitzvos*.

◆§ Quantifying the Eternal

Mitzvos need no explanation. Our Sages teach "One who [in referring to the *mitzvah* of *shiluach haken* (the chasing away of the mother bird before taking her eggs or chicks)] says: "even young birds merit your kindness" is silenced (*Mishnah B'rachos* 5:3).

The purpose of understanding a *mitzvah* is not to comprehend what is accomplished with the *mitzvah* but rather to perceive the lessons to be drawn from the *mitzvah*. Hashem does not need us to care for His creatures, He has countless means at His disposal. The purpose of the *mitzvah* of *shiluach haken* is that we internalize feelings of compassion (see *Ramban, Devarim* 22:6). Thus, when we investigate the reason behind any of the *mitzvos* it is not to explain the mitzvah but to discover what we may draw from it. The understanding of the rationale of the *mitzvah* elevates its performance from a mere physical act to an act that makes a spiritually significant impact on our lives.

Since any theory or explanation advanced as a rationale for a *mitzvah* is merely conjecture, one can never draw *halachic* conclusions from any interpretation of a *mitzvah*, even one presented by earlier authorities. As valid as any interpretation may be, it certainly does not reflect the complete spectrum of the meaning of the *mitzvah*. Just as the Torah itself is infinite, so too is each of its *mitzvos*. Yet, simultaneously, since we are enjoined to ponder the meaning of *mitzvos*, any hypothesis about their rationale, congruent with the known principles of Torah guidelines, is valid and enhances the effect of the *mitzvah* upon man.

Furthermore, one should never be tempted to detach the moral lesson of the *mitzvah* from its performance. One may feel that once he has penetrated the meaning of the *mitzvah* and drawn from it inspiration and wisdom, he may neglect the actual performance of the *mitzvah* ritual. This is incorrect. As the *Ramban* (*Emunah U'bitachon,* Chapter 19) teaches: If one experiences a spiritual awakening he must concretize it if it is to have any permanence. It is insufficient to be a good Jew in heart or mind. Torah is a *Toras Chaim*, a Torah of life, and all its exalted ideas must find active expression and actualization in daily life. The obligation to keep the *mitzvos* is therefore independent of any understanding of them. One who performs a *mitzvah* without any thought of its meaning has nevertheless fulfilled his obligation, albeit in a diminished form, while one who contemplates and internalizes, but ignores the *mitzvah* act, has in no way discharged his responsibility and remains liable for a sin of omission and its accompanying penalty. The principle of *naaseh v'nishma* does not only mean that we accept the Torah without preconditions, but also that *nishma*, the hearing and understanding of the *mitzvah* follows and is secondary to the *naaseh*, its actual fulfillment. Internalizing the *mitzvah* is only meaningful when coupled with the performance of the *mitzvah*. This is in tandem with the axiom of *Pirkei Avos* (3:12) "Anyone whose wisdom exceeds his good deeds — his wisdom will not endure." Just as the fire of the candle cannot exist without a wick on which to kindle, so the most profound and exalted concepts contained in the Divine wisdom of *mitzvos* must find physical expression in order to be sustained.

☙ Taam – Reason and Taste

Mitzvos generally may be classified into two separate categories: *Chukim*, laws whose underlying rationale remains an unknown entity to the human being and *mishpatim*, those to whose reason man has been made privy, allowing him an awareness of the positive impact they have on society at large and on the individual's personal quality of life. (See *Rambam*, ibid.)

In Scriptures the basic portion of food necessary for minimal human survival is called *lechem chuki* (*Mishlei* 30:8) from the word *chok* (statute). Just as one's nutritional needs may be met even via intravenous feeding, so too the minimal purpose and goal of *mitzvos* is more than sufficiently provided by the mere physical act of *mitzvah* fulfillment, which is in itself a show of subservience to the Almighty. Doing a *mitzvah* even without knowing its meaning provides us with our basic spiritual sustenance requirements.

Yet, just as one has little appetite for nourishment imbibed in such a fashion and does not relish such tasteless food, so too the sense of excitement, intellectual identification and emotional attachment that should be part and parcel of doing a *mitzvah* is extremely difficult to achieve without knowing its reason.

It is for this reason that *taam* has a dual meaning: *taste and reason.* The *reason* makes the *mitzvah* appetizing and "tasty" to the heart and mind so that not only the body but the totality of the Jew — body, mind, soul and emotions — serve Hashem, in fulfillment of the words of King David, "All my limbs will say 'Hashem who is like You?' " (*Psalms* 35:10).

It is with this in mind that we approach the task of investigating the *mitzvos* of *kashrus*.

◈ Medicine for the Body or Salve for the Soul?

There have been attempts made to attribute the laws of *kashrus* to reasons of health. These ideas were expressed by no less an authority than *Rambam* in his *Moreh Nevuchim* (Part III, Chapter 48). According to *Rambam*, all foods forbidden by the Torah are unwholesome and unhealthy.

Most other traditional scholars have rejected this theory outright. *Abarbanel* (*Vayikra* 11), argues that attributing the laws of *kashrus* to medicinal reasons, makes the Torah a mere medical text. This is obviously not the case as there are many poisonous herbs that are not prohibited by the Torah. If the purpose of *kashrus* is no more than a health issue, why were these herbs not included in its prohibitions? Furthermore, non-Jews who eat all the foods forbidden to us appear no less healthy than Jews who abstain from these foods. A similar argument is made in *Sefer Akeidas Yitzchok* (60), which also strongly criticizes *Rambam's* view. If in fact the laws of *kashrus* were based on health, the Torah would not distinguish between Jew and non-Jew, as the Psalmist (145:9) declares "His mercies are on all His works." Why were the laws of *kashrus* not incorporated into the seven Noahide laws? *Abarbanel* notes the fact that the Torah uses the word *tamei* in regard to prohibited foods; the word "tamei" signifies spiritual defilement not physical harm. Obviously, *Abarbanel* concludes, the *mitzvos* are not intended to heal bodies and provide for their material welfare but to heal the soul and cure its illnesses.

Perhaps *Rambam* wrote these theories (as is the case with much of the *Moreh*) only as a means of explaining the Torah to those who were steeped in Aristotelian philosophy. He apparently did not believe these reasons to be primary considerations. *Ramban* also cites the medical aspect merely as a secondary factor, as is apparent from his commentary to *Vayikra* 11:13 and *Devarim* 14:3. Indeed, it is highly implausible to attribute the laws of *kashrus* to medical and health reasons. The Torah is the word of G-d, eternal and inviolable. To relegate the *mitzvos* to medical reasons robs them of these qualities. Medical knowledge is an evolving science which is refutable, while Torah is objective and immutable truth. To attribute *kashrus* to explanations that may be disproved is defining the eternal with the temporal, a rather stilted equation.

☙ Consecrated Consumption

One of the most recurrent activities, and at times overwhelming responsibilities, of any observant Jew is eating. The Torah places extreme emphasis upon all aspects of eating. The food itself and the manner in which it is eaten is microscopically scrutinized by the Torah and *Chazal*. In *Kabbalistic* and *Chassidic* schools of thought *"achilah b'kedushah"* — (consecrated consumption), plays an extremely important role in one's service of *Hashem*.

R' Tzadok HaKohen of Lublin writes that the primal desire of man is to eat of the forbidden. Adam and Chava succumbed to that desire, and as a result it has remained pre-dominant in the human psyche since that eventful day. The overwhelming sway of this desire dawned upon Adam when God confronted him with his treason. "The woman whom You gave to be with me, she gave me of the tree and I ate" (*Bereishis* 3:12). While the meaning of the word וָאוֹכֵל is, *and I ate*, the form literally means, *and I will eat*. The Midrash (*Bereishis Rabbah* 19:22) explains this as a new awareness that dawned on Adam. At the moment of truth he realized how powerful a current had now been unleashed. He knew that he would eat the forbidden again, because food and its pursuit were now an intrinsic part of his "nature." Thus it was through "eating" that man emerged from *Gan Eden* into the darker world of sinfulness.

The night of the fifteenth of Nissan celebrates the birth of the "revised" and "corrected" version of humanity — *Knesses Yisrael* — the Jewish nation. For this reason their initiation to *kedushas Yisrael* — the sanctity of Israel — occurs by means of consecrated consumption. The *mitzvah* of eating the *Korban Pesach* (Passover sacrifice), as well as the numerous other food-related *mitzvos* delegated to the holiday of Pesach, are indispensable in the formation of the "second edition" of man. Through *achilah b'kedushah* man's primal desire and basic flaw is redirected toward a higher purpose. This is the beginning of the corrective process.

Why is it that the focal point of man's free choice revolves around *achilah*?

Food — The Focus of Conflict

On the most basic level the act of eating facilitates the remarkable fusion of body and soul. Man is defined as an earthbound creature who has the potential to reach heaven. It is through the life sustaining process of eating that the "dust of the earth" is transformed into "a living soul." צַדִּיק אוֹכֵל לְשׁוֹבַע נַפְשׁוֹ (*Mishlei* 13:25), the *tzaddik* (righteous individual) eats for the purpose of satiating the soul. Man is unique in his stature as a creation combining the lowest and simplest in nature — earth, and the most sacred and spiritual — the Divine itself. Man in his physical body shares the nature of the animal kingdom but his soul reflects the heavenly angels. The goal of the human experience is to subdue the beast in man and to live one's life in accordance with a standard unique to humans alone. The goal of a Jew goes beyond that: to bring holiness from the soul to the body, to raise the mundane to a level of spirituality, and to sublimate and transform the temporal into the sublime.

"The heavens belong to Hashem and the earth was given to man" (*Psalms* 115:16). Said the *Chiddushei HaRim "and the earth was given to man* — to turn it into heaven." At the same time however, the animal in man wishes to overpower and rule over the spirit, to make heaven into earth. Thus, life is a struggle between the animalistic and spiritual aspects of man.

In essence human existence is a partnership between body and soul in which each "partner" seeks controlling interest. All the vicissitudes of man's life — his triumphs and failures, ascents and descents — are linked to this ongoing struggle. The ultimate victory is achieved when man, who rules over the animal kingdom, can subdue and transform the animal within himself.

Thus, the act of eating, which grants life to the human being, is itself the point of fusion between the spiritual and physical. It is the place where the combatants engage, where the ongoing struggle to forge a productive relationship between the physical and the spiritual is at its fiercest. Since eating, more than any other *mitzvah* brings about the integration of these two opposing forces, it stands forever at the crossroads of life (See *Ruach Chaim* 3:3).

Perhaps this helps to explain why the *Zohar* refers to the time of eating as a "time of war." This primal desire is the "front line" in the ongoing battle for primacy between body and soul. This may explain the connection between the words *lechem* (bread) and *locheim* (warrior).

◆ Strategies for Sanctity[1]

In the battle for supremacy of the spiritual, two strategies are available to man. Man may either practice abstinence, seeking to totally decimate the innate desire for consumption, or he may seek to redirect and focus that inclination by sublimating it to a higher purpose.

The Talmud (*B'rachos* 8b) describes the halachic obligation to eat on the eve of Yom Kippur. "He who eats on the ninth [of Tishrei] is considered to have fasted on the ninth and the tenth" (Yom Kippur occurs on the tenth). The Sages seem to infer that eating on the ninth is itself deemed, independent of the Yom Kippur fast, as two days of fasting. Why would eating be considered more sanctified than abstinence. Is not Yom Kippur the holiest day of the year?

The underlying idea is that everything God created has an integral role in the Heavenly symphony. All of Creation sings to God, and man is the master conductor. The non-eating of Yom Kippur is risk-free, but the greater glory of Hashem is served on *Erev* Yom Kippur, when man eats in a sanctified *mitzvah* fashion. Rather than excluding consumption from the Godly symphony, we set a tone whereby food adds to its harmonious melody.

Rabbi Yehudah HaNasi the redactor of the Mishnah is the prototype of this approach to life. Of his own life he said "I have not derived any pleasure in this world, never having tasted any delicacies" (*Kesubos* 104a). This is a rather intriguing statement considering the Talmud's statement regarding his extreme wealth: that all seasonal foods were to be found at his table during both winter and summer (*Avodah Zarah* 11a). This type of conspicuous consumption would seem to be the antithesis of *kedushah*, and yet he is known for posterity as *Rabbeinu HaKadosh* (our holy Rabbi) due to his extreme piety and holiness.

Perhaps we need to free ourselves of foreign ideas and focus on a Torah definition of *kedushah* in order to resolve this seeming anomaly.

◆ People of Holiness

The Kotzker Rebbe explains the verse, "People of holiness you shall be for me" (*Shemos* 22:30) not as an exhortation to be angels, devoid of

---

1. Much of this section is based upon the ideas of R' Tzadok HaKohen of Lublin

any darker side, but rather to be *people* of holiness, fully human yet totally sanctified. *Kedushah* means not abstinence but rather full participation in all facets of life albeit without any pursuit of personal pleasure. God is not looking for angels; of those He has no lack. It is human beings, with all their frailties and foibles, living on an inspired and exalted plane, that give the Almighty endless pleasure.

It is in this sense that *Rambam* calls the section of his *Mishneh Torah* that deals with the laws governing morality in relationships and the laws of *kashrus* — *Kedushah* (holiness). True *kedushah* is extending the spirit of Hashem and the enhancement of His honor to the areas of life which are most prone to egoistical pleasure-pursuit and hedonism.

Rebbi Yehudah HaNasi had a table filled with the finest of gastronomic delights yet he could honestly attest about his own lifestyle, "I derived no personal pleasure whatsoever." All of his eating was solely for *mitzvah* purposes, in order to sustain a body that carries a soul — Hashem's instrument in implementing His will in our world. This is the true *kadosh*, a real live person vibrantly living an exalted existence.

In a similar vein the Midrash (*Vayikra Rabbah* 34) characterizes Hillel the Elder. Whenever Hillel the Elder took leave of his students to go home for his meal they would accompany him. They asked him, "Rebbi, where are you going?" to which he replied, "to show kindness to the guest in my house." "But master do you have a guest every day?" they inquired. He answered "Isn't the soul but a guest in the body? The body remains in this world while the soul is like a guest — here today, gone tomorrow — moving on to the World to Come."

Hillel came to teach his students the proper approach to what could become a hedonistic obsession. Man in this world is like a guest at an inn. The horses are already hitched to the wagon, ready to leave. There is no time for anything more than a quick bite, a snatched drink — and off on the road.

The message of Hillel was that food is a medium with which to show kindness to the soul — by giving it life. Therefore "Eat to live — don't live to eat!"

☙ Timtum Halev

It was said among the students of Rabbi Yishmael "sin dulls the heart, as it says "do not make yourself *tamei* through them (prohibited species) lest you shall become contaminated through them." Do not read it *"venitmeisem"* וְנִטְמֵתֶם, (you shall become contaminated) but as *"venitamtem"* וְנִטַמְתֶּם (you shall become dull hearted) [*Yoma* 39a]. (The word *"venitmeisem"* is written without the *aleph*, hence it may be read differently.)

The issue of *kashrus*, in light of the above, is at the core of the struggle. The food one eats has a profound impact upon one's nature. Modern medicine has only recently discovered that the DNA present in every cell controls the nature of that organism. Similarly, every cell possesses a spiritual nature which is carried through the food chain. One who eats any particular animal ingests its nature and characteristics as well. The fact that this is not recognized by current medical knowledge is of no moment. Science has only begun to scratch the surface of the mysteries of the human body and knows little of the unquantifiable spirit. It requires no great leap of faith to speculate that in due time science will discover the truth that we have accepted as faith for three thousand years.

Hence, food is central to the struggle between the animal instincts in man and his soul. Certain foods strengthen the animal traits. Vegetative matter has no character and cannot affect man in any way. Animal matter, however, carries the nature of the animal and may be harmful to the spirit of man by influencing and strengthening his own animal traits or imparting to him a harmful nature. Ingestion of animal matter may affect a Jew adversely through absorption of debasing and defiling elements which will corrupt his soul. Absorption of these carriers of corruption will make it most difficult to grow in sanctity and closeness to *Hashem* through the ascendancy of soul and the transformation of the body. It is no wonder that all vegetative species are permitted by Torah law. These have no *nefesh* or character that can be absorbed by one who eats them. Indeed, the animals permitted by the Torah are all ruminators that subsist on vegetative matter alone. Thus the food chain is one of simple foods that cannot affect man in a significant manner. Species of animal and fowl that are carnivorous are those forbidden by the Torah, since one who eats of their meat will be influenced by their cruel nature. While we cannot expect to understand why each of the forbidden species is prohibited, we can understand and accept that *Hashem*, who created all these species, understands their nature and prohibited those that may impact negatively in a spiritual sense. [For further study see *Horeb* by Rabbi Samson Raphael Hirsch (chapter 68) and commentary to *Vayikra* by Rabbi Dovid Zvi Hoffmann (vol. #I p. 310).]

◆§ Triumph of the Soul

> "For not by bread alone does man live rather through the word of God does man live"
>
> (*Deuteronomy* 8:3).

In all of Creation it is through the word of God that all was brought into being and it is His utterance that sustains the existence of all that He wrought (see *Psalms* 33:6). It is the inherent word of God, the sustaining pulse of all of existence, which is imparted to man through the vehicle of food. This is what provides man with life.

In food of a forbidden nature it is the negative that controls and subverts the nature of man. The laws of *kashrus* regulate human intake, allowing the spiritual life-giving element in food to connect with all that is Divine in man.

The *Baal HaTanya* writes that all forbidden foods receive their vitality from the lowest, most evil forces in Creation. They are completely imprisoned and bound (*assur*) by the forces of negativity and are for this reason called *ma'achalos assuros* — forbidden foods. Thus, if one ingests these foods unwillingly, even with the intent that they provide him with the strength to serve his Maker — nevertheless the vitality contained therein is entrapped by the evil and can make no contribution toward energizing man in his search for the spiritual.

Permitted foods are referred to as *devarim mutarim*, for their vitality is unbound and unleashed (*muttar*) in order to propel man in his quest upward (see *Tanya* Chapters 6-7).

> If one looks more deeply into the matter one will see that the world was created for man's use. In truth, man is at the center of a great balance. For if he is drawn after the world and is distanced from his Creator he becomes ruined and ruins the world with him. However if he exercises self-control and cleaves to his Creator, using the world only as an aid in service of the Almighty, he is uplifted and uplifts the world with him. . . And if he shall be the warrior, victorious on all fronts, he will be the man of perfection meriting to cleave to his Creator, to leave the corridor and enter the palace to bask in the radiance of life (R' Moshe Chaim Luzzato, *Mesilas Yesharim*, Ch. 1).

CHAPTER ONE

מַאֲכָלוֹת אֲסוּרוֹת

Non-Kosher Foods

- □ An examination of the various types of non-kosher foods.
- □ Biblically prohibited foods.
- □ Rabbinically prohibited foods.
- □ The prohibition of eating non-kosher foods.

Introduction

The rules of *kashrus* encompassed in this work are vastly more complex than simply which foods one may eat or one may not eat. Were that the primary issue, a work of this intricate nature would be unnecessary; a simple food list would suffice. Thus, the complex nature of *hilchos kashrus* necessitates a comprehensive analysis of the fundamental issues.

Even a superficial reading of the *Shulchan Aruch* reveals that many of the most difficult and complex *dinim* of *kashrus* relate to questions of mixtures of forbidden and permitted foods. Therefore much of this work will focus on those problems.

> *The reader should be cautioned that the purpose of this work is neither to replace a moreh hora'ah, which is impossible, nor to thoroughly teach the halachos of kashrus, which can only be accomplished through years of study. One should not use this book to resolve halachic questions. This work is meant solely to acquaint the reader with the basic principles of kashrus so that he may recognize a halachic question and ask it intelligently. In addition, one who has studied these halachos from their primary sources will find this work valuable in reviewing the many difficult and complex issues in hilchos kashrus. Although the reader may expect clear resolution of all his halachic questions, as he experienced in our work on Hilchos B'rachos, he should recognize the fundamental difference between hilchos b'rachos and hilchos kashrus. The issues in hilchos b'rachos are general questions that recur regularly. One who masters the basic theories can easily apply them to most circumstances. Hilchos kashrus, however, is governed by hundreds of principles that overlap one another. Most questions require the knowledge of rules regarding many different aspects of the issue. These may vary from case to case, resulting in entirely different rulings even in very similar situations. The average layman is unequipped to render halachic decisions regarding these questions, and so it should be. These problems rightfully belong in the domain of a capable halachic authority. Thus, the reader should not expect to find the solution to every kashrus question that may arise in his kitchen. He will, however, find a concise explanation of the issues and rules. Those questions that are relatively straightforward will be adequately discussed and guidance will be given. Those questions that may*

vary depending upon the individual case will be explained in a more general manner.

The first step in studying *hilchos kashrus* is to identify different types of forbidden foods *(ma'achalos asuros)*, their origin and their basis. Only then can we begin to understand the myriad factors and components that are the very fiber of *hilchos kashrus*.

The prohibition of foods may be divided in three groups: a) those prohibitions of direct Biblical origin, b) those Rabbinical prohibitions predicated by concern lest one transgress a Biblical prohibition, and c) those prohibitions entirely of Rabbinic derivation. This work relates primarily to the Biblical prohibitions of cooked meat and dairy foods and those Rabbinic prohibitions rooted in the concern that one may transgress the Biblical prohibitions. We will not study, in this volume, other Biblical prohibitions such as the prohibition of eating non-kosher meats or other Rabbinic prohibitions based on Biblical prohibitions such as the laws of *chalav akum* (non-Jewish milk) or the prohibition of *gevinas akum* (non-Jewish cheese). Nor will we examine Rabbinic ordinances such as the laws of *pas akum* (non-Jewish bread) and *bishul akum* (non-Jewish cooking) which are entirely of Rabbinic derivation. We hope, please G-d, to examine those *halachos* in the following volumes of this work. In this chapter, we will explore the general principles that govern *all* the laws of *kashrus*, whether of Biblical or Rabbinic origin. The following two issues will be discussed:

□ Various types of prohibited foods.
□ The amount and type of eating that is prohibited.

I. Types of prohibited foods

It is necessary to identify the various types of non-kosher foods before we can even begin to study their *halachos*. Some of these foods will be mentioned in the following chapters, while some are not within the scope of this work.

A. Biblically prohibited foods — primary prohibitions

1) *Beheimah temeiah*, בְּהֵמָה טְמֵאָה — non-kosher animals:
The Torah[1] forbids us to eat any land animal (or the milk of

1. *Vayikra* 11:3-8.

that animal[2]) that does not have two distinctive *simanim* (signs, indications) that attest to its *kashrus*. The animal must both chew its cud (ruminate) and have completely cloven hooves.[3] Cows, goats, sheep, deer, bison, gazelle, antelope, ibex, addax and giraffe are animals that have both of these characteristics and are considered *beheimah tehorah* ("clean"), kosher animals[4] and need not be inspected individually.[5] A pig does not chew its cud although it has split hooves. A camel chews its cud but has no split hooves. Both of these animals (and certainly an animal possessing neither of the *simanim*, e.g., a donkey or horse) are therefore considered *beheimah temeiah* — ("unclean") non-kosher animals.[6] It has been noted that to this day no species have been discovered that has split hooves but does not chew its cud besides the pig. Similarly, except for the camel, *shafan* and *arneves*,[7] no species has been discovered that chews it cud but has no split hooves. These are precisely the only species cited in the Torah as having one *siman* but not the other.[8]

2. *Rambam: Hilchos Ma'achalos Asuros* 3:1. Henceforth, all references to *Rambam* are to *Hilchos Ma'achalos Asuros* unless noted otherwise.

3. See *Y.D.* 79:1 for identifying features of an animal that chews its cud.

4. In the opinion of many authorities, one may not eat any animal for which we have no tradition as to its permissibility, even though it possesses the proper *simanim* (see *Shach* 80:1, *Chochmas Adam* 36:1, *D.T.* 80:3 and *Chazon Ish: Y.D.* 11:4,5).

5. *Rambam* 1:8.

6. See *Y.D.* 79.

7. We have no tradition identifying the species of *shafan* and *arneves*. Perhaps they are extinct today. The various definitions of *shafan* and *arneves* as rabbit, hare and rock-badger, are modern Hebrew innovations and have no relation to the Biblical meaning. The llama is considered part of the camel family.

8. The Talmud *(Chullin* 60b) comments on *Moshe Rabbeinu's* incredible knowledge of the different animal species. "Was *Moshe Rabbeinu* a hunter or an archer? This refutes those who maintain that the Torah is not of Divine origin." See *Malbim (Vayikra* 11:4) who notes that the Torah endangered its credibility by listing only four animals that possess a single *siman:* the *gamal* (camel), *arneves* and *shafan* that ruminate but have no cloven hooves, and the *chazir* (pig) who possesses the single characteristic of the split hoof. He cites the Talmudic *(Chullin* 59a) conclusion that since the Torah lists only these species, apparently no other species exist that have split hooves and do not ruminate. Thus, the Talmud rules (as cited in *Shulchan Aruch* 79:1) that if one is in the desert and finds an animal with a mutilated mouth and one cannot discern whether or not it is a ruminator, he should examine whether the hooves are split. If the hooves are split and he is certain that the animal is not a pig, he may eat it. Similarly, one who finds an animal with mutilated hooves should examine its mouth to determine whether it is ruminant. If

2) *Ouf tameh,* עוֹף טָמֵא — non-kosher birds:

The Torah[9] similarly differentiates between kosher and non-kosher birds. Unlike animals, the Torah gives no *simanim* to differentiate between kosher and non-kosher birds. The Torah merely lists twenty-four types of forbidden birds; all other birds are assumed to be kosher.[10] Sinaitic oral tradition does provide signs to identify non-kosher birds.[11] However, since we lack the experience to apply these rules, we are permitted to eat only those birds[12] traditionally accepted as kosher.[13] All variations of the common chicken are accepted as kosher.[14] Similarly, common domestic ducks, geese[15] and doves are considered kosher. Many *Sefardic* communities have a tradition that the quail is a kosher fowl. With the appearance of turkeys, *Poskim* questioned whether a reliable tradition exists about their kashrus. Common custom today accepts turkeys as kosher fowl.[16] There is no definitive tradition about the status of a pheasant,[17] peacock,[18] guinea hen, partridge, swan, or

---

it is ruminant and the animal is certainly not a *gamal, arneves* or *shafan,* he may eat it. The Talmud explains: "*Hashem* is the Master of the universe. He knows that no other non-ruminating beast exists with cloven hooves besides the pig and no other ruminators with non-cloven hooves exist besides *gamal, arneves* and *shafan*". In addition, the Torah lists only ten species that have both *simanim.* Naturalists have explored every corner of the globe and have discovered many new species that were unknown to the ancients. To date, they have not discovered any new species that ruminates and has cloven hooves or possesses only one of the two characteristics. Does this not attest to the Divine origin of the Torah?

9. *Vayikra* 11:13-19.

10. *Rambam: Ma'achalos Asuros* 1:14.

11. Enumerated in Y.*D.* 82:2.

12. Or eggs of those birds (*Rambam* 3:1).

13. See Y.*D.* 82, regarding conflicting traditions. See 82:4, where *Shulchan Aruch* rules that one who finds himself in a community that has a tradition of eating a particular species of fowl may eat that species although he plans to eventually return to his own community which has no such tradition. This differs from the usual rule that one is bound to his own tradition, since, in this case, the tradition of not eating these fowl is simply for lack of a definite tradition, not a definitive tradition to treat these fowl as non-kosher (*Shach* §10).

14. See *D.T.* 82:24.

15. See *D.T.* 82:27.

16. See *D.T.* 82:26.

17. *Igros Moshe:* Y.*D.* 2:34 as opposed to *Melamed L'hoil* II:15,16.

18. See *S.D.* 82:8, *Kaf HaChaim* 82:18.

certain species of wild ducks, geese,[19] pigeons and doves;[20] therefore, they should not be eaten. The eggs of any non-kosher fowl are also forbidden to be eaten.[21]

3) *Neveilah*, נְבֵילָה — carrion:
Even a kosher animal or fowl (the laws of *neveilah* do not apply to fish[22]) may not be eaten unless it is slaughtered[23] in the prescribed manner. An animal slaughtered improperly[24] or an animal that died in any other manner is a *neveilah* and may not be eaten. The laws of *shechitah* (slaughtering) are complex and are discussed in the *Shulchan Aruch* at length.[25] The kashrus of the *shechitah* depends upon the type of knife used, its sharpness and the manner in which one performs the *shechitah*.

---

19. See *S.D.* 82:8 and Responsa *Har Tzvi: Y.D.* 75.

20. See *D.T.* 82:35.

21. Y.*D.* 86.

22. Y.*D.* 13:1.

23. Although it is not within the framework of this *sefer*, note should be taken of the controversy surrounding the question of dulling the animal's senses before *shechitah*. It is our belief that the Torah proscribed the most humane method for slaughtering an animal. It is from the Torah itself that mankind derived the concept of avoiding *tzar baalei chaim* (inflicting pain upon living creatures). It is thus peculiar that over the last hundred years many attempts, successful and unsuccessful, were made to prohibit *shechitah* as inhumane to animals. It is even more bizarre that many of these laws were instituted in the very same countries that showed themselves indifferent to Jewish blood and suffering. Anti-Semitism wears many masks. In some of these countries, *shechitah* was permitted providing the animal was stunned (either electrically or through a blow to the head) beforehand. *Halachic* authorities, however, were unanimous in their refusal to permit *shechitah* under these circumstances. Several reasons were cited: to require stunning of the animal would constitute acknowledgment that *shechitah* itself is inhumane. Acknowledgment of this untruth would constitute a grave *chilul Hashem* (desecration of Divine honor). In addition, stunning the animal may render it a *treifah*. See collected letters of R' Chaim Ozer Grodzinsky vol. II p. 732, Responsa *Sridei Eish* vol. I.

24. There are five basic disqualifications of *shechitah:* 1) *Shehiyah* (hesitation): the *shechitah* must be performed in one continuous act without hesitation. 2) *Chaladah* (a covered knife): the *shechitah* knife may not be covered with skin, feathers, wool or cloth during the *shechitah*. 3) *D'rasah* (pressing): the *shechitah* must be accomplished by the sharpness of the knife. Any undue pressure applied to the knife invalidates the *shechitah*. 4) *Hagramah* (cutting outside of the prescribed area): if the knife cuts beyond that area, the *shechitah* is invalid. 5) *Ikur* (uprooting): if the trachea and esophagus are uprooted from their place in the animal's neck before completion of the *shechitah*, the *shechitah* is invalid.

25. Y.*D.* chapters 1 through 26.

Any improper pause[26] or undue pressure[27] during the *shechitah* act or the use of a knife with an imperfect cutting blade[28] are among the conditions that render the animal a *neveilah*. Due to the complexity of these *halachos* and the severe transgression involved in eating *neveilah*, only a G-d fearing *shochet* (ritual slaughterer) who has proven his knowledge of these *halachos* and ability to do *shechitah* properly is accepted as a *shochet*.[29] It is customary to require a prospective *shochet* to receive a "*kabalah*" (certification) from a recognized *halachic* authority attesting to his ability, knowledge,[30] piety and trustworthiness.[31]

4) *Treifah*, טְרֵיפָה — mortally injured:[32]
Any animal or fowl[33] which, as a result of a birth defect, disease or inflicted wound, suffers from a mortally defective organ or limb (or an animal close to death[34]) may be considered a *treifah*. These defects are enumerated by *Chazal*[35] based on Sinaitic tradition. A defect not listed by *Chazal* does not render the animal a *treifah* even if according to current medical knowledge the animal is certain to die shortly.[36] Conversely, a defect that is listed by *Chazal* renders the animal *treifah* regardless of current medical opinion.[37] For example: an animal lacking certain organs, an animal with certain organ walls perforated or certain bones fractured is considered a *treifah*. Thus, even if

---

26. Y.D. 23.

27. Y.D. 24.

28. Y.D. 18.

29. Y.D. 1:1.

30. *Rema:* Y.D. 1:1.

31. *D.T.* 1:44.

32. See *Rambam* 4:6-8, that although *treifah* literally means an animal assaulted by a wild animal and mortally injured, the *halachos* of *treifah* apply regardless of the source of those injuries.

33. The laws of *treifah*, however, do not apply to fish.

34. Regardless of whether this is as a result of sickness, old age and frailty, the animal may be considered a *treifah*. The pertinent rules are discussed in Y.D. 17. However, many sages refrained from eating an animal close to death even when *halachically* permitted (Y.D. ibid., see also *Rambam* 4:11,12).

35. See a list in *Rambam: Hilchos Shechitah* 10:11.

36. *Rambam* ibid. 10:12. See also *Chazon Ish:* Y.D. 5:3.

37. *Rambam* ibid. 10:13.

one slaughters a kosher animal properly, it may nevertheless be unkosher to eat if it is afflicted by any of these injuries. Although every animal and fowl is assumed to be free of any of these injuries[38] and need not be examined,[39] the lung[40] of an animal[41] must be examined after slaughtering to ascertain that the animal suffers no abnormality that renders it a *treifah*. This examination is called "*bedikah*" or "*bedikas ho'reiah*"[42] These *halachos* are discussed at great length in *Shulchan Aruch: Yoreh De'ah.*[43] The rules of *treifah* are of great relevance in the slaughtering house but rarely affect the Jewish home since most meats are delivered prepared and packaged. One must, however, be aware of certain rules of *treifus* as they affect the *kashrus* of fowl, since one may purchase a complete fowl that has broken limbs. One who notices a broken wing or leg or a discolored drumstick should consult a *moreh hora'ah.*

5) *Sheretz,* שֶׁרֶץ — swarming insects and rodents:
The Torah[44] prohibits us from eating any rodents, worms, amphibians or creeping, swimming or flying insects.[45] One who eats fruits or vegetables in which worms, ants or mites are commonly found must examine the fruit carefully before eating.[46] One type of insect, however, is permitted. The Torah[47] describes the features of certain species of locust that are

---

38. If there is reasonable suspicion that the animal may be a *treifah*, it must be checked (*D.T.* 39:6).

39. *Y.D.* 39:1, *Shach* §1. See *Igros Moshe: Y.D.* 1:19, as to whether a simple superficial examination is required.

40. *Y.D.* ibid.

41. See *Rambam: Hilchos Shechitah* 11:12.

42. The lungs are examined for the presence of any *sirchah* (adhesions). A lung found free of adhesions is called "*chalak*" (smooth) or "*glatt*" in Yiddish. Hence, the term "glatt kosher." A lung containing adhesions must be checked by a competent *bodek* (ritual inspector) or shown to an experienced *moreh hora'ah* to ascertain whether the animal is kosher or a *treifah*. If the adhesions are of the type that do not render the animal a *treifah*, the animal is kosher but not "glatt." Today, the term "glatt" is popularly used to describe a more punctilious standard of kashrus, not relating necessarily to lung adhesions.

43. Chapters 29 through 60.

44. *Vayikra* 11.

45. Insects that are visible only through a microscope are not prohibited (*Yechaveh Daas* 6:47).

46. *Y.D.* 84:8.

47. *Vayikra* 11:21.

permitted; these are enumerated in *Shulchan Aruch*.[48] However, today we lack a definite tradition about which species are allowed and therefore do not eat locust.[49] Certain *Sefardic* communities do have a tradition as to which locust are kosher.

6) *Dag tameh,* דָּג טָמֵא — non-kosher fish:
The Torah[50] permits only those fish that have fins and scales; any other fish is prohibited. Some fish have very small scales[51] and still others lose their scales upon being removed from the water; they are, nevertheless, permitted.[52] Swimming creatures that are not fish (i.e., sea horse or squid) are included in the prohibition of *sheretz hamayim.*[53]

7) *Dam,* דָּם — Blood:
The Torah[54] forbids eating the blood of even a kosher animal or fowl. Thus, after slaughtering, all meat to be cooked must be salted beforehand.[55] Certain organs require special treatment to rid them of their blood.[56] The liver is so permeated with blood that only broiling can remove that blood.[57] Fish blood is permitted unless it is gathered in a vessel, in which case it may be confused with animal blood and is forbidden by Rabbinic decree unless it is recognizable as fish blood (e.g., it contains fish scales).[58]

---

48. *Y.D.* 85:1.

49. *Rashi: Vayikra* 11:21, *Tur* 85, citing *Rosh, Taz* 85:1. See *D.T.* §12, who notes that (similar to the *halachah* regarding fowl cited above) one who finds himself in a community that has a tradition of identifying kosher locust may eat those locust although he plans to eventually return to his own community.

50. *Vayikra* 11:12.

51. The scales must be visible to the naked eye, albeit under optimal conditions (e.g. strong sunlight). If, however, the scales are visible only through a magnifying glass or microscope, the fish is a *dag tameh.* See *Tiferes Yisrael (Boaz: Avodah Zarah* 2:3), *Yechaveh Daas* 6:47.

52. *Y.D.* 83:1. Similarly, fish that presently have no scales but will develop them in the future, are permitted. Any fish that has scales certainly has fins. Thus, if one finds a piece of fish that has scales, one may assume that it had fins as well (*Y.D.* 83:3).

53. *Rambam* 2:12.

54. *Vayikra* 7:26,27, 17:10-12, *Devarim* 12:23.

55. *Rambam* 6:10.

56. *Y.D.* 71, 73, 74.

57. *Y.D.* 73:1.

58. *Y.D.* 66:9.

8) *Cheilev,* חֵלֶב — fats:

The fats on certain internal organs must be removed from a kosher slaughtered cattle, sheep or goat[59] before the meat may be eaten. This prohibition applies to commonly domesticated animals only *(beheimah)* (i.e., cattle, sheep and goats), not to fowl *(ouf)* or wild forest animals *(chayah)*.[60] Removal of the forbidden fats is a difficult task and must be done by a skilled expert. This process is called *nikur* and is usually done in the slaughtering house. At times, butchers themselves must do *nikur*. Thus, it is not sufficient to merely obtain meat with a proper slaughtering supervision; one must also determine that the butcher is a skilled, knowledgeable and G-d-fearing individual who does *nikur* under proper Rabbinical supervision.

9) *Gid hanasheh,* גִּיד הַנָּשֶׁה — the sciatic nerve:

The Torah[61] prohibits eating the *gid hanasheh* — the sciatic nerve in both hind thighs of any kosher land animal (domesticated or wild).[62] The difficult process of the removal of the nerve and the fat surrounding it is also called "*nikur*" and must be done with great care by a G-d-fearing skilled expert.[63] In most countries, the hind part of an animal is not eaten at all thereby avoiding entirely the difficult process of removing the prohibited fats and nerves.

10) *Eiver min hachai,* אֵבֶר מִן הַחַי — a limb from a living creature:

One may not eat a limb[64] of an animal or fowl that was removed while the animal was alive.[65] Although this prohibition does not apply to fish, one should nevertheless not eat part of a fish while the fish is alive.[66] Incidentally, the law of *eiver min hachai* is the only law of *kashrus* that applies to non-Jews as well.[67] Thus, a Jew may not provide a non-Jew with *eiver min hachai* meat since, by doing so, he assists him in

59. The fats of other animals is permitted *(Rambam* 7:1).

60. *Y.D.* 64:1.

61. *B'reishis* 32:33.

62. *Rambam* 8:1.

63. See *Rambam* 8:7.

64. If only the meat (i.e., not the bone) of a limb was cut from a living animal, the meat is considered *treifah* and covered under that prohibition instead *(Rambam* 4:10, 5:2).

65. *Rambam* 5:1.

66. *Y.D.* 13.

67. *Rambam: Melachim* 9:10.

transgressing a Torah law.[68]

11) *Tevel,* טֶבֶל — produce from which the tithes were not removed: One may not eat fruits and vegetables grown in *Eretz Yisrael* unless the required *terumos* and *maasros* were set aside.[69] It is common today that fresh fruits and vegetables (or even orange juice concentrate) are imported from the Holy Land. These fruits may not be eaten without setting aside these tithes beforehand. One should consult a *moreh hora'ah* as to the proper procedure for tithing.

12) *Orlah,* עָרְלָה — fruits of the first three years:
One who plants a fruit tree, whether in *Eretz Yisrael* or not, may not eat any produce of the first three years growth. One who replants a tree may also be required to wait three years before eating any of the fruits. A *moreh hora'ah* should be consulted. One should also consult a *moreh hora'ah* to determine when the three years have elapsed. In addition, one should inquire about the particular *dinim* of a grape vine.

13) *Chadash,* חָדָשׁ — new (fresh) grain:
The Torah prohibits eating any of the five types of grain (wheat, barley oats, spelt and rye) that took root after the sixteenth of *Nissan* until the following sixteenth of *Nissan.* There is a difference of opinion whether this Biblical prohibition applies to grains grown outside of *Eretz Yisrael.* There is, therefore, considerable controversy whether one must refrain from eating grain foods, even outside of *Eretz Yisrael,* unless one can establish that they took root before the sixteenth of *Nissan.* It is not within the scope of this work to render a *halachic* decision since different contemporary authorities have opposing views on this matter. One should consult his *moreh hora'ah* regarding the proper conduct on this subject.[70]

14) *Yayin nesech,* יַיִן נֶסֶךְ — wine of libation:
One may not drink or derive any benefit from wine that has been poured in a sacrificial manner to an *avodah zarah* — idolatry. In addition, this prohibition applies to anything served to an idol in a sacrificial manner.[71] Other non-Jewish wines are

68. *Pesachim* 22b.

69. *Rambam* 10:19.

70. See *O.C.* 489:10, *M.B.* §45, *B.H.* s.v. *"af"*.

71. *Rambam* 11:1.

forbidden through Rabbinic injunction and will be discussed below.

B. Biblically prohibited food — prohibited combinations

1) *Basar b'chalav,* בָּשָׂר בְּחָלָב — combined meat and milk:
   Although meat or milk of kosher animals is permitted, a cooked combination of meat and milk is prohibited. One may not even derive benefit from such a combination.[72] The details of this *halachah* will be discussed in Chapter Seven.
2) *Kilayim,* כִּלְאַיִם — different species grown together:
   One may not plant vegetables or grains near one another: this is called *kilaei zeraim.* One also may not plant any vegetable or grain near a grape vine: this is called *kilaei hakerem.* Two distinctions between the two are: the former is forbidden only in *Eretz Yisrael* and does not cause the produce to become prohibited. The latter applies in any country and causes the produce to become prohibited to be eaten or derive benefit *(hana'ah)* thereof.[73]

C. Foods prohibited by Rabbinic injunction

As noted above, some Rabbinic prohibitions are based on Biblical laws while some are independent of any Biblical source. Of the former, some are Rabbinical extensions of Biblical prohibitions and some are Rabbinically prohibited out of concern lest one transgress a Biblical prohibition.

1) Foods forbidden as an extension to Biblical prohibitions:
   Chazal extended the Biblical prohibition on many foods to include foods not covered by the Biblical law itself. For example:
   a) The Torah prohibition of *basar b'chalav* includes only meat and milk of a *beheimah tehorah* — a kosher domestic[74] animal (e.g., cow, sheep and goat). *Chazal*

---

72. *Rambam* 9:1.

73. See *Rambam: Hilchos Kilayim* ch. 1. The prohibition of deriving benefit from *kilaei hakerem* is Biblical in origin, while the prohibition of planting *kilaei hakerem* in other countries is Rabbinic.

74. The term "domestic" is used here as a definition of the species, not of the individual animal's characteristics. Thus, a trained domesticated pet deer is still considered a *chayah.*

extended the prohibition to include meat and milk from a *chayah* — a non-domestic animal (e.g., deer) and fowl.[75]

b) *Chazal* broadened the prohibition of *gid hanasheh* to include parts of the nerve and the fats surrounding it which are not included in the Biblical prohibition.[76]

c) The Torah prohibition of *kilaei hakerem* applies only to produce of *Eretz Yisrael. Chazal,* however, extended the prohibition to other lands as well.[77]

2) Foods prohibited lest one transgress a Biblical prohibition: According to Torah law, one may not eat any food if the likelihood exists that one may thereby come to transgress a Torah prohibition. If, however, that likelihood is not apparent or seems very far-fetched, the food may be Biblically permitted. *Chazal*, however, prohibited certain foods out of concern that eating them may cause one, even in a remote instance, to violate a Biblical law. Thus, while Biblical law does not forbid that food, Rabbinic law does. These laws will be discussed in a later volume. Examples of these foods are:

a) *Chalav Akum,* חָלָב עַכּוּ"ם — non-Jewish milk:
Milk that was not milked in the presence of a Jew is forbidden by Rabbinic injunction. *Chazal* feared that the non-Jew may have mixed non-kosher milk (i.e., milk from a non-kosher animal) into the milk.

b) *Gevinas Akum,* גְּבִינַת עַכּוּ"ם — non-Jewish cheese:
Chazal prohibited cheese made by non-Jews since their cheese is, with all probability, produced with non-kosher rennet.[78]

c) Wine touched by a non-Jew:
Chazal prohibited (even to derive benefit from) the wine of a Jew if it was touched and moved[79] (or even if it may have been touched) by a non-Jew. *Chazal* were concerned that the non-Jew may have poured some of the

---

75. *Rambam* 9:4.

76. *Rambam* 8:1.

77. *Rambam* 10:8.

78. These cheeses, however, are not prohibited by the Biblical law of *basar b'chalav* as will be explained in Chapter Two, note 66.

79. See *Shach Y.D.* 124:20 as to whether only touching the wine renders it *yayin nesech.*

wine as an offering to his *avodah zarah.*[80] These *halachos* are complex and of importance to anyone who has non-Jewish cleaning help.

3) Foods prohibited by Rabbinic law independent of any direct Biblical basis:

Certain foods were prohibited because *Chazal,* as the spiritual guardians of *Klal Yisrael,* felt that eating these foods may be harmful or affect the spiritual purity of the Jewish people, not because of any direct problem with eating that food.[81] Among these foods are:

a) *Bishul Akum,* בִּישׁוּל עַכּו״ם — non-Jewish cooking:
One may not eat food cooked by a non-Jew. *Chazal* feared that this may precipitate an inappropriately close personal relationship between Jew and non-Jew.

b) *Pas Akum,* פַּת עַכּו״ם — non-Jewish bread:
Similarly, *Chazal* prohibited eating bread baked by a non-Jew.

c) *Stam yainom,* סְתַם יֵינָם — non-Jewish wine:
One may not drink wine of a non-Jew, even if the wine was not poured to *avodah zarah.* This prohibition is also based on the concern that drinking his wine may cause a personal relationship between Jew and non-Jew.[82]

d) *Sakanah,* סַכָּנָה — dangerous foods:
Certain foods were prohibited by *Chazal* out of concern for safety.[83] Indeed, *Chazal* were more stringent regarding a *sakanah* — danger, than a prohibition.[84] Among these prohibitions is the prohibition of eating fish with meat.[85]

---

80. *Rambam* 11:4.

81. See *Rambam* 17:9.

82. This refers to a non-Jew that is not an idol worshipper. If the non-Jew is an idol worshipper one may not even derive benefit from his wine, see *Rambam* and *Kesef Mishna* 11:7. See *Rema* 123:1 regarding the fact that it is uncommon today to pour wine for *avodah zarah.*

83. See *Rambam: Hilchos Rotzeach* 11:4,5. See *Darcei Teshuvah* 116:57 and Responsa *Shoel Umashiv* II,3:122 for a discussion as to whether this is a Biblical or Rabbinic prohibition.

84. *Chamira sakanta me'isura* — a danger is more severe than a prohibition *(Chullin* 10a).

85. *Y.D.* 116:2.

Summary of Section I

☙§ Prohibited foods may be divided into two general categories:

□ Prohibitions of Biblical origin.
These can be subdivided into two groups:

1) Primary prohibitions such as non-kosher animals, fowl and fish, *neveilah* (carrion), *treifah* (a mortally injured animal or fowl), *sheretz* (swarming insects and rodents), blood, *cheilev* (certain fats), *gid hanasheh* (the sciatic nerve), *eiver min hachai* (a limb from a living creature), *tevel* (produce from which tithes were not removed), *orlah* (fruits of the first three years), *chadash* (new grain) and *yayin nesech* (wine of libation).
2) Prohibited combinations such as *basar b'chalav* (combined meat and milk) and *kilayim* (different species grown together).

□ Foods prohibited by Rabbinic injunction.
These can be subdivided into two groups:

1) Those with a Biblical basis, such as the Rabbinic extensions to the prohibition of *basar b'chalav, gid hanasheh, kilayim, yayin nesech,* and the prohibitions of *chalav akum* and *gevinas akum.*
2) Those without a Biblical basis, such as *bishul* and *pas akum* (foods cooked or baked by a non-Jew), *stam yainom* (wine of a non-Jew) and those foods considered by *Chazal* to be dangerous.

II. The prohibition of eating non-kosher food

A. A punishable transgression

According to Biblical law, one who eats non-kosher food is liable for punishment or sacrificial atonement only if the following conditions are met:

1) A *shiur,* שִׁיעוּר — the required amount:
Biblically, the act of eating is considered an *achilah,* אֲכִילָה (the Biblical definition of eating) only if one eats a *kizayis,* כְּזַיִת (a

half egg's volume — somewhat more than one fluid ounce) of that food or one drinks a *riviyis*, רְבִיעִית (somewhat more than three fluid ounces) of the forbidden liquid.[86] The *kizayis* is measured exclusive of what may remain between one's teeth. Thus, one who eats an exact *kizayis* is not liable for punishment.[87]

2) The time-span of eating:
Certainly one who eats half a *kizayis* one day and completes it the following day has not performed the act of *achilah*. The *kizayis* must be eaten in a span of time that constitutes one eating act. Sinaitic tradition has defined this to be the amount of time necessary to eat wheat bread in the volume of three (or four) eggs[88] while sitting in the most comfortable manner — *k'dei achilas pras*, כְּדֵי אֲכִילַת פְּרָס.[89] Halachic authorities assume this to be approximately four (or perhaps nine) minutes. Similarly, drinking a *riviyis* must be completed in the time span normally required to drink a *riviyis*.[90] One who does not conclude eating or drinking within the prescribed time is not liable for punishment and needs no atonement even though he violated Torah law.

---

86. One who eats (or drinks) a combination of forbidden foods (e.g., a half a *kizayis* of *neveilah* and a half a *kizayis* of a non-kosher animal) is not liable for a punishment. However, one who eats a *kizayis* combined from different types of non-kosher animals, or a combined *kizayis* of *neveilah* of different types of animals (or/and fowl) or even a combined *kizayis* of *neveilah* and *treifah* is liable for punishment (*Rambam* 4:17). In the former case the prohibitions are not similar (i.e., *neveilah* and *beheimah temeiah*), thus a *kizayis* was not eaten of any one prohibition. In the latter case the prohibitions are the same (i.e., *neveilah* of a sheep and a cow), thus a full *kizayis* of *neveilah* was eaten (the prohibitions of *neveilah* and *treifah* are similar and combine into one full *kizayis*).

87. See *Chullin* 103b and *Rambam* 14:3. However, any food remaining in one's palate (*bein hachanichim*, בֵּין הַחֲנִכַיִם) is included in the measurement of the *kizayis* (ibid.) See *Rashi* and *Rabbeinu Gershom* who define "*chanichim*" as the palate. *Rashi* explains that since one enjoys the taste of the food stuck to the palate it is included in the *kizayis* measurement. See *Mishnah B'rurah* 328:7 who defines "*chanichim*" as the gums.

88. *Rambam* 14:8.

89. *B'rachos* 41a.

90. *Rambam: Hilchos Ma'achalos Asuros* 14:9, *Hilchos Terumos* 10:3. See, however, *Raavad: Hilchos Terumos* ibid., who contends that the time span for drinking is *k'dei achilas pras*. See *Sidei Chemed* vol. 4 p. 396. There is disagreement among *Poskim* whether the time span of drinking a *riviyis* is uniform to all drinks or whether each drink has a particular time span in accordance with the drinking custom of that drink. See responsa *Maharam Shick: O.C.* 86 and *Mishneh L'melech: Hilchos B'rachos* 3:12.

3) The manner of eating:
   One of the axiomatic principles of the Torah states that any action described in the Torah refers only to that action as it is normally done. An action performed in an unnatural or unusual manner has no *halachic* validity.[91] Accordingly, one who eats a prohibited food in an unnatural manner has not transgressed Biblical law.[92] Some possible applications of this principle are:
   a) Swallowing food without chewing is considered within the criteria of natural eating.[93] However, swallowing hot, scalding food is not considered an act of eating.[94]
   b) Authorities disagree whether or not eating raw meat constitutes a natural eating act.[95]
   c) Eating foods into which repugnant matter has been added, causing it to become inedible,[96] is not considered an act of eating.[97]
   d) Gluttonous eating is not considered a natural act of eating. Thus, one who has overeaten and feels a revulsion towards food and subsequently eats non-kosher food has not transgressed a Biblical prohibition.[98] If, however, he is merely satiated but feels no revulsion

---

91. See a general discussion of this principle in *Eglei Tal* (introduction to section 3).

92. The Talmud *Pesachim* 24b states that one who eats in an unnatural manner is not liable for punishment. Although one might interpret this to mean that the offense, although not punishable, is nevertheless Biblically prohibited, it seems clear from the *Rambam: Yesodei Ha'Torah* 5:8, that it is Biblically permitted (see *Mishneh L'melech* ibid. s.v. *"avul shelo")*.

93. *Nodah B'Yehudah* I: *Y.D.* 35, *Chelkas Yoav: Y.D.* 9, as opposed to *Toras Chaim: Chullin* 120b who infers that swallowing whole food is considered unnatural eating. See, however, *Bais Ha'otzar* 153, citing *Mizrachi: Shemos* 34:26, who seems to support the view of *Toras Chaim.*

94. *Rambam* 14:11.

95. See *Minchas Chinuch* 7 and *Reshash: Menachos* 100a.

96. Even if only as a result of a repulsive odor, *Yad Yehudah* 103:2k. See, however, *D.T.* 103:7.

97. *Rambam* 14:11. If however, the food itself spoiled or rotted thereby becoming inedible, it completely loses its status as forbidden food. The ramifications of this concept and the distinction between the two concepts (i.e., the idea of an unnatural eating act vs. the idea of food losing its forbidden status) will be discussed below (see Chapter Three footnote no. 6).

98. *Yoma* 80b.

towards the food, any subsequent eating is considered a natural act of eating.[99]

These *halachos* are limited to those prohibitions in which the Torah uses any form of the word "*achilah*" — eating. Those prohibitions in which the word "*achilah*" is not used include foods eaten even unnaturally. Thus, *basar b'chalav* (meat and milk cooked together) and *kilaei hakerem* (grains grown in a vineyard) are Biblically prohibited even when eaten unnaturally.[100]

B. A Biblically forbidden, but not punishable, transgression

Although, one who eats non-kosher foods is liable for punishment only if all the requirements are met, he may have transgressed a Biblical prohibition even when those conditions are not met. For example:

a) *Chatzi shiur*, חֲצִי שִׁיעוּר — (half) less than the required amount: We noted above that one is Biblically liable for punishment only if he eats the required amount (a *shiur* within a specific time span). The Talmud[101] cites a dispute debating whether or not one is Biblically prohibited from eating less than a *shiur*. The *halachic* ruling follows the stringent opinion. Thus, even one who eats a minute amount of non-kosher food has transgressed a Biblical prohibition even though he is not liable for punishment.[102] Similarly, one who does not conclude eating the non-kosher food within the prescribed time has violated the prohibition of *chatzi shiur*.

b) *Taam k'ikar*, טַעַם כְּעִיקָר — the taste is like the essence: One who does not partake of the actual non-kosher food but merely eats a food into which a noticeable non-kosher taste is absorbed also transgresses a Biblical prohibition. Whenever sufficient non-kosher taste is absorbed into permitted food to make the taste noticeable, the permitted food assumes the prohibited characteristic of the non-kosher food. This is known by the Talmudic principle, "*taam k'ikar*" (the taste is like the essence). The principle of *taam k'ikar* and the means by which

99. *Tosfos: Pesachim* 107b s.v. "*dilma*".

100. *Rambam: Yesodei Ha'Torah* 5:8, *Chinuch* 113.

101. *Yoma* 74a.

102. *Rambam* 14:2.

taam (taste) is transmitted *(nosen taam)* from one food to another, will be discussed at length in Chapters Four and Five.

Summary of Section B

☙ One who eats non-kosher food is liable for punishment only under the following conditions:

- ☐ He eats a *kizayis* (somewhat more than one fluid ounce) of non-kosher food or a *riviyis* (somewhat more than three fluid ounces) of a non-kosher liquid.
- ☐ He eats this amount within the span of four minutes or drinks it within the time span normally required to drink a *riviyis*.
- ☐ He eats the non-kosher food in a natural manner. For example: one who eats scalding hot food, food that has become repugnant and thereby inedible, or one who eats the food in a gluttonous, repulsive manner has not committed a Biblical transgression.

Nevertheless, even one who eats less than the required amount *(chatzi shiur)* or does not complete eating the food within the prescribed time has violated Biblical law. Similarly, one who merely eats food that has absorbed a noticeable taste of non-kosher food has violated Biblical law. This concept is known as *taam k'ikar*.

CHAPTER TWO

בִּיטוּל

Nullification of Non-Kosher Foods

- □ *Bitul b'rov.*
- □ *Bitul b'shishim.*
- □ Foods that cannot become *batel.*
- □ Subsequent adjustments to the ratio.
- □ *Efshar l'sochto.*
- □ *Chatichah na'asis neveilah.*
- □ Intentional *bitul.*

Introduction

One of the fundamental issues in *kashrus* concerns the issue of *bitul* (nullification) of forbidden foods. Whenever non-kosher food becomes[1] mixed into a larger amount of kosher food, the non-kosher food becomes *batel* (nullified). We will, in this work, use the term *"bitul"* to connote nullification and *"batel"* to connote nullified, as these are the terms used in classic *halachic* literature.

Nullification of non-kosher foods is possible in two ways: *bitul b'rov* — nullification in a simple majority, and *bitul b'shishim* — nullification in a ratio of sixty to one. These two types of *bitul* correspond to two different situations of mixture. *Bitul b'rov* is the ordinary means by which the minority becomes *batel* in the majority. According to Torah law, a food has the characteristic of its majority. Thus, a food mixture of which the majority is kosher may be eaten. This method, however, can be applied only when the taste of the non-kosher food is not noticeable in the mixture. If the taste of the non-kosher food is noticeable in the mixture, the Biblical principle of *taam k'ikar* applies. Literally, this means that the taste (of the non-kosher food) is considered as (non-kosher) food itself. In effect, the kosher food assumes the prohibited characteristic of the non-kosher food and is Biblically prohibited. This concept will be explored at length in Chapter Four. The *bitul* process must therefore nullify not only the non-kosher food itself but its taste as well. Generally speaking, when the two combined foods are similar tasting (referred to in *halachic* literature as *"min b'mino"*[2] — lit., a kind in its own kind), the former method of *bitul b'rov* is applied, since no noticeable transfer of taste occurs. Whenever two foods dissimilar in taste (*"min b'sheaino mino"* — lit., a kind in another kind) are cooked together, they impart their tastes to one another and the latter method of *bitul b'shishim* is required. These two types of *bitul* will be discussed in the following sections.

Note: In the opinion of most *Poskim*,[3] when a non-

1. See Section V below, that one may not initially cause *bitul* to happen.

2. Pertaining to these *halachos*, *"min b'mino"* is defined as similar tasting foods, not foods with similar names (*Shach* 98:6, as opposed to *Rema* 98:2. While *Taz: Daf Acharon*, offers a different interpretation of *Rema*, *Poskim* follow the opinion of *Shach*, see *S.D.* 98:6). It will be noted in the course of our discussion that, pertaining to some other *halachos*, *min b'mino* is defined as foods with similar *names* (see note 44 below).

3. With the exception of *Issur V'heter* 57:15, who rules that it is a meritorious act to refrain from eating a mixture containing non-kosher food which became *batel*.

kosher food becomes *batel*, the mixture may be eaten even by the most scrupulous.[4] Indeed, some authorities soundly censure one who hesitates to eat the mixture, as this shows a heretical reservation about the effectiveness of *bitul*.[5]

I. Bitul b'rov, בִּיטוּל בְּרוֹב – nullification in a majority

These *halachos* are based on *Tur* and *Shulchan Aruch Yoreh De'ah* 109.

Whenever two similar tasting foods become mixed, the non-kosher food may become *batel*[6] in a simple majority[7] of kosher food. This is true even if the non-kosher food remains intact but is unrecognizable among the pieces of kosher food.[8] *Chazal* derived the principle of *bitul*

4. See *D.T.* 116:109 who cites opposing views on this. See also *B'nei Yisaschar: Adar* 2:7, who presents a Chassidic rationale that it is indeed a meritorious act to eat the mixture. See also *R' Zadok HaKohen: Machsheves Charurtz* p. 182.

5. See *Pischei Teshuvah* 116:10, citing the *Toras HaAsham*. He cites opposing views as well.

6. *Poskim* note that *bitul* becomes effective only after the mixture becomes known, i.e., someone noticed the fact that non-kosher food fell into kosher food. *Shach* 109:12 implies that this restriction is Biblical in origin (*Yad Yehudah* cited in *D.T.* 99:97, questions this premise). Apparently, *bitul* is not merely a technical matter, it is a Torah edict that the mixture is permitted. Thus, if no one is aware of the mixture, the Torah edict has not taken effect. See *D.T.* 99:97, 109:65, who cites a difference of opinion among *Poskim* as to whether the awareness of any Torah-observant Jew suffices or only that of the owner of the mixture.

7. Classic *halachic* sources describe *bitul b'rov* as "*chad bitrei*" one (piece mixed) into two (pieces). This seems to imply that a ratio of two-to-one is required for *bitul b'rov*. Indeed, this is the opinion of some authorities. Many *Poskim*, however, rule that a simple majority is sufficient. See *Shach* 109:6, *Chochmas Adam* 51:4 and *Pischei Teshuvah* 109:1. (The mixture must certainly contain three pieces. If only two pieces become mixed together the question of *bitul* is moot, since if we know that the *heter* was the majority we obviously know which is the *issur*. Thus, the question applies to a case of three pieces that became mixed and the two smaller pieces together contain a greater volume than the larger piece. See *S.D.* ibid. and *Minchas Kohen* II, 2:1.) See also *D.T.* 109:22, who cites opinions that in regard to a Biblical prohibition, a ratio of two-to-one is required whereas regarding a Rabbinic prohibition, a mere majority is adequate.

8. The foods need not even be mixed together or even close to one another. Indeed, even three unrecognizable pieces of meat in three different rooms or stories of a house are *batel b'rov* (*M.Z.* 109:1, *D.T.* 109:4).

b'rov from the Torah[9] mandate that one must follow the majority opinion in a court of law.[10] Just as a court verdict follows the majority opinion, so too, the characteristic of the mixture follows the majority ingredient.[11]

> *Note: This rule applies to cold, solid mixed foods. If the non-kosher food is a liquid that is blended into, or a solid cooked with, kosher food, the* halachah *varies, as will be discussed below.*

A. The underlying principle

Rishonim disagree about the underlying principle of *bitul b'rov.* In the opinion of most authorities,[12] *bitul b'rov* is based upon the simple probability that each individual piece of food that will be removed from the mixture came from the kosher majority. Others[13] contend that *bitul b'rov* is a unique principle by which the non-kosher food completely loses its identity and becomes permitted matter. The difference between these two views is enormous. According to the first opinion, perhaps one may not eat *all* the mixture since, in doing so, he certainly eats the non-kosher food as well. According to the second view, however, one may eat all the mixture, even at once, since there is no longer any non-kosher food. *Poskim* present a diversity of opinions reflecting various positions on this fundamental question. The foremost opinions are as follows:

1) In the opinion of *Rashba,*[14] *bitul b'rov* is based on the logical premise that when any part of the mixture is removed, we may assume that it has come from the majority. Thus, each piece, as eaten, is assumed to be from the permitted majority. Indeed, even the last piece may be eaten by the same person since, we may assume that it is from the majority as well. Although, eating the last piece presumes that the non-kosher food was previously eaten, the same person may[15] eat the last piece since

9. *Shemos* 23:2.

10. *Rashi: Beitzah* 3b, *Taz* 109:1, *Shach* 109:6.

11. For an in-depth analysis of the relationship of these two concepts, see *Shaarei Yosher* 3:4.

12. The opinion of *Rashba* and others, cited below.

13. *Rosh* cited below.

14. *Toras HaBayis* 4:1 and *Ran* cited in *Beis Yosef* 109.

15. There is, however, reason for one who is punctilious to avoid eating, or even giving another Jew, the last piece. See *Beis Yosef* 109 citing *Maharam.* See opinions ii) and iii) cited in text below.

it is now assumed to be kosher. *Rashba* does concede, however, that one may not[16] eat the entire mixture at once. To do so would leave no alternative other than to assume that non-kosher food is now being eaten.[17] This is the opinion *halachically* accepted by most authorities.[18]

2) Other *Rishonim*[19] contend that *one person* may not eat the entire mixture even if he were to eat each piece individually. He may eat the mixture only if he leaves uneaten a piece equal in size to the original non-kosher food. This piece may, however, be eaten by another Jew. Although we noted that the previous opinion is *halachically* accepted, one should initially, follow this opinion and leave one piece uneaten.[20]

3) Yet other *Rishonim*[21] take a more stringent position. They require that one of the pieces not be eaten by *anyone* but should be discarded or sold to a non-Jew. Thus, one may assume that perhaps that piece was the prohibited piece. *Poskim* rule that while this is a meritorious act, it is not a *halachic* requirement.[22]

4) A fourth opinion is that of the *Rosh*[23] who takes a more lenient and radically different view of *bitul b'rov*. In his opinion, *bitul b'rov* does not entail an assumption that any part removed from the mixture is from the majority. Rather, *bitul b'rov* brings about the complete transformation of the non-kosher food into kosher food. The non-kosher food has been nullified and has

16. This prohibition, however, is Rabbinic in origin. According to Torah law, one may even eat the entire mixture at once (*Taz* 109:1, see *M.Z.* See a dissenting view in *Tosfos Rid: Bava Basra* 31b). Even *Rashba* concedes that according to Torah law each piece actually becomes permitted, see *Pri Migadim* in his introduction to *Hilchos Taaruvos* 1:3.

17. This applies only to *bitul b'rov*. However, in a case of *bitul b'shishim*, when the mixture is blended together, even *Rashba* would concede that one may eat the entire mixture at once (*Chavas Daas* 109:3,5). See *Pri Migadim* (in his introduction to *Hilchos Taaruvos* 3:5 and *Shaarei Yosher* 3:9 for further discussion of this topic.)

18. The first opinion in *Y.D.* 109:1.

19. *Smag* I:141 and *Tosfos: Chullin* 100a s.v. *"beriah"*, cited in *Beis Yosef* 109 and second opinion in *Y.D.* 109:1.

20. *Rema* 109:1.

21. *Rashi: Avodah Zarah* 74a, cited in *Rema* ibid.

22. *Rema* 109:1, see also *Beis Yosef* 109. Once one discards one piece, the remaining pieces may be eaten even at once (*Pischei Teshuvah* citing *Nodah B'Yehudah*).

23. *Chullin* 7:37, and *Smak* and *Maharam Rotenburg* cited in *Beis Yosef* 109. See also *Bedek HaBayis* 4:1 (17a in Warsaw edition).

completely lost its identity. Therefore, the entire mixture may be eaten by one person even at once.

Halachic authorities follow the opinion of *Rashba* cited in 1) above. Thus, one may not eat all the pieces at once.[24] In addition, one person should initially not eat all the pieces even at separate times.[25] Furthermore, it is meritorious to discard or give to a non-Jew a piece from the mixture equal in size to the original non-kosher food.[26]

B. Prohibited foods that require a greater proportion than a majority

Although in Torah law all (similar tasting) prohibited foods are subject to *bitul b'rov* — nullification in a mere majority. *Chazal* required a greater ratio for certain prohibited foods when they are mixed with their own type.[27] Among those foods are:

1) *Terumah,* תְּרוּמָה (the share given to a *Kohen* of most produce), *challah,* חַלָּה (the share given to a *Kohen* from dough) and *bikurim,* בִּיכּוּרִים (the share given to a *Kohen* from the first ripened seven-species fruit) require a ratio of one hundred parts permitted food to one part *terumah, challah* or *bikurim.* In addition, a part corresponding to the original *terumah* etc. must be given to a *Kohen.*[28]

2) *Orlah,* עָרְלָה and *kilaei hakerem,*[29] כִּלְאֵי הַכֶּרֶם require a ratio of two hundred parts permitted food to one part prohibited food.[30]

---

24. Y.D. 109:1. See *Rema* 109:2 who contends that in a situation of loss one may rely on the opinion of *Rosh* (see *Pri Migadim* in his introduction to *Taaruvos* 1:3).

25. *Rema* 109:1.

26. See *Kaf HaChaim* 109:24.

27. If they are mixed with another type of food *min b'sheaino mino* they are *batel b'shishim* (see *Ran* and *Tosfos: Nedarim* 58a).

28. *Rambam* 15:13. The reason that one must give a part to a *Kohen* is because of the monetary claim *Kohanim* have to that share. To use the entire mixture would constitute *gezel hashevet* — depriving the *Kohanim* of their share *(Tosfos: Bava Metzia* 53a). While prohibited matter may become nullified through *bitul b'rov,* monetary claims cannot (see *Tiferes Yisrael* ibid.).

29. See definitions in Chapter One section I.

30. *Rambam* 15:14.

Summary of Section I

⁂ In any mixture of similar tasting cold, dry foods, the non-kosher food becomes nullified *(batel)* in a simple majority of kosher food.

In the opinion of most authorities, this is based on the probability that any food removed from the mixture is from the majority. Accordingly, the following limitations may apply.

- □ Most *Rishonim* agree that the entire mixture may not be eaten at once.
- □ Some *Rishonim* contend that, in any case, the entire mixture may not be eaten by one person.
- □ Yet other *Rishonim* rule that the last piece of the mixture may not be eaten by anyone; it must be discarded.

Although this is the accepted *halachic* opinion, a minority of *Rishonim* view *bitul* as the complete transformation of the non-kosher food into permitted food. Thus, in their opinion, all restrictions cited above do not apply.

Certain prohibited foods require a ratio greater than a simple majority. *Terumah, challah* and *bikurim* require a ratio of one hundred parts permitted food to one part forbidden food. *Orlah* and *kilaei hakerem* require a ratio of two hundred to one.

II. Bitul b'shishim, בִּיטּוּל בְּשִׁשִּׁים — nullification in a ratio of sixty

These *halachos* are based upon *Tur* and *Shulchan Aruch* Y.D. 109:

A. The Torah law

We noted above that *bitul b'rov* can be applied only to those mixtures in which the taste of the non-kosher food is not noticeable. If, however, the taste of the non-kosher food is noticeable, we encounter the principle of *taam k'ikar* — the taste (of the non-kosher food) is considered as (non-kosher) food itself. (This concept will be discussed in detail in Chapter Four.) Thus, the kosher food assumes the prohibited characteristic of the non-kosher food and is Biblically prohibited. Mere nullification of the non-kosher food is inadequate if any non-kosher taste remains. Consequently, the *bitul* process must nullify the non-kosher food and its taste as well. Primarily, *bitul b'shishim* is required only when these *two* features are combined: a) the foods are dissimilar in taste *(min b'sheaino mino)*. If, however, the foods are similar tasting, the taste of one is not noticeable in the other; thus, *bitul b'rov* suffices. b) the foods are either liquids or solids that are blended or cooked together. If, however, the foods are solids that are neither blended nor cooked together, they do not impart taste to one another; thus, *bitul b'rov* is adequate. If *either* of these two factors is missing, *bitul b'shishim* is not Biblically mandated.

B. The Rabbinic prohibition

Chazal extended the requirement of *bitul b'shishim* to cases that resemble the primary Biblical case in some aspect. *Chazal* were aware of the difficult nature of these *halachos*. They were concerned that one may confuse the rules pertaining to similar tasting foods with those of dissimilar ones. A mistake of this nature may cause one to transgress a Biblical prohibition.[31] Thus, although in Torah law *bitul b'shishim* is required only when dissimilar tasting foods are cooked or blended together, *Chazal* extended the requirement to situations that resemble the Biblical case in either of these factors (i.e. dissimilar tasting foods or foods that were cooked together, see footnote for further explanation).[32] Hence,

31. Accordingly, *Shach* 109:9, contends that if a dry non-kosher food that is prohibited by Rabbinic law only is mixed with even a dissimilar tasting dry kosher food, *bitul b'rov* is always effective. A mixture of this type will never entail a Biblical prohibition. See, however, *Minchas Yaakov* 20:16 who disagrees. See also *Minchas Yaakov* 75:14 as to whether this applies to those Rabbinic prohibitions that have no Biblical basis (see also *D.T.* 109:47). However, a mixture of similar tasting liquids or blended (or cooked) solids requires *bitul b'shishim* even if the prohibited matter is only prohibited by Rabbinic law (see *Gilyon Maharsha* to *Shach* ibid. and *Pri Migadim* in his introduction to *Hilchos Taaruvos* 2:1.

32. See *Minchas Kohen* II;2:1, who explains that *Chazal* extended the requirement of *bitul b'shishim* to any case which resembles the Torah requirement of *bitul b'shishim*. Thus, since the Torah requires *bitul b'shishim* in a case of *taam k'ikar* — dissimilar mixtures cooked or blended together, *Chazal* extended this requirement to similar mixtures blended or cooked together and to dissimilar mixtures which are neither cooked nor blended, since each of these resembles the Torah requirement in one aspect. If, however, the mixture is neither similar nor blended together, *Chazal* left *bitul b'rov* intact since no resemblance exists to the Torah requirement. In addition, according to the first three opinions cited above, whenever the mixture is blended together, one who eats any part of it necessarily eats from the non-kosher piece as well *(Minchas Kohen* ibid.).

similar tasting foods that are blended or cooked together[33] or uncooked, dissimilar tasting foods,[34] require *bitul b'shishim*. Each of these instances resembles the Biblical case (i.e., cooked, dissimilar foods) in *one* aspect. However, uncooked (and unblended), similar tasting foods do not resemble the Biblical case in *any* manner. Since they will not be confused with the Biblical case, they may become nullified with a mere *bitul b'rov*.[35] In short: *Chazal* required *bitul b'shishim* in any situation that would have constituted a problem of *taam k'ikar* if the mixture had been of dissimilar foods or if the mixture was cooked together. Therefore, the following rules apply:

> *[In each of the following cases a blending of taste would have occurred had the foods been dissimilar in taste. Therefore* bitul b'rov *cannot be employed even for similar tasting foods. In the last case, a blending of taste would have occurred had the foods been cooked, therefore,* bitul b'shishim *is required].*

1) If a non-kosher liquid falls into a majority of kosher liquid, the entire mixture is forbidden even though they have similar tastes. *Bitul b'shishim* is required.
2) Similarly, if a non-kosher solid food falls into a majority of kosher food in a manner that it or some of its fat blends into the kosher food, *bitul b'shishim* is required against any part of it that blended into the kosher food. Here, too, *Chazal* did not differentiate between similar and non-similar tasting foods.
3) If non-kosher solid foods fall into hot kosher food or are cooked with kosher food, they require *bitul b'shishim* even though the kosher food is the majority of the mixture. Heat causes a transfer of taste between the foods. Again, no distinction is made between similar and non-similar tasting foods.
4) Even a mixture of dry, similar tasting foods that had previously become *batel b'rov* may lose the status of *bitul* if it is subsequently cooked together. While it may seem odd that a prohibited food that became *batel* should revert to its prohibited status, it is actually within the logic of the rules of *bitul*. We noted that

33. *Y.D.* 109:2.

34. *Rema* 109:1.

35. This represents the opinion of the majority of *Rishonim*. *Beis Yosef* 109, however, cites the opinions of *Rashi*, *Raavad* and *Rambam* 15:4, who contend that even uncooked, similar tasting foods require *bitul b'shishim*.

in the opinion of most authorities *bitul b'rov* is not the actual transformation of the non-kosher food into kosher food. The non-kosher food retains its status. We merely assume that any part (or perhaps all parts) removed from the mixture is of the permitted majority. Thus, if the mixture is cooked and the non-kosher taste is spread throughout, the entire mixture may be prohibited; a *moreh hora'ah* should be consulted. (As noted above, whenever a blending of tastes occurs, *Chazal* did not differentiate between similar and dissimilar tasting mixtures.)[36] After becoming aware of the mixture one may cook it in two separate pots[37] or add kosher food to attain *bitul b'shishim.*[38] The specific *halachos* of *bitul b'shishim* will be discussed in Chapter Four.

5) If dissimilar tasting foods are mixed, *bitul b'rov* is inadequate even if the foods are cold, dry and even though no taste was transferred. If the foods had been cooked or blended a transfer of taste would have occurred, thus *bitul b'shishim* is required.[39]

Summary of Section II

◆§ *Bitul b'rov* can be applied only to those mixtures in which the taste of the non-kosher food is not noticeable. Whenever the

---

36. *Rashba* cited in *Beis Yosef* ibid. *Y.D.* 109:2. We noted above that according to the opinion of *Rosh* (cited in *Beis Yosef* ibid.) the non-kosher food has become transformed into kosher food. Thus, according to his opinion, even if the mixture is subsequently cooked it may be eaten. See *Rema* 109:2, who rules that in a situation of loss one may rely on this opinion. *Sefardic* Jews do not rely on the opinion of *Rosh* even in a situation of loss (*Kaf HaChaim* 109:40). *Rosh* does concede that the principle of *bitul b'rov* takes affect only after the mixture is noticed. Thus, if no one was aware of the non-kosher food being mixed into the kosher food before the mixture was cooked, it may not be eaten. The blending of tastes and the principle of *taam k'ikar* preempts and thwarts *bitul b'rov*. Thus, although in the case of similar tasting foods the taste is not noticeable, nevertheless, as noted above, *Chazal* were unwilling to differentiate between similar and dissimilar tasting foods in this case. Consequently, according to both *Rashba* and *Rosh* similar and dissimilar tasting foods are governed by parallel rules. According to *Rashba*, this applies regardless of whether the *bitul* took effect before or during the cooking, while according to *Rosh*, this applies only if the *bitul* has not taken effect prior to the cooking.

37. *Shach* 109:12. In this manner, one may assume that any one pot does not contain the non-kosher food.

38. *Y.D.* 109:2. This is not considered intentional *bitul* of forbidden foods (see Section V below) since, essentially, each piece is permitted on its own (*Taz* 109:3 and *Shach* 109:13 citing *Ran*).

39. *Rema* 109:1, see *Shach* §9.

taste of the non-kosher food is noticeable, the kosher food assumes the prohibited characteristic of the nonkosher food *(taam k'ikar)* and is Biblically prohibited.

1) The Torah Law:
According to Torah law *bitul b'shishim* is required only when: a) the foods are dissimilar in taste *(min b'sheaino mino)*; b) the foods are blended or cooked together. If the foods are solids that are neither blended nor cooked together, *bitul b'shishim* is not Biblically mandated.

2) The Rabbinic prohibition:
Chazal extended the requirement of *bitul b'shishim* to situations that resemble the Biblical case. Accordingly, *bitul b'shishim* is required in the following cases:
   - □ Similar tasting foods that are blended or cooked together.
   - □ Similar tasting liquids that are mixed together.
   - □ Dissimilar tasting foods, even if they are neither cooked nor blended together.
   - □ A mixture of dry similar tasting foods that had previously become *batel b'rov* may require *bitul b'shishim* if it is subsequently cooked together. A *moreh hora'ah* should be consulted.

CHART 1
BITUL
WHETHER B'ROV OR B'SHISHIM

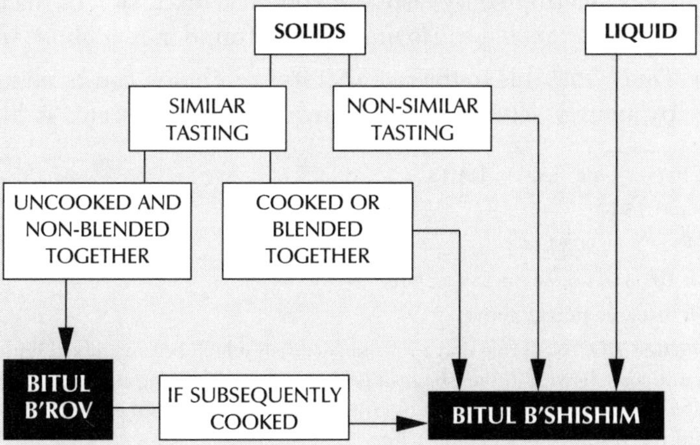

III. Prohibited foods that cannot become batel

Certain prohibited foods cannot be nullified even if mixed with a far greater proportion of kosher foods. This may be due to the unique nature of their prohibition, the prominent nature of the food or because the non-kosher food is somehow noticeable in the mixture.

A. Foods that cannot become batel due to the nature of their prohibition

Bitul b'rov or even *bitul b'shishim* cannot be used with regard to certain prohibited foods because of their unique nature, for example: their prohibition will disappear in the course of time or they are not actually prohibited, merely restricted. *Bitul* applies only to prohibited food, not to foods whose prohibition is of a limited nature. Other foods may not be subject to *bitul* because of the severity of their prohibition. For example:

1) *Davar sheyesh lo matirim*, דָּבָר שֶׁיֵּשׁ לוֹ מַתִּירִים — a food that will, in time, become permitted cannot become *batel* in another food similar in type. For example, *chadash*[40] cannot become *batel* since it will become permitted on the second day of *Pesach*.[41] It can, however, become *batel b'shishim* when mixed with food of a different type.[42] Here, similarity of foods is determined by name not by taste.[43] In the rest of this chapter, however, similarity is determined by taste.[44] A complete discussion of the principle of *davar sheyesh lo matirim*[45] is found in *Shulchan Aruch*.[46]
2) *Tevel*, טֶבֶל, due to the fact that its prohibition can be eliminated by merely setting aside the required *terumah* etc., is likewise

40. See Chapter One, Section I,A,13.

41. *Rambam* 15:10.

42. Ibid. §12. Y.*D.* 102:1.

43. *Shach* 102:3. As opposed to *Taz* §10.

44. *Shach* 98:6, see note 2 above.

45. *Poskim* (see Y.*D.* 102:3) rule that a non-kosher dish which became mixed with kosher dishes is not considered a *davar sheyesh lo matirim* even though it could be *kashered* (see Section D below). *Kashering* can be costly and difficult; thus the ability to *kasher* is not within the realm of *yesh lo matirim*.

46. Y.*D.* 102.

considered a *davar sheyesh lo matirim*. Thus, it cannot become *batel* in any amount of similar tasting food. It can, however, become *batel b'shishim* when mixed with dissimilar foods.[47]

3) *Avodah zarah*, עֲבוֹדָה זָרָה — Anything that has been worshiped as an idol or anything that has been offered in worship to an idol is forbidden and cannot become *batel* in any amount.[48]

4) *Yayin nesech*, יַיִן נֶסֶךְ, due to its association with *avodah zarah*, cannot become *batel* in any amount of wine. It can become *batel*, however in other foods with a sixty to one ratio — *batel b'shishim*.[49]

5) Fruits of *sheviyis*, שְׁבִיעִית (the Sabbatical year) due to the fact that they are essentially not prohibited but are merely subject to certain *halachic* restrictions, cannot become *batel* in any amount of similar tasting food. They can, however, become *batel b'shishim* when mixed with non-similar foods.[50]

6) *Chametz*, חָמֵץ during *Pesach* cannot become *batel* in any amount of similar or dissimilar tasting food.[51] Two reasons are offered for this stringent stance toward *chametz*. Firstly, *chametz* is not forbidden forever; it becomes permitted after *Pesach*. Thus, *chametz* is a *davar sheyesh lo matirim*.[52] Secondly, the prohibition of *chametz* is unusually severe. The Torah punishes one who eats *chametz* with *kares* and prohibits even the mere possession of *chametz*.[53]

B. Foods that cannot become batel because of the prominent nature of the food

Certain foods cannot become *batel* with either *rov* or *shishim* because they are considered significant, either in size or nature. These exceptions are all of Rabbinic origin. In Torah law, non-kosher food becomes *batel* regardless of its prominence.[54] Examples of these foods are:

---

47. *Rambam* 15:6.

48. Y.*D*. 140.

49. *Rambam* ibid.

50. *Rambam* 15:8.

51. *Rambam* 15:9. See *Shulchan Aruch: Orach Chaim* 447 for the details of this *halachahh*.

52. *Rambam* ibid. see also §12.

53. *Ramban: Milchamos, Pesachim* 30a. See *Magen Avraham* 447:5.

54. *Rema* 110:1.

1) *Beriah,* בְּרִיָּה — a complete creature such as an insect, an egg that contains an unhatched bird[55] or even a complete limb torn from a living animal cannot become *batel.* The ramifications of this *halachah* are explained in *Shulchan Aruch.*[56]

2) *Chatichah haruyah l'hischabed,* חֲתִיכָה הָרְאוּיָה לְהִתְכַּבֵּד — a piece of meat of a size and condition fit to serve to company cannot become *batel.* This *halachah* is also explained in *Shulchan Aruch.*[57]

3) *Davar she'biminyan,* דָּבָר שֶׁבְּמִנְיָן — an object that is sold solely by *unit* is considered prominent and cannot become batel when mixed into its own type. For example: a whole egg of a non-kosher bird that became mixed into other kosher eggs is not *batel b'rov* since eggs are sold by *unit* (a dozen). The ramifications of this *halachah* are found in *Shulchan Aruch.*[58]

4) *Davar chashuv,* דָּבָר חָשׁוּב — certain prominent foods cannot become *batel. Davar she'biminyan* is a type of *davar chashuv.* Others are listed in *Shulchan Aruch.*[59]

C. Situations in which the non-kosher food cannot become batel because it is noticeable

At times, a non-kosher food cannot become *batel* because it is noticeable in some manner in the mixture. The fact that the non-kosher food is somehow noticed in the mixture is the equivalent of its taste being noticeable and prevents its *bitul.*[60] For example:

1) The non-kosher food is noticeable:
If small slivers of non-kosher food fall into a majority of kosher liquid, the mixture may not be eaten. The non-kosher food is noticeable by touch and cannot become *batel* even though it cannot be removed (i.e., the mixture cannot be strained or sifted).[61]

---

55. See *Shach* 100:2.

56. *Y.D.* 100.

57. *Y.D.* 101. See 101:3 as to whether or not the piece must be cooked to be considered *chatichah haruyah l'hischabed*. See also *Rema* and *Taz* §5.

58. *Y.D.* 110:1.

59. *Y.D.* ibid.

60. See *Minchas Kohen* II, 3:3.

61. *Chochmas Adam* 51:3.

2) The non-kosher food is removable:
Even if the non-kosher food is not noticeable, it must be removed if possible. For example: the mixture should be sifted if possible. Similarly, non-kosher fat that became mixed with kosher food can be removed by cooling the mixture and causing the fat to jell.[62]

3) *Chazusa*, חֲזוּתָא:
A non-kosher food that was added to a mixture to give it color cannot become *batel.*[63] No distinction is made between similar tasting and dissimilar tasting mixtures.[64]

4) *Davar hama'amid*, דָּבָר הַמַּעֲמִיד:
A non-kosher food which solidifies or jells the food with which it combines cannot become *batel.*[65] For example, cheese that was curdled with non-kosher rennet may not be eaten although the amount of rennet used is minimal and its taste is unnoticeable.[66] The effect of the non-kosher rennet on the cheese is noticeable and prevents its *bitul.*[67] No distinction is made between mixtures of similar tasting or dissimilar tasting foods.[68]

D. Bitul b'rov regarding dishes

A common occurrence in a kosher home is a dish or piece of flatware that became *treif* and subsequently mixed with other dishes. *Poskim* rule that the dish becomes *batel* in the majority of kosher dishes.[69] Later authorities, however, advise that one should not use the dishes until a

62. *Rema* 98:4, *Chochmas Adam* 51:2.

63. See *Minchas Kohen* II 3:3, who contends that this rules applies only if the ingredient was added for the purpose of giving color. See also *M.Z.* 100:1 s.v. *"amnam"*.

64. *Minchas Kohen* ibid.

65. In the opinion of most *Poskim* this rule is Rabbinic in origin, see *Chok Yaakov* 442:16.

66. *Rambam* 16:26. However, *davar hama'amid* applies only to prohibited foods, not foods which, when combined, will produce prohibited food (e.g., meat and milk). Thus, kosher rennet (produced from the stomach lining of a kosher cow) may be used in the cheese-making process and presents no *basar b'chalav* problem (see *Y.D.* 87:11 and *Shach* §35).

67. See *Avodah Zarah* 35a.

68. *Rambam* 16:26.

69. *Y.D.* 102:3. See *Taz* and *Shach* §8, as to why the dish is not considered a *davar sheyesh lo matirim*, see *M.Z.* §8 as to why it is not considered a *davar she'biminyan*.

twenty-four-hour period has elapsed since the non-kosher use.[70] Still other authorities suggest that one remove one dish to be *kashered*. We may presume that perhaps the non-kosher dish was *kashered*.[71] See Chapter Ten (Section A,9) regarding dairy cutlery found with the meat cutlery (or the reverse).

Summary of Section III

- The following prohibited foods cannot become *batel* due to the unique character of the prohibition: *Davar sheyesh lo matirim* (a thing that will, in time, become permitted), *tevel, yayin nesech,* fruits of *sheviyis,* and *chametz* during *Pesach.*
- The following prohibited foods cannot become *batel* because of their prominent nature: *Beriah, chatichah haruyah l'hischabed, davar she'biminyan* and *davar chashuv*.

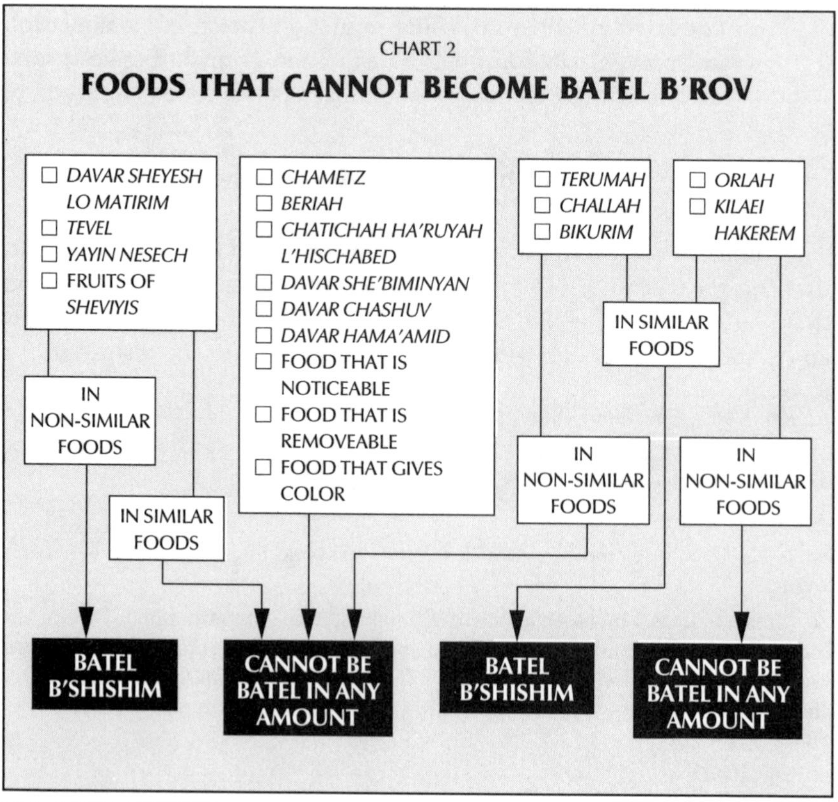

70. *Shach* 102:8.

71. *Shach* ibid. *Aruch HaShulchan* 102:18.

⁂ Certain prohibited foods cannot become *batel* since they are, in some manner, noticeable. When the prohibited matter is either a) noticeable although unremovable, b) removable although it is unnoticeable c) added to the mixture to give it color or d) added to either solidify or jell the mixture it is not *batel*.

IV. Subsequent adjustments to the ratio of the kosher and non-kosher foods

Frequently, after a non-kosher food has been nullified in a majority or a sixty to one ratio, additional non-kosher food falls into the mixture. Should one then consider the nullified non-kosher food as non-existent since it has become *batel?* Or perhaps the non-kosher food was merely in a dormant state, i.e., it was inactive and unable to affect the mixture but nevertheless retained its potential non-kosher status. Consequently, it may later combine with any additional non-kosher matter to affect the mixture. Similarly, consider the question in reverse. Non-kosher food fell into a mixture that was insufficient in quantity to nullify it. As a result, the entire mixture became prohibited. Can additional kosher matter combine with the original kosher food to nullify the non-kosher food? Or perhaps once the original mixture became prohibited (since it did not contain sufficient kosher food to nullify the non-kosher food), the entire mixture assumes a non-kosher status. Consequently, the original kosher food is not only unable to combine with additional kosher food to effect a *bitul*, it actually becomes non-kosher food. Thus, one requires a ratio of sixty times the original mixture to effect a *bitul*. In this section, we will discuss these two possibilities: additional non-kosher food added to a mixture containing nullified non-kosher food, and kosher food added to a mixture containing non-kosher food that initially lacked the required amount for *bitul*.

A. Additional prohibited matter after bitul has taken effect — chozer v'niyur, חוֹזֵר וְנֵעוֹר

If additional non-kosher food is added to a mixture after *bitul* has taken effect, the *bitul* must be re-evaluated. If the kosher food no longer contains enough to nullify the amount of non-kosher food, the original *bitul* is no longer effective.[72] *Chazal* name this phenomenon *chozer*

72. *Rema* 99:6.

v'niyur — a reawakening (of the original non-kosher food). Although the non-kosher food has already become *batel,* the mixture must now be judged in accordance with the new circumstances.[73] For example: a piece of non-kosher meat became *batel* in two pieces of kosher meat. If, subsequently, another piece of non-kosher meat fell into the mixture, the mixture may not be eaten since a *rov* (majority) no longer exists.[74] Similarly, if non-kosher fat became *batel* in a sixty ratio of kosher food, the *bitul* is revoked if more non-kosher fat is subsequently added to the mixture.[75]

B. Kosher food added to a mixture that lacked the proper amount for bitul

If non-kosher food fell into and was cooked with an amount of kosher food that was insufficient to effect a *bitul,* any subsequent, inadvertent[76] addition of kosher food raises two fundamental questions. a) May the *bitul* be reevaluated according to the new ratio? Thus, although the original mixture lacked the required ratio for *bitul,* the additional kosher food perhaps further dilutes the non-kosher taste and effects a *bitul.* This question is the subject of a Talmudic dispute and is known as the issue of *"efshar l'sochto,"* אֶפְשָׁר לְסוֹחְטוֹ — the possibility of extracting (the non-kosher taste from the kosher food). b) Assuming that the non-kosher taste cannot be extracted and the original mixture retains its non-kosher status, what effect does it have on the additional

73. This is the opinion of the majority of *halachic* authorities. A minority of *Poskim* contend that since the non-kosher food has become *batel,* it is no longer considered non-kosher. Therefore, it cannot combine with any non-kosher food subsequently added (see the minority opinions cited in *Shach* 99:21).

74. *Rema* 99:6. See *Shach* 99:21, who disagrees with *Rema* and rules that if the mixture was of similar tasting foods and one became aware of the mixture before the additional non-kosher food fell in, one may be lenient in a situation of serious monetary loss. In his opinion, the concept of *chozer v'niyur* applies only to dissimilar tasting foods. Other authorities do not concede this point and follow the opinion of *Rema* (see *D.T.* 99:95).

75. If, however, the additional non-kosher food was of a different type than the first, e.g., an ounce of non-kosher fat became *batel* in sixty ounces of potatoes and subsequently an ounce of blood falls into the mixture, the potatoes may be eaten. The taste of the fat and the oil are not similar and do not reinforce one another. Indeed, the fat is considered as an addition to the volume of the potatoes to enable them to nullify the blood, while the blood is added to the volume of the potatoes to enable them to nullify the fat (*Taz* 99:13, *Shach* §20).

76. It is forbidden to knowingly add kosher food to a mixture so as to bring about a *bitul,* see below, Section V.

kosher food? Is the original mixture viewed as a non-kosher entity of its own or is it merely viewed as kosher food with an infusion of non-kosher taste? This is the Talmudic question of *"chatichah na'asis neveilah,"* חֲתִיכָה נַעֲשֵׂית נְבֵילָה — the (original) piece becomes a non-kosher entity.[77]

It should be noted that both of these questions pertain only to cooked mixtures or mixtures of liquids and solids.[78] *Dry uncooked mixtures are subject to neither the question of* efshar l'sochto *nor* chatichah na'asis neveilah.[79] *The reason for this is quite simple: A dry non-kosher food that falls into an equal amount of kosher dry food does not impart its taste to the kosher food. The mixture may not be eaten because we do not know which piece is kosher and which piece is not. The kosher food, however, is essentially unaffected.*[80] *Thus, if more kosher food falls into the mixture and increases its ratio to a majority, the non-kosher matter is* batel.

1) *Efshar l'sochto:*
The Talmud[81] cites a difference of opinion as to whether a food that absorbed non-kosher taste can be purged of that taste when cooked with additional kosher food. For example: we know that when milk is cooked with meat, the prohibited food of *basar b'chalav* results. We know, too, that if the volume of the meat is sixty times that of milk, the milk is *batel* and cannot affect the kashrus of the meat. Accordingly, if one fluid ounce of milk fell into a pot of thirty fluid ounces of meat, the entire mixture becomes *basar b'chalav*. If, subsequently, the original mixture becomes combined and is cooked with another thirty ounces of meat, we are confronted with the question of

---

77. In Rabbinic literature, the term *"chatichah na'asis neveilah"* is often used in the place of *efshar l'sochto* since they are so similar in concept. In addition, *chatichah na'asis neveilah* presupposes *efshar l'sochto* (i.e., were we not to assume *efshar l'sochto asur*, we could not rule *chatichah na'asis neveilah).*

78. If, however, both the kosher and non-kosher ingredients are liquid, in the opinion of many *Poskim* both *efshar l'sochto* and *chatichah na'asis neveilah* do not apply. For a discussion of the various explanations of this opinion, see *Yad Yehudah* 92:24a. See *Rema* 92:4, who relies on these opinions only in cases of non-*basar b'chalav* mixtures, and only in cases of severe financial loss. See *Taz* §15 and *S.D.* ibid.

79. *Rema* 92:4.

80. This explanation is offered in *Badei HaShulchan* 92:83.

81. *Chullin* 108a.

efshar l'sochto. Should we assume that the original milk now becomes diluted into the total sixty ounces of meat and becomes *batel ("efshar l'sochto mutar")?* Or perhaps the milk remains in the original thirty ounces of meat. Even if the milk is extracted, perhaps the meat retains its non-kosher status *("efshar l'sochto asur"). Poskim* rule that the milk cannot be extracted from the original mixture. Therefore, the first thirty ounces of meat remain forbidden. Indeed, even if the original mixture is cooked with an amount fit for *bitul b'shishim* (sixty times the original mixture[82]), the original thirty ounces of meat retain their prohibited status.[83] In the opinion of prevailing *Poskim,*[84] the rule of *efshar l'sochto asur* applies to *all* prohibited foods[85] as well as to *basar b'chalav.*[86]

82. 1,860 ounces.

83. *Y.D.* 92:2,3.

84. *Y.D.* 106:1, *Poskim* are troubled by the apparent contradiction in the ruling of the *Shulchan Aruch* 92:4. See *Shach* 92:11 and *S.D.* there.

85. *Efshar l'sochto,* however, does not apply to permitted foods. For example: onions that were cooked with meat and subsequently cooked with *parve* food in a dairy pot require *bitul b'shishim* in ratio to the absorbed meat only, not the onions *(Beis Yosef* 94, citing *Smak).* See *Shach* 94:23 and *Taz* 96:5 who rule that even the onion may be eaten, while *Kreisi U'pleisi* 94:8 disagrees. See also *R' Akiva Eger* (gloss to *Shach* ibid.), *S.D.* (ibid.) and *D.T.* 94:79 as to the status of the onions if they were cooked with actual milk, not only in a milk pot.

86. In the case of *basar b'chalav,* the logic is relatively simple. *Basar b'chalav* is prohibited not merely because of the remaining milk absorbed into the meat. Rather, the mixture of meat and milk has produced a new prohibited entity — *basar b'chalav* (see Chapter Seven footnote no. 8, that this is subject to a dispute between *Taz* 105:13 and *Shach* §17). Therefore, removing the absorbed milk cannot alter the prohibited status of the meat. The concept of *efshar l'sochto asur* does, however, pose a difficulty in relationship to other non-kosher foods. Why can't the non-kosher taste infused in the original mixture be extracted? *Poskim* present two possible explanations: perhaps the infused taste simply does not leave the food in which it was embedded. (For this reason, in the opinion of some *Poskim,* the rule of *chatichah na'asis neveilah* does not apply to a liquid mixture since it blends together completely. See *Rashba* cited in *Beis Yosef* 92.) Or, perhaps, although some of the taste may leave the food, some taste will certainly remain. *Chazal* were unwilling to permit the food as long as any non-kosher taste remains (see *S.D.* 92:11. See also *D.T.* end of 92:40, who cites a difference of opinion whether the rule of *efshar l'sochto* regarding other prohibited foods is Biblical or Rabbinic in origin. *Pri Migadim* in his introduction, ibid., rules that in regard to *basar b'chalav, efshar l'sochto* is Biblical, while in regard to other prohibitions *efshar l'sochto* is Rabbinic). See *Yad Yehudah* 92:16a for an in-depth analysis of the concept of *efshar l'sochto.*

2) *Chatichah na'asis neveilah:*
Once it has become established that the non-kosher taste cannot be extracted from the original mixture *(efshar l'sochto asur)*, we must be concerned with its effect on the new cooked mixture. Should the entire original mixture be viewed as prohibited matter which requires *bitul?* Consequently, should we require eighteen hundred and sixty ounces of kosher food to nullify the original thirty one ounces of *basar b'chalav?* This concept is known as "*chatichah na'asis neveilah*" — the original piece (or mixture) becomes a prohibited entity that generates non-kosher taste of its own. Or perhaps the original thirty ounces of meat are prohibited merely because of the absorbed milk. The meat, however, is essentially not prohibited matter and does not transmit prohibited taste of its own (indeed, it combines with any additional kosher food to nullify the prohibited taste). Therefore, thirty ounces of additional food are adequate to nullify the effect of the milk. Consequently, although the original thirty ounces retain their non-kosher status *(efshar l'sochto asur)*, the second thirty ounces are permitted (if they can be clearly separated). *Halachic* consensus[87] rules that in meat and milk mixtures *(basar b'chalav)*,[88] we assume the mixture to be a prohibited entity of its own *("chatichah na'asis neveilah")*. Accordingly, we require a ratio of sixty against the meat and milk mixture. In mixtures of other non-kosher foods,[89] there is no clear consensus among *Rishonim*

---

87. The opinion of almost all *Rishonim*, excluding *Raavad* and apparently, *Rif*, cited in *Beis Yosef* 92.

88. This is the theory of *Rabbeinu Efraim* cited in *Tosfos: Chullin* 100a. The differentiation between *basar b'chalav* and other non-kosher foods is based on the unique nature of *basar b'chalav*. Meat and milk are, separately, permitted foods. The prohibited food of *basar b'chalav* is created when the two are cooked together. Thus, both the meat and the milk become prohibited foods (we do not assume that the meat is kosher food infused with non-kosher milk and the milk is kosher food infused with non-kosher meat taste — see Chapter Seven, Section I,A). Other non-kosher foods, however, are essentially prohibited. Therefore, when they are absorbed into kosher food, we may view the food as kosher food infused with non-kosher taste (see *Taz* 92:9 and *Shach* 92:10).

89. There is much discussion in the *Poskim* as to whether *chatichah na'asis neveilah* pertains to utensils that absorbed non-kosher taste. See *Y.D.* 98:5 and *Rema* 92:4. See Chapter Four, notes 30, 34-36.

whether the mixture requires *bitul* in sixty times the entire mixture or merely sixty times the volume of the original non-kosher food.

The *Shulchan Aruch*[90] follows the lenient opinion and rules that *chatichah na'asis neveilah* applies to *basar b'chalav* only. Therefore, in mixtures of other non-kosher foods, while the original mixture retains its prohibition, it combines with any additional kosher food to dilute the original non-kosher taste. *Sefardic* Jews follow this opinion.[91] *Rema,*[92] however, follows the opinion of those *Rishonim* who contend that *chatichah na'asis neveilah* applies[93] to all[94] non-kosher mixtures.[95] He concedes that this extension is Rabbinic in nature.[96] *Ashkenazic* custom follows this ruling.

Summary of Section IV

- Additional prohibited matter — the question of *chozer v'niyur*: If non-kosher food is added to a mixture after *bitul* has taken effect, the original *bitul* is no longer effective. This is known as *chozer v'niyur* — a reawakening (of the original non-kosher food). No distinction is made whether the original *bitul* was *bitul b'rov* or *bitul b'shishim*. In either case, the mixture must now be judged in accordance with the new circumstances.
- Additional kosher food — the question of *efshar l'sochto* and *chatichah na'asis neveilah:*

  a) *Efshar l'sochto:*
  If non-kosher food fell into an amount of kosher food

90. Y.D. 92:4.

91. *Kaf HaChaim* 92:16.

92. Y.D. 92:4.

93. *Chatichah na'asis neveilah* usually applies only when the mixture took place in two stages, i.e., the non-kosher food first mixed with some kosher food and subsequently mixed with more kosher food. There are, however, instances when *chatichah na'asis neveilah* applies even to a mixture that took place in one stage. For example, if non-kosher food was cooked in a pot of kosher food in a manner that the non-kosher taste was absorbed into one piece of kosher food before the others. See *Rema* 92:4, *Taz* §12 and M.Z. ibid.

94. We noted above that *chatichah na'asis neveilah* applies only to cooked mixtures or mixtures of solids with liquids. See note no. 78 regarding liquid mixtures.

95. Including those foods prohibited by Rabbinic law (*Taz* 92:11, see M.Z. ibid.).

96. *Taz* 92:11, *Shach* 92:12.

that was insufficient to effect a *bitul,* the addition of permitted food cannot further dilute the non-kosher taste and effect a *bitul* of the original non-kosher food. This is known as "*efshar l'sochto asur.*" In the opinion of prevailing *Poskim,* the rule of *efshar l'sochto asur* applies to *all* prohibited foods as well as to *basar b'chalav.*

b) *Chatichah na'asis neveilah:*
Since the non-kosher taste cannot be extracted from the original mixture, the entire original mixture may be viewed as prohibited matter which requires *bitul.* This is known as "*chatichah na'asis neveilah*" — the original mixture becomes a prohibited entity. Therefore, we require *bitul* in sixty times the original mixture. According to *Sefardic* custom, this applies to *basar b'chalav* only. In mixtures of other non-kosher foods the original

CHART 3

ADJUSTMENTS TO THE BITUL RATIO

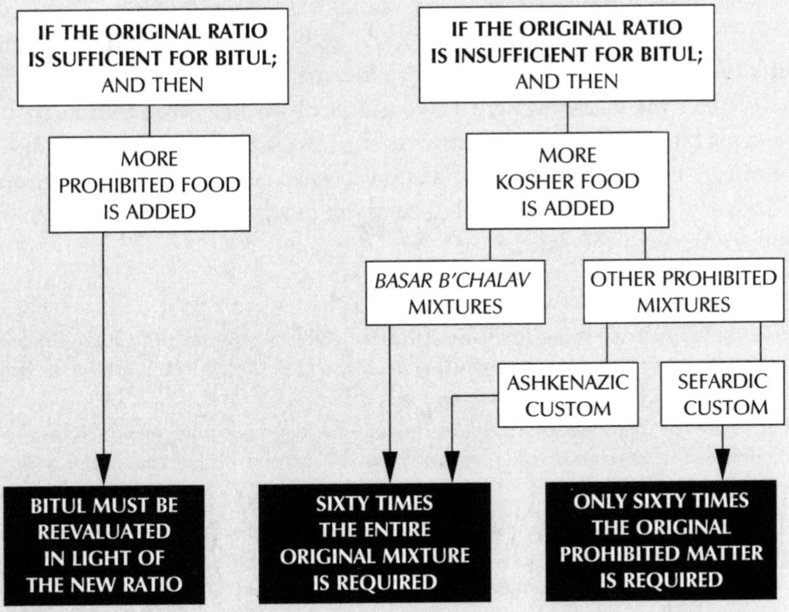

mixture combines with any additional kosher food to nullify the original non-kosher taste. *Ashkenazic* Jews follow the opinion that *chatichah na'asis neveilah* applies to all non-kosher mixtures. See Chapter Four, Section II,E for additional applications of the *chatichah na'asis neveilah* principle.

Both *efshar l'sochto* and *chatichah na'asis neveilah* pertain to cooked mixtures or mixtures of liquids and solids only. A dry non-kosher food that falls into kosher dry food does not impart its taste to the kosher food and is not subject to either the question of *efshar l'sochto* or *chatichah na'asis neveilah.*

V. Intentional bitul — a word of caution

These *halachos* are based upon *Tur* and *Shulchan Aruch* Y.D. 99:5.

A. The prohibition

Although we have discussed the various methods of *bitul*, one may not intentionally cause *bitul* to take place. *Chazal*[97] warn *"ain m'vatlin issur lechatchilah,"* אֵין מְבַטְּלִין אִיסוּר לְכַתְּחִילָה — one may not initially nullify forbidden foods.[98] One may not intentionally mix[99] a non-kosher piece of meat with two pieces of kosher meat. Similarly, one may not blend a non-kosher ingredient into kosher food sixty times its volume.[100] Even in the event that non-kosher food falls into an amount of kosher food that is insufficient to effect *bitul*, one may not add kosher food to increase the ratio.[101]

---

97. *Beitzah* 4b.

98. In the opinion of some *Rishonim*, this is a Biblical prohibition. Other *Rishonim* contend that it is Rabbinic in origin (see *Beis Yosef* 99, *Shach* 99:7, *Chochmas Adam* 52:6).

99. If, however, the intention of the mixing is for some other purpose which cannot be accomplished in another manner, one may mix in the non-kosher food, see *Taz* 99:7.

100. Y.D. 99:5.

101. Y.D. 99:5. Even if he plans to remove the non-kosher food itself *(Aruch HaShulchan* 99:21). One should note that *Sefardic* custom permits the addition of kosher food to a mixture containing non-kosher food that is prohibited by Rabbinic prohibition only. *Ashkenazic* custom, however, does not differentiate between Biblical and Rabbinic prohibitions (see *Rema* 99:6 and *Kaf HaChaim* 99:68).

B. The penalty for intentional bitul

One who intentionally causes a *bitul* of non-kosher food[102] may neither partake of that food[103] nor sell it[104] to another Jew.[105] *Chazal* mandated that the one who executed the *bitul* cannot derive any benefit from his transgression.[106] Others, however, may eat from the mixture, unless it was specifically nullified for their sake.[107]

The following are cases in which this rule does not apply:

1) One who intentionally nullified non-kosher food without realizing that it is forbidden to do so may eat the mixture.[108]
2) We noted above that if a piece of non-kosher food becomes mixed into similar tasting kosher food, it becomes *batel b'rov*. We also noted that the mixture may not be cooked. One may, however, add more kosher food and effect *bitul b'shishim* and subsequently cook the entire mixture.[109]

One should never attempt to add kosher food to a prohibited mixture without consulting a *moreh hora'ah.* The question of *chatichah na'asis neveilah* is very relevant to this question as are many other factors which are not within the scope of this work.[110]

---

102. If, however, the food was prohibited by Rabbinic prohibition only, additional factors may be considered. A *moreh hora'ah* should be consulted (see *M.Z.* 99:12).

103. *Y.D.* 99:5. *Poskim* disagree as to the status of the pot in which it was cooked (see *R' Akiva Eger* ibid. and *Kaf HaChaim* 99:46, see also *Ma'adanei HaShulchan* 99:38).

104. Neither he nor a member of his household may partake of the food (*Taz* 99:10). He may, however, give it to another Jew or sell it to him for a price no more than that paid by a non-Jew. In either case, he derives no benefit from his prohibited act (*Shach* 99:12, see *S.D.* ibid.).

105. He may sell it to a non-Jew for its full price, since he thus derives no benefit from the *bitul* (*Darcei Moshe* 99:3). If the food was of the type from which one may not derive benefit (*issur hana'ah*), i.e., *basar b'chalav*, one must deduct the value of the non-kosher food from the total price *S.D.* 99:12, s.v. "*va'akati*" and *M.Z.* end of §12.

106. *Rashba* cited in *Beis Yosef* 99.

107. *Y.D.* 99:5. If the one for whose sake the food was nullified was unaware of this, some *Poskim* permit his eating the food (see *Taz* 99:10, see, however *Yad Yehudah* 99:23k).

108. *Y.D.* 99:5, see *Taz* §7. Similarly, one who was told by a *moreh hora'ah* that he may nullify the non-kosher food may eat the mixture (the error of the *moreh hora'ah* is not the fault of the inquirer. If, however, one asked a learned person who was not versed in practical *halachah*, the food may not be eaten (*Pischei Teshuvah* 99:5). *Halachic* questions should be presented to an experienced *moreh hora'ah* well versed in practical *halachah*.

109. *Y.D.* 109:2. Since each piece is permitted on its own (see note no. 38 above).

110. See *Rema* 99:5.

CHAPTER THREE

אֵינוֹ רָאוּי לַאֲכִילָה

Inedible Foods

- □ Foods which putrefied.
- □ Naturally inedible foods.
- □ *Nosen taam lifgam.*
- □ *Non ben-yomo* utensils.

Introduction

These *halachos* are based on the Talmud *Avodah Zarah* 67, *Tur* and *Shulchan Aruch; Yoreh De'ah* 103.

Any forbidden food,[1] whether of Biblical or Rabbinic origin, which becomes unfit to eat,[2] loses its status as a forbidden food.[3] This rule is derived from the verse in the Torah[4] which tells us to dispose of a *neveilah* — carcass — by giving or selling it to a non-Jew. *Chazal*[5] understood the intent of the Torah is to include in the prohibition of *neveilah* only a carcass that a non-Jew would find fit to eat.[6] Thus any

1. Even foods from which one may not derive benefit *(asur b'hana'ah)* are permitted if they are inedible and become mixed into permitted food *(Chavas Daas* cited in *D.T.* 103:1).

2. Although *halachic* definitions are usually determined according to the particular culture and place. The definition of edibility in context to these *halachos* must be concluded according to normal human behavior. Thus, food that may culturally be considered unfit to eat in one country is nevertheless considered edible if it is essentially edible. Bitter substances that normal people in normal circumstances would not eat are considered inedible even though starving people may eat them out of desperation. This definition was given by Rav Y.S. Eliashiv (through a third party).

3. There is a major uncertainty as to whether or not (or to what degree) *Rambam* 14:11, accepts this principle. The *Rambam* seems to include inedible food in the general principle of eating in an unnatural manner. See below for the distinctions between the two. See a discussion of *Rambam's* position in *Nodah B'Yehudah* I: Y.D. 26, *Kreisi U'pleisi* 87:15, *Chidushei HaGrach* on *Rambam* ibid., Responsa *Chasam Sofer:* Y.D. 98, *Chavas Daas* 103:1 and *Yad Yehudah* 103:8a. Our discussion in this work follows the opinion of *Rashba* as explained in *Minchas Kohen* II:9, and later *Poskim* and apparently followed in the rulings of the *Shulchan Aruch* 103:2.

4. *Devarim* 14:21.

5. *Avodah Zarah* 67b.

6. It is most important to note that this *halachah* differs in a most significant manner from the *halachah* cited above about unnatural eating. While the exclusion of eating in an unnatural manner relates to the act or the person *("gavrah"* גַּבְרָא in Talmudic terminology), the exclusion of inedible foods relates to the food or object *("cheftzah"* חֶפְצָה*).* The contrast between the two is profound. 1) As we noted above, eating foods that are inedible is not considered an "eating" act; however, this applies only to items that the Torah prohibited with use of the word *"achilah"* — (eating). There are other items whose consumption is prohibited with use of other terms in the Torah. Since the term *"achilah"* is not utilized in regard to those prohibitions, they would not be excluded from the prohibition merely by reason of their inedibility. The *halachah* presently under discussion teaches us that *any* item completely inedible is excluded from

food unfit for human consumption is excluded from any prohibition pertaining to eating. This principle applies in a variety of manners depending upon the following circumstances:

- When the substance of the non-kosher food is present:
  In this case, one must contend with the actual substance of the prohibited food. Therefore, the food retains its forbidden status until it becomes completely inedible.
- When only the taste of the non-kosher food is present:
  In this case, one need only contend with the non-kosher taste present in the kosher food. Thus, even if the food mixture is edible, it is nevertheless permitted if the non-kosher food affects the mixture in a detrimental manner.[7] This distinction will be explained in detail below.

---

the Torah prohibition, not merely because the eating act is not considered "eating" but because the matter is excluded from the prohibition (see *Shaagas Aryeh* 75). 2) If we were to exclude inedible foods merely because the eating act is not considered "eating", it would apply only to the prohibition of eating. One may still be prohibited from deriving benefit from the item if it is an item which is *asur b'hana'ah* (prohibited from deriving benefit). If, on the other hand, inedible items are excluded from the prohibition, as *Chazal* derived from the verse pertaining to *neveilah*, it may be that the item was removed entirely from the realm of prohibited foods. One may therefore be permitted to derive benefit from it as well. [This is, however, quite less than certain. Although the prohibited food is inedible and thus excluded from the prohibition of eating, it may nevertheless retain its status as pertaining to other *halachos*. For example, although a *neveilah* loses its prohibited status once it is unfit for human consumption, it retains the status of *neveilah* regarding the *halachah* of *tumah* (spiritual defilement), see *Rambam: Hilchos Avos Hatumos* 1:13 who rules that the *neveilah* retains its status as far as *tumah* is concerned until it has become unfit for even a dog's consumption. Therefore, the question remains, should we compare the prohibition of benefit to that of eating or that of *tumah?* See *Mishneh L'Melech: Hilchos Avel* 14:21, and *Chidushei HaGrach: Rambam* 14:11. See also *Yad Yehudah* 103:8a for a most comprehensive discussion of this and related topics. *Yad Yehudah* presents a convincing proof that the prohibition of benefit remains. He cites the Talmud *(Temurah* 34a) that the ashes of most forbidden foods retain their prohibition of benefit. Ashes are certainly inedible, and yet they retain their prohibition.] 3) A prohibited food which became rotten and inedible and thereby lost its prohibition perhaps will not regain that status even if it was somehow made edible again. Were it merely a matter of an unnatural eating, however, once the food is made edible, it returns to its prohibited status (see *Chavas Daas* 103:1, *Yad Yehudah* 103:11a citing *Re'ah* in *Bedek HaBayis)*. For further study, see *Nodah B'Yehudah* I: Y.D. 26, *Kreisi U'pleisi* 87:15, *Chidushei HaGrach: Rambam* (ibid.), Responsa *Chasam Sofer:* Y.D. 98, and *Chavas Daas* 103:1.

7. *Taz* 103:1.

I. When the actual substance of the non-kosher food is present

A. Prohibited food which became inedible

A prohibited food which putrefied[8] or, for any reason,[9] became completely unfit to eat, loses its status as a forbidden food. If, however, it is somewhat edible, albeit with difficulty, it retains its non-kosher status. Nevertheless, in the opinion of some *Poskim*,[10] Rabbinic law prohibits eating even completely inedible non-kosher foods unless they are combined with kosher food.[11] Thus, the *halachos* are as follows:

1) Non-kosher food which has completely spoiled and become inedible is permitted by Torah law but prohibited by Rabbinic injunction unless one must eat it for medicinal purposes and no

---

8. The discussion here pertains to food which spoiled on its own as opposed to food which was spoiled through addition of foreign matter. In the former case, the food itself loses its status as forbidden food. In the latter case, the food itself is edible and retains its prohibition; however, one who eats it in its spoiled state transgresses no Torah prohibition since the eating act is an unnatural act. See *Chavas Daas* 103:1 and *Yad Yehudah* 103:8a, 11a who make this distinction.

9. Even if only because it assumed a repulsive odor (*Yad Yehudah* 103:2k, see, however. *D.T.* §7). *Yad Yehudah* derives this from *Rambam*. However, as noted above in note 3, *Rambam* may not consider inedible foods a category of their own. Eating inedible foods is merely a form of unnatural eating. According to those *Poskim* who disagree with *Rambam*, one might argue that food which assumed a repulsive odor should be compared to foods which became spoiled as a result of an addition of foreign matter and do not belong to this category, as noted above citing *Chavas Daas*.

10. See *Minchas Kohen* 1:9, who derives this from the language of *Rambam* 14:11). See also *M.Z.* 103:1. Perhaps one may question the contention of *Minchas Kohen* based on *Rambam* since it is not certain that *Rambam* accepts the entire principle that foods lose their prohibited status because of inedibility, see discussion in note 3 above. See also *Yad Yehudah* 103:8a who explains this Rabbinic prohibition on the basis of the fact that one who eats even inedible foods has accorded them the status of food (*ach'shevei*). A source for this explanation may be found in *Rosh: Pesachim* 2:1. Incidentally, based on this reason, *Rosh* rules that forbidden foods may not be eaten even if they are inedible for a dog. It is odd that *Rosh* is not cited by these *Poskim*. *Yad Yehudah* and *D.T.* §5, however, cite opinions who contend that inedible foods are completely permitted. See also *Minchas Yaakov: Toras Chatas* 46:9.

11. *Y.D.* 103:2. See *Minchas Kohen* and *M.Z.* ibid.

kosher substitute is available. Thus, one may use cod liver oil even if his sickness is not life threatening.[12]

2) Non-kosher food which has spoiled and become completely inedible[13] *and* mixed into kosher food may be eaten even if the non-kosher food is a majority of the mixture,[14] providing that the non-kosher food cannot be separated and removed.[15]

3) Non-kosher food which has spoiled and become inedible (even if not completely inedible) and mixed into *a majority* of kosher food is considered as if the substance of the non-kosher is not existent and is discussed in Section II below.

B. Prohibited foods that are naturally inedible

Many food prohibitions of the Torah pertain to objects which are basically not eaten. For example: most insects and rodents are particularly loathsome and are not eaten. Nevertheless, one who eats a *kizayis* of these insects is liable for punishment. The fact that the Torah forbids these insects is evidence that the Torah, in this case, is not concerned with the fact that they are inedible.[16] Similarly, the *gid*

12. *D.T.* 103:5. This is consistent with *Rema* 155:3. The basis for this is presumably because the concept of *ach'shevei* (see note 10 above) cannot apply when the food is eaten solely for medicinal purposes. See *Yad Avraham: Y.D.* 155:3 and *D.T.* 84:195. See, however, *Shaagas Aryeh* 75, who apparently forbids use of inedible foods even in case of illness.

13. At times, the forbidden food may not be completely inedible. In that case, a majority of kosher food may be required, See *Taz* and *M.Z.* 103:2.

14. *Minchas Kohen* 1:9, *M.Z.* 103:1. See, however, *Chavas Daas* 103:4, for a dissenting opinion. See *M.Z.* ibid. and *D.T.* 103:20 for an explanation of why the prohibition disappears with the addition of merely a small amount of permitted food. We chose to follow this opinion since it is clearly set forth in the *Minchas Kohen*. If, however, the amount of kosher food is insignificant, perhaps even the lenient opinions would concede that the mixture is prohibited (this would depend upon the opposing explanations presented by *M.Z.* and *D.T.*).

15. *D.T.* 103:6.

16. See *Avodah Zarah* 68b, *Tosfos* s.v. *"d'ha"*, see also *Beis Yosef* Y.D. 104. If, however, the inedible insect or worm became rotten or otherwise spoiled (i.e., it is now inedible for two reasons: its natural repulsive nature and its acquired spoiled taste), it is subject to a dispute among *Poskim*. Some authorities maintain that since the Torah prohibited insects in spite of their inedibility, any additional spoilage is irrelevant. Others maintain that while the Torah disregarded the natural inedibility of the insect, it does not ignore the additional spoilage (see *D.T.* 103:12).

ha'nasheh — the sciatic nerve, is not considered edible; nevertheless, it is forbidden by the Torah.[17]

Therefore, one may not eat any food (e.g., fruit or vegetable) in which a whole worm or insect is present even if the taste of the insect is repulsive.[18] The food may be permitted in one of the following conditions:

1) If the insect is removed (even after being cooked with the food) the food may be eaten.[19] (Incidentally, if one finds three or more insects in any food, one must assume that the food is infested with insects. The food may not be eaten unless it is sifted or strained beforehand.)[20]
2) If the insect is incomplete and not noticeable, it is *batel* (nullified) and the food may be eaten. However, if it is possible to strain the food and remove the insect, one is required to do so.[21]

II. When only the taste of the non-kosher food is present

We noted earlier that non-kosher food can affect kosher food even if the substance of the non-kosher is not present.[22] Whenever

---

17. *Y.D.* 65:9.

18. A complete creature cannot become nullified (*Y.D.* 100:1) unless it becomes completely inedible (*Rema* 103:1. See a dissenting opinion cited in *Aruch HaShulchan* 100:17, 103:11). However, an insect which is inedible in its original state is prohibited notwithstanding the fact that it is inedible, as noted above. See a discussion of the various opinions on this subject in *Matamei HaShulchan* 103:2. If the insect or worm becomes rotten and inedible besides its normal inedible state, it is subject to the difference of opinion cited in note 16 above.

19. The food certainly contains more than sixty times the volume of the insect. In addition, the taste of the insect is usually detrimental to the food (*Y.D.* 107:2). See, however, *Shach* 107:7 for a dissenting opinion. Common custom is to follow the lenient opinion of the *Shulchan Aruch* (*S.D.* ibid., who notes that it is a meritorious act to refrain from eating the food. He is, however, referring to a case where the taste is not *batel b'shishim*).

20. *Y.D.* 84:9.

21. *Y.D.* 104:3.

22. Actually, whenever the non-kosher taste is noticeable it is assumed that some of its substance must be present. This amount, however, is usually negligible (see *Yad Yehudah* 103:9a).

non-kosher taste is absorbed into a permitted food to the degree that its taste is noticeable, the permitted food assumes the prohibited characteristic of the non-kosher food. This is possible in one of three ways:

- □ Non-kosher food mixed into a majority of kosher food. In this case, the non-kosher food alone would be nullified by the majority of kosher food. However, the fact that the non-kosher food imbues its taste into the kosher food renders the food non-kosher.
- □ Non-kosher food cooked together with kosher food but subsequently removed. In this case, the non-kosher food itself cannot affect the status of the kosher food. However, the fact that its taste was absorbed by the kosher food renders the food non-kosher.
- □ Foods cooked in a *treif* vessel. Although the kosher food never came in contact with the non-kosher food, the non-kosher taste absorbed into the pot is infused into the kosher food.

In any of these cases, the non-kosher food can only impart its non-kosher status to the kosher food if it improves the taste of the kosher food. The principle of *taam k'ikar* only applies where the infused taste is beneficial to the food into which it is absorbed.[23] In the cases cited above, the non-kosher food need not render the food completely inedible. The mere fact that it adversely affects the kosher food negates its ability to confer its prohibited characteristic on the kosher food. This phenomenon is known as *nosen taam lifgam*, נוֹתֵן טַעַם לִפְגַם (imparting an unsatisfactory taste). Although the source of this rule is identical with that of inedible foods cited above, its *halachos* vary. When only the taste is present (even in a very significant amount[24]) it is not necessary for the non-kosher food to render the kosher food completely inedible in order for the food to remain permissible. In any situation where the non-kosher food affects the kosher food in a detrimental manner, it cannot impart its non-kosher status.[25] For example:

---

23. See explanations of *Rashba* and *Ran* and the practical differences between their views, cited in *Beis Yosef; Y.D.* 103.

24. *Taz* 103:3 and *Shach* §5.

25. *Y.D.* 103:2.

A. Mixtures containing non-kosher taste

If an inedible non-kosher food is cooked and blended into a majority of kosher food, the kosher food may be eaten if its taste was impaired, even slightly, by the non-kosher food.[26] Similarly, if the non-kosher food was the majority but it was subsequently removed, the kosher food may be eaten.[27]

In addition, the following considerations apply:

1) Even if the non-kosher food itself is pleasant tasting, it cannot affect the kosher food if, in combination, it adversely affects the taste of the kosher food.[28]

2) Even if the non-kosher food would not, in itself, ruin the kosher food were it not for the presence of a third ingredient, it is nevertheless considered *nosen taam lifgam.*[29]

3) If the non-kosher food has no effect on the kosher food i.e., it affects it neither in a positive nor a negative manner, it cannot be considered *nosen taam lifgam*.[30]

4) If the non-kosher food significantly adds to the volume of the mixture and thus provides more benefit (through the increased amount of food) than detriment (through the impaired taste), the mixture is not permitted, in the opinion of some *Poskim,* unless it becomes completely inedible.[31]

---

26. Y.*D.* 103:2. See *D.T.* 103:8 who cites opinions that the concept of *nosen taam lifgam* can be applied only to those mixtures mentioned by *Chazal* as being *nosen taam lifgam.* This opinion is, however, not accepted by most *Poskim.*

27. If, however, non-kosher gravy remained, it must be treated as non-kosher food itself i.e., it requires nullification in a majority of kosher food vs. the gravy (see *Yad Yehudah* 103:11k).

28. Y.*D.* 103:1.

29. Y.*D.* 103:3. See *D.T.* 103:51.

30. *Shach* 103:2 See *D.T.* 103:16, who cites opposing view regarding this case and makes a distinction between a non-kosher food which possesses a taste of its own but does not affect the food into which it is mixed, and a food which possesses no taste. In the former, the mixture is prohibited; in the latter, the mixture is permitted. See *S.D.* 103:2 who differentiates between a case of where the actual non-kosher food becomes mixed with the kosher food and a case of where only non-kosher taste was absorbed.

31. See *Y.D.* 103:2 who cites the opinion of *Ran* as the second opinion. See *D.T.* 103:26, as to whether or not the opinion of *Ran* is accepted by *Poskim.* See *Kaf HaChaim* 103:17 who rules that in an instance of difficulty, one may follow the lenient opinions.

5) If the immediate effect of the non-kosher food is to improve the taste of the mixture even though it subsequently has a negative effect, the food may not be eaten. The principle of *nosen taam lifgam* applies only if the non-kosher food affects the kosher food negatively, continuously from the time of the original mixture.[32]

6) Similarly, if the immediate effect of the non-kosher food is negative but subsequently it improves the taste of the mixture, one may not eat the food once the negative effect ceases.[33] One may, however, eat the food while the effect is still negative.[34]

7) If, however, the non-kosher food that had become rotten and completely inedible improves only when ingredients are added to make it edible the food may be eaten.[35]

8) Although the food may be eaten, the vessel in which it was cooked requires *kashering*.[36] *Poskim* were concerned that one may use the vessel to cook food which is not harmed by the offensive taste.[37]

As noted above, these rules are limited to a situation where only the *taam* (taste) of the prohibited food poses the problem. If, however, the substance of the prohibited food is present in a significant amount (i.e., it has not become nullified by a majority of kosher food[38]) or in the event that it cannot be nullified (i.e., it is something of importance,[39] see above), it retains its prohibited status until it has become completely inedible,[40] as noted above.

---

32. *Y.D.* 103:2. Thus, even after the taste has spoiled, the food may not be eaten (*Shach* §7. See *S.D.* ibid. that this prohibition is only Rabbinic).

33. Ibid.

34. *Shach* 103:7 and *S.D.* ibid. Although other authorities disagree (see *D.T.* 103:32).

35. *Chavas Daas* 103:1 and *Yad Yehudah* 103:11a. Since the non-kosher food retains its negative character but is merely overwhelmed by additional kosher food, the mixture is permitted. The non-kosher food is still, in itself, *nosen taam lifgam* (*D.T.* 103:31).

36. *Rema* 103:2.

37. *Biur HaGra* 103:8. If, however, the non-kosher food was completely inedible, the vessel need not be *kashered* (*S.D.* 103:11).

38. *Y.D.* 103:2.

39. *Rema* 103:1 see *Shach* §1 and *D.T.* §12.

40. *Taz* 103:1.

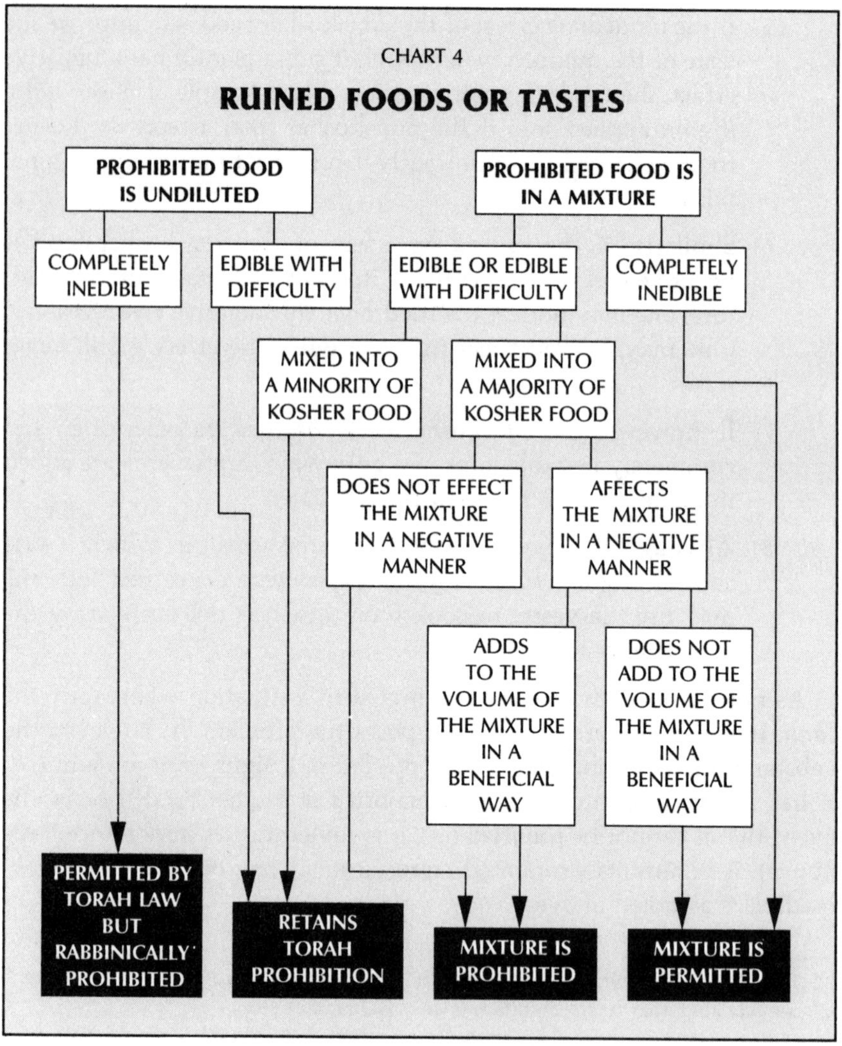

B. Non-kosher taste absorbed in vessels

Whenever food is cooked in a vessel, the vessel absorbs taste of that food and infuses it into any food subsequently cooked in that vessel. If, however, the taste remains in the vessel[41] for a longer period of time, it becomes *pagum*, פָּגוּם (stale) and affects any food cooked in that pot in

41. Only taste absorbed into a vessel becomes *pagum*. Taste absorbed into food never loses its potency. Thus, potatoes boiled with non-kosher meat and subsequently warmed in a pot, even after twenty-four hours, renders that pot non-kosher (*D.T.* 103:75).

a negative manner — *nosen taam lifgam*.[42] *Poskim* disagree as to the length of time required for the taste to become stale. In the opinion of some *Poskim*, the passage of a complete night is sufficient.[43] Others require the passage of a twenty-four-hour period.[44] This second, more stringent opinion is most widely accepted by *Poskim*.[45] Thus, if food is cooked in a pot that was used for hot, non-kosher food in the previous twenty-four hours (*ben-yomo,* בֶּן יומו — lit. of the day), the food may not be eaten. If food is cooked in a non-kosher pot that was not used during the previous twenty-four hours (*aino ben-yomo,* אֵינו בֶּן יומו), the food is permitted. Similarly, if meat is cooked in a milk pot that was not *ben-yomo*, the meat is permitted.[46]

Accordingly, it may seem that one should not be required to *kasher* any non-kosher vessel: it can merely be set aside for the twenty-four-hour respite. However, *Chazal* ordained that any non-kosher[47] vessel must be *kashered* before it is used for kosher food. Similarly, a dairy vessel in which meat was cooked requires *kashering* before it may be used for a kosher food. *Chazal* were concerned that if one were permitted to use the vessel after the twenty-four hour respite, one may inadvertently use it during the first twenty-four hours as well.[48]

---

42. *Avodah Zarah* 75b.

43. A passage of merely part of the night is insufficient, e.g., if the pot was used in the first hour of the night, passage of that night does not affect the taste (*Rashi*, as interpreted in *Tosfos: Avodah Zarah* 76a) and *Ran* (cited in *Tur* 103). See *Chochmas Adam* 55:4 that a complete night begins at sundown. See *S.D.* 103:19 that it ends at dawn (*alos hashachar*).

44. *Rashbam* cited in *Tur* 103.

45. *Y.D.* 103:5.

46. See *Issur V'heter* 44:1, that this rule is applied only in an ex-post-facto (*bidieved*) situation of foods, i.e., food was already cooked in a non-kosher non-*ben-yomo* pot. If, however, only water was cooked in the pot, it may not be used with other foods since the loss of water is insignificant. In the event that one specifically cooked the water for drinking purposes, it may be used since this case is also considered *bidieved* (see *Beis Yosef* 95).

47. Even if the vessel was used for a food prohibited only by Rabbinic decree (*issur d'rabbanon*) or even for a food whose status as Rabbinically prohibited is not certain (*safek d'rabbanon*), see R' Akiva Eger, gloss to *Y.D.* 103:5. See, however, *S.D.* 103:17 who apparently is lenient regarding a *safek d'rabbanon*.

48. *Avodah Zarah* 75b. See *S.D.* 103:17 and *Yad Yehudah* 103:23a that even an earthenware vessel which cannot be *kashered*, and even if it is no longer a *ben-yomo*, it nevertheless cannot be used and must be discarded (though *Chazal* permitted the *ex-post-facto* situation of the food that was cooked in the vessel, they did not permit the *ex-post-facto* situation of the vessel itself). See also *Yad Yehudah* (ibid.) for a discussion of the opinion of *Chacham Tzvi* 75,81, that after the respite of twelve months, any

Although we stated that a pot which is not *ben-yomo* cannot impart its non-kosher taste, one should note the following considerations:

1) Food not immediately removed from the vessel:
The twenty-four-hour respite is determined from the time that the non-kosher food stopped infusing its taste into the vessel. Therefore, if upon completion of the cooking the non-kosher food was not immediately removed from the vessel, one must determine the twenty-four hours from the time that the food was no longer hot *(yad soledes bo)*.[49] In addition, if a non-kosher liquid remained in the vessel for twenty-four hours or more, one must calculate the respite from the time the liquid was removed.[50]

2) Food residue on the vessel:
The question of *ben-yomo* applies only to a clean vessel. An unwashed[51] vessel retains non-kosher food residue and transmits the taste of that residue to any food cooked in the pot regardless of passage of time. Only absorbed taste becomes stale after twenty-four hours have passed. Actual food (or even the minute food residue on a vessel) is unaffected.[52] All vessels[53] may be assumed to be clean unless known to be unwashed.[54]

3) Sharp foods:
Sharp foods (e.g., onions or garlic) have the ability to revitalize a stale taste absorbed from the vessel. Therefore, if a sharp

---

taste is completely dried and ruined (see also *Chochmas Adam* 55:4). *Yad Yehudah*, however, concludes that the option of waiting twelve months applies only to wine vessels. He does concede that a sharp food cannot revitalize a taste that remained in a vessel for twelve months. Other *Poskim* take a more lenient view. See *Matamei HaShulchan* 91:19 for a discussion of the possibility of *kashering* earthenware or china in cases of significant loss. See also *Igros Moshe: Y.D.* 2:46.

49. *D.T.* 103:76. See Chapter Five, Section II for a definition of the degree of heat.

50. *Yad Yehudah* 103:29k. See *Pischei Teshuvah* 93:5. See also *Shach* 103:16 who cites opinion of *Maharshal* that whenever food is in the utensil even the absorbed taste does not become stale. *Shach*, however, rejects this view.

51. See *Yad Yehudah* 103:24a, as to the status of a vessel that was washed but not scrubbed.

52. First opinion in *Y.D.* 103:5, unless, of course, the passage of time renders the foods completely inedible.

53. With the exception of a knife, as will be discussed in Chapter Twelve.

54. *Shach* 103:15. If possible, however, one should inquire as to whether or not the vessel was indeed washed (see *D.T.* 103:78). See *Yad Yehudah* 103:30k, who notes that not all *Poskim* agree with *Shach*.

food[55] is cooked in even an *aino ben-yomo* non-kosher pot, the food may not be eaten.[56] See Chapter Twelve, Section II, C for a more extensive discussion of this point.

4) Water cooked in the vessel in the interim:
The twenty-four-hour respite pertains only to the non-kosher foods cooked in the pot. Use of the pot for kosher foods (e.g., water) during those twenty-four hours should not pose a problem. However, since the water cooked in the *ben-yomo* pot absorbed non-kosher taste and became prohibited, perhaps the water itself should be treated as prohibited matter which can, in turn, impart its prohibited taste to another food. This depends upon the question of *chatichah na'asis neveilah* (the object itself becomes prohibited matter) discussed above in chapter 2. Were we to treat the water as non-kosher matter itself, the twenty-four hours should be calculated from the time the water was cooked. If, however, the water merely *contains* non-kosher taste but is not non-kosher itself, the twenty-four hours should be calculated from the time the original non-kosher food was cooked. For example: Non-kosher meat was boiled in a pot at 8:00 PM Sunday evening. Subsequently water was boiled in the pot Monday morning and potatoes were boiled in the pot at 8:30 PM Monday night. If we were to calculate the twenty-four hours starting from the cooking of the non-kosher food the potatoes are permitted. However, if we were to calculate the twenty-four hours starting from the boiling of the water, the potatoes are forbidden. Since these *halachos* are difficult and subject to controversy, one should consult a *moreh hora'ah*.[57]

---

55. I.e., either the entire food is sharp or it contains enough sharp ingredients to give the entire mixture a sharp flavor (*Taz* 103:9, see *Yad Yehudah* 103:33k).

56. *Y.D.* 103:6. See *D.T.* 103:81 whether this principle is Biblical or Rabbinic in origin and as to whether this principle should be applied to foods whose status as sharp foods is not certain. See *Yad Yehudah* 103:23a, that a sharp food cannot revitalize a taste that remained in a vessel for twelve months. When a *davar charif* is cooked in a non-*ben-yomo* pot, the taste previously absorbed in the pot remains non-*ben-yomo* taste. Thus, if non sharp food is subsequently cooked in the pot, it is unaffected (*Shach* 95:7). In addition, if a sharp non-kosher food is cooked in a pot and subsequently, after twenty-four hours, a non sharp kosher food is cooked in the pot, it is permitted. A taste from sharp foods, just as any taste, becomes stale with the passage of time (*Rema* 122:3).

57. See *Y.D.* 103:7. The question hinges on three considerations: 1) Perhaps *chatichah na'asis neveilah* applies only to *basar b'chalav* (meat and milk mixtures) but not to other forbidden foods (the opinion of *Rabeinu Efraim* cited in *Beis Yosef* 103). 2) Perhaps *chatichah na'asis neveilah* has no relevance to this question. While *chatichah*

This much, however, is clear: a meat or dairy vessel is considered *aino ben-yomo* once twenty-four hours have passed from the original cooking of the meat or milk, regardless of any *parve* food or water cooked in between.[58]

Summary

⁂ Any forbidden food which becomes unfit to eat has lost its status as a forbidden food.

1) When the actual substance of the non-kosher food is present:
   a) Prohibited food which putrefies and has become completely unfit to eat, has lost its status as a forbidden food. Nevertheless, it is prohibited by Rabbinic injunction unless: a) one must eat it for medicinal purposes and no kosher substitute is available, or b) it was mixed into kosher food and cannot be separated and removed.
   b) Prohibited foods that are naturally inedible such as loathsome insects and rodents are nevertheless prohibited by Torah law. Therefore, a worm or insect found in any food must be removed unless the insect is incomplete, not noticeable and unremovable with a strainer. Once the insect is removed the food may be eaten.

---

na'asis neveilah can cause the water to become prohibited it cannot alter the status of *aino ben-yomo* since the water itself is not the original prohibited matter (the opinion of *Smak* cited ibid.). 3) Perhaps, in this case, we can rely on the position of *Rashi* that passage of a night is sufficient to ruin the absorbed taste. Based on these considerations, *Poskim* rule that if a complete night passed between the original non-kosher cooking and the boiling of the water, the vessel is considered *aino ben-yomo* after a passage of twenty-four hours from the original cooking, regardless of whether that was *basar b'chalav* or other non-kosher foods. Correspondingly, if the vessel was a meat pot used to boil milk after passage of a complete night and subsequently used to boil water, it is considered *aino ben-yomo* after passage of twenty-four hours from the boiling of the milk (*Y.D.* 103:7). This is based on the last two considerations. Similarly, if the vessel involved is not one of *basar b'chalav,* one may follow the lenient position in a case of even a minor loss (*Rema* 103:7, as explained in *Shach* §20). This is based on the first two considerations. If, however, the vessel was used for *basar b'chalav* and subsequently used to boil water before the passage of a complete night, it is considered a *ben-yomo* until the passage of twenty-four hours from the boiling of the water (*Y.D.* ibid. see *Shach* §18 as opposed to *Darcei Moshe* 103:2). In a situation of serious loss, one may follow the lenient position even in this case (*Shach* 103:20).

58. The concept of *chatichah na'asis neveilah* is not applicable to the taste of meat or milk absorbed into the water since each in itself is completely kosher (*Tur* 94, 103, see *Issur V'heter* 34:7).

2) When only the taste of the non-kosher food is present:
This is possible in one of three ways: a) the non-kosher food is mixed into a majority of kosher food. b) the non-kosher food is cooked together with kosher food but is subsequently removed. c) foods cooked in a non-kosher vessel. In any of these cases, the non-kosher food cannot impart its non-kosher status to the kosher food unless it improves the taste of the kosher food. However, if it adversely affects the kosher food, the food continues to be kosher even though it remains edible. This phenomenon is known as *nosen taam lifgam* (imparting an unsatisfactory taste). For example:

a) If a non-kosher food is blended into a majority of kosher food or if the non-kosher food was the majority but it was subsequently removed, the kosher food may be eaten if its taste was immediately impaired, even slightly, by the non-kosher food.

□ Even if the non-kosher food itself is pleasant tasting and even if it would not ruin the kosher food were it not for the presence of a third ingredient, it cannot affect the status of kosher food since, in combination, it adversely affects the taste of the kosher food.

□ If the non-kosher food affects the kosher food in neither a positive nor a negative manner, it cannot be considered *nosen taam lifgam*.

b) Non-kosher taste absorbed in vessels — *nosen taam lifgam:*
Taste that remains in a vessel for a period of twenty-four hours has become *pagum* and affects any food cooked in that pot in a negative manner — *nosen taam lifgam*. Thus, if food is cooked in a non-kosher pot that was not used in the previous twenty-four hours *(aino ben-yomo)* the food is permitted.

□ The twenty-four-hour respite applies only to a clean vessel. An unwashed vessel transmits the taste of its residue regardless of passage of time. All vessels may be assumed to be clean unless known to be unwashed.

□ Sharp foods have the ability to revitalize a stale taste absorbed from the vessel. Therefore, if a sharp food is cooked in even an *aino ben-yomo* non-kosher pot, the food may not be eaten.

CHART 5

CALCULATION OF BEN–YOMO

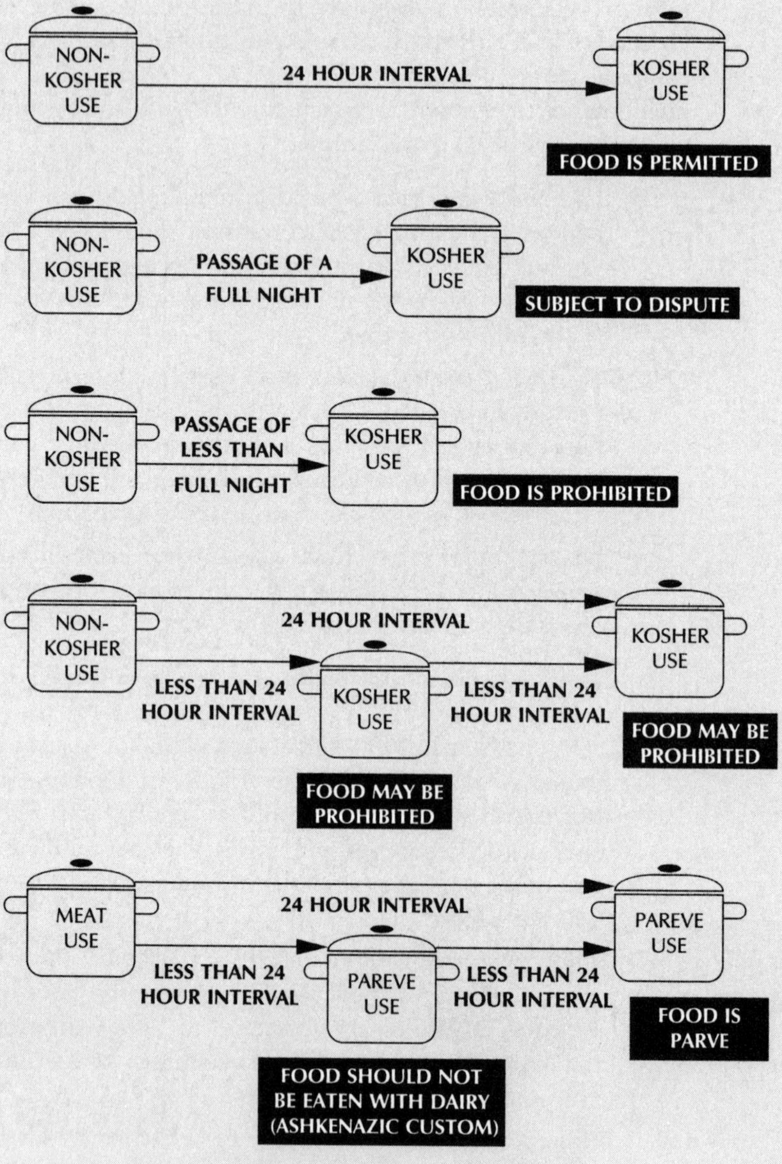

CHAPTER FOUR

טַעַם כְּעִיקָר
Non-Kosher Tastes

- The principle of *taam k'ikar*.
- Sampling the mixture to detect non-kosher taste.
- Nullification through *bitul b'shishim*.

Introduction

A central issue in *hilchos kashrus* concerns the infusion and absorption of taste. Whenever non-kosher food comes in contact with kosher food, there is a potential transfer of taste from the non-kosher food to the kosher food. In this chapter, we will discuss the concept of *taam k'ikar* — the principle by which the kosher food is affected by the non-kosher taste it has absorbed. We will also explore the possibility of sampling food to detect the presence of non-kosher taste. Finally, we will discuss the requirement of *bitul b'shishim* (nullification in a sixty-to-one ratio) — the means through which the problem of *taam k'ikar* is overcome.

At the core of the issue of taste infusions is the principle of *taam k'ikar*, which means that the taste of the (non-kosher) food is considered as its essence. Kosher food imbued with a noticeable taste of non-kosher food is considered the equivalent of the non-kosher food itself. One may not eat kosher food that has absorbed non-kosher taste since, in doing so, he will taste the non-kosher taste.

We noted in Chapter Two that non-kosher taste may affect kosher food under several different circumstances: a) The non-kosher matter may have completely blended into the mixture, b) the non-kosher matter may have been cooked together with the kosher food and infuse the kosher food with its taste before having been removed. c) The kosher food may have been cooked in a utensil that was infused with non-kosher taste and thereby absorbed some of the taste infused in the utensil. In any of these cases, the principle of *taam k'ikar* rules that the kosher food has assumed a non-kosher status.

Rishonim disagree as to whether the principle of *taam k'ikar* is Biblical or Rabbinic in origin. In the opinion of some *Rishonim,* this depends upon whether the actual substance of the non-kosher food or only its taste is present in the mixture. It further depends upon the ratio of kosher and non-kosher matter in the mixture and upon the amount of the mixture one eats. A detailed analysis of divergent viewpoints is not within the scope of this work; however, the *halachic* consensus assumes that *taam k'ikar* should usually be treated as a Biblical precept. We refer the reader to the footnotes.[1] We will limit our discussion to the practical steps that must be taken regarding situations of *taam k'ikar*.

---

1. A comprehensive discussion of the varying positions can be found in *Minchas Kohen* II, 1:2-6. In short: i) In the opinion of *Rashi, taam k'ikar* is of Rabbinic nature whenever

I. Sampling the mixture to detect non-kosher taste

These *halachos* are based on *Tur* and *Shulchan Aruch; Yoreh De'ah* 98:1.

We noted in Chapter Two that when non-kosher matter falls into dissimilar tasting kosher food, it is assumed to have imparted some of its taste into the kosher food. We noted, too, that *bitul b'shishim*, a nullification in a sixty-to-one ratio, is required to make the mixture permissible. We assume that the taste of the non-kosher food is unnoticeable when it is mixed into kosher food sixty times its volume. The sixty-to-one ratio, however, is not absolute. Any ratio in which the non-kosher flavor is unnoticeable is adequate to eliminate the problem of *taam k'ikar*. Thus, theoretically, by sampling the mixture one should be able to determine whether or not the non-kosher taste is recognizable and eliminate the problem of *taam k'ikar*.[2]

---

the non-kosher matter is a liquid or a solid that has dissolved. ii) In the opinion of *Ran*, whenever the non-kosher matter is present in the mixture (even if dissolved), the mixture is Biblically prohibited if the non-kosher taste is noticeable. If the non-kosher taste is not noticeable, *bitul b'shishim* is only Rabbinically required. iii) In the opinion of the *Rambam*, if the non-kosher matter is mixed into the food in a ratio of one *kizayis* to three *kibeitzim* (egg volumes), it is Biblically prohibited to eat three egg volumes of the mixture. According to the *Shulchan Aruch: O.C.* 486, a *kizayis* is one half an egg; thus, the ratio is one to six (or one to eight, see *M.B.* 208:43). Others *(Magen Avraham,* ibid.) contend that in the opinion of *Rambam*, a *kizayis* is one third of a *kibeitzah* and thus the ratio is one to nine (see *Chochmas Adam* 51:8). iv) In the opinion of *Rabbeinu Tam*, even if none of the non-kosher matter is present in the mixture, but the kosher food absorbed non-kosher taste, the food is Biblically forbidden. Furthermore, in his opinion, one who eats a *kizayis* of kosher food imbued with only the taste of non-kosher matter is liable for the punishment of *malkos* (forty lashes). This is the most stringent opinion regarding *taam k'ikar* found in the *Rishonim*. v) *Rashba, Raavad* and *Rabbeinu Chaim* agree in principle with *Rabbeinu Tam*, but disagree as to the precise conditions under which one who eats the affected food is liable for *malkos*. As noted above, *Minchas Kohen* offers an exhaustive analysis of each of these opinions and their sources in the Talmud. See also *Pri Chadash: O.C.* 442:1, 453:2.

2. One who wishes to research the differing opinions among *Rishonim* (and their Talmudic sources) pertaining to the issue of a non-Jewish taster *(k'feilah)* is referred to *Minchas Kohen* II, 1:7. A summary of the primary opinions is as follows: a) In the opinion of *Rashi: Chullin* 97a, and *Rosh* (as cited in *Minchas Kohen)* the sampler, whether a Jew or a non-Jew, must be a professional chef. An amateur is incompetent to judge with certainty whether the taste is noticeable. In addition, a non-Jewish sampler must be unaware that his testimony has any relevance with regard to *halachahh*. b) In

A. The problem

Poskim have raised the following objections to the use of sampling in order to determine the presence of non-kosher taste through sampling:

1) Sampling by a Jew:
If the non-kosher taste is indeed noticeable, the mixture may not be eaten. Therefore, one who samples the mixture risks violating the prohibition. Thus, a Jew cannot taste the mixture to determine whether a non-kosher taste is present. At times, however, this objection may not be valid. For example: If *terumah* fell into permitted food, perhaps it may be sampled by a *Kohen* since he is permitted to eat *terumah*. Similarly, if milk fell into *parve* food, perhaps it may be sampled by any Jew to determine whether the mixture tastes of milk and is thus considered a dairy food.[3] In addition, perhaps simple sampling of a non-kosher mixture with the tip of the tongue may be permitted to determine whether the non-kosher flavor is noticeable.[4]

2) Sampling by a non-Jew:
A non-Jew may anticipate our concern that the mixture is prohibited and wish to "please" us with his assurance that the food is permitted. Thus, his word is suspect. Furthermore, one may not rely upon a non-Jew in any matter pertaining to *halachah*. This is due to our attitude towards *mitzvos*. We

---

the opinion of *Ran: Chullin* ibid. (this appears to be the opinion of *Tosfos* as well), the requirement of a professional taster is based upon the need for his credibility, not his expertise. Even an amateur is able to detect a noticeable taste in food (a non-noticeable taste is of no concern). However, a non-Jewish amateur cannot be trusted to provide reliable information. A professional, however, would never compromise his professional integrity by providing inaccurate information. Thus, even (and especially) if the non-Jew is aware of the importance of his testimony, he is believed. Similarly, a Jew may sample the mixture (where permitted) even though he is an amateur. (Although an amateur may not notice a subtle taste, any taste not recognizable to the amateur is not *halachically* considered a noticeable taste -*Tur* 98). An amateur non-Jew, however, may not be relied upon. c) In the opinion of *Rashba* (cited in *Beis Yosef* 98) even an amateur non-Jew is trusted if he is unaware of the importance of his testimony. d) In the opinion of *Rambam* 15:30 (as noted in *Beis Yosef* 98 and explained in *Minchas Kohen*, see *S.D.* 98:2), any non-Jew may be trusted to sample the mixture. No one would provide false information where the deceit will become apparent as soon as the food is eaten and the non-kosher taste is noticed.

3. See *Shach* 98:5.

4. See *Taz* 98:2, *Pischei Teshuvah* 98:1.

believe that the performance of a *mitzvah* or the violation of a prohibition is a matter of cosmic effect that can only be properly appreciated by one who accepts and abides by those precepts. A non-Jew, however honest and trustworthy he may be, cannot appreciate the enormous consequences of his information. Therefore, a non-Jew who samples a mixture and claims that the non-kosher taste is unnoticeable cannot be believed. In the opinion of some authorities, this objection would not apply if the non-Jew is unaware of the fact that the question of taste is of any concern to us *(masiach lefi tumo)*.[5] Other authorities contend that even in this case, the non-Jew cannot be believed.[6] However, if the non-Jew is a professional chef who would ruin his reputation if he were to provide inaccurate information,[7] there may be grounds to accept his testimony.

B. The halachah

The *Shulchan Aruch*[8] rules that one may[9] rely upon the sampling[10] of any non-Jew who is unaware of our concern regarding *kashrus* or upon that of a professional even if he is aware of our concern.[11] *Ashkenazic*[12] custom,[13] however, does not permit reliance upon any non-Jew to

5. The opinion of the *Shulchan Aruch* 98:1. See *Taz*, § end of note 2, concerning a case where the non-Jew is aware of our interest but not necessarily concerning kashrus.

6. *Taz* 98:2.

7. In this case, the fact that he is aware of our concern increases his reliability *(Ran*, cited in *Beis Yosef* 98).

8. *Y.D.* 98:1, as understood by *Shach* §2.

9. Moreover, *Shulchan Aruch* seems to rule that if a non-Jew is available, one may not rely on *bitul b'shishim*, see *Shach* 98:4.

10. See *Matamei HaShulchan* 98:2 as to whether even a non-Jewish professional is relied upon if he tasted the food without actually swallowing.

11. See *Taz* 98:2 and *Shach* 98:2 who note the contradiction between this ruling of *Shulchan Aruch* and the Talmudic *(Bava Kama* 114a) rule that *masiach lefi tumo* is unacceptable with regard to any Biblical prohibition. Thus, since *Shulchan Aruch* rules that *taam k'ikar* is a Biblical precept, the testimony of a non-Jew should be unacceptable. *Shach* answers that this case is unique since the non-Jew realizes that when the Jew eats the mixture, he will certainly notice any non-kosher taste. Therefore, the non-Jew is careful to offer an honest evaluation.

12. See *Kaf HaChaim* 92:2 and 98:2 that in this instance even *Sefardic* custom follows the stringent opinion of *Rema*.

13. See *R' Akiva Eger* gloss to *Rema* who finds a rationale for this custom. See also gloss *Yad Efraim* (ibid.).

sample food mixtures;[14] instead, *bitul b'shishim* is required in all circumstances. Some authorities question whether in this day and age we have the ability to properly identify the non-kosher taste in a mixture. In their opinion, one may not even rely upon the sampling of a Jew.[15] Other authorities rule that one may rely upon the tasting of a Jew (where permitted, as described in 1, above) to determine the presence of taste in the mixture.[16] However, a Jew is not permitted to taste a mixture of non-kosher food with his tongue to ascertain the presence of non-kosher taste. *Poskim* raise two objections: Perhaps sampling non-kosher food with one's tongue is prohibited,[17] and secondly, a simple tongue tasting may be insufficient to determine the presence of taste. The food must be taken into the mouth and perhaps even swallowed. This is certainly forbidden to a Jew since the mixture may have non-kosher taste.[18]

It should be clear by now that solving a problem of dissimilar tasting mixtures through sampling is, in most cases, either impossible or unacceptable. Thus, the only way the mixture may become permissible is through *bitul b'shishim*.[19] If, however, the mixture was sampled and the non-kosher taste was noticeable, the mixture may not be eaten, even though it was *batel b'shishim*.[20] Mixtures of similar tasting foods can never be sampled to determine the presence of any non-kosher flavor since they do not impart a noticeable taste into one another. Thus, mixtures of similar tasting food always require *bitul b'shishim*. We proceed now to a discussion of the principles of *bitul b'shishim*.

---

14. *Rema* 98:1. This is not merely because *Chazal* required *bitul b'shishim*, for even in the event that the kosher food may contain sixty times the non-kosher taste, a non-Jew may not check for non-kosher taste. For instance, if kosher food was cooked in a non-kosher pot, a non-Jew may not sample the food even though if he detects no taste we may assume that the taste was indeed *batel b'shishim*. See *Beis Yosef* (beginning of 93) who argues that in this case even those who normally reject the sampling of a non-Jew should accept it. *Rema* 93:1, however, does not accept a non-Jew's sampling, even in this case (see *Shach* §1).

15. *Levush* cited in *Shach* 98:5.

16. *Shach* 98:5, see *Chavas Daas* §26.

17. See *Pischei Teshuvah* 98:1.

18. See *Taz* 98:2, and *Matamei HaShulchan* 98:2, for a discussion of the various opinions on this matter.

19. In the opinion of *Rashi: Chullin* 98a, *bitul b'shishim* may be relied upon only if sampling is impossible or if the sampling has not indicated any non-kosher taste.

20. *Shach* 98:4.

Summary of Section I

☙ It is usually impossible to determine the presence of non-kosher food in a mixture through sampling:

- ☐ A Jew may not taste the mixture to determine whether a non-kosher taste is present since he may not taste non-kosher food. Even sampling non-kosher food with one's tongue is prohibited. In the opinion of some authorities, a *Kohen* may not determine, through sampling, whether a food mixture has the taste of *terumah* since we lack the ability today to properly identify the taste in a mixture.
- ☐ A non-Jew may not be trusted to taste the food since he does not understand the importance of *kashrus*. In the opinion of the *Shulchan Aruch*, one may rely on the sampling of a culinary professional or on that of any non-Jew who is unaware of our concern with regard to *kashrus*. *Ashkenazic* custom does not permit reliance upon any non-Jew to sample food mixtures.
- ☐ Mixtures of similar tasting foods certainly cannot be sampled to determine the presence of any non-kosher flavor since one does not impart a noticeable taste into the other. Therefore, mixtures of similar tasting foods always require *bitul b'shishim*.

Thus, the only way the mixture may become permissible is through *bitul b'shishim*. If the mixture is sampled and the non-kosher taste is noticeable, the mixture may not be eaten even though it is *batel b'shishim*.

II. Nullifying the non-kosher taste through bitul b'shishim

These *halachos* are found in *Tur* and *Shulchan Aruch* 98:4,5.

The principles of *bitul* (nullification) of prohibited foods has been discussed at length in Chapter Two. In this section, we will examine *bitul b'shishim* (nullification in a ratio of sixty) as it pertains to nullification of non-kosher taste. As noted above, the only practical and acceptable method of guaranteeing that no non-kosher taste is present in a mixture is through *bitul b'shishim*. If non-kosher food falls into kosher food that is sixty times its volume, we assume that the non-kosher taste is not noticeable.

A. When is bitul b'shishim required

The issue of *taam k'ikar* and *bitul b'shishim* seemingly pertain only to dissimilar tasting foods mixed together. Similar tasting mixtures should not require *bitul b'shishim* since no taste is imparted. Nevertheless, as explained in Chapter Two, *Chazal* were concerned that one may confuse similar with dissimilar tasting mixtures and therefore they required *bitul b'shishim* even for similar tasting mixtures.[21] The distinction between the two is that while *bitul b'shishim* may be a Biblical requirement for a mixture of dissimilar tasting foods, it is merely a Rabbinic requirement for similar tasting foods since *bitul b'rov* meets the Biblical requirement.[22]

CHART 6

BITUL B'ROV — B'SHISHIM

	LIQUIDS OR SOLIDS COOKED OR BLENDED TOGETHER	SOLIDS NOT COOKED OR BLENDED TOGETHER
DISSIMILAR TASTING MIXTURES	***BITUL B'SHISHIM*** **REQUIRED BY TORAH LAW**	***BITUL B'SHISHIM*** **REQUIRED BY RABBINIC LAW**
SIMILAR TASTING MIXTURES	***BITUL B'SHISHIM*** **REQUIRED BY RABBINIC LAW**	***BATEL B'ROV***

21. *Y.D.* 98:1. We noted, as well, that even Rabbinically prohibited foods require *bitul b'shishim* when mixed with dissimilar tasting foods. When these foods are mixed with similar tasting foods, their status is subject to a dispute among *Poskim* (see *Pri Migadim* in his introduction to *Hilchos Taaruvos* 1:3 and *D.T.* 109:47).

22. The practical difference would pertain to a case where the permitted food certainly constitutes a majority of the mixture but may not contain sixty times the volume of the prohibited food. If the foods are dissimilar in taste, the mixture is forbidden. If the foods are similar tasting and it is impossible to determine whether or not the mixture contains a sufficient amount for *bitul b'shishim*, the mixture is permitted (*Y.D.* 98:2).

B. The effect of bitul b'shishim

In Chapter Two, we discussed the distinction between *bitul b'rov* (nullification in a simple majority), which nullifies the non-kosher matter when no taste is transferred, and *bitul b'shishim*, which is required whenever a transfer of taste occurs. The ratio of sixty parts kosher food to one part non-kosher food is assumed to dilute the non-kosher taste to a degree that it is no longer noticeable. Although, in reality, not all food tastes are equally potent, *Chazal*, basing their decision upon Biblical sources,[23] mandated that all foods require a sixty-to-one ratio for nullification, regardless of how potent their taste may be.[24]

C. The measurement of the sixty-to-one ratio

The sixty-to-one ratio should be measured by volume, not by weight. If both the kosher and non-kosher matter are of equal density (i.e., they are similar in ratio of size to weight), one may measure the ratio by weight.[25] A simple method to measure the proper ratio is the following: if, for example, the non-kosher matter is one cubic inch, then imagine a cube of four inches on each edge. The cube contains sixty four times the original cube of non-kosher matter.

CHART 7

MEASUREMENT OF THE SIXTY RATIO

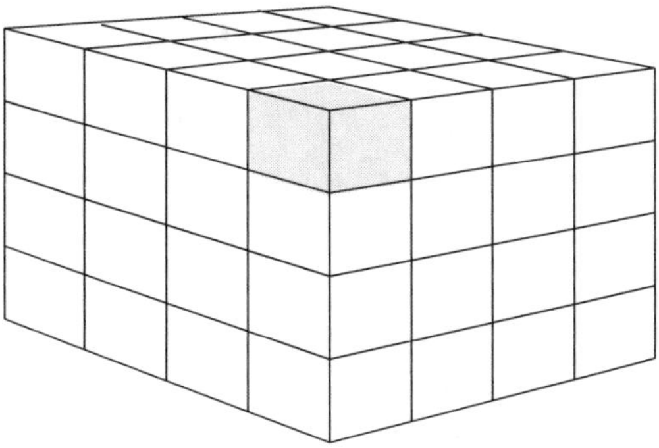

23. *Chullin* 96a.

24. See *Tosfos: Chullin* 98b s.v. *"l'chumra"*.

25. See *Pischei Teshuvah* 98:2.

D. The amount of non-kosher taste imparted into the kosher food

When kosher and non-kosher matter are combined in an indistinguishable mixture, the non-kosher matter usually cannot be removed. Consequently, the non-kosher matter must be nullified in a sixty-to-one ratio. We then have no doubt as to measuring the effect of the non-kosher taste: the entire taste of the non-kosher matter is blended into the mixture. When, however, the non-kosher matter is noticeable and removed (as we noted in Chapter Two, Section III,C *bitul* is not functional when the non-kosher matter is noticeable or removable), there is considerable doubt as to measuring its effect on the mixture. This much, however, is certain: mere removal of the non-kosher matter does not eliminate its effect. The non-kosher taste has already been imparted into the kosher food.[26] *Bitul b'shishim* is therefore necessary. The question thus arises: How is one to measure the volume of the non-kosher taste infused into the kosher food? The Talmud[27] rules that since it is impossible to ascertain the precise amount, one must assume that *all* of the taste of the non-kosher matter[28] was imparted into the kosher food.[29] Consequently, a sixty to one ratio is required against the entire non-kosher matter. For example: if a *kizayis* of non-kosher meat fell into a pot of kosher soup and was subsequently removed, the soup may not be eaten unless it contains sixty times the *kizayis* of meat.

E. The amount of taste imparted from non-kosher utensils

When a non-kosher spoon is placed in hot kosher food or when

26. Although the non-kosher matter appears to be its original size, perhaps it absorbed kosher liquid in place of the matter it imparted into the kosher food (*Taz* 98:7).

27. *Chullin* 97b.

28. *Y.D.* 98:4. See *Aruch HaShulchan* 98:51, who notes that this is not an arbitrary stringent ruling, but rather the logical essential *halachah*. See *Shach* 98:10, who contends that one should not differentiate between Biblically and Rabbinically prohibited foods.

29. *Y.D.* 98:4. Nevertheless, if the non-kosher matter subsequently falls into another kosher food, we require *bitul b'shishim* again (and so infinitely, *Rema* 98:4, see reasons in *Chochmas Adam* 51:7 and *Aruch HaShulchan* 98:58). If, however, the non-kosher matter falls into the original mixture twice, a double *bitul b'shishim* is not required (*Rema*, ibid., for an explanation; see *Biur HaGra* ibid., *Chochmas Adam* and *Aruch HaShulchan* ibid.).

kosher food is cooked in a non-kosher pot, we are again faced with the question of measuring the amount of non-kosher taste transferred. *Halachah* rules that in this case as well, although the spoon is removed, one must assume that the entire non-kosher taste absorbed in the spoon or pot was imparted into the kosher food.[30] However, a non-kosher utensil differs from non-kosher food in one particular aspect. While non-kosher food is thoroughly non-kosher, non-kosher utensils are non-kosher only to the extent of the non-kosher taste they absorbed. We must therefore differentiate between those utensils whose degree of absorption may be defined (i.e., we can determine the maximum taste absorbed into the utensil) and those whose degree of absorption cannot be defined. The *halachos* are as follows:

1) A defined absorption:

A utensil never before used for non-kosher food that was used for a specific amount of non-kosher food (e.g., a *kizayis)* has not absorbed more than the defined amount of taste (a *kizayis).* Consequently, if that utensil is used to cook kosher food, one need be concerned only with the defined amount of taste. Thus, if kosher food is sixty times the original amount of non-kosher food, the kosher food may be eaten.

We noted in Chapter Three, Section II,B that a non-kosher utensil unused for twenty-four hours is *nosen taam lifgam* and has lost the ability to impart its non-kosher taste. Thus, it is the equivalent of an unused utensil. If, after being unused for twenty-four hours, it is used to cook a *kizayis* of non-kosher food, and subsequently (within twenty-four hours) used for sixty *zaysim* kosher food, the non-kosher taste is *batel b'shishim* and the food is permitted. We do not require sixty times the volume of the utensil.[31]

Similarly, if a *parve* utensil (or a meat utensil that was not used for meat during the previous twenty-four hours) is used with a *kizayis* of hot milk and subsequently (within

30. *Y.D.* 98:4. Although this is the accepted ruling, authorities rule that under certain circumstances, we do not measure against the entire volume of the vessel (see *Kaf HaChayim* 94:11). *Poskim* also note the opinion of *Raavad* who differentiates between vessels that can be *kashered* and those that cannot. In the former case, we do not measure against the entire vessel. In the latter case, we must measure against the entire vessel (see *Shach* 98:12). See *M.Z.* 94:1, who contends that even when only a Rabbinic prohibition is involved, we cannot calculate the amount of taste that was imparted; rather, we must measure in proportion to the entire vessel.

31. *Y.D.* 98:5.

twenty-four hours) used for hot meat, *bitul b'shishim* is required against the *kizayis* of milk only.[32]

2) An undefined absorption:
If the utensil in question is a non-kosher utensil that was used during the previous twenty-four hours for an undetermined amount of non-kosher food or used on several occasions during the previous twenty-four hours, it is considered completely imbued with non-kosher taste. If kosher food is cooked in this utensil within twenty-four hours of the non-kosher use, we require *bitul b'shishim* over the volume of the entire utensil.[33]

3) The issue of *chatichah na'asis neveilah:*
Another example of an undefined absorption relates to the concept of *chatichah na'asis neveilah*. For example: a dairy utensil that is used for an undetermined amount of dairy food and subsequently (within twenty-four hours) used for a *kizayis* of hot meat is considered completely imbued with non-kosher taste. We are familiar with the concept of *chatichah na'asis neveilah* by which the previously kosher food is not merely kosher food imbued with a non-kosher taste but becomes a non-kosher entity of its own (see Chapter Two, Section IV,B). Accordingly, the kosher dairy taste[34] previously absorbed in the dairy utensil has become (through the absorption of meat) a non-kosher entity of *basar b'chalav*. Therefore, the vessel is considered imbued not merely with a *kizayis* of meat taste, but totally imbued with *basar b'chalav* taste. Thus, if the utensil is subsequently (within twenty-four hours) used for kosher food, we require *bitul b'shishim* over the volume of the entire

---

32. *Y.D.* ibid.

33. *Y.D.* 98:4. This assumes that the utensil was able to absorb the non-kosher taste throughout. If, however, the utensil absorbed the non-kosher taste only into its *klipah*, e.g., it was used with cold non-kosher salty foods (*Rema* 98:4) or through *iruy* (*Shach* 98:13), we require *bitul b'shishim* only against that *klipah*.

34. *Poskim* reject the notion that a vessel itself (i.e., the body of the vessel, not merely the taste absorbed in it) can be considered *neveilah*. For example: if one cooks a *kizayis* of non-kosher food in a new pot, the pot itself cannot become *neveilah*. Thus, one needs sixty times the volume of the *kizayis* only. The question of *chatichah na'asis neveilah* is relevant only to kosher taste absorbed into the vessel which subsequently mixes with non-kosher taste. Although the vessel itself cannot become *treif*, the tastes absorbed therein can. See *Shach* 98:21. See *Taz* §8 who contends that in the opinion of *Mordechai* an earthenware vessel can itself be considered *neveilah*. See footnote no. 36.

utensil.[35] One faced with this question should consult a *moreh hora'ah*.[36]

In instances that require *bitul b'shishim* over the entire volume of the utensil, *Poskim* differentiate between foods cooked in the vessel (e.g., a pot) and foods into which the utensil (e.g., a ladle) was placed. In the first case, we require *bitul b'shishim* against the entire pot,[37] even though it was only half filled.[38] We assume that taste from the entire vessel is imparted into the food. In the latter case, however, we require *bitul b'shishim* only against that part of the ladle inserted into the pot.[39] We assume that the taste imbued in the ladle handle cannot be absorbed into the food since there was no direct contact between them.[40] See Chapter Eleven, Section G for the practical applications of this *halachah*.

---

35. *Y.D.* 98:5. *Shulchan Aruch* does, however, cite the opinion of *Ramban* that *chatichah na'asis neveilah* cannot be applied to taste absorbed in a vessel. Thus, in his opinion, *bitul b'shishim* is required only against the *kizayis* of meat.

36. *Rema* cites the opinion of *Mordechai* that the concept of *chatichah na'asis neveilah* as applied to utensils pertains only to earthenware utensils that cannot be *kashered*. Taste absorbed in utensils that can be *kashered* (i.e., metal or wood utensils) cannot become *neveilah*. *Taz* 98:8 and *Shach* §21 disagree in interpretation of the *Mordechai*. According to *Taz*, the *Mordechai's* opinion is a restrictive opinion. He contends that *chatichah na'asis neveilah* applies to any utensil, earthenware or metal, that was used in the previous twenty-four hours. An earthenware utensil, however, is subject to *chatichah na'asis neveilah* even if it is new and unused. *Taz* follows this restrictive opinion with regard to *basar b'chalav* but follows the lenient opinions with regard to other non-kosher foods, since essentially *chatichah na'asis neveilah* applies only to *basar b'chalav*. According to *Shach* §21 (and in *Nekudas Hakesef)* the opinion of *Mordechai* is a lenient opinion. Thus, even an earthenware utensil is not subject to *chatichah na'asis neveilah* unless it was used in the previous twenty-four hours, while metal utensils are never subject to *chatichah na'asis neveilah*. *Shach* rules that in a case of significant financial loss, one may rely on this lenient opinion, while under normal circumstances one should follow the stricter opinion and apply *chatichah na'asis neveilah* even to metal utensils (see *S.D.* §21). The opinion of *Mordechai* under discussion should not be confused with that of *Raavad* cited in note no. 30 above (see *Shach* 98:21).

37. *Poskim* assume that a pot does not contain sixty times its own mass *(Shach* 98:11) unless the pot is exceptionally large and made of thin metal *(Shach* 93:1).

38. *Kaf HaChaim* 98:48.

39. Or, in the opinion of others, into the food. This will be discussed in Chapter Eleven, Section G. One may assume that only the part of the ladle normally inserted into the food was inserted *(Shach* 94:1), i.e., the round part *(S.D.* ibid.).

40. *Y.D.* 98:4, as opposed to the opinion of *Rabeinu Peretz* (cited as second opinion in *Y.D.* ibid.) who contends that since a metal spoon is thoroughly heated, it imparts all of its taste into the food. See Chapter Eleven, note 94.

Summary of Section II

ॐ The following are the principal rules of *bitul b'shishim*:

- ☐ All mixtures of kosher and non-kosher foods require *bitul b'shishim*, regardless of whether they are mixtures of similar or dissimilar tasting foods.
- ☐ The requirement of *bitul b'shishim* for dissimilar tasting foods may be Biblical, while the requirement of *bitul b'shishim* for similar tasting foods is merely Rabbinic.
- ☐ *Bitul b'shishim* is assumed to dilute the non-kosher taste to a degree that it is no longer noticeable.
- ☐ All food mixtures require *bitul b'shishim*, regardless of how potent their taste may be.
- ☐ *Bitul b'shishim* is measured by volume, not by weight.
- ☐ When non-kosher matter falls into kosher food and is subsequently removed, one must assume that *all* of the taste of the non-kosher matter was imparted into the kosher food.
- ☐ When kosher food is cooked in a non-kosher pot, we require *bitul b'shishim* against the entire body of the pot. If the pot was used within the previous twenty-four hours for only a specific amount of non-kosher food, we require *bitul b'shishim* merely against that amount of non-kosher food.
- ☐ If a dairy utensil was used for a *kizayis* of hot meat, it is considered completely imbued with non-kosher taste, since the dairy taste previously absorbed in the dairy utensil has become *basar b'chalav*. If the utensil is subsequently used for kosher food, we require *bitul b'shishim* over the volume of the entire utensil.

CHAPTER FIVE

נוֹתֵן טַעַם
Infusion of Taste

An examination of the means by which tastes are transferred.

□ Transfer of taste through heat.

□ *Kli rishon, kli sheni* and *iruy.*

□ *Davar gush* and *davar charif.*

□ *Tatai gavar.*

□ Transfer of taste through soaking — *kavush k'mevushal.*

□ Transfer of taste through salting — *meliach k'roseiach.*

□ Transfer of taste through aroma — *reicha milsa.*

□ Transfer of taste through steam — *zeiah.*

Introduction

When two foods come in physical contact with one another, no taste is transferred from one to the other without a medium through which taste can be transferred. In addition, a thorough transfer cannot be achieved unless the foods are induced to infuse and absorb taste. Taste may be transferred only through a liquid or fatty medium. Among the conditions that bring about infusion of taste are heat, salting or soaking. In this chapter we will discuss these two issues: the medium that enables transfer and the conditions that cause taste transfer. These *halachos* relate to non-kosher food that comes in contact with kosher food and may impart its non-kosher taste to the kosher food. Similarly, if meat and dairy foods come in contact, they may impart taste into one another and produce *basar b'chalav*, or if *parve* foods come in contact with either meat or dairy, they may absorb taste and become meat or dairy foods.

I. Mediums that permit taste transfers

A. Liquids

The most common medium through which taste is transferred is liquid. Liquid (when hot) is absorbed throughout the food and carries with it any taste found in the liquid. Similarly, the liquid imparts taste from the food into the liquid or from one food to another when both are in liquid.[1]

B. Fatty foods

Although fatty foods lack the physical quality of liquids to saturate foods, *Chazal* considered fat capable of being absorbed into foods (when hot) and imparting its taste into the food. Thus, fatty foods also serve as a conduit for taste infusions. Accordingly, if hot non-kosher food comes in contact with hot kosher food, if either food is fatty, non-kosher taste is imparted throughout the kosher food. If the kosher

1. *Y.D.* 105:4. See *D.T.* §102, who cites opinions that the surfaces must be actually wet. Mere dampness, however, is not sufficient to enable transfer of taste throughout the food.

food contains sixty times the volume of the non-kosher food, it is permitted. Nevertheless, a *k'dei netilah,* כְּדֵי נְטִילָה (between 2 and 2.5 centimeters, approximately one inch) should be removed from the surface of kosher food at the area of contact with the non-kosher food.[2]

C. Dry lean foods

Dry lean foods permit only a minimal amount of transfer even when heated. When two hot, dry surfaces touch one another, taste can only be imparted into a *k'dei netilah* of the outer surface. The foods lack the medium to enable the taste to penetrate any further. Thus, if a piece of lean non-kosher meat falls on a piece of lean kosher meat roasting or baking in an oven, a *k'dei netilah* is removed from the kosher meat.[3] In *halachic* literature, this is referred to as a transfer of taste through *tzli,* צְלִי — roasting. Since it is difficult, at times, to determine which foods are considered fatty and which lean, common custom is to treat most foods as fatty foods. A *moreh hora'ah* should be consulted.[4]

Accordingly, if non-kosher food falls upon a piece of kosher food cooking in a pot, its status would depend upon whether the foods are considered fatty or lean, whether the food in the pot was submerged (or even partially submerged) in the liquid, and whether the pot was stirred or covered immediately after the non-kosher food fell into the pot. These *halachos* are complex and a *moreh hora'ah* should be consulted.[5]

Summary of Section I

⁂ Since hot liquids are absorbed throughout a food, they are able to impart taste from liquid to food (and the reverse) and from food to food if both are in the liquid. Fatty foods also serve as

---

2. *Y.D.* 105:5.

3. *Y.D.* 105:4.

4. *Rema* 105:5, see *Kaf HaChaim* §68, who notes that even Sefardic Jews follow the opinion of *Rema* in this case. See *Shach* §16, who contends that this custom applies even to those foods that are lean and cannot be confused with fatty foods. If, however, the prohibition of the food is merely Rabbinic, one may be lenient with a food that is certainly lean and cannot be confused with fatty foods. See *Yad Yehudah* §44k, who argues that any food that is certainly lean (with the exception of *chametz* on *Pesach)* may be treated as lean foods that do not transfer taste beyond a *k'dei netilah*. See *Chochmas Adam* 60:7, and *D.T.* §105:123, regarding whether one may be lenient in a case of lean food when significant loss is involved.

5. See *Y.D.* 105:4, and commentaries.

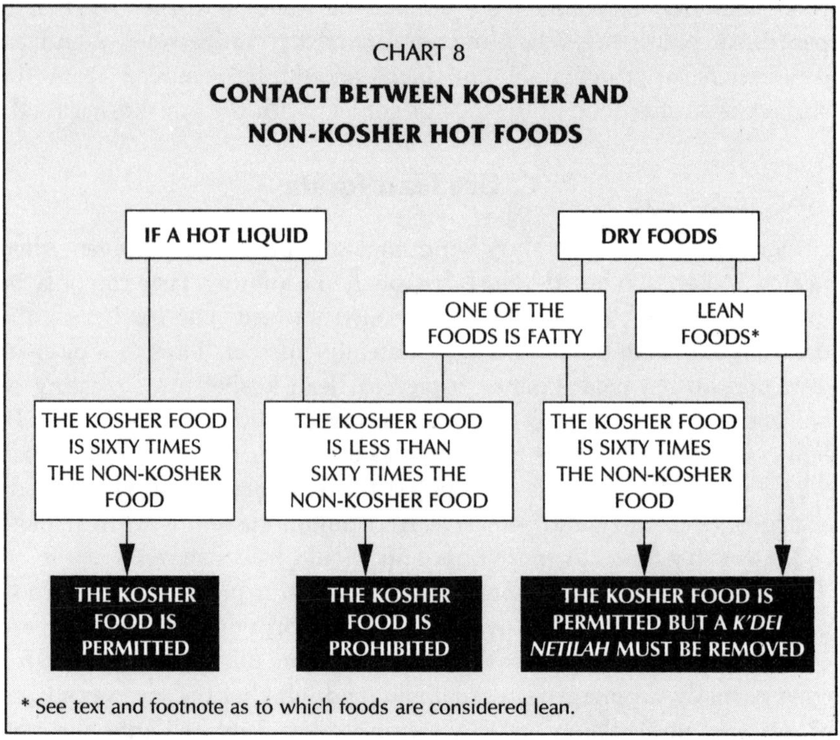

a conduit for taste infusions. Thus, if either of two foods is fatty, taste is imparted from one to another. Two dry lean foods can impart taste only into a *k'dei netilah* of their outer surface. Since it is difficult to know which foods are considered fatty and which are lean, common custom is to treat most foods as fatty foods.

II. Transfer of taste through heat

These *halachos* are based upon *Tur* and *Shulchan Aruch* 105:2,3.

Even when a medium is present to permit infusion of taste, the infusion cannot take place without the conditions that cause taste transfer. First and foremost among the means by which taste is imparted and absorbed is heat. The Torah teaches us that heat has the ability to cause taste to be imparted from one matter into another.[6]

A. The minimum degree of heat

The minimum degree of heat required to cause transfer of taste is defined by the Talmud[7] as *"yad soledes bo"*[8], יַד סוֹלֶדֶת בּוֹ — the degree of heat from which the hand recoils for fear of being burnt.[9] According to some authorities, this connotes heat sufficient to cause immediate recoil even though it would not immediately scald the skin[10]. Other authorities describe *yad soledes bo* as the degree of heat that would scald the hand after sustained contact[11] or the degree of heat that would scald the sensitive abdominal skin of a day-old child.[12] Common custom is to treat any food that one would eat without cooling beforehand as not *halachically* "hot" and thus not capable of transferring taste.[13] Contemporary authorities assume that any food cooler than 110° fahrenheit (43° centigrade) cannot transfer taste.[14] *Poskim* note a higher degree of heat called *"yad nichvas bo,"* יַד נִכְוֵית בּוֹ (the degree of heat that would immediately scald the hand) which may be effective even in cases where *yad soledes bo* cannot bring about a taste transfer.[15]

---

6. The question has been raised; does the transfer of taste by heat require a minimum amount of time? If non-kosher food falls into a hot pot of kosher food and is removed immediately, may the kosher food be eaten? See *D.T.* 105:65, who cites many opinions on the matter. The *halachic* consensus is to assume that the transfer of taste is instantaneous. In a case of serious financial loss, a *moreh hora'ah* should be consulted. See also *Aruch HaShulchan* 105:43 and *Matamei HaShulchan* 91:10, 105:11.

7. *Shabbos* 40b.

8. See a discussion in M.Z. 68: end of 9, as to whether the proper text of the Talmud should read *"soledes,"* סוֹלֶדֶת or *"sholetes,"* שׁוֹלֶטֶת. He analyses the ramifications of each text.

9. *Rashi* 40b.

10. See *Darcei Teshuvah* 105:51.

11. Ibid. If, however, one is able to hold one's hand in the hot water for a short while, the water is not considered *yad soledes bo* (see *Yad Yehudah* 105:16k).

12. O.C. 318:14. See *Issur V'heter* 34:20, who notes that these two definitions are synonymous.

13. See *D.T.* 105:51. and *Kaf HaChaim* 105:30.

14. *Igros Moshe: O.C.* 4:74 (*bishul* [3]). In the opinion of Rav Shlomo Z. Auerbach (*Minchas Shlomo* 91:8) any heat less than 113° fahrenheit (45° centigrade) is not *halachically* considered "hot." See *Metzudas Tzion: Kitzur Shulchan Aruch* ch. 72 who contends that 104° should perhaps be considered *yad soledes bo*. *Igros Moshe* (ibid.) notes that 160° (71° centigrade) is certainly *yad soledes bo*. See also *Matamei HaShulchan* 105:7.

15. E.g., in a *kli sheni*, see *Taz* 105:4, *Chayei Adam* 20:4, *Chochmas Adam* 59:6.

B. Heat as opposed to bishul

It should be noted that the term *"yad soledes bo"* is used to define "heat", both with regard to transfer of taste and with regard to the definition of *bishul* — cooking. These two subjects, however, are not synonymous. "Heating" is a broad term that applies to many forms of warmth and can cause a transfer of taste in many circumstances. *"Bishul"* is a term more restricted in its definition and application. For example:

1) *Bishul* on *Shabbos:*
   One is forbidden to do an act of *bishul* (cooking) on *Shabbos.* However, merely warming food to the degree of *yad soledes bo* does not necessarily violate *Shabbos.* This would depend upon the source of the heat that brought about the warmth. For example: One may warm food in direct sunlight on *Shabbos* even if it attains the degree of *yad soledes bo.* Similarly, one who warms food in a *kli sheni* (a vessel into which the original boiling pot was emptied) has not, in the opinion of many *Poskim,* violated the *Shabbos* even if the food attains the heat of *yad soledes bo.* Nevertheless, in either of these cases the heat may have generated a transfer of taste.
2) *Bishul basar b'chalav:*
   One is forbidden to cook meat and milk *(basar b'chalav)* together. This too, depends upon the source of the heat. Solar cooking or even cooking in a natural, hot spring may not violate the Biblical prohibition of cooking *basar b'chalav*. These *halachos* are discussed at length in Chapter Seven, Section II,A. However, either of these forms of cooking may bring about a transfer of taste.

C. Situations of heat

Although heat brings about a transfer of taste, not every situation of heat is necessarily sufficient to cause taste to be transmitted. We will discuss the various situations of heat in relation to their ability to effect a taste transfer.

1) A *kli rishon,* כְּלִי רִאשׁוֹן:
   Any food cooked in a *kli rishon* has the ability to discharge or absorb taste throughout the food,[16] regardless of whether or not

16. *Y.D.* 105:2.

the pot remains over the fire[17] or whether the food continues to cook.[18] In the opinion of some *Poskim,*[19] a *kli rishon* while over the fire is potent[20] even if it is not *yad soledes bo;* others disagree.[21] *Halachic* authorities rule that if the *kli rishon* was not *yad soledes bo*, a *klipah* (a thin removable surface) should be removed from the kosher food.[22] If one is in doubt as to whether the *kli rishon* was *yad soledes bo,* a *moreh hora'ah* should be consulted as to the status of the food.[23] In the event that a cold food falls into a *kli rishon,* the principle of *tatai gavar,* which will be discussed shortly, may apply. A utensil that falls into non-kosher liquid in a *kli rishon* or a dairy utensil that falls into a *kli rishon* meat soup must be *kashered.* If the *kli rishon* was no longer *yad soledes bo,* a *moreh hora'ah* should be consulted.[24]

2) A ladle:
Poskim disagree as to the status of a ladle that was inserted into a *kli rishon,* filled and then removed. Some contend that the ladle may be a *kli rishon,* while others consider it a *kli sheni*. If the ladle remained in the pot for a while,[25] all *Poskim* agree that

17. *Rashi: Shabbos* 40b, *Chochmas Adam* 59:1. See *Aruch HaShulchan* 105:18, who notes that even those who contend that a *kli rishon* cannot do *bishul* regarding *Shabbos* unless it remains over the fire (see Chapter Seven, footnote no. 31) agree that it transfers taste even when it is no longer over the fire.

18. *Beis Yosef* 105.

19. *Maharshal (Yam Shel Shlomo: Chullin* 8:71). See also *Pischei Teshuvah* 105:6.

20. See *Matamei HaShulchan* 105:6, as to whether this view applies only to a *kli rishon* which had already attained the heat of *yad soledes bo* but subsequently cooled, or even to a *kli rishon* that, although sitting over the fire, has not yet attained *yad soledes bo*. It seems clear from *Aruch HaShulchan* 105:18 that, according to those opinions, this rule applies even in the latter case. See also *Taz* 94:1.

21. *Taz* 94:1. This principle is merely Rabbinic in origin. Thus, one may follow the lenient ruling in a situation of doubt *(M.Z.* 68: end of 9).

22. *Shach* 105:5 (see M.Z. 68:9, s.v. *"amnam")*, *Chochmas Adam* 59:1. This applies only to food since food absorbs easily. A utensil, however, will not absorb even into its *klipah* unless heated to *yad soledes bo (Chochmas Adam* ibid.). Incidently, *Chochmas Adam* does not differentiate between a non *yad soledes bo kli rishon* that is presently over the fire and one that has been removed from the fire. A *moreh hora'ah* should be consulted.

23. See *Atzei Ha'olah* II, p. 23b no.4.

24. See M.Z. 68: end of 9. *Chochmas Adam* 59:1, rules that it need not be *kashered* but merely rinsed (see *Kaf HaChaim* 105:27). See also *Matamei HaShulchan* 91:8.

25. *Poskim* offer no exact length of time required to give the ladle the status of a *kli rishon.* Presumably, once the ladle is thoroughly heated in the pot, it should be considered a *kli rishon.*

the ladle is considered a *kli rishon*.[26]

3) A *kli sheni*, כְּלִי שֵׁנִי:
Once the liquid is poured from the original pot used for cooking (*kli rishon*) into a second vessel (*kli sheni*), it no longer has the ability to cause *bishul*.[27] This is true regardless of whether or not the liquid retains the heat of *yad soledes bo*. *Rishonim* explain that the cool body of the second vessel continuously cools the cooked liquid and prevents it from causing *bishul*.[28] In the opinion of most[29] *Rishonim*, the heat of a *kli sheni* cannot cause a discharge or absorption of taste.[30] For example, if kosher food falls into non-kosher hot liquid in a *kli sheni*, the food can be washed and remains kosher. Others contend that although a *kli sheni* cannot cause *bishul*, it can induce an absorption of taste into a *klipah* of the food; thus, a *klipah* must be removed.[31] Still others assert that a *kli sheni*[32] can induce absorption into the entire food; therefore, the entire food is forbid-

---

26. See *Taz* 92:30 and *S.D.* there.

27. *Shabbos* 40b.

28. *Tosfos: Shabbos* 40b. A vessel warmed in a microwave oven presents an interesting question since the vessel neither cools nor warms the food. Unlike other ovens in which the vessel becomes warm from the fire itself, a microwave oven heats only the food which then heats the vessel. Thus, a vessel removed from the microwave oven is perhaps not a *kli rishon* since the vessel cannot preserve its heat. (Indeed, one could question whether it becomes a *kli rishon* even while cooking in the microwave.) This would depend upon our interpretation of the *Tosfos*. If we were to interpret *Tosfos* to imply that the main criterion is the fact that the vessel of a *kli rishon* continues to warm the food, it would follow that a microwave dish is not a *kli rishon*. If, however, we were to deduce that the primary consideration is the fact that the vessel of a *kli sheni* cools the food, a microwave dish should be considered a *kli rishon* since it does not cool the food. Essentially, the question is: what is the status of food that is neither warmed nor cooled by the vessel? This issue is discussed by *Chavas Daas* 92:27. His question pertains to a ladle that was immersed in a *kli rishon* until it became hot and was subsequently removed. Should the ladle be considered a *kli rishon* or a *kli sheni?* In the opinion of *Taz* 92:30 that a ladle is considered *kli rishon*, perhaps a utensil in a microwave oven is also considered *kli rishon*.

29. See *Aruch HaShulchan* 105:19.

30. The first (and primary) opinion in *Shulchan Aruch* 105:2, *Rema* 92:7, 105:3, *Rashbam*, *Rabbeinu Tam* and others cited in *Shach* 105:5.

31. *Rashba* cited as second opinion, ibid.

32. In the opinion of some *Poskim*, even a *kli sh'lishi* (the third vessel into which the liquid from the *kli sheni* was poured) is equal in status to a *kli sheni*. In their opinion, as long as the liquid is *yad soledes bo*, it may cause a transfer of taste (see *Pri Chadash* 68, *Chasam Sofer* cited in *Pischei Teshuvah* 94:7, *Chazon Ish: O.C.* 52:19. The *Shaar Hatziyun: O.C.* 451:10, however, implies that a *kli sh'lishi* certainly cannot bring about a transfer of taste. See also *Igros Moshe: O.C.* 4:74 [*bishul*, 15]).

den.[33] Since *halachic* authorities disagree as to the proper conduct in this matter, a *moreh hora'ah* should be consulted.[34] The following are some additional rules pertaining to a *kli sheni:*

a) *Yad nichvas bo:*
If the liquid in the *kli sheni* is so hot as to scald a hand placed in it *(yad nichvas bo)*, some authorities rule that it certainly must be treated as a *kli rishon*.[35]

b) A *kli sheni* that is not *yad soledes bo:*
Although we noted earlier that in the opinion of some authorities, a *kli rishon* retains its potency even when it is no longer *yad soledes bo*, a *kli sheni* that is not *yad soledes bo* certainly cannot induce a transfer of taste. Thus, if kosher food falls into a non-kosher *kli sheni* that was not *yad soledes bo*, it need only be thoroughly rinsed.[36]

c) A *davar gush*, דָבָר גוּש (solid food):
In the opinion of some *Poskim*, solid food removed from a *kli rishon*[37] and placed in a *kli sheni* retains the status

---

33. *Maharshal: Chullin* 7:71, cited in *Taz* 105:4, and *Shach* 105:5. This also seems to be the opinion of *Tur* 105 (see *Beis Yosef*). *Maharshal* concedes, however, that a *kli sheni* cannot cause two concurrent transfers of taste *(maflit u'mavliah k'echod)* i.e., two cold foods placed in it do not transfer taste to one another (ibid.). Thus, if a piece of non-kosher food falls into a bowl of soup, the soup is prohibited. If, however, a piece of kosher food and a piece of non-kosher food both fall into a bowl of hot water, the kosher food may be rinsed and eaten. *Shach* 105:5 rejects the opinion of *Bach* who contends that a *kli sheni* can cause two concurrent transfers and can infuse taste into the entire food.

34. *Taz* (ibid.) rules that one should follow the stringent opinion of *Maharshal* in all cases except those of serious financial loss *(hefsed merubah)*, see *Chavas Daas* 105:10c. *Chochmas Adam*, 59:6, seems to imply that in **any** case of financial loss, one may follow the lenient opinions. *Beis Meir*, 105:2, rules that whenever the non-kosher food is merely Rabbinically prohibited, one may follow the lenient position even if no financial loss is involved. See *Aruch HaShulchan* 105:19, who apparently takes an even more lenient position. In all cases that a lenient opinion is followed, the food should be washed thoroughly to remove any non-kosher residue. If one is in doubt whether the food fell into the *kli sheni*, it may merely be rinsed. Similarly, if there is doubt whether the *kli sheni* was *yad soledes bo*, the food may merely be rinsed *(M.Z.* 68: end of 9).

35. *Taz* 105:4, *Chayei Adam* 20:4, *Chochmas Adam* 59:6, see *Matamei HaShulchan* 105:8, who cites a dissenting opinion.

36. *Minchas Yaakov* 33:1, *Taz* end of 105:4, *M.Z.* ibid.

37. A solid food that was roasted over the fire certainly retains its status as a *kli rishon* even after it has been removed from the fire. However, if the roasted food is placed on a cool surface after its intense heat has dissipated, it is no longer considered a *kli rishon*, even though it is *yad soledes bo* (see *Aruch HaShulchan* 105:26, in his interpretation of *Rema* 105:3). In the opinion of the *Maharshal* cited below, the food retains the status of

of a *kli rishon*. These authorities argue that only a liquid is affected by its transferral to a *kli sheni* since the walls of the vessel cool the liquid. A solid, however, retains its form and does not come in contact with the walls of the vessel and is thus unaffected by them, therefore, it remains a *kli rishon*.[38] Other *Poskim* do not differentiate between liquids and solids.[39] *Halachic* authorities follow the more stringent view unless significant loss is involved.[40]

d) A *davar charif*, דָּבָר חָרִיף (sharp food):
Sharp foods[41] that fall into a *kli sheni* may be governed by more stringent rules; a *moreh hora'ah* should be consulted.[42]

4) Pouring from a *kli rishon* — *iruy*, עִירוּי.
We have heretofore discussed the status of the liquid after it comes to rest in the second vessel *(kli sheni)*. However, while liquid is being poured from one vessel to another, it is neither a *kli rishon* (since it is no longer being warmed by the original vessel) nor a *kli sheni* (since it is not yet cooled by the second vessel). *Rishonim* disagree as to the exact status of the liquid.[43]

---

kli rishon even after it has lost its intense heat (see *Darcei Moshe* 105:4).

38. *Issur V'heter* 36:7 and *Maharshal: Chullin* 7:44, cited in *Taz* 94:14 and *Shach* 94:30, 105:8. See also *Aruch HaShulchan* 94:32.

39. *Rema* 94:7.

40. *Chochmas Adam* 60:12, *Aruch HaShulchan* 105:20.

41. See Chapter Twelve, Section II,C for a definition of which foods are considered *davar charif*.

42. In the opinion of *Chavas Daas* 105:10c, all *Poskim* concede that a *davar charif* imparts and absorbs taste when placed into a *kli sheni*. See, however, *Yad Yehudah* 105:18k, for a dissenting opinion.

43. In the opinion of *Rashbam* (cited in *Tosfos: Shabbos* 42b, *Zevachim* 95b), *iruy* is considered a *kli sheni* and cannot actually cook *(bishul)*; it can, however, generate either a discharge or absorption of taste (not both concurrently) into the thickness of a *klipah*. In the opinion of *Rabbeinu Tam* (cited in *Tosfos* ibid.), *iruy* is considered a *kli rishon* and can therefore effect actual *bishul* to the thickness of a *klipah*. *Maharshal* (cited in *Shach* 105:5 who notes that *Maharshal* contradicts himself in his responsa) contends that according to *Rabbeinu Tam, iruy* effects a taste transfer to the entire food, see also *M.Z.* 68:9:3. *Prishah* (cited in *Shach* ibid.) contends that *iruy* effects *bishul* on the entire food. This dispute has little significance with regard to transfer of taste, since we usually follow the stringent opinion that even a *kli sheni* is capable of transferring taste, it does have relevance regarding the prohibition of *bishul* on *Shabbos* and regarding the prohibition of *bishul* of *basar b'chalav*. See *D.T.* 87:17 as to whether the *bishul* of *iruy* is a Biblical law or merely Rabbinic.

CHART 9

TRANSFER OF TASTE THROUGH HEAT
KLI RISHON AND KLI SHENI

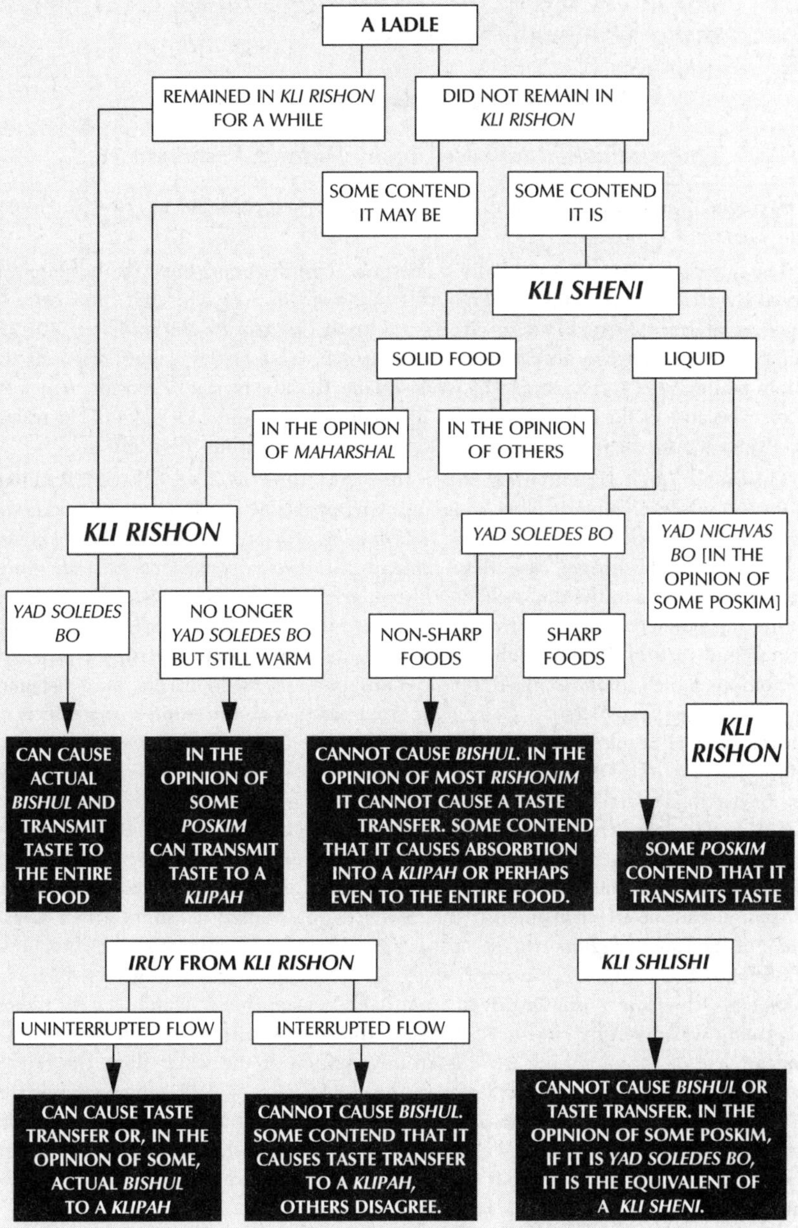

Poskim rule that if hot, non-kosher liquid[44] is poured over cold, kosher food, the taste of non-kosher liquid is absorbed into a *klipah*[45] of the food.[46] One faced with a situation of *iruy* between kosher and non-kosher foods should consult a *moreh hora'ah*. A utensil that becomes *treif* through *iruy* may be *kashered* through *iruy* as well.[47]

D. Contact between hot foods

These *halachos* are based upon Talmud: *Pesachim* 76,

---

44. A single drop, however, cannot affect the food since it cools quickly, see *Shach* 93:6 and *Chochmas Adam* 59:2.

45. The question of *iruy* is essentially a question of *tatai gavar*, since the hot liquid is poured over cold food. Thus, since we rule that even in a case of cold *tatai gavar* a *klipah* is affected, *iruy* likewise effects a *klipah* (see *Aruch HaShulchan* 105:22). Similarly, the reason *iruy* affects only a *klipah* is because of the cooling effect of the bottom matter. See *Chavas Daas* 91:5 who explains that the reason to consider *iruy* a *kli rishon* is because of the connection to the hot walls of the original *kli rishon*. The reason to consider it a *kli sheni* is because the flow is no longer within the walls.

46. This ruling is not definitive, see *Shach* 105:5, *S.D.* 105:5, M.Z. 68:9:3, and *Chochmas Adam* 59:2 who differentiate between an uninterrupted flow i.e., the poured liquid is still connected to the *kli rishon (lo nifsak ha'kiluach)* and an interrupted flow *(nifsak ha'kiluach)*. In the former case, they contend, the *iruy* is considered *kli rishon* and effects actual *bishul* to the thickness of a *klipah*. In the latter case, the *iruy* is considered *kli sheni* and merely causes *one* transfer of taste to the thickness of a *klipah* but cannot effect *bishul*. See M.Z. 68:9:4, who rules that with regard to an interrupted flow, the prohibition of the *klipah* is only Rabbinic. Thus, in a case of doubt, one may disregard the problem. See *Chazon Ish:* Y.D. 9:5, who contends that an interrupted *iruy* effects no transfer of taste at all. Most authorities disagree) (see *Badei HaShulchan* 91:20). *Iruy* cannot, however, effect *two* transfers, e.g., if hot water is poured over a kosher and non-kosher food placed side by side, the kosher food is unaffected. If the liquid is not poured directly over the food but rather reaches the food only after flowing over a surface, a *klipah* must be discarded if the flow was uninterrupted (see *Chavas Daas* 92:23 who contends that even though an indirect *iruy* can cause taste to be absorbed into a *klipah*, it cannot effect *bishul)*. If the flow was interrupted it cannot affect even a *klipah* of the food (See *Biur HaGra* 92:36, in explanation of *Rema* 92:7, and *Chochmas Adam* ibid). Accordingly, hot water flowing from the tap should be considered *iruy kli rishon* since the flow is uninterrupted from the hot water boiler which is a *kli rishon*. This ruling was given by *Harav* Y.S. *Eliashiv* (through a third party). He noted that if in the course of the plumbing there is an interruption of the water flow, the flow is considered *nifsak hakiluach*. See, however, *Igros Moshe*, Y.D. 1:42, who contends that this is far from certain. Responsa *Minchas Yitzchok* 2:100(2), argues that on the contrary, a sink tap is an even stronger form of *iruy* since the boiler may be actively heating the body of water while it flows from the tap (unlike common *iruy kli rishon* which refers to a vessel that is removed from the fire).

47. O.C. 451:5.

Tur and *Shulchan Aruch* 91:4 and 105:3.

1) Foodstuffs placed atop one another:
When kosher and non-kosher foods[48] are placed atop one another, the *halachah* distinguishes between a case of two hot foods and a case of one hot food and one cold food. Placing two hot foods atop one another does not diminish their heat. Consequently, they infuse taste into one another. A hot and a cold food, do immediately affect one another. Thus, the question is: does the hot food warm the cold food more quickly than the cold food cools the warm food? The Talmud[49] rules that a distinction must be made based upon which of the two foods was on top and which was underneath.[50] The Talmud cites a difference of opinion whether *tatai gavar*[51], תַּתָּאִי גָּבַר ("the bottom overpowers" the top) or *elai gavar*, עִילָּאִי גָּבַר ("the top overpowers" the bottom).[52] *Rishonim*[53] rule that one should follow the opinion of *tatai gavar*.[54] This is reflected in the

48. Or a liquid poured over a solid food, or a solid food placed in a liquid. If, however, one liquid is poured into another, their respective tastes immediately blend into one another, regardless of their heat. Thus, the only remaining consideration is the respective amount of each liquid, i.e., whether the kosher liquid is sixty times the non-kosher liquid. Nevertheless, *Poskim* do discuss the effect of the heat on one another with regard to the prohibition of *bishul* on *Shabbos* and *basar b'chalav*. For example: if a larger amount of cold liquid is poured into a smaller amount of hot liquid, should we assume *tatai gavar* and *bishul* has occurred or should we assume that the greater amount of cold liquid immediately cools the hot liquid? See *Chavas Daas* 91:5, *D.T.* 91:15, *Taz O.C.* 318:18, *Magen Avraham* 318:35, *Machtzis Hashekel* and *P.M.* (ibid.).

49. *Pesachim* 76a.

50. This depends upon their respective positions at the time of the original mixture. For example: A solid food falls and is completely submerged into a liquid. The solid is nevertheless considered the upper and the liquid is considered the lower of the two, even though the liquid is now above the solid *(Shach* 91:23).

51. Two reasons are given for the dominance of the lower food: a) The top food weighs upon the bottom and b) heat rises by nature *(Issur V'heter* 29:1). These reasons reflect the opinion of the *Issur V'heter* that *tatai gavar* applies only to two foods when placed atop one another, not when they are placed side by side. See 3) below.

52. The positions of *Shmuel* and *Rav* respectively (ibid.).

53. *Rashi* and *Tosfos: Pesachim* 76a, *Tur* 91.

54. *Poskim* grapple with the obvious question: Why is no consideration given to the amount of the relative foods? Certainly, a large amount of hot food would warm a considerably smaller amount of cold food beneath it. Similarly, a large amount of cold food cannot be heated by a small amount of hot food beneath it (see *Yad Efraim*, beginning of *Y.D.* 76). Accordingly, *Aruch HaShulchan*, 91:11,12, rules that *tatai gavar* applies only to equal amounts of hot and cold matter. See also *Yad Yehudah*

halachos that follow. One should note that "hot" is defined as food (or liquid) that is heated to the level of *yad soledes bo* and is presently in (or being directly poured from) a *kli rishon.*[55] "Cold" is defined as any heat less than *yad soledes bo*. When we discuss food placed atop another hot food, we refer to food placed atop hot solid food immediately after it was removed from a *kli rishon*.[56] When we discuss hot liquid poured over food, we refer to the direct, uninterrupted pouring of liquid *(iruy)* from a *kli rishon*. In addition, we noted earlier that a medium of transfer is required to enable the tastes to travel from one matter to another. Thus, whenever we speak of a transfer of taste between two solid foods, a liquid or fatty medium is required to induce this transfer. We will therefore, address the subject of both dry and fatty foods as well as liquids in the course of our discussion.

a) Both foods are hot:
Two hot, solid foods placed atop one another, one kosher and one non-kosher, effect a complete transfer of taste from one to the other regardless of whether the non-kosher food is on top or underneath. However, we noted earlier that two solids cannot thoroughly impart taste to one another without a liquid or fatty medium. Thus, only a *k'dei netilah* (approximately one inch) need be removed from the surface of the kosher meat that touched the non-kosher food. If either one of the foods is

---

105:21k,12a, who, in addition to the question above, poses the problem that an abundance of liquid poured over solid matter completely surrounds it. Thus, the liquid flows under the solid and becomes the *tatai* (see above note 50). Nevertheless, *Yad Yehudah* notes that it appears that *Poskim* make no distinction between the relative amounts of the foods. See *D.T.* (91:18, see also 105:75) who rules that one follow the stringent inference of each position. Thus, if the bottom food is hot, one should follow the principle of *tatai gavar*, regardless of the ratio of the amount of hot to cold food. If, however, the bottom food is cold, one cannot follow the principle of *tatai gavar* if the amount of the upper, hot food is significantly greater than the cold food.

55. If the hot liquid is in a *kli sheni* or even a *kli sh'lishi*, its status would depend upon the opinions cited in C,4 above (see *Rema* 105:3). Similarly, a hot, solid food may be considered a *kli rishon* even after it is removed from the pot, see above C,3. A *moreh hora'ah* should be consulted in either of these cases.

56. If, however, the food was placed atop the hot food only after it was placed into a *kli sheni* or has cooled a bit, the hot food is considered a *kli sheni (Rema* 105:3). See above C,3 that according to *Maharshal* a solid food retains the status of *kli rishon* as long as its heat is *yad soledes bo* (see *Shach* 105:8).

fatty, non-kosher taste is transmitted throughout the kosher food. We noted in Section I, C above that customarily most foods are treated as fatty foods. Similarly, if hot meat and hot cheese are placed atop one another, they absorb taste from one another and are both prohibited. If hot kosher liquid is poured[57] over hot non-kosher food, or hot non-kosher liquid[58] is poured over hot kosher food, the entire kosher food or liquid is prohibited.[59] Similarly, if hot milk is poured over hot meat or hot meat falls into hot milk, both meat and milk have become *basar b'chalav* and must be discarded.[60] If either the milk or the dairy contains a volume of sixty times the other, a *moreh hora'ah* should be consulted.[61] See Chapter Eleven, Section E, regarding cold milk that spilled over meat.

b) Only the bottom food is hot:
Halachah follows the Talmudic opinion of *tatai gavar*. Thus, the bottom food in the *kli rishon* warms the top food and enables it to impart or absorb[62] taste throughout[63] both foods.[64] Consequently, regardless of whether

---

57. One may not initially pour kosher liquid into hot non-kosher food since the stream of poured liquid connects the kosher and non-kosher foods (*Rema* 105:3). This leaves even the liquid remaining in the poured vessel in a questionable status (see *Taz* §6 and *Shach* §11 for differing explanations to this *halachah*, see also M.Z. §6. See Chapter Eleven, Section F). If one did pour kosher liquid into non-kosher food, the poured liquid is subject to the discussion below. The liquid remaining in the poured container retains its kosher status, see M.Z. ibid. and *D.T.* 105:97.

58. The liquid must be of a quantity to serve as a medium of transfer to enable the taste to penetrate the entire solid food; otherwise, the taste cannot travel beyond a *klipah*, see *Yad Yehudah* 91:12k,11a.

59. Y.*D*. 105:3.

60. Y.*D*. 91:4.

61. We must contend with the additional problem of absorption of milk into the meat, see Chapter Eleven, Section E, regarding meat that fell into cold milk.

62. See *Tur* 105, who explains that the lower matter requires less heat to impart its taste into the upper matter than for it to absorb taste from the upper matter. This is reflected in the wording of the *Shulchan Aruch* (*Y.D.* 105:3).

63. The reader is reminded again that according to *halachah*, if neither of the foods is fatty, only a *k'dei netilah* is affected. However, our custom is to treat most foods as fatty foods. See Section I,C.

64. See *D.T.* 105:70, who cites a difference of opinion regarding a case when the top food clearly did not become thoroughly hot.

the non-kosher food is on top or underneath, if the bottom food is *yad soledes bo*, the kosher food is prohibited.[65] If cold cheese is placed atop hot meat (or cold meat atop hot cheese), both must be discarded. Similarly, regardless of whether cold milk falls over hot meat or cold meat falls into hot milk, both must be discarded.[66] In the event that either the meat or the milk contained sixty times the volume of the other, a *moreh hora'ah* should be consulted.[67]

c) Only the top food is hot:
Following the principle of *tatai gavar*, we assume that cold[68] food overpowers and cools hot food placed above it.[69] Thus, the taste is not transferred from one to another. Nevertheless, the Talmud explains that prior to its being cooled, the hot top food is able to absorb or impart taste to the thickness of a *klipah*. Therefore, regardless of whether the non-kosher food is on top or underneath, a *klipah* of the kosher food absorbs non-kosher taste and is prohibited.[70] If hot kosher food

---

65. Even if the kosher upper food is wider than the non-kosher lower food *(Issur V'heter* 29:1).

66. *Y.D.* 91:4. See *Chavas Daas* 91:5 as to whether the top food is heated sufficiently to act as a *tatai* towards additional cold food placed upon it.

67. At times, even when there is *bitul b'shishim*, a *k'dei netilah* must be removed (see *Rema* 105:5 and *Chochmas Adam* 60:7).

68. *Poskim* disagree as to the status of hot food that was placed over food in a *kli sheni* that was *yad soledes bo*. Some contend that it should be compared to hot placed over hot. Thus, it causes a transfer of taste throughout the food *(Minchas Yaakov* 51:1, 56:21). Others contend that it is compared to hot placed over cold and causes a transfer of taste only to a *klipah (Chavas Daas* 91:8c). Authorities rule that when pertaining to a Biblical prohibition, one should follow the stringent opinion unless serious financial loss is involved *(M.Z.* 68:9[4], see also *M.Z.* 92:25 and *S.D.* 94:22). In the event that the *kli sheni* was not *yad soledes bo*, all *Poskim* agree that it is considered cold *(M.Z.* 92:25).

69. However, a hot *kli rishon* placed on a cool surface remains a *kli rishon* as long as it remains *yad soledes bo*. The heat retained in the walls of the utensil prevent the food from being significantly cooled by the cool surface *(Chavas Daas* 91:5b). See *M.Z.* 92:22 and *S.D.* §32 (citing *Toras Chatas)* that if the upper hot food (or pot) is still being heated by a source of heat it is not subject to the rules of *tatai gavar* since it will not be cooled by the lower cold food.

70. *Y.D.* 91:4. See *M.Z.* 91:5, that this is Rabbinic in origin. Therefore, in a case of doubt whether any hot liquid actually fell, one need not discard the *klipah* if that would cause any financial loss. If the food was cooked without removing the *klipah*, a *moreh*

falls into a non-kosher liquid, a *klipah* must be removed and the remaining food should be thoroughly rinsed.[71] In the opinion of some authorities, if hot kosher liquid falls on cold non-kosher food, the liquid retains its kosher status.[72] They contend that since the *klipah* immediately mixes with all the liquid, it is not prohibited.[73] Others argue that a *klipah* of the kosher liquid becomes prohibited;[74] thus, if the liquid does not contain sixty times its thin outer surface, it is prohibited. Similarly, if hot milk is poured over cold meat or hot meat falls into cold milk, a *klipah* of the meat must be discarded. The remainder of the meat may be permitted;

CHART 10

FOODS PLACED ATOP ONE ANOTHER
E.G., MEAT PLACED ON CHEESE

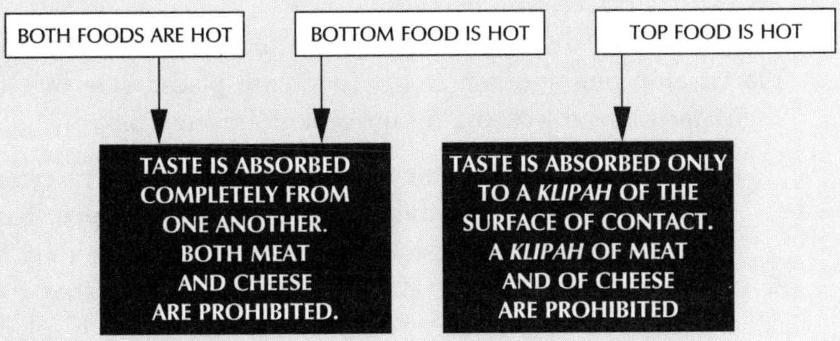

---

hora'ah should be consulted (see *Rema* 91:4 who rules that the food is permitted. *Taz* §7, however, contends that the entire food is prohibited, while *Shach* §8 differentiates between a recognizable *klipah* and an unrecognizable *klipah* (as the *klipah* of a liquid which immediately blends with the rest of the liquid). Later authorities accept *Rema's* ruling only in a case of an uninterrupted *iruy* (see *M.Z.* 91:7 and *S.D.* 101:6).

71. *R' Akiva Eger*, gloss to *Y.D.* 91:4.

72. *Y.D.* 91:4, following the opinion of *Rabbeinu Tam (Tosfos: Pesachim* 76a).

73. *Shach* 91:8. See *M.Z.* 68:9:3, who applies this principle to the question of *bishul* on *Shabbos* regarding a case of *iruy* over liquid, i.e., may one pour hot liquid over cold liquid? Does the hot liquid cook a *klipah* of the cold liquid underneath thereby violating the prohibition of *bishul*?

74. *Taz* 91:7 following the opinion of *Riva (Tosfos: Pesachim* 76a).

however, a *moreh hora'ah* should be consulted since even cold meat that falls into cold milk may become prohibited due to the absorption of milk into its crevices (see Chapter Eleven, Section E). Even if the milk contains sixty times its *klipah*, a *moreh hora'ah* should be consulted.[75]

2) *Tatai gavar* regarding utensils:
The rules of *tatai gavar* pertain to utensils as well as foods, e.g., if cold food is placed into an empty hot pot or hot food is placed onto a cold plate. This question pertains to *basar b'chalav* as well, e.g., if cold meat is placed into a hot dairy pot or hot meat is placed onto a cold dairy plate. These *halachos* depend upon whether the utensil is *ben-yomo*, whether the utensil or the food is the non-kosher element, whether the utensil or the food or both are hot, whether liquid is present and whether the food is fatty. These *halachos* are complex and a *moreh hora'ah* should be consulted.[76]

3) Foodstuffs placed side by side:
Heretofore we discussed the *halacha* of a hot and cold food placed atop one another. If the foods are placed side by side, their status is subject to a disagreement among *Poskim*.[77]

   a) In the opinion of some *Poskim*, only hot food placed on the bottom has the ability to heat the entire upper food. Thus, if hot non-kosher food and cold kosher food are placed side by side, only a *klipah* of the kosher food must be removed.[78] Similarly, if hot meat is placed alongside cold cheese (or the reverse), a *klipah* of each must be removed.[79]

   b) Other *Poskim* disagree. They contend that if hot non-kosher food is placed alongside cold kosher food, non-kosher taste is imparted throughout[80] the kosher

75. In the opinion of *Chochmas Adam* (42:10), one may follow the lenient opinion in a case of serious financial loss. See also Chapter Eleven note 62.

76. See *Rema* 105:3 and *Chochmas Adam* 57:1-8.

77. *Poskim* grapple with the question of whether we are referring to two foods placed on hot surface or two foods placed on a cold surface, see *Chavas Daas* 92:24 and *D.T.* 105:85.

78. Ibid.

79. *Taz* 105:5 and *Shach* §9, see *Gilyon Maharsha*.

80. If one of the foods are fatty or according to our custom of treating most foods as fatty.

food. If, however, the non-kosher food is cold and the kosher food is hot, the non-kosher food imparts taste to only a *klipah* of the kosher food.[81] Similarly, if hot meat and cold cheese are placed alongside one another, the entire cheese is prohibited and a *k'dei klipah* of the meat must be removed. If the cheese is hot and the meat is cold, the meat is prohibited and a *k'dei klipah* of the cheese is removed.[82] Many authorities follow this ruling if no serious loss is involved.[83]

c) If two hot[84] foods are placed alongside one another, they certainly transfer their tastes throughout one another.[85]

4) Lack of a medium of transfer:
As noted above, these *halachos* all relate to a situation where the proper medium exists for heat to transfer taste. If the foods in contact do not possess a medium by which they transfer taste, only a minimum of taste is imparted. Therefore, if even two hot, dry, lean foods are placed atop one another, only a *k'dei netilah* of the kosher food is affected. A *moreh hora'ah* should be consulted since, as noted above, Section I,C even certain lean foods may be treated as fatty foods.

E. Contact between cold foods

If no heat is present, no transfer of taste has occurred and no *kashering* is required. The question is merely in how must the kosher food be cleaned to remove any non-kosher residue? *Poskim* differentiate between dry, damp and fatty foods.[86]

1) Dry cold foods:
If both foods are completely dry, the kosher food does not

---

81. *Maharshal* cited in *Taz* §5 and *Shach* §9.

82. M.Z. §5.

83. *Taz* §5 and *Chochmas Adam* 60:11. See, however, *Shach* §9 and *Aruch HaShulchan* §27 who follow the lenient ruling of *Rema*.

84. As noted in note 56 above, in the opinion of *Rema*, 105:3, this applies only if they come in contact prior to being placed into a *kli sheni*. In the opinion of *Maharshal*, solid foods retain the status of *kli rishon* as long as they are *yad soledes bo* (see *Shach* 105:8).

85. *Issur V'heter* 29:2, *Rema* 105:3.

86. Extremely salty foods are covered by different guidelines which are enumerated in *Y.D.* 91:5-8, see Section III,B.

require washing, since no non-kosher residue will adhere to it.[87]

2) Damp cold foods:
If either (and certainly if both) food is even slightly damp, the kosher food must be rinsed.[88] If the food was cooked without rinsing, a *moreh hora'ah* should be consulted.[89]

3) Fatty cold foods:
If either of the foods are fatty, the kosher food must be scrubbed well to remove any non-kosher residue.[90]

4) Cold milk and meat:
If cold meat falls into cold milk or cold milk spills over cold meat, the meat may absorb some milk. This depends upon whether the meat is raw or cooked, smooth or with crevices and whether the meat is bland or spiced. The question will be discussed in detail in Chapter Eleven, Section E.

Summary of Section II

The minimum degree of heat required to cause transfer of taste is *yad soledes bo*. Contemporary authorities assume that any food cooler than 110° fahrenheit (43° centigrade) is certainly not *yad soledes bo*.

Although heating to *yad soledes bo* may cause transfer of taste, it does not necessarily qualify as *bishul*. Not every situation of warming food to the degree of *yad soledes bo* necessarily violates *Shabbos* or the Biblical prohibition of cooking *basar b'chalav*. Not every situation of *yad soledes bo* necessarily causes even a total transfer of taste.

- ☐ A *kli rishon* has the ability to discharge or absorb taste even after the pot is removed from the fire and perhaps even if it is not *yad soledes bo*.
- ☐ A *kli sheni* no longer has the ability to cause *bishul*, even

87. *Shach* 91:1, *Chochmas Adam* 42:1.

88. *Y.D.* 91:1. Scrubbing, however, is unnecessary (*Chavas Daas* §1 and *Aruch HaShulchan* §1, see *Yad Yehudah* §1a).

89. See *Taz* §1, *Chavas Daas* §2c, and *Chochmas Adam* 42:2, who contend that the food is permitted. See, however, *Yad Yehudah* 6a.

90. *M.Z.* §1, *Chochmas Adam* 42:1. Although we be noted (Section I,C and Section III,B) that, with regard to cooking and salting, we do not differentiate between fatty and lean foods, we do distinguish between then with regard to *kavush* (*Shach* 105:1); thus, in regard to contact between cold foods we certainly may differentiate.

if it retains the heat of *yad soledes bo*. *Rishonim* disagree whether a *kli sheni* can cause a discharge or absorption of taste. A *kli sheni* that is not *yad soledes bo* certainly cannot induce a transfer of taste.

- □ In the opinion of some *Poskim*, solid food removed from a *kli rishon* and placed in a *kli sheni* retains the status of a *kli rishon*.
- □ *Rishonim* disagree as to the exact status of the liquid being poured from a *kli rishon* — *iruy*.
- □ Two hot, solid foods placed atop one another, or even a cold food placed atop a hot food, transfer taste to one another to the thickness of approximately one inch *(k'dei netilah)*. If either one of the foods is fatty, taste is transmitted throughout each of the foods. Customarily, most foods are treated as fatty foods.
- □ If hot food is placed atop cold food, the hot food is able to heat a *klipah* of the bottom food. Thus, taste is absorbed only into a *klipah* of either food.
- □ If two hot foods are placed alongside one another, they transfer their tastes throughout one another. If one of the foods is hot and the other is cold, their status is subject to a disagreement among *Poskim*.
- □ If two cold, completely dry foods, one kosher and one non-kosher, touch one another, the kosher food does not require washing. If either of the foods are even slightly damp, the kosher food must be rinsed. If either of the foods are fatty, the kosher food must be scrubbed well to remove any non-kosher residue.

III. Other types of taste transfers

A. Transfer of taste through soaking — Kavush k'mevushal, כָּבוּשׁ כִּמְבוּשָּׁל

These *halachos* are based upon *Tur* and *Shulchan Aruch* 105:1,2:

The Talmud[91] teaches us that any food that has soaked in a liquid effects the same transfer of taste that occurs when the two are

91. *Chullin* 97b, 111b, *Pesachim* 76a.

cooked together.[92] This is known in Talmudic terminology as *kavush k'mevushal* — soaking is the equivalent of cooking. Thus, if a non-kosher food[93] soaked in a kosher liquid or a kosher food soaked in a non-kosher liquid, the kosher liquid or food absorbs non-kosher taste. A kosher food that soaked in a liquid in which a non-kosher food previously soaked or is presently soaking is likewise affected by the non-kosher taste.[94] In each of these cases, the status of the kosher food is determined by the ratio of kosher to non-kosher food.[95]

In the opinion of practically all *Poskim*, the *kavush k'mevushal* principle is of Biblical origin.[96] Thus, if one is in doubt as to whether or not a food soaked for twenty-four hours, the stringent possibility must be assumed.[97]

> One should note, however, that although *kavush* effects the equivalent of cooking, it is not considered an act of *bishul*.[98] For example, one who soaks a food on *Shabbos* has not violated the Biblical prohibition of cooking.[99] Similarly, one

---

92. See *D.T.* 105:10,14, who cites a difference of opinion as to whether the transfer of taste is a continuous process that is completed at the end of twenty-four hours or whether the transfer occurs only at the end of the twenty-four hours.

93. Even if the food was solidly frozen at the time it was placed in the liquid (*Yad Yehudah* 105:1a). See *D.T.* 105:5, for a discussion as to whether *kavush k'mevushal* applies only to non-kosher tastes or to kosher tastes as well. For example: does milk soaked in a vessel render it a dairy vessel? See M.Z. 87:1, *Chavas Daas* 105:3c and *Yad Yehudah* 105:4k.

94. *D.T.* 105:2 citing *Minchas Yaakov*.

95. As in the case of cooked mixtures, if the amount of kosher food is sixty times that of non-kosher food, the kosher food may be eaten. One need not remove even the surface that came in contact with the non-kosher liquid (*D.T.* 105:17, see *D.T.* ibid. for a discussion as to whether *chatichah na'asis neveilah* is applicable to *kavush k'mevushal*). See *Rema* 105:1 as to whether those parts of the food that are not submerged into the liquid are subject to the rule of *kavush k'mevushal*.

96. See *D.T.* 105:13.

97. *Rema* 105:1, see *Taz* no. 3 and *Pischei Teshuvah* no. 3, regarding the utilization of this principle.

98. See M.Z. (105, end of 1) that although cooked blood is only Rabbinically forbidden, blood that was extracted from meat through soaking is Biblically forbidden since it was not actually cooked. See also *D.T.* 105:16. The *Aruch HaShulchan* 105:15, however, seems unsure regarding this question.

99. *Chochmas Adam* 58:1, as opposed to *Kreisi U'pleisi* 105:2 who contends that in the opinion of *Rambam*, *kavush k'mevushal* applies to the prohibition of cooking on *Shabbos* as well. One may also infer this from *Rashi: Pesachim* 44b. See also *Sidei Chemed* (*Ma'areches Chaf* no.43, vol. III, p. 119). *Chochmas Adam* does, however,

who soaks meat in milk has not transgressed the Biblical prohibition of cooking *basar b'chalav.*[100] However, the meat and milk are Rabbinically prohibited since they absorbed taste from one another.[101]

1) The required period of time:
Although the Talmud offers no precise time span for *kavush k'mevushal* to be effective, most *Rishonim*[102] agree that a soaking of twenty-four hours effects a transfer of taste. Kosher food that soaked in non-kosher liquid for less than twenty-four hours is washed and is permitted.[103] The soaking must be for twenty four consecutive hours. If the food is removed from the liquid, even momentarily, and then returned, no transfer of taste occurs, even if the total soaking time was twenty-four hours.[104] Similarly, if the food is soaked in running water, it is not considered *kavush* since the water has changed.[105] Whenever the soaking is for a period of less than twenty-four hours,[106] the solid food must merely be washed.[107] See, however, Chapter Eleven, Section E that at times meat soaked in non-

---

concede that in the opinion of *Rambam, kavush* constitutes a Rabbinic prohibition of cooking. See *M.B.* 318:37, who rules that one may prepare foods through soaking without noting that the food should not be soaked for twenty-four hours. See gloss in Chapter Fourteen, "*kavush k'mevushal*" for further exploration of this point.

100. *Pesachim* 44b, *Rema* 105:1.

101. *Rashi: Pesachim* (ibid.), *Y.D.* 91:8.

102. See *Beis Yosef* *Y.D.* 105.

103. *Y.D.* 105:1.

104. Although *Chavas Daas* 105:2c, *R' Akiva Eger* 105:1 and *Pischei Teshuvah* 69:33 follow the lenient ruling (see also *D.T.* 105:8), *M.Z.* 105:1, relies on it only in a case of serious financial loss. See *Yad Yehudah* 105:2k,1a, who contends that if the interruption is short, the *kavush k'mevushal* process is not interrupted. *Yad Yehudah* perceives *kavush k'mevushal* as depending entirely upon the softening of the solid matter; thus, a momentary interruption of the soaking does not interfere with the process. It is for this reason too that *Yad Yehudah* argues that flowing water can effect *kavush k'mevushal*. He also contends that if meat soaked in a vessel for twenty-four hours and only then milk falls in, the *kavush k'mevushal* effect is immediate since the meat was previously soaked and softened.

105. *Pischei Teshuvah* ibid. As noted above *Yad Yehudah* (ibid.) disagrees.

106. If, however, the non-kosher solid started dissolving, the liquid may become prohibited even if the soaking did not last twenty-four hours (*D.T.* 104:5, 105:20).

107. *Y.D.* 105:1. See *D.T.* 105:23, for a more stringent opinion. If, however, the kosher and non-kosher foods did not come into direct contact, but merely soaked in the same liquid, the kosher food need not be rinsed (*D.T.* 105:21).

kosher liquid for even a short time may absorb liquid and become prohibited.

2) The type of liquid:
In the opinion of almost all *Rishonim, kavush k'mevushal* applies even to bland liquids (see 3, below regarding brine and vinegar).[108] However, the liquid must be in a liquid or near liquid state. Honey is considered liquid with regard to *kavush k'mevushal*.[109] Butter, solid fat[110] and frozen liquids[111] do not bring about a transfer of taste. Two wet solids placed side by side do not absorb from one another. Nevertheless, one should remove an inch *(k'dei netilah)* of each adjacent surface.[112] A non-kosher liquid that mixed with a kosher liquid immediately imparts its non-kosher taste and is not subject to the limitations of *kavush k'mevushal*.[113]

3) Salt brine and vinegar:
Kosher foods that soaked together with non-kosher foods in salt brine absorb the non-kosher taste in a period shorter than twenty-four hours.[114] In the opinion of some authorities, soaking in brine for eighteen minutes effects *kavush k'mevushal*, while others contend that soaking for even six minutes may suffice.[115] A *moreh hora'ah* should be con-

108. The opinion of *Rosh* and others, cited in *Bais Yosef* 105, as opposed to the apparent opinion of *Rashi* (cited in *Bais Yosef* ibid.) that *kavush k'mevushal* applies only to foods soaked in vinegar or salt brine. *Kreisi U'pleisi* 105:2, attempts to prove that *Rambam* concurs with the opinion of *Rashi*.

109. *Chochmas Adam* 58:1. See *D.T.* 105:3, who cites opposing opinions on this matter. He agrees, however, that if solid matter can move freely in the honey, the honey is considered liquid. We omitted *Chochmas Adam's* ruling regarding molten butter and fat since, as *D.T.* notes, it is rare for butter to retain that state for twenty-four hours.

110. *Chavas Daas* 105:1c. *Pri Migadim: M.Z.* 105:1, cites *Rosh* who categorizes liquids, with regard to *kavush k'mevushal*, as anything in which a solid can move.

111. This is subject to a dispute among *halachic* authorities. See *M.Z.* (ibid.), who essentially agrees that frozen liquid does not cause a transfer of taste, although he hesitates to rule leniently except in a case of substantial monetary loss. In *S.D.* 69:60, he takes a more stringent view. *Yad Yehudah* 105:1a, follows the lenient view without reservation. See also *D.T.* 105:3.

112. *M.Z.* 105:1.

113. *M.Z.* ibid.

114. *Y.D.* 69:18, 105:1.

115. See *D.T.* 105:42.

sulted.[116] Some *Poskim* contend that vinegar is similar in potency to salt brine and effects *kavush k'mevushal* in a short period of time.[117] Others argue that vinegar is no different than other liquids.[118] Others differentiate between strong and weak vinegar.[119] Later authorities rule that initially one should follow the stringent opinion. In the event of monetary loss, one may rely on the lenient opinions.[120] A *moreh hora'ah* should be consulted. If the foods were soaked in vinegar for less than six minutes, a *klipah* should be removed.[121] If foods are soaked in salt brine for less than six minutes, there is no problem of *kavush k'mevushal* but we must contend with the effect of the salt. In most circumstances foods soaked in salt brine are prohibited immediately. This will be discussed in the next section.

4) *Kavush k'mevushal* regarding utensils:
Just as foods absorb and transmit taste through *kavush k'mevushal,* so too, vessels may absorb or transmit taste through soaking.

    a) Non-kosher liquids soaked in a kosher vessel:
    If a non-kosher liquid is contained in a kosher vessel for a twenty-four-hour period, the vessel absorbs non-kosher taste. *Poskim* disagree as to which substances are affected by soaking. Some argue that this applies to earthenware[122] and other porous materials (e.g., wood,

---

116. In case of serious loss, there may be a difference between fatty foods and lean foods soaked in salt brine. See the following section regarding the rules of *meliach k'roseiach.*

117. *Y.D.* 105:1.

118. *Shach* 105:2, contends that the power of salt brine is not due to *kavush k'mevushal* but to *meliach k'roseiach;* thus, vinegar cannot share its status.

119. *Magen Avraham* 447:28.

120. See *D.T.* 105:40. Incidentally, *Mishnah B'rurah* 447:71, follows the lenient opinion of *Shach*.

121. *Y.D.* 105:1.

122. Some *Poskim* differentiate between new and previously used earthenware (see *D.T.* 93:37 as to whether a utensil is considered previously used if it was used only once or twice). Used earthenware absorbs only in twenty-four hours, while new earthenware absorbs more quickly (see *Taz* 93:2 and *Pri Chadash* 105:1). *M.Z.* 105:1 contends that the absorption is immediate, while in *M.Z.* 93:2 he writes that it takes place only after twelve hours or perhaps one hour. Although *Shach: Nekudas Hakesef* 93:2, rules that even new earthenware does not absorb taste before twenty-four hours, *M.Z.* follows the opinion of *Taz* (ibid.). [See also *D.T.* 93:37.] See also *M.Z.* 105:1, regarding glazed earthenware. *Poskim* assume that glass utensils are not subject to the principle of *kavush k'mevushal* (see *Yad Yehudah* 105:4k, *D.T.* §11). Nevertheless, regarding *Pesach,* we

leather and stone)[123] only,[124] while others extend the principle to metals as well.[125]

b) Kosher liquids soaked in a non-kosher vessel:
Poskim disagree whether or not a kosher liquid that soaked in a non-kosher vessel is affected by the non-kosher taste absorbed in the vessel. Soaking is effective only after twenty-four hours, thus, no transfer of taste will occur beforehand. However, since the non-kosher taste that had previously been absorbed into the vessel becomes stale *(pagum)* after a period of twenty-four hours, it can no longer impart its non-kosher taste to the liquid (see footnote).[126]

Summary of Section A

☙ Any food that has soaked in a liquid consecutively for twenty-four hours effects the same transfer of taste as when the two are cooked together — *kavush k'mevushal*.

- ☐ Nevertheless, soaking is not considered an act of *bishul*. One who soaks a food on *Shabbos* or one who soaks meat

---

treat glass as earthenware (see *Rema O.C.* 451:26).

123. *Yad Yehudah* 105:1a. Even wooden utensils absorb only after twenty-four hours (*M.Z.* 105:1).

124. See *D.T.* 105:11.

125. See *M.Z.* 105:1, who cites a difference of opinion regarding metal utensils. However, in *M.Z.* 93:2, he rules that metal utensils do absorb through soaking (see *M.Z.* 68 end of 9). See also *Chavas Daas* 105:3c, who rules that metal does not absorb through soaking. *Yad Yehudah* 105:4k, follows this lenient ruling if the liquid was not sharp.

126. The point of contention is whether *kavush k'mevushal* causes the taste to be absorbed exactly at the end of the twenty-four-hour period, whereas the taste becomes stale only *after* twenty-four hours have passed. Thus, if the soaking started immediately after the vessel was used with non-kosher food, it may impart its taste through *kavush k'mevushal*. Or perhaps the spoiling of the taste takes place exactly at the end of twenty-four hours, and thus a transfer of non-kosher taste of a vessel through *kavush k'mevushal* is impossible. See *B'er Heitev* §1 who argues that the liquid soaking in the vessel does not permit the absorbed taste to become stale. See *Magen Avraham* 447:16 who contends that the taste transfer and staleness are simultaneous *(ba'in k'echad)*. Thus if the kosher liquid is placed in the vessel immediately after the non-kosher liquid was removed, the kosher liquid becomes prohibited. *Chavas Daas* 105:3c, follows this opinion, while *Mishnah B'rurah* 447:39 follows the lenient opinions. See *D.T.* 105:14, for a discussion of the various opinions in this matter. See Chapter Eleven note no. 17 regarding salty or sharp liquids and for a further discussion of these issues.

CHART 11

KOSHER AND NON-KOSHER FOODS SOAKED TOGETHER

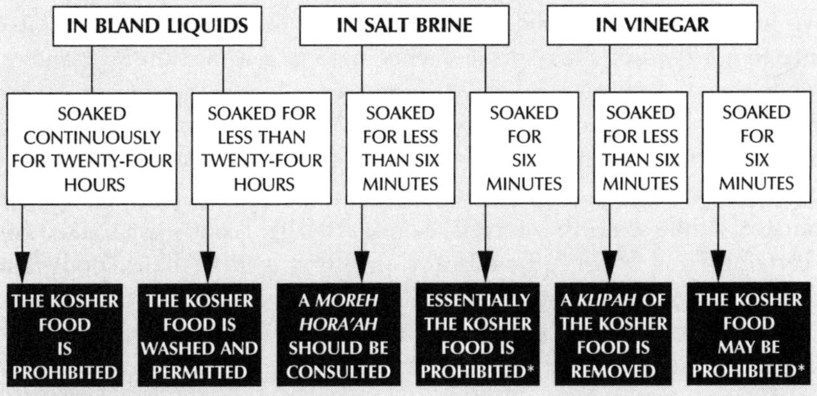

* A *moreh hora'ah* should be consulted.

in milk has not violated the Biblical prohibition of cooking on *Shabbos* or cooking *basar b'chalav*.

- ☐ *Kavush k'mevushal* applies even to bland liquids. However, the liquid must be in a liquid or near liquid state.
- ☐ Foods soaked in salt brine or vinegar for eighteen or perhaps even six minutes transmit and absorb taste.

B. Transfer of taste through salting — *Meliach k'roseiach,* מְלִיחַ כְּרוֹתֵחַ

These *halachos* are based upon *Tur* and *Shulchan Aruch* 91:5:

The Talmud[127] teaches that salting, in the proper amount, can effect a taste transfer. This is known in Talmudic terminology as *meliach k'roseiach* — salting is the equivalent of heat. However, salting differs from soaking with regard to the area affected by the taste transfer. We noted in the beginning of this chapter that any transfer of taste requires both a medium to permit the taste transfer (e.g., liquid) and a condition to induce that transfer (e.g., heat). Whereas soaking fulfills both of these

127. *Pesachim* 76a, *Chullin* 97b.

conditions, i.e., the liquid provides both the medium and the condition of transfer, salting produces the condition but not the medium since the foods are not submerged into a liquid.[128] While soaking can impart taste throughout the food, salting can impart taste only to a *klipah* of the food. In this sense salting is the exact equivalent of heating: likewise, two hot, dry and lean foods that touch one another transfer their tastes only to a *klipah* of their surfaces since they lack a medium of transfer. While this is theoretically true, it is questionable whether or not we are capable of distinguishing between fatty and lean foods, as will be explained later in this section. Another difference between salting and soaking is in regard to the amount of time necessary to effect a taste transfer. While soaking is effective only after the foods have soaked for a certain period of time, the efficacy of salting is immediate. Foods that are salted together transfer taste to one another instantly.[129]

The reader should note that our discussion relates to wet salt which is potent and capable of effecting a taste transfer. Dry salt, however, has no effect on foods. Even if the salt on the food was damp, but dried before the kosher and non-kosher food came in contact, it loses its power.[130] Thus, if dry salted meat and cheese touch one another, they require only rinsing.[131]

1) The amount of salting necessary to impart taste:
   The Talmud[132] considers salting as heating only if the salting is so potent that the food is inedible because of the salt upon it. *Poskim* note three levels of salting: a) the salting of meat for preservation, b) the salting of meat to remove its blood in preparation for boiling in a pot, c) the salting of meat to remove its blood in preparation for broiling over (or under) an open flame.[133]

---

128. This is apparent from the terms used in the Talmud: *kavush k'mevushal* -soaking is like *boiling*, *meliach k'roseiach* — salting is like heating (see *Chullin* 97b).

129. *Rema* 70:6, *Taz* §17, *Shach* §46, 87:27, 91:11, 105:3, even though *Shulchan Aruch* 91:5 seems to hold otherwise (see *Aruch HaShulchan* 91:27-30).

130. This is true even if the foods subsequently became damp (*Y.D.* 91:5, see *Pri Toar* §13).

131. *Kaf HaChaim* §48.

132. *Pesachim* 76a, *Chullin* 112a.

133. In the case of boiling in a pot, the meat remains in contact with the blood that is discharged during the boiling process. Thus, since the blood is prohibited, it must be removed by salting prior to any cooking lest the blood be absorbed into the meat. However, when meat is broiled in a manner that the blood may drip away freely, one is not required to salt the meat beforehand. Nevertheless, the custom is to salt the meat lightly even before broiling.

a) Salting for preservation:
Meat that is salted for preserving purposes is the most potent form of salting. Meat salted in this manner has the ability to impart its taste to a *klipah* of any food with which it comes in contact. The meat retains this power until the salt is removed by soaking the meat in water. However, merely rinsing the meat of its salt cannot eliminate the effect of the salt.[134]

b) Salting for boiling:
One may not boil meat unless it was salted beforehand to remove any blood. Meat that was salted for boiling purposes has the ability to impart its taste on contact to the *klipah* of any food. However, once the meat is washed of the salt it cannot impart any taste.[135] Although most meats commercially sold today are salted, they are not considered salty since they are washed of their salt prior to packing.

c) Salting for broiling:
The process of broiling removes blood from meat. Therefore, one who wishes to broil meat is required to salt it only lightly. This light salting is insufficient to effect a taste transfer. However, since we are not capable of differentiating between different levels of salting, *Ashkenazic* custom is to consider even this level of salting capable of imparting taste. In a situation of serious financial loss, one may consider salting in preparation for broiling as not actual salting.[136]

2) To what degree can salting impart taste:
As noted above, salting replicates only the heat necessary for a taste transfer. A full transfer of taste also requires a medium to impart the taste throughout the food. Thus, salting two lean foods together can transfer taste only to a *klipah* of the surface

---

134. *Y.D.* 91:5.

135. *Y.D.* 91:5. See *Rema* (ibid.) with regard to salt that remains on the meat after all the blood has been removed, see *Shach* §11.

136. *Rema* 91:5. See *Kaf HaChaim* §38 who notes that according to *Sefardic* custom one may follow the lenient opinion even in a case of minor loss. *Kaf HaChaim* §37 also notes that this discussion pertains to a significant amount of salt, albeit an amount less than that required for boiling. If, however, only a bit of salt was sprinkled on the food, it is inconsequential.

of contact. Fatty foods, however, provide the salt with the proper medium to carry the infusion of taste thoroughly.[137] Even if non-kosher lean food is salted together with kosher fatty food, the kosher fatty food imparts its fattiness to the non-kosher food which then imparts its taste to the kosher food.[138] *Poskim* note that since it is difficult to judge which foods are fatty one should treat all foods as fatty foods.[139]

3) If only one of the foods is salty:
If only one of the foods is salty, taste can only be imparted from the salty food to the non-salty food, but not the reverse. Thus, if the non-kosher food is salty, it imparts its taste to the kosher food. However, if the kosher food is salty it is unaffected by the non-kosher food. The kosher food is merely rinsed and may be eaten.[140] No distinction is made whether the non-kosher food is on top or underneath.[141] In the opinion of some *Poskim,* even if only the kosher food is salty, it absorbs the non-kosher taste.[142] *Poskim* rule that in a case of loss, one may follow the lenient opinion.[143]

Summary of Section B

☙ Salting can effect a taste transfer equivalent to heating — *meliach k'roseiach*.

- ☐ Meat that is salted for preserving purposes and not soaked to remove the salt imparts its taste to a *klipah* of any food it touches.
- ☐ Meat that is salted only for boiling (or even for broiling) purposes retains this power until it is washed of the salt.
- ☐ Two lean foods salted together transfer taste only to a

137. *Y.D.* 70:4, 91:6.

138. *Y.D.* 70:4.

139. *Rema* 91:5, 105:9. Even *Sefardic* Jews follow *Rema* in this matter (*Kaf HaChaim* 105:111). Distinctions are made between different levels of lean foods and between Biblical and Rabbinic prohibitions. These are discussed in the commentaries to *Rema* 105:9, and are not within the scope of this work.

140. *Y.D.* 70:3, 105:10.

141. *Y.D.* 70:3, 91:5, *Chochmas Adam* 43:6. See *Shach* 70:22 and 91:12 who notes that this refers to lean foods only. This is relevant to the opinion of *Shulchan Aruch* not to *Ashkenazic* custom which follows *Rema* 105:11.

142. The opinion of *Ran* cited in *Y.D.* 70:3, and *Rema* 105:10.

143. *Rema* 105:10, see *Shach* 70:20 and *Chochmas Adam* 43:5.

klipah of the surface of contact. Fatty foods carry the infusion of taste throughout the food. Since it is difficult to judge which foods are fatty, one should treat all foods as fatty foods.

CHART 12

MELIACH K'ROSEIACH

TASTE TRANSFER THROUGH SALTING

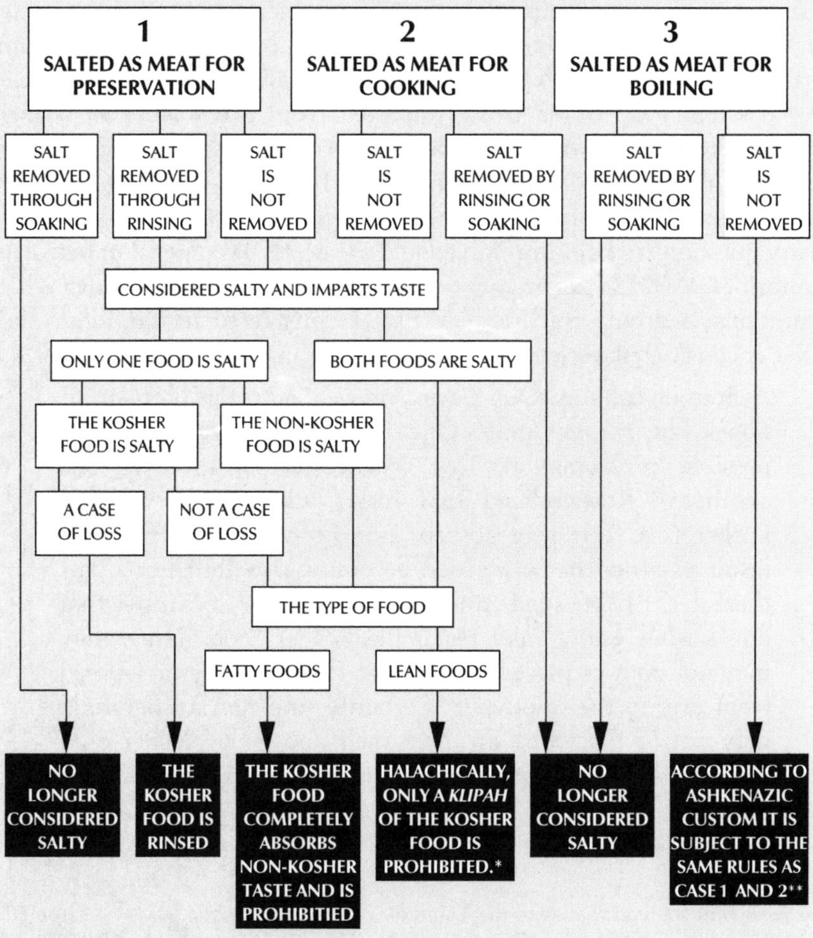

* Actualy, we consider all foods to be fatty food and are thus prohibited. In case of loss a *moreh hora'ah* should be consulted.

** In case of serious loss it may be considered not salty. A *moreh hora'ah* should be consulted.

C. Transfer of taste through aroma — *Reicha milsa,* רֵיחָא מִילְתָא

These *halachos* are based upon *Tur* and *Shulchan Aruch; Yoreh De'ah* 108.

When two foods are baked simultaneously in an oven, there is a possibility of aroma being imparted from one to the other. This issue, known by the Talmudical term of *"reicha milsa"* (aroma is significant), is the subject of Talmudical debate.[144] The consensus of opinion among *Rishonim* and the *halachic* conclusion as presented in *Shulchan Aruch*[145] is that *lechatchilah* (a priori) — initially — one should avoid any possibility of aroma being imparted from non-kosher to kosher foods.[146] However, *bidieved* (ex-post-facto) — in the event that kosher food did absorb aroma from non-kosher food, we assume *reicha lav milsa* (aroma is insignificant) and the food may be eaten. However, many questions remain unresolved and are issues of contention between authorities. What foods impart taste through their aroma? Under what conditions is aroma imparted? What is considered *lechatchilah* and what is considered *bidieved?*

A note of caution: Our discussion relates to the problem of non-kosher aroma only. One must be attentive to other possible problems. a) The foods must not touch one another.[147] Kosher food that roasts while touching non-kosher food certainly absorbs non-kosher taste. This may result in either the entire food becoming prohibited or a part thereof.[148] b) The foods must not be placed in a manner that non-kosher gravy may reach the kosher food. Thus, they may not both be placed on the oven floor if gravy can spread from one to the another.[149] Certainly, the non-kosher food may not be placed on an oven shelf above the kosher food lest non-kosher gravy drip upon the kosher food. c) In

---

144. *Pesachim* 76b.

145. *Y.D.* 108:1.

146. *Rishonim* contend that even the Talmudic opinion that *reicha lav milsa* (aroma is insignificant) concedes that initially they should not be roasted together (see *Rif: Chullin* 32b).

147. *Y.D.* 108:1.

148. See *Y.D.* 105:4-7.

149. See *Rema* 97:1.

addition, if the food being cooked contains liquid, it produces steam. One must thus contend with the problem of *zeiah* — steam, which will be discussed in the following section.

1) Which foods impart taste through their aroma?

   a) Fatty meats:
   Chazal were concerned with the aroma of fatty foods, דָּבָר שָׁמֵן. Lean foods impart no significant aroma. Thus, fatty non-kosher meat should not be roasted in the oven simultaneously with kosher meat. Indeed, fatty kosher meat should not be roasted with even lean non-kosher meat since the fatty aroma of the kosher meat may transfer the taste of the non-kosher meat to the kosher meat.[150]

   b) Lean meats:
   In the opinion of many authorities,[151] two lean meats may be roasted concurrently. However, since it is difficult to determine what constitutes lean meat, many authorities advise that one should not roast even two lean meats concurrently.[152]

   c) Breads:
   One may bake a kosher bread in the oven together with a non-kosher bread since breads have no fatty aroma.[153] Similarly, one may burn the *challah*[154] set aside from the dough while the bread is baking in the oven even though *challah* may not be eaten. *Poskim* note that one who avoids even this is praiseworthy.[155]

   d) Sharp foods:
   Sharp foods are especially prone to absorbing aroma. Thus, even in situations where *reicha* would not

150. *Taz* 108:1 and *Shach* §1.

151. *Taz* 108:1, *Shach* §1, as opposed to *Toras Chatas* 35:3.

152. *S.D.* 108:1, see also *Aruch HaShulchan* 108:9.

153. *S.D.* ibid.

154. Colloquially, the *Shabbos* breads are called *challos*. *Halachically* and in this context, however, *challah* refers to the portion of the dough that must be set aside. In previous times, this was given to a *Kohen* who ate the *challah* while spiritually "clean". Today, since we lack the means of becoming spiritually "clean" and, furthermore, we are uncertain who is a *Kohen*, the *challah* is burnt.

155. *S.D.* 108:18(1).

normally be problematic, sharp foods would be affected. Consequently, if either the kosher or non-kosher food[156] is sharp, the kosher food may not be eaten.[157] A definition of sharp foods may be found in Chapter Twelve, II,C.

2) Under what conditions is aroma imparted?
Two foods baked in a confined area are more likely to absorb aroma than those baked in an open area which permits the aroma to dissipate. Thus, foods baked in a large, ventilated oven do not impart taste to one another. However, foods baked in a small, confined oven will impart their taste. Several issues must be addressed: What is a large oven, what is considered an open oven, and how can the transfer of taste be prevented even in a small oven?

   a) A large oven:
   Authorities define a large oven as that with the surface area of approximately 68 square *amos* (approximately 272 square feet or 25.3 square meters). Others contend that the area is measured in total cubic volume of the oven. In their opinion, an oven of 600 cubic *tefochim* (approximately 22 cubic feet or .62 cubic meters) is considered a large oven.[158] Household ovens do not qualify as large according to either of these standards and must be considered small ovens.

   b) An open or vented oven:
   An oven completely open at the top permits any aroma to thoroughly dissipate and therefore presents less of a *reicha* problem.[159] A closed but vented oven that allows

---

156. See *Gilyon Maharsha* in gloss to *Rema* 108:1 who cites the opinion of *Chok Yaakov* that while sharp foods are susceptible to absorb taste through *reicha*, they cannot impart taste. Thus, the *halachah* stated above applies only when the kosher food is sharp not when the non-kosher food is sharp. See also *Shaar Hatziyun: Orach Chaim* 447:7, who notes that *Eliah Rabbah* and *Graz* follow the opinion of *Rema*.

157. *Rema* 108:1. In either case, a *moreh hora'ah* should be consulted.

158. See both opinions in *Binas Adam* 62 (81). See *S.D.* 108:18 who follows the first opinion.

159. *Shach* 108:3. See *S.D.* §3 who notes that one must separate the foods sufficiently so that they not splatter on one another. In addition, he notes, one should not place in the oven similar looking foods, one meat and one dairy, lest they become mixed up.

smoke to escape may nevertheless retain aroma and permit it to travel from food to food.[160]

c) A closed oven:
An oven without any vent or outlet presents a more serious problem of *reicha*. Kosher food roasted with non-kosher meat may become completely prohibited.[161]

d) Covered food:
Even sharp foods baked in a small confined oven cannot impart aroma to one another if either of them are completely covered. For example, if one of the foods is in a pot covered by a lid[162] or if the food is wrapped even in another food, e.g., a meat pie completely enveloped in crust, no aroma is imparted.[163] Initially, one should not bake a covered, sharp meat pie in an oven concurrently with non-kosher food.[164] However, kosher food completely covered in a pot may be baked in the same oven as non-kosher food[165] (the kosher pot should not be placed on a non-kosher surface). One may, therefore, cook kosher food in a non-kosher oven, even while non-kosher food is being cooked there, if it is completely wrapped in aluminum foil.[166] However, the foods should not be placed above one another.

160. *Rema* as cited in *Shach* ibid. See below that in the opinion of *Pri Chadash* §4, the *Shulchan Aruch* disagrees with *Rema*.

161. Unless serious financial loss will be incurred (*Rema* 108:1, see also *Shach* §8).

162. In the opinion of the *Shulchan Aruch* 108:2 foods cooking in a pot are not subject to the rules of *reicha* even if the pot is uncovered and the oven is not vented. *Poskim* disagree whether this is due to the pot walls which prevent the aroma from spreading or to the difference between the roasting process and the boiling process (a practical application of this argument is the question of whether or not *reicha* applies to meat roasted in an uncovered pot without liquid, see *Shach* §16 *Chochmas Adam* 62:2). *Sefardic* Jews follow this lenient opinion of *Shulchan Aruch* and permit meat and dairy foods to be cooked in an oven simultaneously in separate pots (*Kaf HaChaim* §50). *Rema* (ibid.) follows this opinion only regarding a vented oven. We have omitted this aspect of the *halachah* from our discussion since foods boiled in an uncovered pot are subject to the laws of *zeiah* as will be discussed in the following section. Those *Poskim* who make this distinction are referring to a situation where there is no problem of *zeiah*.

163. *Y.D.* 108:1.

164. *Shach* 108:10.

165. Even if the food is sharp (*S.D.* 108:10, *R' Akiva Eger* gloss to *Shach* ibid.).

166. It is advisable to double wrap any food placed in a non-kosher oven since the oven shelves may contain non-kosher residue.

3) The practical *halachah:*
The *halachos* of *reicha* must be divided between *lechatchilah,* לְכַתְּחִילָה — the optimum course of action, and *bidieved,* בְּדִיעֲבַד — dealing with the ex-post-facto situation.

a) *Lechatchilah:*

- □ One may not roast kosher and non-kosher meat concurrently in an oven, even if they do not touch one another and there is no chance of the non-kosher gravy reaching the kosher food.[167] In the opinion of some *Poskim*, no distinction should be made between fatty and lean meats.[168]
- □ Similarly, one may not roast meat and dairy concurrently in an oven even if they do not touch one another and there is no chance of the meat gravy reaching the dairy food.[169]
- □ One may bake kosher and non-kosher breads concurrently in one oven since breads do not emit a significant aroma.[170] Nevertheless, it is meritorious to avoid doing so.[171]

Some ex-post-facto situations are considered *lechatchilah* if one has another course of action. For example:

- □ One who baked bread concurrently with meat may not eat that bread with dairy.[172] Since one has the option of eating the bread alone or with meat, choosing to eat the bread with dairy constitutes *lechatchilah*. If, however, no other bread is available

---

167. *Y.D.* 108:1.

168. *S.D.* 108:1, see also *Aruch HaShulchan* 108:9.

169. *Rema* 108:1.

170. *S.D* 108:1.

171. *S.D.* 108:18(1).

172. *Rema* 108:1. Even if the bread was baked in a loaf pan, it is subject to this *halachah* (the dough usually rises above the walls of the pan and are therefore not relevant to the opinion of *Shulchan Aruch* 108:2, cited in note 162 above, who rules that foods cooked in a pot are exempt from the rules of *reicha*, see *Pri Toar* §2). The question of the status of the *parve* loaf pan (i.e., whether it can be used with dairy) is subject to a disagreement between *Chinuch Bais Yehudah* (cited in *Pischei Teshuvah* 108:2, *Gilyon Maharsha* ibid. and *R' Akiva Eger* ibid.).

to eat with the dairy food, one may use the bread in question.[173]

- ☐ Similarly, bread baked by a non-Jew simultaneously with non-kosher meat should not be purchased. Choosing to purchase the bread constitutes *lechatchilah*. If, however, no other bread is easily available, the bread may be purchased.[174]

These *halachos* apply regardless of whether the oven is large or small, open or closed. In either case one should not initially roast kosher and non-kosher meats concurrently.[175] This is, however, permitted if the roasting is done in a large oven that is completely open at the top[176] (household ovens are neither of the two) or if either of the foods is completely covered.[177]

b) *Bidieved:*

One who baked kosher and non-kosher foods concurrently in an oven may eat the kosher food, regardless of whether the oven was large or small, with or without an opening.[178] There are two significant exceptions to these rules:

- ☐ If the oven is completely closed and non-vented, the food may not be eaten unless serious financial loss will be incurred.[179] It should be noted that all household ovens are vented; thus, this *halacha* has no application to regular ovens. A microwave oven is completely closed and poses a serious problem of *reicha* (besides the problem of *zeiah)*. A *moreh hora'ah* should be consulted.
- ☐ If one of the foods[180] is sharp, the kosher food may not be eaten.[181]

---

173. *Rema* 108:1. Providing that he is unable to eat the bread alone or that the dairy food cannot be eaten without bread *(Kreisi U'pleisi* §6).

174. *Rema* ibid.

175. *Rema* ibid. In the opinion of *Pri Chadash* §4, the *Shulchan Aruch* permits roasting in a large oven that has a partial opening. See also *Chochmas Adam* 62:1,3.

176. *Rema* (ibid.), as per interpretation of *Shach* 108:3 (see note 159 above). It is, however, meritorious to abstain from doing so *(S.D.* §18:1).

177. *Y.D.* 108:1.

178. *Rema* 108:1.

179. Ibid.

☐ The laws of *chametz* on *Pesach* are more stringent in regard to the question of *reicha*. See *Rema: Orach Chaim* 447:1.

If one of the foods is completely covered (even if only covered with crust), the kosher food is permitted in all circumstances.[182]

Due to the complexity of these *halachos*, one who actually bakes kosher food concurrently with non-kosher food or meat with dairy should consult a *moreh hora'ah*.

4) Two additional aspects of *reicha* are not within the scope of this work but warrant mention.

a) Bread placed on a barrel of wine:
The Talmud rules that when warm bread is placed upon a barrel of non-kosher wine, it absorbs the aroma of the wine. This depends upon a) the warmth of the bread, b) whether the barrel is open or closed and c) whether the bread is of wheat or barley flour (barley is more absorbent). These *halachos* may be found in *Shulchan Aruch* and its commentaries.[183]

b) Enjoying the aroma of prohibited foods:
The issue of *reicha* as discussed heretofore relates to the aroma of prohibited foods absorbed into permitted foods. One who subsequently eats the kosher food eats, as it were, the non-kosher taste. This is predicated upon the principle of *taam k'ikar* as discussed in Chapter Four. Inhaling fragrance in itself, however, is not a form of eating or drinking; rather, it is a form of deriving benefit — *hana'ah*. Thus, one may not enjoy the aroma of those forbidden foods from which one may not derive benefit. One may, however, enjoy the fragrance of those foods that are merely prohibited to be eaten *(issurei achilah)*. Thus, the *halachos* regarding fragrances are as follows:

---

180. See *Gilyon Maharsha* cited in note 156 above.

181. *Rema* ibid. Even when baked in a large oven (*Taz* 108:5 and *Shach* §9, as opposed to *Maharshal* cited in *Taz*. See *M.Z.* §5 regarding an open oven.

182. *Y.D.* 108:1. In addition, if the kosher food contains a volume of sixty times the non-kosher food, it may be eaten (see *Rema* ibid.).

183. *Y.D.* 108:4.

- ☐ *Issurei achilah:*
  Fragrances from foods that are merely prohibited to eat, may be enjoyed (see footnote).[184]
- ☐ *Issurei hana'ah:*
  Fragrances of foods from which one may not derive benefit are prohibited. However, some *Poskim* permit enjoying their aroma if the food is primarily eaten, not used for aromas.[185]
- ☐ *Yayin nesech:*
  An exception to this rule is *yayin nesech* — wine of libation. Due to the severity of *avodah zarah,* one may not enjoy the fragrance of *yayin nesech,* even if the wine is not usually used for fragrance.[186]

Accordingly, one who passes a non-kosher bakery or restaurant may pause and enjoy the pleasant aroma. Any non-kosher food in the bakery is probably not among those from which one may not derive benefit and certainly not of a food used primarily for aroma. One passing a house of *avodah zarah* may not derive pleasure from the fragrance of any incense emitted. Indeed, one must, if possible, refrain from passing the building if the fragrance cannot be otherwise avoided.

Summary of Section C

☙ Two foods baked simultaneously in an oven may impart taste from one to another through their aroma - *reicha milsa.* Therefore, one should avoid any possibility of aroma being imparted from non-kosher foods to kosher foods. However, in the event that kosher food did absorb aroma from non-kosher

184. *Pri Chadash* 108:25. See, however, *Biur Halachah* 216:2 s.v. *"hamusak"* who contends that even if the prohibited food is primarily eaten, one should not smell its aroma lest one come to eat of it.

185. *Rashba,* cited in *Shach* 108:27, while other *Poskim* prohibit use of *issurei hana'ah* for fragrance purposes (*Tosfos,* cited in *Shach* ibid.).

186. All of the above is gleaned from *Pri Chadash* 108:25. See, however, *Pri Toar* §6, who contends that one may not enjoy the aroma of anything that is *asur b'hana'ah,* regardless of whether it is usually used for fragrance.

food, we assume that the aroma is insignificant.

- ☐ Fatty non-kosher meat and even lean kosher meat or fatty kosher meat and even lean non-kosher meat should not be roasted simultaneously in the oven. Since it is difficult to determine which meats are considered fatty and which are considered lean, one should not roast even two lean meats concurrently.
- ☐ If either the kosher or non-kosher food is sharp, the kosher food may not be eaten.
- ☐ It is meritorious to avoid baking kosher bread in the oven together with a non-kosher bread, even though breads have no fatty aroma.
- ☐ A large oven completely open at the top presents no problem of *reicha*, while a closed, but vented, oven does pose a *reicha* problem.
- ☐ Kosher food completely covered in a pot or aluminum foil may be baked in the same oven as non-kosher food.
- ☐ One who bakes bread concurrently with meat may not eat that bread with dairy unless no other bread is available.
- ☐ Fragrances from foods that are merely prohibited to eat, may be enjoyed. Fragrances of foods from which one may not derive benefit are prohibited if the food is of a type used for aromas. One may not enjoy the fragrance of *yayin nesech,* even if the wine is not usually used for fragrance.

D. Transfer of taste through steam — *zeiah,* זֵיעָה

These *halachos* are based upon *Tur* and *Shulchan Aruch; Yoreh De'ah* 92:8 and *Rema* 108:1.

Another problem encountered when cooking foods in an oven is the issue of *zeiah* - steam.[187] All liquids and many foods emit steam when cooked or baked. *Halachah* considers the steam of any liquid as having the status of that food. Thus, steam of non-kosher liquid is not harmless,

---

187. The source for this *halachah* is found in *Teshuvos HaRosh* 20:26, cited in *Tur* and *S.A., Y.D.* 92:8. *Rosh,* in turn, bases this on the *Mishnah: Machshirin* 2:2, which rules that the steam of a *tameh* (spiritually unclean) bath transmits the *tumah* to the entire house. *Poskim* are uncertain whether *zeiah* is a Biblical or Rabbinical concept, see responsa *Minchas Yitzchok* 5:20;10.

non-matter vapor; it is actually *treif* and will impart its non-kosher taste and status to anything it penetrates. Similarly, steam of milk that condensed into water is nothing other than milk. It should not be considered pure water distilled from the milk. Accordingly, if this water subsequently mixes with meat, it is the equivalent of milk mixing with meat.

1) The application of this principle is dependent upon the following factors:

   a) Liquids as opposed to solids:
   In the opinion of some authorities,[188] the principle that steam is the food itself applies to liquids only. They contend that steam emitted by foods (even when liquified, i.e., melted butter or chicken gravy) is *halachically* considered plain water and does not have the *halachic* status of the food. While most *Poskim*[189] reject this view, they concede that solid foods produce a negligible amount of steam.[190] Thus, one need not be concerned about *zeiah* when cooking solid food unless steam is visibly rising from the food. In short:

   - □ One must assume that the *zeiah* of all liquids, regardless of their source, carries their taste.
   - □ One may assume that solids do not produce *zeiah* unless steam is actually detected.[191]

   b) Steam returning to the liquid:
   Once the ability of steam to rise and imbue its taste into the surface directly above it is established, we must be concerned with the possibility of condensed steam falling back into the liquid. Thus, even kosher steam may pose a problem if it condenses onto a non-kosher surface while still hot. The condensed water vapor, having absorbed non-kosher taste, may fall into the kosher food rendering it *treif*. *Poskim* disagree as to whether one must be concerned with this potentiality or whether it may be ignored unless one actually notices

188. See *Pischei Teshuvah* 92:6, citing *Pri Migadim* who in turn bases his opinion on *Rambam*.

189. See *Yad Yehudah* §53a and *D.T.* §164.

190. See *Rema: Toras Chatas* 35:6, and *Minchas Yaakov* (35:21).

191. *Igros Moshe*, Y.D. 1:40.

droplets falling into the food.[192] In conclusion:

- □ Steam certainly imparts its taste to a surface in its path.
- □ It is a matter of contention as to whether the steam can impart taste from the upper surface to the food below.

c) Hot as opposed to cold steam:
The reader is well acquainted, by now, with the principle that taste is only transferred through heat. Thus, the problem of *zeiah* pertains only when hot steam reaches the surface directly above a cooking liquid.[193] Hot steam can induce even a cold surface to absorb taste. If, however, the surface is far above the cooking liquid, the steam reaching the surface will no longer be hot enough to effect a transfer of taste. The surface may become damp and covered with condensed non-kosher vapor, but its kosher status is unaffected. Simply washing the surface thoroughly to remove any non-kosher residue will do. This applies to hot steam reaching an otherwise cool surface. However, if the surface was independently heated, it may heat the condensed vapor and absorb its non-kosher taste.[194] Thus:

- □ Non-kosher food cooking beneath a cool surface will impart its taste to that surface if the steam is hot upon reaching the surface. The surface is rendered *treif* and must be *kashered*.
- □ If the steam is no longer hot when reaching the surface, it cannot impart its taste. The surface has not absorbed taste and remains kosher. It must, however, be washed to remove any non-kosher residue.

---

192. See *Dagul Mervavah* 92:8, who implies that one must assume that the vapor fell into the food. *M.Z.* §29, however, rules that it is a matter of concern only if the vapor actually drips into the food. This opinion is shared by *Yad Yehudah* §52a, 69k. See also *D.T.* §165.

193. In the event that one is uncertain whether or not the steam was hot, one may assume that it was not sufficiently hot to effect a transfer of taste. If, however, the cooking took place in a completely closed oven, one must assume that the steam was hot (*R' Akiva Eger* gloss to 92:8, see also *D.T.* §177).

194. *M.Z.* 92:29, *R' Akiva Eger* gloss to *Y.D.* 92:8. See a dissenting opinion in *Yad Yehudah* §55a.

- ☐ If the surface is independently hot (e.g., both utensils are in an oven), the upper surface must be *kashered*, regardless of whether the steam was hot upon contact.

d) A closed as opposed to an open area:
The ability of steam to impart taste or absorb taste from the surface above depends upon whether the steam is in an open area or a restricted area. Steam rising in an open area easily dissipates and is less likely to reach the upper surface in a volume and intensity of heat necessary to cause a transfer of taste. In addition, steam that dissipated sufficiently is less likely to condense on the upper surface and fall back into the cooking liquid. Thus, some authorities rule that although usually one need not be concerned that droplets of condensed steam may fall back into the food, if the cooking takes place in a confined area, we must assume that those droplets acquired taste from the non-kosher surface and may fall into the food.[195]

e) A closed pot:
The problem of *zeiah* depends upon the ability of the steam to travel. Therefore, if the pot is covered in a manner that the steam cannot escape, *zeiah* is of no concern.[196]

2) These concepts present many practical applications to kashrus:

a) A pot lid:
Foods cooked in a pot emit steam. If that pot is covered, the steam gathers and condenses into droplets on the underside of the lid. Thus, if a kosher pot lid is placed over a non-kosher pot that is boiling over the fire, the pot lid may become *treif* and require *kashering*. A non-kosher pot lid placed over cooking kosher foods may similarly render the food *treif*. The steam of the kosher food rises to the pot lid, absorbs its taste and, upon condensation, drops into the food, imbuing it with non-kosher taste. In this case, a *moreh hora'ah* should be consulted. Similarly, a meat pot lid placed over a cooking

---

195. See *Imrei Baruch* cited in *D.T.* §165.

196. *Rema* 92:8.

dairy pot may render the food, the pot, and the lid *treif*. This complex issue will be discussed in Chapter Eleven, Section C.

b) An oven:
Foods cooked in an oven also produce steam which rises to the top of the oven and may give it the status of the food. Thus, non-kosher food cooked in an oven may make the oven *treif*, while milk foods baked therein may render the oven dairy. While this is apparent, the status of food subsequently cooked in the oven is less than certain. Should one assume that the steam of the kosher food condenses on the oven roof, absorbs the non-kosher taste and returns to the food in the form of droplets? Or perhaps, unlike the closed environs of a pot, a vented oven permits the steam to dissipate without condensing on its roof. This question is most relevant to use of an oven for meat and dairy foods and will be discussed in Chapter Nine.

c) An object in the path of steam:
Objects placed in the path of steam escaping from non-kosher food may become *treif* if the steam comes in contact with them while still hot.[197] Indeed, even if the steam is not hot and thus cannot effect a transfer of its taste into the object, it nevertheless coats the object with non-kosher residue which must be removed before the object may be used.[198] Therefore, one should not hang ladles and spatulas above a stove where they may be affected by the steam of meat or dairy foods.[199]

Summary of Section D

☙ The steam *(zeiah)* of any liquid has the status of that food. Thus, the steam of non-kosher liquid is *treif* and the steam of milk is milk.

---

197. *Rema* 92:8.

198. *D.T.* §178, citing *Pri Migadim*.

199. Even if the steam is not hot enough to impart its taste to the ladles, it nevertheless coats the ladles. Although this may be washed off, one may forget to do so. Generally, one may not cause a situation requiring washing, since one may neglect to do so (see *D.T.* §178).

- ☐ One need not be concerned about steam when cooking solid food unless steam is visibly rising from the food.
- ☐ Hot steam imparts its taste to the surface directly above, even if that surface is cold, unless the surface is far above the cooking liquid and is not independently hot.
- ☐ Steam rising in an open area dissipates and usually poses no *zeiah* problem.
- ☐ If the cooking pot is properly covered, *zeiah* is of no concern.
- ☐ If a kosher pot lid is placed over a non-kosher pot that is cooking over the fire, the pot lid becomes *treif* and must be *kashered*. Similarly, a non-kosher pot lid placed over cooking kosher foods may render the food *treif*.
- ☐ One should not hang ladles and spatulas where they may be affected by the steam of meat or dairy foods cooking on the stove.

CHAPTER SIX

נַ"ט בַּר נַ"ט
Secondary Infusions of Taste

□ *Nat-bar-nat d'heteira.*

□ *Nat-bar-nat d'isura.*

□ *Sefardic* and *Ashkenazic* customs.

Introduction

In the preceding chapters, we discussed primary infusionss of taste. In this chapter, we will discuss secondary infusionss. Food cooked in a pot infuses its taste into the pot. When another food is subsequently cooked in that pot (even after it has been scrubbed clean), the original taste is transmitted to the second food. This secondary transfer (i.e., food to pot to food) is known as *nosen taam bar nosen taam,* נוֹתֵן טַעַם בַּר נוֹתֵן טַעַם (lit. infused taste, the son of infused taste) or *nat-bar-nat* for short. Presumably, the taste is weakened as it travels from matter to matter.[1] Before we discuss the *halachic* ramifications of *nat-bar-nat,* it is important that we fully understand its definition and parameters.

I. The theory of nat-bar-nat

These *halachos* are based upon the Talmud: *Chullin* 111b, *Tur* and *Shulchan Aruch; Yoreh De'ah* 95.

A. Defining nat-bar-nat

Food which is fried, roasted or baked in a pot or pan effects an infusions of taste *(nesinas taam,* נְתִינַת טַעַם).[2] When another food is subsequently fried, etc. in that same pot, some of the original taste is

1. There is disagreement as to the underlying logic of *nat-bar-nat*. Is it based upon the assumption that a secondary taste is weakened and unnoticeable, or is it built upon the principle that a secondary taste, even if noticeable, is not *halachically* significant? The practical difference between these two views can be found in a case where the secondary taste is noticeable. In the opinion of many authorities, even a noticeable taste may be ignored if it is *nat-bar-nat* (see *Pri Chadash* 95:3, *Yad Yehudah* §6k). In their opinion, a *nat-bar-nat* taste is not considered actual taste. Others contend that the permissibility of *nat-bar-nat* is based upon the presumption that the taste is weakened and unnoticeable. However, if the taste is noticeable, it is considered potent *(Maharshal* cited in *D.T.* 95:5).

2. *Nosen taam* — infusions of taste as discussed here is understood as just that — *taste* transferred from one matter to another. For example, when milk is boiled in a pot, the pot absorbs milk taste, not actual milk; thus, the question of *nat-bar-nat* applies *(M.Z.* §1, see *D.T.* §9). However, vegetables boiled in milk absorb actual milk, not mere taste. Similarly, vegetables cooked in meat gravy absorb the actual gravy, not mere taste. Thus, if these vegetables are subsequently boiled in a pot, the taste absorbed in the pot is a primary, not a secondary taste *(Yad Yehudah* §1a, see *Issur V'heter* 34:7).

infused into the second food. This infusions of taste from food to pot to food is *nat-bar-nat*. Had the second food been boiled (not fried)[3] in the pot, we would have an additional step of food to pot to water and to food (three *"nats"*). See footnote.[4]

---

3. The issue is whether the food came in direct contact with the pot and imparted its taste directly to the pot or whether it imparted its taste through a liquid medium. Thus, deep-frying is the equivalent of cooking regarding these *halachos*.

4. *Poskim* stipulate several important qualifications regarding *nat-bar-nat*.

□ Two concurrent infusionss:
In the opinion of some authorities, a taste that is transferred twice while cooking and in contact with its original source cannot be considered *nat-bar-nat*. Thus, if milk splatters on the outside of a pot in which potatoes are cooking, the potatoes may not be eaten with meat. Although the milk taste was transferred twice (from milk to pot to potatoes), it is not considered *nat-bar-nat* since the two infusionss were simultaneous *(Chavas Daas* 95;1b, 2c). In the event that the potatoes were subsequently cooked with meat, they are prohibited. Other authorities disagree (see *Yad Yehudah* §7a, *R' Akiva Eger: Drush V'chidush* responsa 7 at end of part one, *Pischei Teshuvah* 95:1, 97:5, *Kaf HaChaim* §12).

□ Taste transfer from food to food:
In the opinion of *Pri Migadim:* M.Z. 95:1, *nat-bar-nat* applies only to taste infused from the original food into a vessel and then into food, not from the original food into food and then into a vessel. (One of the axiomatic principles in *kashrus* is that taste absorbed into a vessel is itself a weakened taste. We noted that a taste absorbed in a vessel becomes stale overnight, whereas a taste absorbed in food retains its potency over time. See *Issur V'heter* 39:6 and *Zair Zahav* ibid.) For example, if hot vegetables were placed upon hot meat thereby absorbing its taste and subsequently cooked in a *parve* pot, the pot is considered a meat pot. Any milk boiled in the pot becomes *basar b'chalav*. *Pri Migadim* explains that the original transfer of taste from meat to vegetable, being a food to food infusions, is potent. Thus, the vegetables impart that primary taste to the pot. See, however, *Chavas Daas* §4, who disagrees. He contends that as long as one of the transfers is into a vessel, we apply the *nat-bar-nat* principle. He does concede (in §2) that if no vessel is involved, i.e., the transfers are solely food to food, the taste is continually considered primary, not secondary. Thus, if a chocolate danish and a meat pie touch one another while baking, the danish may not be eaten with milk. The fact that the meat taste traveled from meat, to crust and to danish is not considered *nat-bar-nat* since the transfers were solely between food and food *(Pri Migadim* ibid. see also *Aruch HaShulchan* §3 and *D.T.* §15,19).

□ Food boiled in water:
Based upon the two concepts cited above, *Poskim* never consider the original taste transfer to the pot as *nat-bar-nat* (i.e., the meat to the water to the pot). The original infusionss were concurrent (i.e., the meat was cooking in the pot while its taste was imparted into the pot). In addition, the taste transfer from meat to water is food to food and thus a more potent infusions (this is subject to the disagreement between *Pri Migadim* and *Chavas Daas* cited above).

□ Taste transfer from vessel to vessel:
We noted that a taste infusions from food to food is stronger than that from food to

B. Two foods boiled together

When two foods are boiled together, the taste infused from one to another is primary, not secondary. The fact that the taste traveled from food to liquid to food does not accord it the status of *nat-bar-nat*.[5]

C. The type of pot under discussion

Our deliberation is limited to the use of a clean pot. A soiled pot is not subject to the principle of *nat-bar-nat* since the food[6] residue adhering to the pot is food, not mere taste. Any pot used for cooking is assumed to be clean unless known otherwise.[7] In addition, the reader should remember that throughout this section (unless noted otherwise) our subject is a *ben-yomo* pot (i.e., a pot used for hot meat or dairy food within the previous twenty-four hours).

D. Forbidden tastes — nat-bar-nat d'isura

When forbidden foods impart their taste, no distinction is made between primary and secondary transfers. Thus, if non-kosher food is cooked in a pot, the pot is *treif*. Any kosher food subsequently cooked in that pot becomes *treif* as well. If this food is then cooked in another pot, the taste is passed on to the second pot, which now also becomes *treif*.[8] Theoretically, this continues endlessly.[9]

---

a vessel. Similarly, an infusions from vessel to vessel is still weaker. Thus, even *Rema*, who, as noted below, takes a more stringent position regarding *nat-bar-nat*, concedes that when only vessels are involved, *nat-bar-nat* may be ignored (*M.Z.* 105:9). Thus, a hot damp *parve* spoon that was placed in a hot meat pot (without meat) remains *parve* and may be used with dairy without *kashering*.

5. See *Rashi: Chullin* 111b and note above.

6. See *Aruch HaShulchan* 95:7, who contends that in a case of *basar b'chalav*, our concern is that no *meat* residue be present on the pot. Thus, if potatoes were cooked with meat, any potato residue that remains in the pot is of no concern. Any meat in the potato residue is considered *taam* (taste), not actual meat. *Aruch HaShulchan* explains that this does not contradict the opinion of *Pri Migadim* cited in note 4 above.

7. *Shach* 95:1.

8. *Taz* 95:1. See *S.D.* 94:22, and *Yad Yehudah* 95:5a, whether this prohibition is Biblical or Rabbinical.

9. See *Issur V'heter* 34:7, and *Smak* (cited in *Beis Yosef* 94) who explain that this is predicated upon the concept of *chatichah na'asis neveilah*. Thus, each infusions of taste creates new prohibited matter that generates primary taste. Nevertheless, even those who contend that *chatichah na'asis neveilah* applies to *basar b'chalav* only, concede that *nat-bar-nat* does not apply to prohibited foods. They argue that while a permitted

E. Permitted tastes – nat-bar-nat d'heteira[10]

When taste of permitted food is infused into a vessel and subsequently imparted into other food, the secondary taste is no longer capable of producing a prohibited entity. The classic example is the following case discussed in the Talmud.[11] If hot fish was placed upon a clean, cold, *ben-yomo* meat[12] plate, the prevailing Talmudic opinion[13] rules that the fish may be eaten with dairy.[14] The meat taste imparted from the plate is merely a secondary taste, i.e., it was transferred from the meat into the plate and from the plate into the fish. Thus, when the fish comes in contact with dairy, the meat taste is already negligible[15] and cannot cause *basar b'chalav*. However, if milk itself is boiled in a meat pot, the milk becomes *basar b'chalav*. Although the meat taste was transferred twice (from meat to pot and then to milk), when the second transfer is effected (i.e., the meat taste is imparted into the milk) it immediately becomes *basar b'chalav*.[16] This, too, is an example of *nat-bar-nat d'isura* since the second taste (the *nat-bar-nat)* is prohibited.[17]

---

taste is weakened once it has been transferred twice, a prohibited taste retains its strength (see *Shach* 94:22). However, in their opinion, the power of each successive infusions should be dependent upon the volume of the original prohibited matter. Eventually, the non-kosher taste is less than a sixtieth of the volume and is insignificant (see *S.D., Mateh Yonasan* and *Dagul Mervavah* ibid.).

10. *Nat-bar-nat d'heteira* should not be defined as secondary taste of permitted foods. Even permitted foods are considered *nat-bar-nat d'isura* if, at the time of the second infusions, they become prohibited. Thus, milk cooked in a meat pot is *nat-bar-nat d'isura* since the moment the meat taste leaves the pot, it encounters the *issur* of *basar b'chalav*. The proper definition of *nat-bar-nat d'heteira* is: a secondary taste that is not as yet prohibited. See *Ran* cited in *Beis Yosef* 95, *Toras Chatas* 57:1,6, *Taz* 95:1, *Shach* §5 and *Minchas Yaakov: Toras Chatas* ibid.

11. *Chullin* 111b.

12. Although one may not eat meat and fish, this fish is nevertheless permitted. The prohibition of fish and meat applies only to eating fish with actual meat, not to eating fish cooked in a clean meat pot *(Taz* §3), see *Chochmas Adam* 68:1.

13. *Shmuel* as opposed to *Rav*.

14. See *Pischei Teshuvah* 87:19 and *Kaf HaChaim: O.C.* 173:3 who contend that, in the opinion of some authorities, fish should not be eaten with dairy. In their opinion, the example of fish is used merely as an illustration (see a similar example in *Taz* 95:3).

15. See responsa *R' Akiva Eger* 207, who cites a difference of opinion whether the meat taste absorbed in the fish is no longer considered a potent meat taste or whether it loses its potency only after it is transferred from the fish.

16. See *Tosfos: Zevachim* 96a. See also *Yad Yehudah* 94:19a, for a comprehensive examination of the issues involved in *nat-bar-nat*.

17. See *Toras Chatas* 57:6 and *Minchas Yaakov* there.

II. The halachah

A. The differing halachic opinions

Rishonim differ as to the implications of this Talmudic ruling. The most prominent opinions are:

1) In the opinion of some *Rishonim*, the rule of *nat-bar-nat* applies solely to a case of hot food placed onto a cold dish or cold food placed onto a hot dish. In either case, only a weak taste is transmitted (since only one item is hot).[18] Thus, when the taste (of the meat or dairy) is further weakened through a secondary infusions, it cannot create prohibited matter (i.e., *basar b'chalav*). If, however, fish is cooked in a *ben-yomo* meat pot or roasted on a meat grill, it is, in their opinion, thoroughly infused with meat taste and may not be eaten with dairy.[19]

2) Others agree with this in principle. They concede that fish fried on a meat grill may not be eaten with dairy since only two transfers are involved (i.e., from the meat to the grill and from the grill directly to the fish). Nevertheless, they permit fish boiled in a meat pot. They contend that the boiling process involves not two taste transfers, but three. The original meat taste is infused into the pot, and subsequently infused from the pot into the water and from the water into the fish.[20]

3) Still others contend that any case of secondary taste is permitted, regardless if the cooking is through boiling or roasting.[21] In their opinion, even an infusions of taste from a hot vessel directly into a hot food is considered *nat-bar-nat*.

---

18. See Chapter Five I,D regarding the issues of *tatai gavar* and *elai gavar*. Although *halachah* accepts the concept of *tatai gavar* (i.e., the bottom warms the top), nevertheless, the amount of taste imparted is less than if both surfaces had been hot *(Pri Migadim, S.D.* §6).

19. The opinion of *Rashi* as quoted by *Rivan* cited in *Tosfos: Zevachim* 96a and *Chullin* 111b. However, *Rashi* in his commentary to *Chullin* 111b, seems to conclude otherwise. *Rema* implies that, according to this opinion, even if the fish was mixed with dairy, it may not be eaten. Nevertheless, *Rema* follows the lenient opinion in an ex-post-facto situation.

20. *Rosh: Chullin* 8:30, citing *Sefer HaTrumos, Smag* and *Smak* cited in *Beis Yosef* 95. See also *Maharshal* cited in *Shach* 95:4.

21. *Rambam, Rashba* and *Ran* as interpreted by *Beis Yosef* ibid.

B. The halachah

The *Shulchan Aruch*[22] follows the most lenient opinion, and permits fish which was boiled or roasted in a meat pot or grill to be eaten with dairy. Similarly, he permits one to stuff chicken with eggs boiled in a dairy pot. However, he concedes that one should not initially boil fish in a meat pot with the intention of eating it with dairy.[23] *Sefardic* Jews follow this ruling. *Ashkenazic* custom follows a more stringent ruling.

> *The reader is reminded that this discussion pertains to a ben-yomo vessel.*

1) Boiled or fried foods:
   Initially, one should not rely upon *nat-bar-nat*. Thus, one certainly may not boil fish in a meat pot if it is to be eaten with dairy.[24] Even if the fish was already boiled in the meat pot, it may not be eaten with dairy since this is essentially *lechatchilah*.[25] In the event that the fish is erroneously[26] mixed with dairy, it may be eaten.[27] If the fish was fried in a meat pan and subsequently mixed with dairy, a *moreh hora'ah* should be consulted.[28]

---

22. *Y.D.* 95:1.

23. *Shach* 95:3, see also *Kaf Hachaim* §1.

24. Even the *Shulchan Aruch* concedes this point, as noted above.

25. As opposed to the opinion of *Shulchan Aruch*, cited above, who permits the fish to be eaten with dairy once it is cooked. See *S.D.* §2, who contends that conceivably in a case that is clearly three *nats*, even *Rema* concedes that the food may be eaten with dairy. He argues that perhaps the reason *Rema* forbids dairy use of foods cooked in a meat pot is because the food may have touched the pot itself (in which case the meat taste in the pot is only two *nats)*. Thus, in a case where there certainly is three *nats*, perhaps even *Rema* permits use of the food with dairy. See, however, *Yad Yehudah* §20a, who contends that one should not differentiate between two, three or many *nats*.

26. If it was intentionally mixed with dairy, there is a question as to whether it may be eaten (see *M.Z.* §4 and *D.T.* §16).

27. *Rema* 95:2. See *Shach* §3.

28. See *Shach* §4, who cites the opinion of *Maharshal* that if the fish is fried or roasted in a meat pot, not boiled (in a liquid), and subsequently mixed with dairy food, it may not be eaten. He contends that the lenient ex-post-facto ruling of *Rema* applies to boiled foods only, because the taste involved in boiling is a triple transfer (see *S.D.* §4. who contends that the liquid in which the food is cooked is subject to the same controversy, since only two "*nats*" are involved. He also notes that rice cooked in water and retained in the pot after the water has evaporated is analogous to fried foods, since at that time

In short: According to Sefardic *custom, once* nat-bar-nat *has been caused, it is considered* bedieved *and may be used with dairy. According to* Ashkenazic *custom, it is not considered* bedieved *until the food is mixed with dairy.*

a) Thus, water boiled in a meat pot may not be used for coffee with milk.[29] If one used the water for coffee with milk, he may drink it.

b) Similarly, one should not melt margarine in a dairy pot for use in challah dough since the challos are usually served during a meat meal.[30] If the margarine is melted in a dairy pot, an *Ashkenazic* Jew should not serve the challos with meat.

c) Foods prepared in a dairy pot may be served in the course of a meat meal providing they are not actually eaten with meat.[31]

2) Foods placed on a meat utensil:
If the fish is not boiled or broiled in a meat utensil, but merely placed, while hot, on a cold meat dish (or placed, while cold, on a hot meat dish),[32] it may be eaten with dairy.[33] However, one should not initially place hot fish on a meat plate (or the reverse) if it is to be eaten with dairy[34] since one may not initially cause *nat-bar-nat*.[35]

---

only two "*nats*" are involved). See *Chavas Daas* §4 who follows the opinion of *Maharshal* when both transfers of taste are without a liquid medium (i.e., the fish is roasted on a grill upon which meat was previously roasted). However, *Chochmas Adam* 48:1, completely disagrees with *Maharshal* and rules that one should not differentiate between boiling and frying. His opinion is supported by *Issur V'heter* 34:5. A *moreh hora'ah* should be consulted.

29. A Sefardic Jew who follows the opinion of the *Shulchan Aruch* is permitted to use the water once it is boiled. However, he should not initially cook the water in a meat pot if it is to be used with dairy.

30. *Kaf HaChaim* §2.

31. See *Rema* 89:3. The basis of these prohibitions is the mixing of meat and dairy tastes. If the foods are not eaten with meat, no mixing of tastes occurs.

32. If, however, both the food and the dish are hot, it is the equivalent of cooking in the pot (*Taz* 95:3 and *Shach* §6, see *Aruch HaShulchan* §12 who disagrees).

33. *Rema* 95:2. See *Taz* §4.

34. *Taz* §4.

35. *Issur V'heter* 34:1.

In the case above, both Sefardic *and* Ashkenazic *custom agree.*

3) Sharp foods:
All of the above applies to non-sharp foods. However, sharp foods, *(davar charif)*, even when cooked in a non *ben-yomo* meat pot and subsequently mixed with dairy food, may not be eaten.[36] We noted earlier (Chapter Three, Section II,B,3) that a *davar charif* negates the advantage of a non *ben-yomo* pot. The sharpness of the food revitalizes the stale taste. Likewise, the sharp taste of the food causes a transfer of primary meat taste, not merely a secondary taste.[37] Thus, one may not mix onions fried in a dairy pan with chopped liver, regardless of whether the pan was a *ben-yomo*. In the event that the onions were mixed with chopped liver, a *moreh hora'ah* should be consulted.[38] We will learn in Chapter Twelve, Section II,C that sharp foods cut or chopped with a knife absorb taste from that knife. Thus, onions chopped with a dairy chopper or cut with a dairy knife may not be used with meat foods, even if the chopper was not *ben-yomo.*[39]

4) Placing the food in a dairy dish:
Although one may not eat fish boiled in a meat pot together with dairy foods, the fish may subsequently be placed, even

---

36. *Rema* 95:2. In the opinion of the *Shulchan Aruch* 96:1,3 if the pot was not *ben-yomo* the mixture may be eaten. See *Kaf HaChaim* 96:10 who contends that *Shulchan Aruch* permits this only in a case of severe loss. If the pot is *ben-yomo*, even the *Shulchan Aruch* concedes that the mixture may not be eaten *(Y.D.* 96:1,3).

37. *Shach* 95:7, *Chochmas Adam* 49:1. This applies only to a *nat-bar-nat* absorbed by a *davar charif*. However, a *nat-bar-nat* taste originating from a *davar charif* is the equivalent of any *nat-bar-nat (Yad Yehudah* 95:1a). See *Shach* ibid. (citing *Rema* 122:3), who notes that the dairy pot in which onions are cooked remains *nat-bar-nat*. Therefore, if, subsequently, other foods are cooked in the dairy pot after twenty four hours and mixed with meat, they may be eaten. See *Kreisi U'pleisi* 96:4, who contends that sharp foods can only elevate a secondary taste to the level of a primary taste. They cannot elevate a third level taste to the level of a primary taste. Thus, if fish is cooked in a meat pot (the fish now has a secondary taste), it may subsequently be cooked with radishes that were cut with a dairy knife.

38. See Chapter Twelve, Section II,C,1 regarding cooked or fried onions and onions mixed with oil. See *Aruch HaShulchan* §15, who rules that if there is doubt as to whether the food is actively a *davar charif*, the mixture may be eaten.

39. *Rema* 95:2. As noted above, in the opinion of *Shulchan Aruch*, if the chopper was not *ben-yomo*, the food is permitted.

while hot, on a dairy dish.[40] However, one should not initially boil the fish in a meat pot with the intention of placing it on a dairy dish while hot.[41] One should not boil water for tea in a *ben-yomo* meat pot if the tea is to be served in a dairy cup. In the event that the water was boiled already, it may be used in a dairy cup.[42]

5) A non *ben-yomo* pot:
As noted, these rules apply to fish cooked in a *ben-yomo* pot. Fish cooked in a non *ben-yomo* pot may be eaten with dairy since we have a double lenient consideration of *nat-bar-nat* and *nosen taam lifgam.*[43] Initially, however, one should not use even a non *ben-yomo* pot if another pot is available.[44] Thus, if hot gravy splattered on a hot coffee urn, the urn should not be used for coffee even when not *ben-yomo*[45] unless no other urn is available.[46] If that water was boiled in the urn, it may be used for coffee.[47] The reader is reminded that this *halachah* of a non

40. *Rema* ibid. One should, however, not pour liquids cooked in a meat pot directly into a dairy dish, see *Rema* 95:3. They must first be poured into a second meat dish and then into the dairy dish. In the event that liquid was poured from a *ben-yomo* meat pot into a dairy dish (or the reverse), a *moreh hora'ah* should be consulted (see *Shach* 95:5 and *Chochmas Adam* 48:13). See Chapter Eleven, Section VI for a detailed discussion of the issues involved.

41. *M.Z.* §4, 5. He notes that *Pri Chadash* disagrees.

42. Although *Rema* 95:3 cites the custom that one not use the water since the loss of water is not significant (see *Issur V'heter* 34:11 cited in *Shach* §14, see also *Shach* 94:19), that refers only to the case of milk and dairy dishes washed together. In that case, the water would be *basar b'chalav* if not for *nosen taam lifgam.* In our case, the water is permissible because it is *nat-bar-nat* and it is not coming in contact with any dairy. See *Minchas Yaakov* 57:27. When this argument was presented to Harav Y.S. Eliashiv he agreed with its conclusion.

43. *Rema* 95:2.

44. *Chochmas Adam* 48:2 (who derives this from the wording of *Issur V'heter* and *Rema*). Although *Biur HaGra* 95:10 seems to permit using a non *ben-yomo* pot, one should follow the opinion of *Chochmas Adam* (heard from Harav Y.S. Eliashiv).

45. If, however, the splatter was very small, one can assume that the urn will always contain sixty times the volume of the splatter *(Binas Adam* 41 [58]).

46. *Chochmas Adam* 48:2. He does, however, imply that if one is able to borrow a pot from a neighbor, he is required to do so.

47. Ibid. This case too (as in note 42 above), differs from that of the *Rema* §3, cited above since in this case the permissibility of the water is based independently on *nat-bar-nat* and *nosen taam lifgam.* In the case of the *Rema,* the two are intertwined i.e., the case is considered *nat-bar-nat* only because of the *nosen taam lifgam*. See *Issur V'heter* 34:6,8 and *Minchas Yaakov* 57:27.

ben-yomo pot does not apply to sharp foods cooked in that pot, as noted above.

6) Use with cold liquids:
One should not store liquids in a dairy container (i.e. a container once used with hot dairy) for a period of twenty four hours if the liquids are to be used with meat. If no other suitable container is available, even a *ben-yomo* dairy container may be used.[48] Sharp liquids should not be stored even in a non *ben-yomo* milk container, even for a short period of time, if they are to be eaten with meat.[49]

7) Use of *parve* utensils with cold meat or dairy:
Halachically, one may use a *parve* utensil for cold meat or dairy foods. No taste will be imparted into the *parve* utensil without heat. Likewise, one need not be concerned that the utensil will be used for *parve* food without being cleaned beforehand, since one usually washes dishes between uses. Thus, one is permitted to whip cream with a *parve* mixer. Some are more scrupulous and refrain from this practice since it may cause confusion and error.
   a) One should not store meat or dairy liquids in a *parve* container for twenty-four hours if he plans to retain those containers for *parve* use.
   b) See Chapter Eleven, Section G regarding one who inserts a meat or dairy ladle into a *parve* pot.

Summary

❧ Food cooked in a pot infuses its taste into the pot. When another food is subsequently cooked in that pot after it has been cleaned, the secondary transfer is known as *nat-bar-nat*.

- ☐ When forbidden foods impart their taste, no distinction is made between primary and secondary transfers.

---

48. See *R' Akiva Eger* gloss to 95:2, who is uncertain whether, in principle, *nat-bar-nat* applies to soaking — *kavush*. In addition, by the time the soaking can effect a transfer of taste (after twenty-four hours), the vessel is no longer a *ben-yomo*. Thus, one may put a *parve* liquid into a meat or dairy container if it is not immediately after the meat or dairy use, see *R' Akiva Eger* ibid.

49. See Chapter Three, Section II,B that sharp foods — *davar charif* — can revitalize a non *ben-yomo* stale taste. See also Chapter Five, Section II,A that soaking in sharp liquids may generate a taste transfer even in less than twenty-four hours.

However, a secondary taste of permitted foods is not capable of producing a prohibited entity.

- □ If hot fish is placed on a clean, cold meat plate, it may be eaten with dairy.
- □ In the opinion of some *Rishonim*, if fish is cooked in a meat pot or roasted on a meat grill, it may not be eaten with dairy. If the fish is boiled in a meat pot, some *Rishonim* permit it to be eaten with dairy. Still others permit any case of secondary taste, regardless if through boiling or roasting.
- □ *Sefardic* tradition permits fish boiled or roasted in a meat pot or grill to be eaten with dairy. According to *Ashkenazic* custom, even if the fish is boiled already in the meat pot, it may not be eaten with dairy. All agree that initially one should not cook fish in a meat pot if it is to be eaten with dairy.
- □ According to *Ashkenazic* tradition, water boiled in a meat pot may not be used for coffee with milk. If one used the water for coffee with milk, he may drink it.
- □ Foods prepared in a dairy pot may be served in the course of a meat meal, provided they are not actually eaten with meat.
- □ A sharp food cooked even in a non *ben-yomo* meat pot and subsequently mixed with dairy food may not be eaten.
- □ One should not boil water for tea in a *ben-yomo* meat pot if the tea is to be served in a dairy cup. If the water was boiled already, it may be used in a dairy cup.
- □ Fish cooked in a non *ben-yomo* pot may be eaten with dairy. Initially, one should not use even a non *ben-yomo* pot if another pot is available.

CHART 13

NAT-BAR-NAT

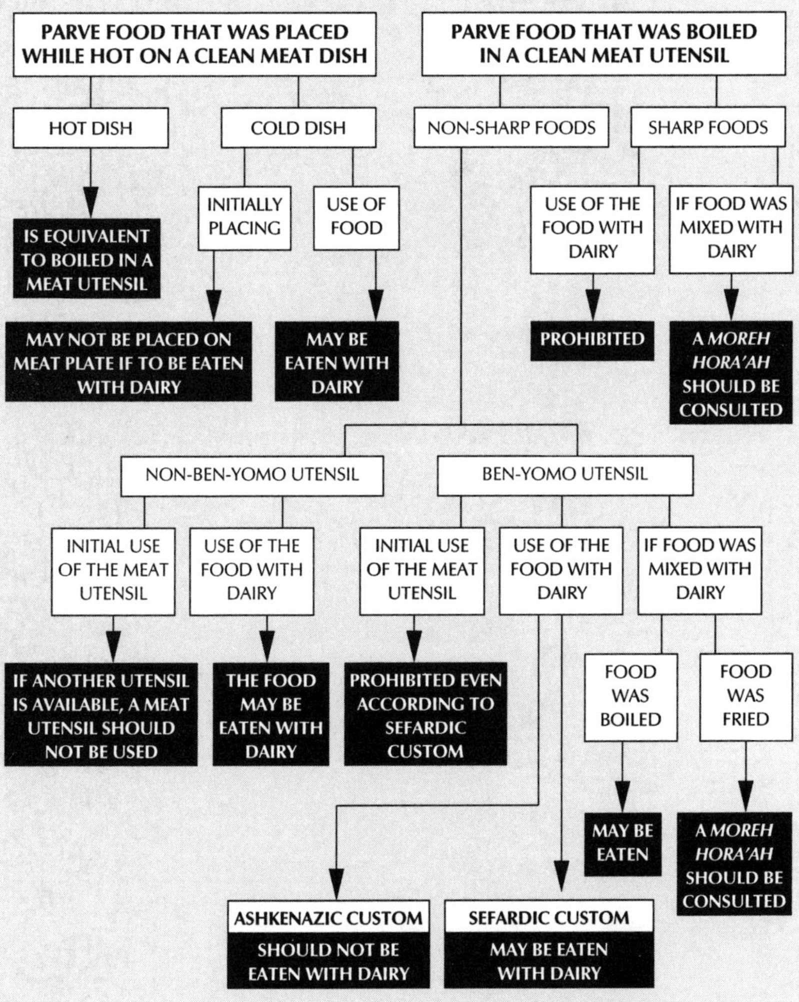

CHAPTER SEVEN

בָּשָׂר בְּחָלָב

The Prohibition of Basar B'chalav

- □ The unique nature of *basar b'chalav.*
- □ The laws of *bitul* as applying to *basar b'chalav.*
- □ Types of meats and milks which constitute *basar b'chalav.*
- □ The three prohibitions regarding *basar b'chalav.*
- □ What forms of cooking are prohibited.
- □ What types of benefits are prohibited.

I. General principles

Introduction

The laws of *basar b'chalav* are among the most extensive, stringent and unusual of all the *halachos* regarding kashrus. *Basar b'chalav* is subject to many rules and principles that are not found elsewhere in *hilchos kashrus*. Oddly, the prohibition of eating *basar b'chalav* is not even mentioned explicitly in the Torah. Rather, the Torah prohibits *cooking basar b'chalav* ("לֹא תְבַשֵּׁל גְּדִי בַּחֲלֵב אִמּוֹ — you shall not cook a kid in its mother's milk") and repeats this prohibition three times in the exact same form[1]. Sinaitic tradition teaches us that the laws of *basar b'chalav* are not limited to either a kid or to its mother's milk but extended to other animals and situations as well. We will first examine the distinctive characteristics of *basar b'chalav*.

A. The novelty of basar b'chalav

The *halachos* of meat and dairy mixtures are unique in many of their aspects. The scope of the prohibition of *basar b'chalav* is virtually[2] unparalleled in Torah law. One may not eat *basar b'chalav* or derive any benefit from it or cook meat and milk together even if one does not intend to eat it. These prohibitions will be examined in this section. *Basar b'chalav* is also exceptional in that it comprises two permitted foods which, only in combination, become prohibited. At times, this aspect affects the prohibition of *basar b'chalav* in a lenient manner, and, at times, it affects it in a stringent manner. Although many attempts have been made to expound upon the meaning and reasons for this unique phenomenon,[3] most explanations seem insufficient. It is

1. *Shemos* 23:19, 34:26 and *Devarim* 14:21.

2. With the sole exception of *kilai hakerem*.

3. See *Rambam: Moreh Nivuchim* (cited in *Rabbeinu Bachaya* 23:19 and *Chinuch* 92) that the ancient custom of idol worshipers was to eat *basar b'chalav* in their temples during their holidays. Thus, the Torah warns us not to eat *basar b'chalav* when we come to the Temple during the three festivals. *Ibn Ezra: Shemos* 23:19, explains that to cook a kid in its mother's milk is similar in its cruelty to slaughtering a cow and its calf in one day and taking the chick in the presence of the mother. Although according to this theory, only milk of the mother should be forbidden, the Torah prohibits milk of all animals since one may not know the milk's source with certainty. A similar exposition is found in the *Rashbam* (ibid.). *Rabbeinu Bachaya* (ibid.) explains that the Torah

easier to accept *basar b'chalav* as a *chok*, a Biblical decree, whose meaning and purpose are beyond our grasp.[4] Basically, the phenomenon of *basar b'chalav* is twofold:

1) Two permitted foods prohibited when combined:
Although meat or dairy products are permitted foods, the Torah specifically forbids the combination of meat and dairy. However, merely combining meat and dairy does not constitute *basar b'chalav* according to Torah law. Only meat and dairy that are **cooked** together become *basar b'chalav*. Meat soaked in or mixed with dairy does not become *basar b'chalav* (according to Torah law) although they certainly absorb taste from one another.[5] *Chazal*[6] refer to the phenomenon of two permitted foods becoming prohibited when combined in a special manner as a *"chidush"* — a phenomenon.[7]

2) The formation of a new entity:
The prohibition of *basar b'chalav* is not merely that of meat and dairy that have become prohibited; rather, cooking meat and milk together creates a new *halachic* entity called *basar*

---

forbids eating blood because it generates a cruel nature in one that eats it. Thus since, according to *Chazal*, milk is formed from blood, it potentially retains this nature. Although milk alone is permitted since it has been transformed into new matter, cooking milk with meat revives its harmful nature. See *Chinuch* (62, 92) who compares *basar b'chalav* to *kilayim* and *shatnez* in that they all constitute tampering with *Hashem's* creation in an attempt to create new compounds. Although one may generally combine elements to create new forms, these compounds were specifically forbidden as they have harmful effects. For further analysis of this idea, see *Horeb* (407, 408). See an additional explanation in *Kli Yakar* (ibid.).

4. See *Ibn Ezra* (ibid.) who offers his explanation with reservation. He more readily assumes that *basar b'chalav* is a *chok*. A similar approach is taken by *Rabbeinu Bachaya* (ibid.) who cites a statement of *Chazal* that in the World to Come *Hashem* will reveal the hidden reason of *basar b'chalav*. *Rabbeinu Bachaya* offers a Kabalistic explanation as to why the reason for *basar b'chalav* will be understood only then.

5. Nevertheless, it is Biblically forbidden to cook the meat, for by doing so one cooks meat and dairy.

6. *Chullin* 108a, *Pesachim* 44b.

7. The Talmud notes that the novelty may be two-fold: a) the mere fact that two permitted objects become prohibited when combined and b) that this prohibition is effective only when they are cooked together. The Talmud explains that the former novelty is not as unique as the second since we find its parallel in the laws of *kilayim*. *Rashi: Chullin* 108a, (as opposed to *Tosfos* there), however, considers *basar b'chalav* a novelty even in terms of the two permitted foods becoming forbidden when combined. See *Lev Aryeh: Chullin* 108a, and responsa *Chasam Sofer: Y.D.* 88, for an explanation of *Rashi's* position.

b'chalav. Thus, if a cup of milk falls into a pot of meat, the entire pot of meat becomes *basar b'chalav*. Hence, even one who eats a *kizayis* of the meat alone is punishable by *malkos* even though he ate an insignificant amount of milk. Similarly, if a piece of that meat falls into a pot of potatoes, all the potatoes are forbidden even though the taste of milk itself in the potatoes is negligible.[8] This concept is known as "*chatichah na'asis neveilah* — the mixture becomes a prohibited entity of its own. This concept has been explored in Chapter Two. The underlying principle here is that *basar b'chalav* is not meat prohibited because of a dairy taste or dairy prohibited by a meat taste; rather, the mixture has generated a new prohibited matter called *basar b'chalav*.[9]

3) Lenient considerations:
We have noted the stringent side of the phenomenon of *basar b'chalav* (i.e., the concept of *chatichah na'asis neveilah*). There is, however, a lenient side as well. This is reflected in the following[10] *halachos:*

a) *Nat-bar-nat:*
We noted in Chapter Six that when *ta'am* — taste — travels from object to object indirectly, it is defined as "*nat-bar-nat*", a secondary infusion of taste (*nosen ta'am bar nosen ta'am* — "infused taste the 'son' of infused taste"). *Chazal* ruled that a secondary infusion of taste can be effective only if it is that of a prohibited food (*nat-bar-nat d'isura*), but a secondary taste of a permitted food (*nat-bar-nat d'heteira*) is considered to have lost its identity and cannot affect another permitted food. Thus, a secondary taste of dairy cannot affect meat

---

8. Indeed, in the opinion of *Shach* 105:17, even if one could remove the absorbed milk from the meat, the meat would remain *basar b'chalav*. Others cited in *Shach* disagree with this contention. See also *Taz* §13.

9. Thus although the rule of *chatichah ha'ruyah l'hischabed* applies only to primary prohibitions, not to matter that absorbed taste from prohibited matter, it does apply to *basar b'chalav* (see Y.D. 101).

10. Another interesting point is noted by *R' Akiva Eger* (responsa 207). He argues that the prohibition of intentional *bitul* (see Chapter Two, Section V) should not apply to meat or dairy prior to their being combined since neither is classified as an *issur* on its own. He concedes (see also *Gilyon Maharsha* gloss to 98:6) that nevertheless it should not be done (i.e., one who wishes to eat potatoes with meat should not even put a small amount of butter in those potatoes).

since the taste of dairy alone is *heteira*.[11] However, a secondary taste of meat and dairy that was cooked together can affect other foods since, once combined, the meat and dairy are *isura*.

b) *Heteira balah:*
Another application of the permitted status of *basar b'chalav* prior to its combination is found with regard to *kashering* a vessel. Normally, a vessel used in direct contact with fire (without a liquid medium) requires the *kashering* method of *libun* (heating in fire).[12] Nevertheless, when *kashering* a kosher meat grill to dairy use, one need not use the method of *libun*. The meat taste, which is *heter*, can be purged merely with *hagalah* (scalding with water)[13] or with *libun kal* (see Chapter Nine, Section I,C).[14]

c) *Chatichah na'asis neveilah:*
We noted above the concept of *chatichah na'asis neveilah* as applied to *basar b'chalav*. Refer to Chapter Two, Section IV,B where this concept is discussed at length. The reader will remember that in the opinion of some authorities, *chatichah na'asis neveilah* applies only to *basar b'chalav* and not to other prohibitions. However, all authorities agree that it does not apply to meat or dairy alone. Thus, if potatoes are cooked with butter they remain potatoes with a dairy taste, not actual dairy. If, subsequently, meat falls into those potatoes, a ratio of sixty times meat to one part butter, is sufficient to nullify the butter taste.[15]

d) *Ben-yomo:*
We noted in Chapter Three, Section II,B that when food is cooked in a *treif* pot that is not *ben-yomo* (i.e., it had not been used for a twenty-four-hour period), the food is unaffected. Any taste absorbed in a pot for that period

11. Or the reverse.

12. O.C. 451:4.

13. See *Shach* 121:8, and gloss of *R' Akiva Eger* (ibid.). See Chapter Eight, Section III,C as to when it is permitted to *kasher* from meat to dairy or the reverse.

14. O.C. 509:4.

15. Y.D. 94:6, see *Rema*.

becomes stale and can no longer affect any food cooked in the pot. Similarly, if milk is cooked in a meat pot that was unused for twenty-four hours, the milk is permitted. However, the two cases are not completely similar. If a non-kosher pot was used even for kosher food, or for water, during those twenty-four hours the pot is considered *ben-yomo.*[16] However, if water or *parve* food was cooked in a meat pot during the twenty-four-hour period, the pot is not considered *ben-yomo.* Thus, if milk is cooked in that pot within twenty-four hours from the cooking of the water, the milk is permitted, providing that twenty-four hours elapsed from the time of the actual meat use.[17]

e) *Efshar l'sochto:*
We learned in Chapter Two, Section IV,B that a non-kosher taste absorbed into kosher food cannot be removed (i.e., the kosher food that absorbed non-kosher taste, if recognizable, remains forbidden even if it is subsequently cooked in a large amount of kosher food). This principle is called "*efshar l'sochto assur*". Nevertheless, if *parve* food that absorbed meat or dairy taste is subsequently cooked in a large amount of other *parve* food, the original *parve* food loses its meat or dairy taste and become completely *parve* once again.[18]

B. The laws of bitul as pertaining to basar b'chalav

The rules of *bitul* apply to *basar b'chalav* as to all other prohibited foods. This *bitul*, however, reflects the uniqueness of *basar b'chalav* in the following manner: Prior to their being combined through cooking, meat and dairy are treated as two permitted foods which are able to nullify one another. Indeed, they are treated leniently with regard to *bitul*, since they are permitted foods *(heter)*.[19] However, once the meat

---

16. See *Y.D.* 103:7. See Chapter Three, Section II,B that perhaps passage of a full night is sufficient to render the pot non *ben-yomo*.

17. *Tur* 94. See chart #5.

18. *Taz* 96:5 and *Shach* 94:23 citing *Maharam Lublin.*

19. Actually, there would be reason to assume that being *heter*, meat and dairy should not nullify one another. See *Tosfos: Nidah* 61b, who notes that *bitul* applies only to permitted matter that mixed into prohibited matter, but two permitted objects (e.g., linen and wool regarding the prohibition of *Shatnez*) cannot nullify one another. However,

and dairy are cooked together, a new prohibited substance *(issur)* is produced which requires *bitul* befitting prohibited matter. This is illustrated by the following:

1) Nullification of meat or dairy prior to cooking:
When dairy falls into an amount of meat sixty times its volume, the dairy, which is yet permitted, is immediately nullified and cannot affect the meat. Similarly, if dairy combines with *parve* food sixty times its volume, it is completely nullified. Any subsequent addition of meat is inconsequential.

2) Nullification of *basar b'chalav*:
Once *basar b'chalav* has been created, both the meat and dairy become prohibited matter and prohibit any food into which they subsequently become mixed unless that food contain sixty times **both** the meat and the dairy. Thus, when confronted with a mixture of one ounce milk, one ounce meat and sixty ounces potatoes, the order in which they became mixed together is critical. If the ounce of milk mixed with the sixty ounces of potatoes prior[20] to the advent of the meat, the milk would be nullified in the potatoes. When, subsequently, the meat is combined it is nullified as well. If, however, the milk first falls into the meat, two ounces of *basar b'chalav* are produced. When, subsequently, they mix with the potatoes, the entire mixture is prohibited since one hundred and twenty ounces are now required to nullify the two ounces of *basar b'chalav*.

Summary of Section I

☙ The prohibition of *basar b'chalav* is unique and virtually unparalleled in Torah law. The novelty *(chidush)* of *basar b'chalav* is essentially twofold:

Tosfos: Avodah Zarah 65b and *Rosh (Avodah Zarah, Hilchos Kilai Begadim* 5, cited in *Shach* 299:1) explains that *basar b'chalav* is an exception to this principle since *basar b'chalav* is created only when there is a transfer of taste from one to the other. Accordingly, *bitul* as regarding dairy and meat cooked together is essentially not an example of classic *bitul;* it is merely a means in which the meat and milk do not impart taste to one another. See Chapter Fourteen, "*Bitul b'rov,* regarding *bitul* of *heter*.

20. Indeed, even if the meat and milk fell simultaneously into fifty-nine ounces of potatoes, both meat and milk combine with the potatoes to nullify one another (see *Rema* 98:9).

- ☐ *Basar b'chalav* is comprised of permitted foods which become prohibited when combined through *bishul*.
- ☐ The prohibition of *basar b'chalav* is not merely that of meat and dairy that have become prohibited; rather, cooking meat and milk together creates a new *halachic* entity called *basar b'chalav*. This concept is known as *"chatichah na'asis neveilah"*.

⁂ There is a lenient side to *basar b'chalav* as well. In contrast to other prohibitions, *basar b'chalav* has the following lenient *halachos:*

- ☐ A secondary taste of meat or milk alone is considered *nat-bar-nat d'heteira* and cannot effect a prohibition of *basar b'chalav*.
- ☐ When *kashering* a grill from one use to another, one need not use the method of *libun*. The meat or dairy taste is *heter (heteira balah)* and can be purged merely with *hagalah* or with *libun kal*.
- ☐ The concept of *chatichah na'asis neveilah* does not apply to meat or dairy alone.
- ☐ If *parve* food or water was cooked in a meat pot, the pot is not considered *ben-yomo* once twenty four hours have passed from the actual cooking of the meat itself even though it is still within twenty-four hours from the cooking of the water.
- ☐ The principle of *efshar l'sochto assur* does not apply to meat or dairy alone.

⁂ *Bitul* as pertaining to *basar b'chalav*:

- ☐ When dairy falls into an amount of meat sixty times its volume, the dairy is immediately nullified and cannot affect the meat.
- ☐ Once *basar b'chalav* is created, both the meat and dairy become prohibited matter and prohibit any food into which they become mixed unless that food contains sixty times both the meat and the dairy.

II. The prohibitions of basar b'chalav

These *halachos* are based on *Tur* and *Shulchan Aruch; Yoreh De'ah* 87.

A. The three prohibitions

Basar b'chalav is unique in that it comprises three prohibitions.[21] One may not cook meat and dairy together, nor may one eat or derive benefit from meat and dairy that were cooked together. The reader should note that not all methods of cooking are identical. Some forms entail a Biblical prohibition while others are Rabbinic ordinances. Still others are subject to contention as to whether they entail a Biblical prohibition. Ordinarily, this would be of little practical interest. A prohibition is forbidden regardless of whether its source is Biblical or Rabbinic. Nevertheless, with regard to *basar b'chalav*, the source of the prohibition is of major consequence. We will learn in the following sections that one may derive benefit from Rabbinic *basar b'chalav*. Thus, the question of whether the particular instance is forbidden by Torah is most significant.

1) Cooking *basar b'chalav*:
One may not cook meat and dairy together. Indeed, one may not even cook meat in a dairy *ben-yomo* pot or dairy in a *ben-yomo* meat pot. One who does either of the above transgresses the Biblical prohibition of *basar b'chalav*.[22] Even one who does not intend to partake of the *basar b'chalav* may not cook it. One may not even cook *basar b'chalav* for a non-Jew. Thus a Jew working as a chef in a non-Jewish establishment must be careful not to cook meat and dairy together or cook meat in a dairy pot (or the reverse).[23] One who cooks a combined *kizayis* of meat

---

21. See *Rambam: Sefer HaMitzvos* II:187, that *basar b'chalav* is considered two of the six hundred and thirteen *Mitzvos:* the prohibition of cooking and the prohibition of eating or deriving benefit thereof. He explains that deriving benefit is merely an extension of eating and should not be counted as an individual *mitzvah* although it is mentioned specifically in the Torah.

22. *Chochmas Adam* 46:1. See also *Pri Migadim* introduction to *basar b'chalav*.

23. See *Pischei Teshuvah* 87:8, who notes that one may cook meat in a dairy pot for a non-Jew if the pot was not *ben-yomo*. He concludes, however, that initially, this should not be done. Indeed, *Rema* 87:6, cites an opinion that one should not light the flame under

and milk[24] has violated a Biblical prohibition[25] and is punished by *malkos* — thirty-nine lashes.[26]

a) What forms of cooking are prohibited:
The Torah uses the word *"bishul"*, which literally translates as "boiling". To avoid confusion, we will employ that word in our discussion. Many *Poskim*, however, contend, that in regard to *basar b'chalav, bishul* includes other types of cooking as well. In addition, there are other methods of food preparation. Are these preparations also included in the prohibition of *bishul*? This will be discussed in the following section. The reader should note that in all the cases listed below, the meat and milk may not be eaten. The issue being examined is only whether one may derive benefit from the food, i.e., whether the prohibition is Biblical or Rabbinic. We must caution the reader again not to decide these questions on his own but to consult a *moreh hora'ah*.

□ Broiling, frying, barbecuing, roasting and baking:
In the opinion of many *Poskim*, broiling, barbecuing, roasting[27] and frying[28] are all considered forms of

---

any pot of a non-Jew even if it contains neither meat nor dairy since the pot may contain both meat and dairy tastes, one who places it over the fire is, in effect, cooking *basar b'chalav* (although one assumes that any non-Jewish owned pot is not *ben-yomo*). *Rema* concedes, however, that this is merely a *chumra*, not *halachically* prohibited. Later authorities note that this *chumra* is not customarily followed *(Shach* 87:18).

24. This may consist of a half *kizayis* of each or any combination of the two that equals a *kizayis*. There is a situation where one might cook a large amount and yet not be liable for *malkos;* one who cooks a half *kizayis* of meat in thirty *kizeisim* of milk is not punishable by *malkos*. The meat volume is a sixtieth of the milk volume, thus it cannot affect the milk and make it *basar b'chalav*. The meat which absorbs significant milk taste is less than a *kizayis* and therefore less than the Biblical *shiur (Minchas Chinuch* 92). See *R' Akiva Eger* (responsa 207) that *basar b'chalav* is forbidden only if both the meat gives taste to the milk and the milk to the meat. Thus, in his opinion, even if the meat was a *kizayis* (in sixty *kizeisim* of milk), no Biblical prohibition is violated since the transmission of taste is only from milk to meat and not from meat to milk (due to *bitul)*.

25. See *Pri Migadim* in his introduction and *Minchas Chinuch* 92, who are uncertain whether cooking a half *kizayis* of *basar b'chalav* is forbidden at all by Torah law.

26. *Rambam* 9:1.

27. *Pri Chadash* 87:2, *Yad Yehudah* §2k and *Chochmas Adam* 40:1. However, *Pri Toar* §3 and *Chavas Daas* §1 rule that these forms of cooking are prohibited only Rabbinically.

28. See *D.T.* §18.

bishul and are Biblically prohibited. Thus, one who grills a cheese hamburger (even for a non-Jew) may have violated the Biblical prohibition of cooking *basar b'chalav*.[29] One should not warm the sandwich of a non-Jewish maid in an oven, even if it is properly wrapped, unless he can ascertain that it contains no *basar b'chalav*.[30]

- □ A *kli rishon* (the original pot):
  If a piece of meat falls into a pot of hot milk even after it has been removed from the fire or if milk spills into a pot of hot meat, it is considered *bishul* in Torah law.[31]
- □ *Iruy* — pouring from a *kli rishon:*
  The reader will remember the question of *iruy* discussed in Chapter Five, Section II,C. We noted that when hot liquid is poured directly from a *kli rishon* onto cold food, it is able to transfer its taste into a *klipah* of the food. Thus, if hot milk is poured over cold meat, a *klipah* of the meat is prohibited. Does this act constitute actual *bishul?* If so, the Biblical

29. Many *Poskim* rule that, in a case of serious loss, if meat and dairy were roasted or fried together they may be sold or given to a non-Jew (see *Arugas HaBosem* §1, *Pri Migadim* M.Z. §1 and *Kaf HaChaim* §53). One may assume that the prohibition is merely Rabbinic and, therefore, its use is permitted. We noted that one may derive benefit from any *basar b'chalav* that is prohibited only Rabbinically.

30. One may not even tell a non-Jew to cook *basar b'chalav*. The prohibition of "*amirah l'Akum*" — telling a non-Jew to do a forbidden act (on *Shabbos)* applies to *basar b'chalav* as well *(Biur Halachah* 307:21). Thus, one may not give one's maid a hamburger patty and a piece of cheese and say "Here, make yourself a cheeseburger." However, if one does not directly tell the maid to cook *basar b'chalav*, it is permitted. For example: one may give the maid a hamburger patty and tell her to broil it even though one knows she will broil it with cheese, providing that she broils it in her own *treif* toaster oven.

31. *Pri Chadash* 87:2. We apply the rule of *tatai gavar* (see Chapter Five, II,D) thus, actual *bishul* has occurred. See, however, *Talmud Yerushalmi: Maasros* 1:4, which implies that *bishul* is effected only when the food is actually over the fire. Thus, once the pot is removed from the fire, Biblical *basar b'chalav* is not effected. Indeed, the *Rogachover Gaon (Tzofnas Pa'aneach: Rambam* 9:1) finds a basis for this view in *Talmud Bavli* as well. See *Aruch HaShulchan* 68:24. See also, R' Akiva Eger (gloss to *Y.D.* end of 91) who rules that beef (that requires intense cooking) cannot become *basar b'chalav* (in Biblical law) unless it is cooked over a flame. Thus, in his opinion, one could derive benefit from beef that fell into a pot of hot milk even though the milk was a *kli rishon* that was *yad soledes bo*.

prohibition of cooking *basar b'chalav* has been violated causing the meat to be Biblically forbidden. Perhaps *iruy* does not constitute actual *bishul* and thus the meat is not Biblically prohibited. Some authorities rule that the meat is Biblically prohibited,[32] while others disagree.[33] All authorities agree that if the stream is indirect (i.e., when the milk flow reaches the meat it is no longer connected to the *kli rishon)*, it is not considered *bishul.*

☐ A *kli sheni* (hot food is placed into a second vessel): A *kli sheni* cannot effect *bishul.*[34] Some authorities maintain that a *kli sheni* cannot even cause a transfer of taste. See Chapter Five, Section II,C for a more thorough discussion of the issues involved.[35]

☐ Hot meat touching hot cheese:
If hot meat and hot cheese touch one another on a plate, no *bishul* has been effected. Thus, one may derive benefit from the meat and cheese.[36] Nevertheless, since taste has been transferred, one who wishes to eat either the meat or the cheese should consult a *moreh hora'ah*. See Chapter Five, Section II,D.

☐ Naturally hot spring water:
Poskim disagree whether naturally hot spring water

---

32. *Pri Chadash* 87:2, who contends that *iruy* is *derech bishul* — normal cooking.

33. See *Yad Avraham* 87:1. See also *Pri Migadim* in his preface to *basar b'chalav* who is unsure whether the *klipah* is Biblically forbidden.

34. Y.D. 105:2.

35. *Poskim* disagree as to whether a hot, solid food placed in a *kli sheni* is treated as *kli sheni* or effects *bishul* as a *kli rishon* (see Chapter Five, Section II,C). In addition, even if the solid food is to be treated as *kli rishon,* some authorities maintain that it cannot effect *bishul* with regard to *basar b'chalav* (see *Chavas Daas* 95:26b).

36. *R' Akiva Eger* (gloss to Y.D. 87:1) and *Pri Migadim* introduction to *basar b'chalav* s.v. *"vehinei"*, citing *Maharshal*. See *D.T.* §15, who cites opinions that this refers only to when the meat and cheese are in a *kli sheni* (he contends that even though hot solid food placed in a dish is considered *kli rishon* in the opinion of *Maharshal* it nevertheless cannot effect *bishul)*. However, if the hot meat and cheese touch one another while in a *kli rishon* they effect *bishul* even if no liquid is present. See *D.T.* (ibid.) regarding whether cold meat put into a *kli rishon* of hot milk *(tatai gavar)* is considered actual *bishul.* Nevertheless, the meat and dairy may not be eaten since they absorbed taste from one another. If hot milk is poured over solid meat, a *k'dei klipah* of the meat is prohibited. If the meat was previously cooked and has crevices the entire meat may be prohibited, see Chapter Eleven, Section E. The milk is permitted in any case.

can effect *bishul*. It is therefore questionable whether one may derive benefit from meat and milk cooked in hot spring water.[37]

- ☐ Smoking:
  Similarly, *Poskim* disagree as to the status of meat that was soaked in milk and subsequently smoked.[38]
- ☐ Salting, soaking and pickling:
  Several forms of food preparation are equated with cooking insofar as they have the ability to cause a transfer of taste. Nevertheless, they cannot effect *bishul*.[39] Therefore, one may soak, salt or pickle meat with dairy in order to sell to non-Jews or feed to animals.[40] However, initially one should avoid mixing meat and dairy in any form.[41]
- ☐ Solar cooking:
  Many authorities compare solar cooking to cooking in hot spring water.[42]

Modern technology has produced new forms of cooking unknown in earlier times. These forms must be examined to determine whether they qualify as *bishul*.

- ☐ Electrical cooking:
  An electric oven or stove top cooks without an open flame. With the advent of electricity and its application to many *halachos*, *Poskim* of the previous generations were obliged to rule whether electricity is considered fire and thus considered *bishul*. Although there were minority opinions otherwise,[43] the prevailing opinion among *Poskim* was to consider a hot electrical element as fire.[44] Thus, for all practical purposes, cooking on an electric stove top is

---

37. See *Aruch HaShulchan* 87:25.

38. Ibid.

39. *Pri Chadash* 87:2.

40. *Pri Toar* 91:17. Nevertheless, since the meat absorbed milk taste, it should not be cooked even alone (*R' Akiva Eger* gloss to Y.D. 87:1).

41. *Rema* 87:6, as interpreted by the *Yad Yehudah* ibid.

42. See responsa *Ohel Avraham* 94.

43. Responsa *Maharsham* 2:247.

44. See responsa *Achiezer* 3:60 and *Chazon Ish*, *O.C.* 50:9.

analogous to cooking over fire and cooking in an electric oven is treated the same as any other oven.[45]

- ☐ A microwave oven:
  Contemporary authorities grapple with the question of whether microwave cooking should be considered *bishul*.[46] No definitive ruling has been accepted on the matter. Thus, one may perhaps derive benefit from meat and milk cooked in a microwave oven, a *moreh hora'ah* should be consulted.

b) The degree of heat necessary for *bishul*:
The degree of heat necessary to effect *bishul* is defined as *yad soledes bo*. See Chapter Five for a detailed definition.

c) The extent of the cooking:
Cooking, as pertains to *basar b'chalav*, is defined as cooking to the extent that the *basar b'chalav* is edible. One who cooks meat and milk to that degree is punished with *malkos*.[47] *Rishonim* disagree as to whether "cooking" is interpreted as fully cooked[48] or one third cooked.[49] *Poskim* follow the latter opinion.[50] This refers to the prohibition of the cooking itself, but, in the opinion of many authorities, the meat and milk become prohibited immediately upon being subjected to heat.[51] Others contend that although the meat and milk may not be eaten, one may derive benefit from the meat.[52]

d) Foods previously cooked:
If meat and milk were first cooked separately and then

---

45. This assumes that the electrical element heats to a glow, hence the analogy to a flame. If, however, the element heats without glowing, the cooking process may perhaps be compared to solar cooking (see *Zer HaShulchan* 87:6).

46. See *Igros Moshe: O.C.* 3:52 who rules that microwave cooking is considered cooking with regard to the prohibition of cooking on *Shabbos*. Presumably, he would hold the same regarding *basar b'chalav*.

47. *Chullin* 108b.

48. *Pri Migadim* in introduction, citing *Rashi*.

49. *Ritva: Chullin* 108b.

50. *Pri Chadash* 87:3, *Chavas Daas* 91:7.

51. *Pri Migadim* ibid. see *D.T.* 87:3 who cites a dissenting opinion.

52. *Chavas Daas* 91:7. This discussion pertains to the meat only, the milk may not be used since it becomes cooked immediately.

subsequently cooked together, the Biblical prohibition of cooking *basar b'chalav* has been violated.[53] If, however, the meat and milk were initially cooked together, many *Poskim* contend that recooking them violates no additional Biblical prohibition,[54] although others disagree.[55]

e) Cooking inedible *basar b'chalav:*
One who cooks meat and dairy in a liquid to which a foul tasting substance was added (prior to cooking) does not transgress the Biblical prohibition. The meat and dairy absorb an unpleasant taste from one another. Cooking in this manner does not constitute "normal" cooking.[56]

2) Eating *basar b'chalav*:
One may not eat *basar b'chalav*. Biblically, this prohibits eating meat and dairy cooked together. Meat and dairy that were soaked together, even for an extended period, are not considered *basar b'chalav* according to Torah law even though they certainly absorbed taste from one another.[57] Meat and dairy cooked in any of the forms noted above (Section 1) as Biblically prohibited are included in the Biblical prohibition of eating *basar b'chalav*. Meat and dairy prepared in a manner that is Rabbinically forbidden is prohibited to be eaten by Rabbinic law only.[58] *Chazal,* however, extended the prohibition of eating *basar b'chalav* to include meat or dairy that absorbed taste from one another in any manner.

3) Deriving benefit from *basar b'chalav*:
One may not derive benefit from *basar b'chalav*.[59] The prohibition of deriving benefit from *basar b'chalav* is limited to Biblical *basar b'chalav* as defined in Section 1. Meat and milk

---

53. Responsa *Chasam Sofer:* Y.D. 82.

54. *R' Akiva Eger* and *Gilyon Maharsha* gloss to 87:1. See also *D.T.* 87:4 and *Sidei Chemed* vol. 1 page 184.

55. *S.D.* 87:18, and 99:11, rules that the prohibition applies in all cases. However, in *O.C., A.A.* 673:1 he contradicts this ruling and in *M.Z.* 105:2, seems to be uncertain.

56. *Pri Migadim* end of preface to *basar b'chalav.*

57. Y.*D.* 87:1.

58. Y.*D.* 87:1.

59. See *D.T.* 30 regarding soap made of *basar b'chalav*. Authorities are uncertain whether, in the opinion of the *Rambam*, deriving benefit from *basar b'chalav* is punishable with *malkos*. See *D.T.* 87:8.

mixtures that are only Rabbinically prohibited may be used for any form of benefit.[60]

a) Examples of beneficial use:

- ☐ One may not engage in any commerce involving *basar b'chalav*. One who owns a restaurant with a non-Jewish clientele, may not serve *basar b'chalav*. Incidentally, one may not engage in commerce involving any foodstuff Biblically forbidden to eat,[61] lest one inadvertently come to eat some of the prohibited food himself.[62] In addition, it may be problematic selling any forbidden food to the public since non-observant Jews may also purchase food.[63]
- ☐ One may not feed *basar b'chalav* to dogs[64] even if the dogs are not his own.[65] The act of feeding itself is use of *basar b'chalav*. Thus, one who owns a dog must ascertain that the dog food contains no Biblically prohibted *basar b'chalav*. If, however, the meat (or milk) is from a non-kosher animal, the food may be used even though it contains both meat and milk.[66]
- ☐ One who erroneously purchased *basar b'chalav* perhaps may not return it for a refund. Returning the food is a form of sale which constitutes beneficial use of *basar b'chalav*. A *moreh hora'ah* should be consulted.[67]

---

60. *Rema* 87:1. See *Taz* §1, *Shach* §2, who both reject opposing view of *Maharshal*.

61. If the foodstuff came into his possession inadvertently (e.g., he inherited it) he may sell and dispose of it; see *Y.D.* 117. See *Taz* §1, whether this is a Biblical or a Rabbinic law.

62. *Shach* §2, and *Taz* §1 citing *Rashba*.

63. See *D.T.* 117:65.

64. *Chochmas Adam* 40:62.

65. *Issur V'heter* 21:12, *Taz* 94:4. See, however, *Shaar HaTziyun* (*O.C.* 448:75), responsa *Bais HaLevi* I:20, *Pischei Teshuvah* 94:5, *D.T.* §48 and *Sidei Chemed* vol. 1 p. 65, for dissenting opinions.

66. See Section B,3 below, that only kosher meat and milk constitute Biblical *basar b'chalav*. One may derive benefit from Rabbinic *basar b'chalav*.

67. If the food was purchased from a Jew, the seller may be required to give a refund even if the food has been discarded, since the sale is not valid (see *Choshen Mishpat* 234:4).

- ☐ If *basar b'chalav* becomes mixed into other foods in a manner that it is not *batel*, the food may not be eaten. In the opinion of some *Poskim*, one may sell the entire mixture to a non-Jew if the value of the *basar b'chalav* is deducted from the price.[68]
- ☐ If *basar b'chalav* is cooked in a pot, it may need *kashering*. In the event that the pot cannot be *kashered* or one chooses not to *kasher* it, the pot may be sold to a non-Jew.[69]
- ☐ One who did, in error, sell *basar b'chalav* may keep the money. Use of the money does not constitute benefit from *basar b'chalav*.[70]

b) Disposal of *basar b'chalav*:
Basar b'chalav must be disposed of in a manner that no one will come to benefit from it. Thus, it may not be discarded into the garbage. It must be buried or disposed of in the toilet or thrown into a river without fish.[71] One may dispose of *basar b'chalav* by burning it.[72]

Summary of Section A

§ The prohibition of cooking *basar b'chalav*:
One may not cook meat and dairy together even if he does not intend to partake of the *basar b'chalav*. One may not even cook *basar b'chalav* for a non-Jew.

a) The following forms of cooking may be included in the Biblical prohibition of *basar b'chalav*.

- ☐ In the opinion of many *Poskim*, broiling, barbecuing, roasting, baking and frying are all considered forms of *bishul* and are Biblically prohibited. No distinction is made whether the cooking is done over a flame or an electrical element. The question of the status of

---

68. *Chavas Daas* 110:2c, see, however, *S.D.* §2.

69. *Pischei Teshuvah* 94:6 citing *Chasam Sofer*, see however, *M.B.* 450:28.

70. *Meiri: Chullin* 113a.

71. See *Issur V'heter* 21:13, who writes that *basar b'chalav* must be disposed of "in a manner that no creature will derive benefit from it. It is therefore inadequate to throw it in the street even where no dogs are found."

72. *Pri Chadash* 94:10.

microwave cooking has not been definitively resolved.

- □ Cooking meat and dairy in a *kli rishon* constitutes a violation of the Biblical prohibition of *bishul basar b'chalav*. In the opinion of some authorities, an uninterrupted pouring *(iruy)* from a *kli rishon* constitutes *bishul* as well, while others disagree. A *kli sheni* cannot effect *bishul*.
- □ *Poskim* disagree about whether cooking meat and dairy in naturally hot spring water, solar cooking or smoking constitute *bishul*:
- □ Salting, soaking and pickling have the ability to cause a transfer of taste, but cannot effect *bishul*.

b) Cooking as pertains to *basar b'chalav* is defined as cooking in a heat of *yad soledes bo* to the extent that the food is edible. *Poskim* rule that once the food has reached one third of being fully cooked, the prohibition has been violated.

c) If meat and milk were cooked separately and subsequently cooked together, the Biblical prohibition has been violated. If the meat and milk were previously cooked together, *Poskim* disagree whether recooking them violates an additional Biblical prohibition.

d) One who cooks meat and dairy in a liquid to which a foul tasting substance has been added does not transgress the Biblical prohibition.

☙ The prohibition of eating *basar b'chalav*:
One may not eat *basar b'chalav*. Only meat and dairy cooked in any form noted above as Biblically prohibited is included in the Biblical prohibition of eating *basar b'chalav*. *Chazal*, however, extended the prohibition of eating *basar b'chalav* to include meat or dairy that absorbed taste from one another in any manner.

☙ The prohibition of deriving benefit from *basar b'chalav*:
One may not derive benefit from any Biblically prohibited *basar b'chalav*. Meat and milk mixtures that are only Rabbinically prohibited may be used for any form of benefit. Thus, one may not engage in any commerce involving *basar b'chalav*. One may not feed Biblically prohibited *basar*

b'chalav to any dog. Dog food that contains only Rabbinically prohibited *basar b'chalav* may be used.

- *Basar b'chalav* must be disposed of in a manner that no one will come to benefit from it.

B. Types of meats and dairy which constitute basar b'chalav

1) The Torah prohibition:
The Torah relates the prohibition of *basar b'chalav* regarding the cooking of a *g'di* (a kid) in his mother's milk. Sinaitic tradition, however, includes all kosher domestic animals[73] in the prohibition of *basar b'chalav*, whether cooked in their mother's milk or the milk of any kosher animal.[74] Meat or milk from a non-kosher or a non-domestic (even kosher) animal *(chayah)*[75] cooked together is not prohibited by Biblical law. Even cow's milk cooked with deer's meat is not *basar b'chalav* according to Torah law since a deer is a non-domestic animal. Similarly, meat of fowl cooked with milk is not forbidden by Torah law.[76]

2) Non-domestic or fowl meat:
Rabbinic law prohibits eating *chayah* or fowl meat cooked in

73. I.e., those type of domestic animals that may be eaten when properly slaughtered. A kosher animal that was improperly slaughtered is theoretically included in the prohibition of *basar b'chalav*. However, we have a principle of *ain issur chal al issur* — one prohibition cannot be effectual on anything that is currently under another prohibition. Thus, *Rambam* 9:6, rules that one who eats *neveilah* (carrion meat) cooked in milk is punished for eating *neveilah* only, not for eating *basar b'chalav*. Nevertheless, since cooking *neveilah* itself is permissible, the prohibition of *cooking basar b'chalav* is in effect on *neveilah* meat. *Poskim* disagree as to whether one may derive benefit from *neveilah* cooked in milk. See *Dagul Mervavah* 87:3 citing *Rambam* who is lenient in a case of loss. Other authorities disagree, see *Pri Migadim* in his introduction. Thus, one should not use pet food containing *basar b'chalav* even though the meat is non-slaughtered. If, however, the meat is from a non-kosher animal, it may be used. One who is faced with a situation of financial loss regarding *basar b'chalav* of non-slaughtered meat should consult a *moreh hora'ah* (see responsa *Chasam Sofer:* Y.D. 92).

74. Y.D. 87:3. See *Ibn Ezra: Shemos* 23:19, who explains the reason for the Torah choosing *g'di*, a kid. He explains that the Torah usually speaks of typical situations although it actually intends to include all cases. Thus, although *basar b'chalav* applies to all kosher animals, the only animal that is tasty when cooked in milk is a kid.

75. E.g., a deer, antelope and perhaps a buffalo.

76. Y.D. 87:3.

milk (from a domestic animal),[77] domestic animal meat cooked in *chayah* milk[78] or even *chayah* or fowl meat cooked in *chayah* milk.[79] In addition, Rabbinic law prohibits even merely cooking fowl meat in milk since people may confuse it *(maris ayin)* with animal meat.[80]

3) Non-kosher animals:
   It was not necessary for *Chazal* to prohibit *basar b'chalav* of non-kosher animals since they are prohibited to be eaten anyway. Some *Poskim*, however, contend that *Chazal* extended *basar b'chalav* to non-kosher animals as well. Hence, in their opinion, all of the rules of *basar b'chalav*, which are more stringent than those of non-kosher meat or non-kosher milk alone, apply to *basar b'chalav* of non-kosher animals as well.[81]

4) Fish:
   Chazal did not extend the prohibition of *basar b'chalav* to fish. Therefore, one may drink milk while eating fish or even fry fish in butter.[82] There is a view that one should not cook fish in dairy products. Although most authorities reject this view, some have the custom to refrain from eating fish with dairy.[83]

5) Whey:
   The clear fluid that separates from the cheese curds during the

---

77. *Y.D.* 87:3. One may not even eat fowl soaked in milk. One might argue that it should be permitted since this is a secondary Rabbinic prohibition: fowl meat is prohibited only Rabbinically and soaked meat and milk are only Rabbinically prohibited. Nevertheless, *Poskim* rule that the fowl may not be eaten *(Pri Toar* 87:14, M.Z. §1).

78. *Pischei Teshuvah* 87:7.

79. See *Rambam* 9:4. It is surprising that later *Poskim* and contemporary authorities make no mention of this *halachah*.

80. See *Rema* 87:4, *Taz* §5 and *M.Z.* ibid. It would follow from the argument set forth by *Taz* that one should not cook non-domesticated animal meat in milk or domesticated animal meat in non-domesticated animal milk. However, *Shach* §7 contends that cooking itself is not prohibited in these cases.

81. *Bach* and *Drishah* 87, see, however, *Taz* §2 and *Shach* §3, who disagree.

82. *Y.D.* 87:3.

83. See *Shach* 87:5, *Pischei Teshuvah* §9 and *D.T.* §48. See *Kaf HaChaim* §24, who differentiates between butter and milk. He rules that one should not cook fish in milk but one may cook it in butter. See *Yechaveh Daas* 6:48 who cites the opinions many *Sefardic Poskim* on the matter. Indeed, some have the custom of cleaning and rinsing the mouth between eating fish and milk. Even those who do not cook fish with dairy may cook fish in a dairy pot.

process of making cheese is called "whey." *Poskim* rule that whey is considered milk and is Biblically prohibited when cooked with meat.[84]

6) Human milk:
Human milk is not included in the prohibition of *basar b'chalav;* nevertheless, one should not cook meat in human milk.[85] In the event that human milk fell into a meat food (and is not noticeable[86]), it is *batel*[87] and the food may be eaten.[88] Thus, if a bottle used by a nursing mother to store her milk is washed with meat dishes, neither the bottle nor the dishes are affected.

7) Artificial milk:
In earlier times, a *parve* milk made of almonds was used in lieu of milk. *Poskim* ruled that one who cooked meat in almond milk must place almonds near the milk[89] so that is should not seem as if he eats *basar b'chalav.*[90] In the opinion of some *Poskim,* this prohibition applies only to domestic animal meat (which, when cooked with milk, is Biblically prohibited), not chicken meat,[91] while others disagree.[92] Similarly, *Poskim* disagree about the status of animal meat that is mixed with, but not cooked with, the almond milk, since that too is only Rabbinically prohibited. Authorities rule that one should follow the stringent opinions; however, some authorities are lenient if the almond milk is used privately, not publicly, because they contend that in this case one need not be

---

84. *Y.D.* 87:8, *S.D.* §23.

85. *Y.D.* 87:4. In the opinion of *Rema* (ibid.) one may cook fowl meat in human milk, see, however, *Shach* §8 who contends that no distinction be made between animal meat and fowl in regard to this *halachah.* See also *Shach* §7 who contends that this *halachah* refers to eating meat with human milk, not merely cooking it.

86. *D.T.* 87:51 citing *Levush.*

87. *Poskim* disagree whether the milk may become nullified in a food in which the milk is the majority. *Bitul b'shishim* is certainly not required *(D.T.* 87:52).

88. *Y.D.* 87:4.

89. In the opinion of the *Shach* §7 this is only required while one eats. One need not place the almonds by the pot during the cooking itself. See, however, *S.D.* §7, who disagrees.

90. *Rema* 87:3.

91. *Rema* ibid. See also *Pri Chadash* §7.

92. *Taz* §5, *Shach* §6 and *Pri Toar* §9.

concerned about any misunderstanding.[93] Some authorities argue that if the almond milk is not actually mixed into the meat, no reminder is required.[94] One who has no almonds to place near the almond milk may nevertheless eat the food.[95] This question applies today in the following forms:

a) Margarine:
Contemporary authorities discuss the question of whether one may use *parve* margarine with meat foods. Certainly, whenever the margarine is blended into the food, it poses no problem. May one, however, eat a salami sandwich with margarine without displaying the margarine wrapper? There is an opinion that contends that since margarine is so common today, no one will actually suspect that the margarine is butter.[96] One may certainly rely on this opinion if the sandwich is being eaten privately.[97]

b) Non-dairy coffee creamer:
A similar question applies to *parve* coffee creamer. Must one place the container of coffee creamer on the table if it is to be served at a meat meal? The opinions cited above regarding margarine apply to creamer as well.[98] In addition, meat is not usually eaten directly with the creamer. The coffee is generally served after the meat has been removed; thus, we have an additional reason to follow the lenient opinions.[99]

c) *Parve* ice cream:
Similarly, ice cream is served after the meat is no longer on the table. Therefore the commonly accepted custom is

---

93. See *Pischei Teshuvah* §10. This case, not being a Talmudic prohibition, is not subject to the usual rule that anything prohibited because of *maris ayin* is prohibited even when done privately.

94. *Shulchan Govoha* cited in *D.T.* §44,45.

95. *Taz* §4, see *Pischei Teshuvah* §10.

96. Responsa *Cheshev Ha'efod* 1:20. See also *Kreisi U'pleisi* §8 and responsa *Maharash Engel* 6:40. See a similar position in *Daas Torah* 87:3, regarding coconut oil used as butter.

97. In which case we have the additional support of the *Pischei Teshuvah* cited above in note 93.

98. See also responsa *Yabia Omer*, *Y.D.* 6:8, who rules leniently in this question.

99. See note 94 above.

to permit *parve* ice cream to be served without display of the carton.[100]

Summary of Section B

- Meat and milk of domesticated kosher animals:
  The meat and the milk of all kosher domestic animals are included in the Biblical prohibition of *basar b'chalav* when they are cooked together.

- Other types of meat and milk:

  - Fowl and non-domestic animals:
    Meat and milk from a non-kosher animal or from a kosher *chayah* or meat of a fowl is not included in the Biblical prohibition. Rabbinic law prohibits eating non-domestic or fowl meat cooked in milk or domestic animal meat cooked in non-domestic animal milk. In addition, Rabbinic law prohibits even the cooking of non-domestic or fowl meat.

  - Non-kosher animals:
    While one may not eat meat or milk from non-kosher animals, *Poskim* disagree whether or not *Chazal* extended the more stringent rules of *basar b'chalav* to include non-kosher animals.

  - Fish:
    Chazal did not extend the prohibition of *basar b'chalav* to fish. Most authorities reject the view that one should not cook fish in dairy products.

  - Whey:
    Authorities rule that whey is included in the Biblical prohibition of *basar b'chalav*.

  - Human milk:
    Human milk is not included in the prohibition of *basar*

100. An additional supporting argument may be that if the ice cream is being served privately, one may not need to worry about *maris ayin* as noted above. If the ice cream is being served publicly (e.g., a wedding) the wrapper cannot be placed at each table since it is bought in large containers. We noted above that if an almond is not available, the food may nevertheless be eaten. While this reason alone may not be grounds to be lenient in this case since one can avoid purchasing the ice cream, it is an additional justification.

b'chalav, but should not be cooked with meat. If human milk falls into meat and is not noticeable, the food may be eaten.

- ☐ Artificial milk:

  One who cooks meat in artificial (e.g., almond) milk must place almonds near the milk. Even one who drinks almond milk while eating meat should place almonds nearby if possible. Contemporary authorities discuss the question of using *parve* margarine, non-dairy coffee creamer and *parve* ice cream with meat foods. Common custom is to permit their use.

CHAPTER EIGHT

Rabbinic Precautionary Measures Regarding Basar B'chalav

- ☐ Eating meat in proximity to dairy.
- ☐ The six hour interlude between eating meat and dairy.
- ☐ Food cooked in a meat or dairy pot.
- ☐ Eating meat after eating cheese.
- ☐ Cutting bread with a meat or dairy knife.
- ☐ The prohibition of dairy breads.
- ☐ Kashering utensils from one use to another.

I. Eating meat in proximity to milk

These *halachos* are based on *Tur* and *Shulchan Aruch; Yoreh De'ah* 88.

In addition to extending the scope of *basar b'chalav* to animals not included in the Torah prohibition, *Chazal* also broadened the extent of the prohibition of eating *basar b'chalav*. *Chazal* were worried that specific situations may cause one to eat meat and dairy together. Some of these concerns may seem far-fetched and not in keeping with *Chazal's* usual reluctance to add prohibitions unless absolutely necessary. Indeed, these *halachos* hardly have a parallel in other prohibitions. For example, one may eat kosher food at a table on which non-kosher food lays.[1] Nevertheless, since both meat and dairy are permitted foods that are normally eaten, *Chazal* felt that *basar b'chalav* requires numerous barriers to guard against transgression of the Torah law.[2] Accordingly, even meat of fowl or non-domestic animals are not exempt from the rules listed below.[3]

A. Eating alone

Rabbinic decree prohibits placing meat upon the table at which one is eating dairy[4] (or the reverse[5]). *Chazal* were concerned that one may absent-mindedly eat some of the meat. If, however, the table is large and the meat is not within hands-reach, this prohibition does not apply.[6]

---

1. An exception to this is non-kosher bread. Since bread is the mainstay of any meal we must be concerned that one may inadvertently eat from the non-kosher bread (*Shach* 88:2).

2. *Shach* ibid. Similarly, two people who vowed a *neder* not to benefit from one another are subject to all these *halachos*.

3. Y.*D*. 88:1.

4. Y.*D*. 88:1, even if the meat is not his (*D.T.* §2).

5. *Shach*. 88:1.

6. See *D.T.* §7 who cites the *Knesses HaGedolah* that the original prohibition related to the types of tables common in times of *Chazal* i.e., small tables seating only one. Our tables, however, that seat more than one person are not governed by this rule. He nevertheless requires some type of symbol to remind one not to partake of the meat. However, if the table is very large and the meat is not within hands-reach, it would seem that a symbol is not required, see *P.T.* §3.

B. Eating in company

Similarly, *Chazal* were concerned that if two people eat at one table, one meat and one dairy, they may offer some of their food to one another and transgress the prohibition of *basar b'chalav*. Therefore, one eating meat[7] may not share a table with one eating dairy. This prohibition is restricted by the following:

1) Non-acquaintances:
   Since only acquaintances are liable to share their food, two strangers may share a table while eating meat and dairy respectively. For a definition of acquaintances, the following guidelines are given:
   a) The two are on friendly terms and would feel comfortable partaking of one another's food[8] even though they may expect payment.[9]
   b) If, however, they are not acquainted or would not permit one another to partake of their food because of mutual animosity, they may eat together.[10]
2) A mark or reminder:
   One may share a table even with an acquaintance if one puts a sign or mark that will effectively remind them that they may not share food. This reminder may take several forms: one may place a separate tablecloth for each individual. This may be done any of the following methods:
   a) They may actually use two separate tablecloths.[11]
   b) One of the parties may use a tablecloth while the other eats on the table itself.
   c) Each may use place mats if they would normally not eat in that manner[12] (i.e., if it is common to use place mats,

---

7. See *D.T.* §16 regarding one who is not presently eating meat but is within six hours of a meat meal. Should he be forbidden to share a table with one eating dairy lest he forget and partake of the dairy food? Most *Poskim* contend that this is not within the scope of the Rabbinic prohibition.

8. *Pri Chadash* 88:2, *Aruch HaShulchan* 88:8.

9. See *Pri Toar* §2.

10. See *Shach* 88:2 and *M.Z.* §2.

11. *Y.D.* 88:2.

12. *D.T.* §20.

they cannot be considered a reminder).[13]

d) One of the parties may lift the tablecloth and place his plate on the table itself.[14]

One may place an object to serve as a separation and reminder between the two. This object must conform to the following:

- The object must be something that is usually not placed on the table,[15] or something not being used at this meal (e.g., a bread loaf).[16]
- The object must be of sufficient size to be noticeable.[17]

3) The distance between the two:
If the two are sitting not within the hand reach of one another (i.e., the food of one is not within grasp of the other), they may eat together.[18]

4) Eating with a non-Jew:
One may eat meat on a table with a non-Jew eating dairy food providing that the dairy food is non-kosher or cooked in the non-Jew's home. If, however, the food is kosher and the Jew and non-Jew are on friendly terms and would feel comfortable eating from one another's food, the prohibition applies.[19]

These *halachos* are very relevant to students eating in a school cafeteria. The fact that each student eats his lunch from his bag is not a sufficient reminder since students usually eat in that manner. One student should open his bag and use it as a mat.

Summary of Section I

- One may not place meat upon the table at which one is eating dairy (or the reverse), unless the meat is not within hands-reach.
- Two people on friendly terms may not eat at one table if one is eating meat and one is eating dairy, unless they place a

13. Unless the place mats themselves are obviously of different types, i.e., the custom in that household is to use different colored place mats for meat and dairy.

14. See *Shach* 195:6.

15. Or not placed on that part of the table (*D.T.* §27).

16. *Rema* 88:2, see *S.D.* §8 and *D.T.* §21 as to whether or not the loaf must be whole.

17. *Kaf HaChaim* §26, *D.T.* §26.

18. *Aruch HaShulchan* 88:8.

19. *Pri Toar* §1.

noticeable object in between to remind them not to share food. They may also use two separate tablecloths or place mats to serve as a reminder or not sit within hands-reach of one another.

- One may eat meat on a table with a non-Jew eating non-kosher dairy food. If the food is kosher and they are on friendly terms, they may not eat together.
- When students are eating together in a school cafeteria one eating meat and one eating dairy, one party should open his bag for use as a mat.

II. Eating meat and dairy after one another

These *halachos* are based on *Tur* and *Shulchan Aruch; Yoreh De'ah* 88.

A. Eating dairy after meat

Chazal were not satisfied with the prevention of meat and dairy being eaten together. They decreed that dairy may not be eaten even *after* eating meat unless one waits a specific period of time. Although this edict is cited in the Talmud, it is subject to different interpretations and explanations.

1) The Talmudic source:
The source for this precept is found in the following two Talmudic passages:[20]

- ☐ Rav Chisda stated: "One who ate meat is forbidden to eat cheese. One who ate cheese may eat meat."
- ☐ Mar Ukvah said: "In this matter I resemble 'vinegar the son of wine' when compared to my father. Father would wait twenty-four hours after eating meat before partaking of cheese. But I, although I would not eat cheese in the same meal as meat, I would eat cheese in the next meal."

These two passages complement one another. One who eats meat may not eat cheese unless he waits at least until the next meal. Certainly, the standard of Mar Ukvah is a minimum

20. Both are found in *Chullin* 105a.

standard since he was self critical of his leniency.[21] One who eats cheese need not wait before eating meat. In addition to the waiting period, the Talmud notes the following other obligations required between eating meat and dairy foods.[22]

- ☐ Rinsing one's mouth:
  One may not eat meat after dairy without rinsing the mouth in-between.
- ☐ Wiping one's mouth:
  One may not eat meat after dairy without first cleansing one's mouth by eating a bulky food that wipes out the mouth.[23]
- ☐ Washing one's hands:
  One who eats cheese must wash his hands before eating meat.

However, when one waits six hours after eating meat, he is not required to rinse or wipe his mouth or wash his hands.

2) The opposing interpretations:
Rishonim disagree as to the meaning of Mar Ukvah's waiting for the next meal. In the opinion of some,[24] the essential element is **waiting** an amount of time after eating meat. This span of time is measured by the usual span of time between the day and evening meals which is six hours.[25] Other *Rishonim*[26] contend

21. This is the opinion of most *Rishonim* and the accepted opinion. However, *Rabbeinu Tam* cites *Halachos Gedolos* (cited in *Tosfos: Chullin* 104b) who contends that the first verse merely prohibits eating cheese after meat without cleaning one's mouth and hands. One who cleans his mouth and hands may eat cheese immediately after meat. One who eats cheese, however, may immediately eat meat without any preparation. In the opinion of *Rabbeinu Tam*, Mar Ukvah's objection to eating cheese after meat refers only to one who did not clean his hands and mouth. One who cleans his hands and mouth properly may eat cheese immediately after meat. He also speculates that perhaps Mar Ukvah was applying a stringent standard to himself but did not intend to present this as *halachah*.

22. The Talmud mentions these in regard to one who wishes to eat dairy after meat. However, since we follow the opinion that one must wait six hours after eating meat, these *halachos* apply only to one who ate dairy and wishes to eat meat afterwards (see *Tosfos: Chullin* 104b, s.v. *ouf*). See Section III, below.

23. Although modern hygiene has provided more efficient methods of cleaning one's mouth, e.g., flossing or brushing one's teeth or gargling with mouthwash, they alone perhaps do not accomplish the desired effect. Eating bulky food actually wipes the mouth surface and removes any cheese residue and is the only *halachically* acceptable method.

24. *Rambam* 9:28, *Rashba*, *Rosh: Chullin* 8:5.

that the essential point is not to eat meat and dairy in the same meal. Once the meat meal is finished, dairy may be eaten.[27] Nevertheless, even according to this opinion, one must recite *Bircas HaMazon* (or the proper *b'rachah acharonah* if the meal was not a bread meal[28]), wait a minimum of one hour after eating meat[29] and clean one's mouth, as noted above, by eating and drinking.[30]

3) The *halachic* consensus:
The overwhelming majority of *Poskim* require that one wait six hours between meat and dairy. However, *Sefardic* and *Ashkenazic* tradition differ in acceptance of the six-hour respite. According to *Sefardic* tradition, the six-hour respite is *halachically* required. It follows those opinions that interpret the Talmud in that manner. *Ashkenazic* tradition follows the lenient opinion in theory. Nevertheless, in practice, the six-hour respite was accepted almost universally among *Ashkenazic* Jews as well.[31] *Poskim* declare that this is the proper conduct for anyone "imbued with the spirit of Torah."[32] However, certain communities continued to follow the original *Ashkenazic* custom of reciting a *b'rachah acharonah*, waiting only one hour and cleaning the mouth.[33] This custom is found today among original Dutch Jews. Jews originating from Germany continue

---

25. A scholar (such as Mar Ukvah) usually ate his morning meal in the sixth hour of the day (see *Shabbos* 10a). Thus the evening meal was normally six hours later (see *Biur HaGra* 89:2).

26. *Tosfos: Chullin* 105a, *Hagaos Ashri: Chullin* 8:5, *Hagaos Maimoni (Maachalos Asuros* 9:28).

27. The implication of this approach is that one who eats dairy first may eat meat afterwards even in the same meal. See footnote no. 84.

28. *Shach* 89:6.

29. This additional requirement is cited by *Rema* 89:1. The *Taz* §3, notes that he was unable to find the source of this requirement. See however, *Biur HaGra* §6, who notes that its source is found in the *Zohar* who prohibits eating meat and milk in the same hour. This *Zohar* is also cited in *Divrei Chamudos: Chullin* 8:23.

30. *Rema* 89:1. See *Shach* §7, who contends that one who waits an hour is not required to clean his mouth. See, however, *S.D.* §7.

31. *Aruch HaShulchan* 89:7.

32. *Shach* 89:5.

33. *Rema* 89:1, according to the view of *Taz* §2, *Yad Yehudah* §9k and *M.Z.* §2 as opposed to *Shach* §7 and *Chochmas Adam* 40:13.

today their tradition of waiting three hours after eating meat.[34] This custom is perhaps based on the theory that during a short winter day the span between meals is shortened corresponding to the length of the day. Thus, the shorter waiting span should be sufficient at any time of the year.[35] While these customs are acceptable for one whose family tradition is such, others may not choose to follow these customs. The accepted tradition among the majority of Jews to wait six hours is binding upon everyone, unless his tradition is clearly otherwise. One who changes his custom to follow a more lenient custom is soundly censured by *halachic* authorities.[36]

4) Extenuating circumstances:
Since waiting six hours after eating meat is, for *Ashkenazic* Jews, a matter of custom rather than *halachah*, it may be disregarded in cases of difficulty, for example:

   a) Illness:
   Halachah dictates that forbidden foods may be eaten only in cases of life-threatening illness. However, one suffering from an ailment that requires him to eat dairy foods often (e.g., an ulcer) needs to wait only one hour after eating meat. The requirement of waiting six hours is merely a custom[37] and does not interfere with medical necessity. There are, however, two provisos: he must recite a *b'rachah acharonah* on the meat[38] and he must cleanse his mouth in the proper manner (i.e., eating solid food and drinking).[39]

   b) A nursing woman:
   A nursing mother who needs to drink milk often has a

34. This custom is cited in *Rabbeinu Yeruchum: Issur V'heter* no. 39.

35. See *D.T.* §6.

36. *Chochmas Adam* 40:13, *Aruch HaShulchan* 89:7.

37. Even *Sefardic* Jews who consider the six-hour wait a *halachic* requirement may be lenient in case of illness (*Yechaveh Daas* 3:58).

38. *Chochmas Adam* 40:13. He also requires that one manually clean the teeth (flossing or brushing), apparently, to compensate for not waiting six hours. It is unclear whether he requires rinsing the mouth as well. Other authorities, however, do not mention the requirement of manually cleaning the teeth.

39. *Aruch HaShulchan* 89:7.

status similar to that of one who is ill and is governed by the same rules.[40]

c) A baby or child:
The rules of waiting six hours regarding children depends upon the following age groups:

- □ An infant:
One need not wait six hours when feeding a baby approximately three years or younger. A child of this age is too frail to delay his milk drinking.[41] One may even feed him dairy immediately after meat if this is beneficial to the child.[42]

- □ A young child:
A child older than approximately three years is no longer considered frail and should wait an hour, if possible, before eating dairy. In addition, a child must be trained in proper performance of *mitzvos*. Therefore, one should train the child according to his ability to wait additional time, increasing the time each year.[43]

- □ An older child:
A child above the approximate age of six should wait six hours after eating meat. Nevertheless, if the child requires milk, thirsts for milk or insists upon eating a dairy product, he may do so if he is younger than nine[44] or ten[45] years.[46] A nine or ten year old child

40. See *Salmas Chaim* 286 [2:4]. No *hataras nedarim* (annulment of vows) is required, since she plans to eventually return to her original custom (see *Dagul Mervavah: Y.D.* 214).

41. See *Tosfos: Shabbos* 121a.

42. This is the common custom. See responsa of R. M. Stern in appendix to *Pischei Halachah, Kashrus* who notes that the child's mouth should be cleaned externally of any meat residue.

43. Ibid.

44. For a robust child.

45. For a more slight child.

46. See responsa *Chelkas Yaakov* 2:88,89; 3:147, for a discussion of the various issues involved. On the one hand, a minor, or even an infant, may not be fed non-kosher foods. On the other hand, dairy after meat is essentially not non-kosher. Furthermore, one may speculate whether the six-hour respite has the status of a vow and whether that vow is binding upon minors.

should wait six hours even though he is not *bar-mitzvah*. However, a frail child who requires milk need wait only an hour, recite the *b'rachah acharonah* and clean his mouth.[47]

d) One who recited a *b'rachah* over milk:
One who in error recites a *b'rachah rishonah* over milk during the six-hour interval may, in the opinion of many authorities, partake of a bit of milk so as not to cause a *b'rachah levatalah* (a *b'rachah* in vain), providing that one hour has passed.[48] Incidentally, one who ate, in error, even a large amount of dairy before the end of the six-hour period has not changed his status and must wait the remainder of the six-hour waiting period before eating any additional dairy.

5) The measurement of six hours:

a) Six, five or five and one half hours?
As noted above, the vast majority of Jews wait six hours between eating meat and milk. *Poskim* interpret this to mean six full hours.[49] There are some who wait only five and one half hours or only somewhat more than five complete hours. Indeed, some authorities of the past generation are alleged to have ruled that five and a half hours suffice. While many follow this interpretation, it is difficult to find a basis for it in *halachic* literature.[50]

---

47. *Aruch HaShulchan* 89:7.

48. See *Sidei Chemed* vol. 5 p. 290, responsa *Be'er Moshe* 4:24, or perhaps even before passage of one hour, see responsa *Yechaveh Daas* 4:41.

49. See *D.T.* 89:6.

50. See responsa *Yabia Omer* (vol. 1, *Y.D.* 4) who tries to find some basis for waiting five and one half hours. He concludes that where necessary one may follow this custom, but only after eating fowl. He bases his ruling on the fact that in earlier times people had no clocks and certainly approximated the six-hour period. Thus, he contends, an approximation is adequate. This argument is difficult to accept. While the case can be made that one who approximates that six hours have elapsed may eat dairy (see below), this cannot be compared to one who knows that only five and one half hours have passed. Others are quoted as having based their opinion on the language of *Rambam* 9:28, who writes *"k'mo sheish shaos"* ("about six hours"). This nuance of *Rambam* (and *Rashba)* has been previously noted by the *Bircei Yosef* (89:3), who interprets it in a different manner. In addition, our custom of waiting six hours is not based on *Rambam* since we follow the *Ashkenazic* tradition that *halachically*, one hour suffices. We wait six hours as a matter of custom accepted by previous generations. Thus, the question

b) Whether an exact calculation:
   If one is unsure of the exact time he completed his meat meal, he must, in the opinion of some authorities, wait until he estimates that six hours have certainly passed.[51] Other authorities permit eating dairy on the basis that six hours may have passed.[52]

c) Whether measured from the end of the meal:
   The six-hour interlude is measured from the cessation of actually eating meat, not the end of the entire meat meal. Thus, one who finished his Shabbos meal at 2:00 pm but ate no meat after 1:00 pm, may eat dairy at 7:00 pm.[53]

6) The purpose of the interlude:
   Common misconception associates the proscribed six-hour interval to the time required to digest the meat eaten. Although there is mention of this concept in classic *halachic* literature,[54] it

---

should be a matter of clarifying the custom. Thus, since there is no basis in *Shulchan Aruch* and its commentaries for eating dairy in less than six hours, we must assume that the accepted custom was to wait a full six hours, any nuance in the wording of the *Rambam* should be irrelevant.

51. *Yad Yehudah* §1.

52. See *D.T.* §5.

53. See *Aruch HaShulchan* 89:4 who rules that one must count six hours from the end of the meat meal to the beginning of the dairy meal even if he had not eaten meat at the end of the meal and plans to eat no dairy at the beginning of the dairy meal. This view has no basis in *Poskim* and is rejected by all contemporary authorities. Indeed, it seems illogical. We will note in the following paragraph of text that the waiting between meat and dairy is **either** a measurement of time (six hours) to guarantee that no meat or taste remains in the mouth or the concept of interrupting the meat and dairy so that they are not eaten in one meal. The *Aruch HaShulchan* has, in effect, combined these two opposing views and therefore requires a six-hour interruption between the meals.

54. See *Kreisi U'pleisi* 89:3, who contends that the digestive process starts 1.2 hours after eating and continues for six hours (he bases this on *Magen Avraham: O.C.* 184:9). Thus he maintains that the two opinions cited in *Rishonim*, whether to wait one or six hours, argue whether the interlude depends upon the beginning of the digestive process or the end. While this opinion of *Kreisi U'pleisi* is not shared by other *Poskim*, it is interesting to note a story told of the *Chasam Sofer* (cited in *sefer Zichron L'Moshe* p. 181). It seems that the *Chasam Sofer* held that the six hour interlude was dependent upon digestion of the meat. In addition, he assumed that the digestive process quickens during sleep. Thus, if one ate meat late at night and rose early the next morning, he may eat dairy even though six hours have not passed since he ate the meat. Accordingly, one morning the *Chasam Sofer* prepared a coffee with milk even though six hours had not passed from his meat meal. Before he was able to drink the coffee, however, the cup overturned

is not the accepted rationale. *Rishonim* present various reasons for the six-hour interlude. In the opinion of some,[55] meat leaves a fatty residue in the throat and palate for a period of six hours. Others[56] maintain that particles of meat may remain lodged between the teeth. The fatty residue or meat particles may mix with any dairy food eaten afterwards. Once six hours have passed, one may eat dairy since the fatty residue has certainly been dissolved by saliva. Similarly, any remaining meat particles are sufficiently decomposed by salivic acids and are no longer considered meat.

7) The distinction between the reasons:
Poskim note the following practical differences between these reasons.

- ☐ If one did not actually swallow the meat but only chewed it (in previous times, when prepared baby foods were unavailable, a mother would chew meat to feed her baby), if one were to follow the first reason, one need not wait six hours before eating dairy. According to the second reason, however, the six hour respite is required since meat may have lodged between the teeth.
- ☐ If one finds meat lodged between his teeth after waiting six hours, he must remove that meat before eating dairy, according to the first reason. Those that follow that theory do not acknowledge that meat will decay in the mouth over a six-hour period. If, however, we assume that the purpose of waiting six hours is to allow the meat to decay, apparently, meat remaining in the mouth for six hours is no longer considered meat. Thus, one may eat dairy without removing the meat.[57]

8) The practical *halachah*:
Poskim rule that one should follow both theories. Thus, the following rules apply:

   a) One who merely chews meat:

---

spilling its contents to the floor. Seeing this, the *Chasam Sofer* remarked, "apparently, in heaven they do not accept my ruling." See *Piskei Teshuvah* (Pietrokov 1937) ch. 285, who cites a lenient opinion regarding this question.

55. *Rashi: Chullin* 105a.

56. *Rambam* 9:28.

57. See *Tur* 98.

Even one who merely chews meat without swallowing may not eat dairy before six hours.[58] Even one who did not chew actual meat but rather food cooked with meat fat must wait six hours before eating dairy.[59]

b) One who merely tastes:
One who merely tastes meat with his tongue and immediately removes it from his mouth, need not wait six hours.[60] Thus, one who wishes to follow the commendable custom of tasting *Shabbos* food before *Shabbos*, but wishes to eat dairy afterwards, should taste with the tongue only.

c) One who swallows a meat vitamin:
One who swallows a meat vitamin may drink milk immediately afterwards since the reasons cited above do not apply.[61]

d) Meat found between one's teeth:
One who finds meat lodged between his teeth even after six hours must remove it[62] and clean[63] and rinse his mouth[64] before eating dairy. It is unnecessary to wait an additional six hours.[65]

e) Dentures:
One who uses dentures may treat them as regular teeth regarding the *halachos* of *basar b'chalav*. It is

---

58. *Y.D.* 89:1. See *Aruch HaShulchan* that in this case one who cleans his teeth thoroughly need not wait six hours.

59. Although in this case one need not be concerned with meat lodged between the teeth, nevertheless, one should not differentiate (*M.Z.* §1).

60. *D.T.* §10, *Aruch HaShulchan* §14. He must nevertheless clean and rinse out his mouth.

61. The custom to refrain from dairy after meat in all circumstances applies to eaten food, not to swallowed vitamins (*Igros Moshe: Y.D.* 2:26). *Igros Moshe* differentiates between this and one who swallows meat. One who swallows meat, even without chewing, must wait six hours since meat is usually chewed. Vitamins, however, are generally not chewed.

62. *Y.D.* 89:1.

63. By eating *parve* bulky food *Shach* §4.

64. *Rema* 89:1.

65. *Shach* §3. See gloss to *Y.D.* by *Haflaah* who contends that if the meat found between the teeth was swallowed, not removed, an additional six hours are required. He notes, however, that common custom is not to wait six hours even in that case.

unnecessary to kasher the dentures from meat to dairy since food placed in the mouth is certainly not *yad soledes bo*.[66]

9) Which meat foods require the six-hour respite?

a) Foods cooked with meat:
One who ate *parve* foods cooked with meat (but eats no actual meat),[67] meat gravy[68] or even clear meat or chicken broth[69] may not eat dairy before the conclusion of six hours.[70] One may not even eat *parve* foods cooked with dairy before the conclusion of the six hours.[71] The accepted custom is to wait six hours in all these cases even though neither of the aforementioned reasons apply. Thus, one who eats a potato from the *Shabbos* chulent (that contained meat) must wait six hours before partaking of dairy.

b) Foods cooked in a meat pot:
Parve foods cooked in a meat pot without meat, present two questions: i) May one eat dairy immediately **after** eating the *parve* food or must one wait six hours? ii) May one eat dairy **together** with the *parve* food?

i) Eating dairy afterwards:
One who eats *parve* food that was cooked in a meat pot without any meat need not wait six hours before eating dairy.[72] This is true regardless of whether or

---

66. See responsa *Maharsham* 1:197, *D.T.* 89:11, *Igros Moshe: O.C.* 1:5, *Yabia Omer: O.C.* 3:24, *Yechaveh Daas* 1:8, *Tzitz Eliezer* 9:25. *Maharsham* does require that dentures be *kashered* for *Pesach* by pouring boiling water over them. *D.T.* cites an opinion that it is proper to keep separate sets of dentures one for meat and one for dairy.

67. This case differs from that noted above. In this case one ate no meat or meat gravy, only foods that absorbed taste from meat. In the event that the meat was less than a sixtieth of the *parve* food its taste is certainly insignificant and can be disregarded.

68. See *Taz* §5, who cites a difference of opinion regarding meat gravy. *M.Z.* §5 notes that one who treats meat gravy as meat is praiseworthy. According to the opinions cited below regarding chicken broth, one should certainly wait six hours after eating meat gravy.

69. *Kaf HaChaim* 89:52,53.

70. *Rema* 89:3.

71. *Yad Avraham* citing *Maharshal*. See also *Kaf HaChaim* 89:56 for dissenting opinions. He notes, however, that the custom is to be stringent in this question.

72. *Rema* 89:3. Cleaning the mouth or hands is likewise unnecessary (*Kaf HaChaim* §61).

not the pot is well scrubbed. Any slight meat residue is certainly negligible and therefore *batel*.[73] Even one who eats sharp food cooked in a meat pot is not required to wait six hours.[74]

ii) Eating dairy with the *parve* food:
We noted earlier that a taste imbedded in a pot for twenty four hours becomes stale and can no longer affect food cooked in that pot. Thus the question of whether one may eat dairy with the *parve* food depends upon whether or not the pot is a *ben-yomo*, i.e., it was used for hot meat during the previous twenty four hours. A comprehensive discussion of this topic can be found in Chapter Six and Chapter Nine, Section II. A short summary follows:

□ A *ben-yomo* pot:
According to *Ashkenazic* tradition, one may not eat dairy with a *parve* food that was cooked in a meat pot. This is true even if the pot was thoroughly washed.[75] Nevertheless, one may put the food on a dairy dish even while hot.[76]

□ A non-*ben-yomo* pot:
If, however, the meat pot was not used for hot meat during the previous twenty four hours, one may eat the *parve* food with dairy.[77] Nevertheless, one should not cook *parve* food in a non *ben-yomo* meat pot if he plans to eat the food with dairy.[78] However, one who has no suitable *parve* or dairy pot may use a non-*ben-yomo* meat pot.[79]

---

73. *Shach* 89:19.

74. *R' Akiva Eger* cited in *D.T.* 89:42.

75. *Rema* 95:2. Although we previously learnt that *nat-bar-nat* is permitted, nevertheless, initially, one should not rely on this leniency (ibid.). In the opinion of the *Shulchan Aruch* 95:1, however, one may eat the food together with dairy.

76. *Rema* ibid.

77. *Rema* ibid.

78. *Chochmas Adam* 48:2. See *Biur HaGra* 95:10, who seems to permit using a non *ben-yomo* pot. The wording of *Issur V'heter* 34:6 and *Rema* (ibid.) seem to support *Chochmas Adam's* view.

79. Ibid. *Chochmas Adam* implies that if one is able to borrow a *parve* pot, he is required to do so.

□ Sharp foods cooked in a meat pot:
We noted in Chapter Three, Seciton II,B that sharp foods have the ability to revitalize a stale taste. Thus, the previous lenient *halachah* regarding a non-*ben-yomo* pot does not apply to sharp foods.[80]

c) Foods cut with a meat knife:
The *halachos* regarding food cut with a meat knife are complex. The rules vary depending upon whether the food is hot or cold and whether or not the knife is used to cut sharp foods. These are discussed at length in Chapter Twelve.

10) Which foods may not be eaten after meat?

a) Foods cooked with dairy:
Many *Poskim* note that common custom is to refrain from eating *parve* foods cooked with dairy within six hours of eating even foods merely cooked with meat.[81]

b) Foods cooked in a dairy pot:

□ Bland foods:
Bland *parve* foods cooked in a dairy pot may be eaten immediately after meat.

□ Sharp foods:
One must wait six hours after eating meat before eating sharp foods cooked in a dairy pot or cut with a dairy knife.[82]

Summary of Section A

☙ The almost universally accepted tradition among Jews is to wait six hours before eating dairy after meat. Dutch Jews have the custom of eating dairy after reciting a *b'rachah acharonah*, waiting only one hour and cleaning the mouth, while German Jews wait only three hours after eating meat. One whose tradition is to wait six hours may not change his custom for a

80. *Rema* ibid.

81. *R' Akiva Eger*, gloss to 89:3 citing *Maharshal*. See also *Yad Yehudah* §27k and *Kaf HaChaim* §57.

82. *Pri Migadim: O.C., A.A.* 494:6, cited in *D.T.* 89:42. See, however, *Yad Yehudah* 89:5a, who is lenient in the event that the pot was not *ben-yomo*.

more lenient one. Nevertheless, the custom may be disregarded in the following circumstances:

- ☐ One suffering from an ailment (or a nursing woman) that requires him to eat dairy foods often, may eat dairy after waiting one hour, reciting a *b'rachah acharonah* on the meat and cleansing his mouth.
- ☐ One need not wait six hours when feeding a baby approximately three years or younger. A child older than approximately three years should wait an hour, if possible, before eating dairy. A child above the approximate age of six should wait six hours after eating meat, unless the child requires milk or thirsts for milk. A nine or ten year old child should be treated as an adult.
- ☐ One who in error recites a *b'rachah rishonah* over milk during the six-hour interval should partake of a bit of milk providing that one hour has passed.

☙ *Poskim* note that one must wait six full hours from the time one stopped eating meat. Some have the custom to wait only five and one half hours or only five hours. Some authorities permit one to approximate the passage of six hours, while others require that one be certain that six hours have passed.

☙ *Rishonim* present two reasons for the six-hour interlude; a) meat leaves a fatty residue in the throat and palate for a period of six hours. b) particles of meat may remain lodged between the teeth. After six hours have passed, the fatty residue has been dissolved by saliva and any remaining meat particles have been decomposed by salivic acids and no longer considered meat.

☙ Even one who merely chews meat (or food cooked with meat fat) without swallowing may not eat dairy before six hours. One who merely tastes meat with his tongue and immediately removes it from his mouth, is not required to wait six hours. One who swallows a meat vitamin may drink milk immediately afterwards.

☙ One who ate *parve* foods cooked with meat or one who eats clear meat or chicken broth may not eat dairy (or even eat *parve* foods cooked with dairy) before the conclusion of six hours.

- One who ate *parve* food that was cooked in a clean meat pot (even if it was not scrubbed well) is not required to wait six hours before eating dairy.
- According to *Ashkenazic* tradition, one may not eat dairy with a *parve* food that was cooked in a clean meat pot unless the meat pot was not *ben-yomo* from meat use. One should not initially cook *parve* food in a non *ben-yomo* meat pot if he plans to eat the food with dairy unless he has no other suitable pot.

B. Eating meat after dairy

As noted above, there are two reasons given for the six-hour interval between eating meat and dairy. However, one who eats dairy need not wait six hours prior to eating meat. Dairy foods do not leave a fatty residue in the throat and palate nor do they remain lodged between the teeth. Nevertheless, one may not eat meat immediately after dairy without the following preparations:

1) After drinking milk:
One who drank milk and wishes to eat meat should rinse out his mouth to wash away any milk residue.[83] Some authorities require that one recite a *b'rachah acharonah* over the milk prior to eating meat.[84] The purpose of this is to separate the milk and meat into two meals. Many have the custom to wait one half an hour between the two.[85]

2) After eating cheese:
One who eats cheese must do all the above. In addition, since cheese adheres to other surfaces, he must eat[86] solid food[87] to

---

83. Wiping one's mouth and washing one's hands is unnecessary. *D.T.* 89:31 citing *Reshash: Chullin* 103:2.

84. *Magen Avraham* 494:6 rules that a *b'rachah acharonah* is not required, while *Darcei Teshuvah* 89:14 cites many authorities who do require it. This is also the opinion of *Maharsham* 3:126. See note no. 27 above.

85. This is based on the *Zohar* cited above who prohibits eating meat and milk within the same hour (see *Maharshal, Yam Shel Shlomo: Chullin* 8:6). This custom assumes that the hour mentioned is an approximation.

86. See *Kaf HaChaim* §39, who cites a difference of opinion whether or not one must swallow the food or merely chew (and discard) it.

87. With the exception of: flour, dates and green vegetables.

clean his mouth[88] and he must wash his hands[89] to cleanse them of any cheese adhering to them.[90]

3) After eating "hard" cheese:
One who eats "hard" cheese must wait six hours before eating meat.[91] "Hard" cheese is defined as cheese that has aged for six months.[92] This cheese leaves a fatty residue[93] and has a very strong taste that remains in the mouth for a long period.[94] Most commercial cheeses produced in this country do not possess this characteristic. However, one who eats the type of cheese commonly called "swiss cheese" or the equivalent must wait six hours before eating meat.[95] One who eats "hard" cheese that has been melted into food (e.g., lasagna) need not wait six hours.[96]

Summary of Section B

- One who drinks milk and subsequently wishes to eat meat should rinse out his mouth. Some authorities require that he also recite a *b'rachah acharonah* over the milk beforehand.
- In addition, one who ate cheese must wash his hands and eat solid food to clean his mouth before eating meat.

---

88. *Y.D.* 89:2. One with wide spaces between his teeth or one with braces on his teeth, should clean his mouth thoroughly between eating cheese and meat (see *Maharshal, Yam Shel Shlomo: Chullin* 8:6).

89. See *S.D.* §20, who notes that even one who ate cheese with a fork should nevertheless wash his hands, even though he is not obligated to do so. See also *Bircei Yosef: Shiyurei B'rachah* §15 who notes that this is the common custom.

90. *Y.D.* 89:2. The *Shulchan Aruch* rules that if one is able to visually inspect his hands, they need not be washed. Nevertheless *Shach* §9 cites opinions and notes that common custom is to wash one's hands in any case. See *Kaf HaChaim* §45, who notes that even one who wishes to eat only fowl should wash his hands.

91. *Rema* 89:2.

92. *Shach* ibid. §15.

93. *Aruch HaShulchan* 89:11.

94. *Taz* 89:4.

95. See gloss by Rav Moshe Stern to *Pischei Halachah: Kashrus*. While many cheese varieties are available, few carry kosher certification. It is difficult to evaluate which of those varieties should be categorized as "hard cheese".

96. *Yad Yehudah* 89:30k. It would seem that this applies only to cheese melted **into** food, but if the cheese is melted **onto** food (i.e., it is still visible as a separate entity), it retains its status. Thus, one who eats cheese melted onto toast or a cheese omelette made with hard cheese is required to wait six hours before eating meat.

☙ One who eats "hard" (e.g., "swiss") cheese must wait six hours before eating meat.

III. Additional separations between meat and dairy

A. Use of utensils of one type for another

In addition to the ordinances enacted by *Chazal, poskim* mandated many additional restrictions relating to use of utensils and foods with meat and dairy. The underlying rationale of these laws is the concern that residue of meat may remain and combine with dairy (or the reverse).

1) Cutting cheese with a meat knife (and vice-versa):
One should not cut either cheese with a meat knife or meat with a dairy knife.[97] One who does either of the above must remove the surface of food and clean or perhaps *kasher* the knife. The *halachos* regarding a knife are discussed in Chapter Twelve.

2) Cutting bread with a meat or dairy knife:
One may not cut bread with a meat knife if he plans to eat that bread with a dairy meal. Conversely, one may not cut bread with a dairy knife for use with a meat meal.[98] *Poskim* were concerned that fatty residue may have remained on the knife and the residue is then transmitted to the bread.[99] Since the issue involves actual meat (or cheese) residue, no distinction is made between a *ben-yomo* or non-*ben-yomo* knife. One who must use a meat knife to cut bread for a dairy meal should do *ne'itzah* (thrusting into the ground)[100] beforehand if possible. The process of *ne'itzah* is discussed in detail in Chapter Twelve, Section III as are many other relevant *halachos*. In the event that a meat knife was used without *ne'itzah*, the cut surfaces of the bread should be scraped.[101] *Poskim* relate that the common

97. *Y.D.* 89:4.

98. *Y.D.* 89:4.

99. *Beis Yosef* ibid.

100. *Shach* 89:22, *R' Akiva Eger* ibid. The *Aruch HaShulchan* §16, and the *Chochmas Adam* 40:14, however, follow the opinion of the *Taz* 89:6, that wiping the knife thoroughly is sufficient.

101. *M.Z.* 96:14. If meat merely touched the crust of the bread, the crust need only be washed (*Pischei Teshuvah* 91:4).

custom is not to rely on *ne'itzah* but to cut bread for a dairy meal with a dairy knife only (and vice-versa).[102] *Poskim* commend the custom of punctilious individuals who keep a separate *parve* bread knife.[103]

B. Separation of meat and dairy utensils

1) The tablecloth:
One may not eat dairy on a tablecloth used for a meat meal (or the reverse)[104] since meat residue remaining on the cloth may touch the dairy food. Most authorities do not differentiate between foods eaten directly on the cloth and those eaten only on plates.[105] One need not, however, keep separate tablecloths for meat and dairy. A tablecloth used for meat may be thoroughly washed and subsequently used for dairy.[106] Nevertheless some have the custom of using separate tablecloths for each type. *Halachically*, one is permitted to eat both meat and dairy cold meals directly on the table providing that one wipes the table clean.[107] Similarly, a plastic tablecloth may be wiped and cleaned of any residue and reused for dairy. Nevertheless, common custom is not to eat meat and dairy on the same table or plastic tablecloth surface.[108]

2) Salt dish:
Before the advent of salt shakers, salt was usually placed on the table in a dish into which the food was dipped. Therefore, one could not use the same salt dish for both meat and dairy.[109] Today, because salt shakers are used, this reason no longer applies. Thus, it is not necessary to use separate shakers for meat

---

102. *Rema* 89:4.

103. *D.T.* 89:53.

104. *Y.D.* 89:4.

105. *Minchas Yaakov* 76:17. See, however, *Radvaz* cited in *P.T.* 89:8.

106. *Magen Avraham* 173. See *D.T.* 121:66.

107. One usually wipes a table (and a plastic tablecloth) clean between meals. Thus, we assume that it will be cleaned between meat and dairy use (see *Y.D.* 91:2). A linen (or any other material) tablecloth cannot be cleaned properly without laundering.

108. Some institutions (e.g., schools or camps) use either side of a heavy plastic tablecloth, one side for meat and one for dairy. While this may be *halachically* permitted, it is not an advisable practice.

109. See *Rema* 88:2.

and dairy. Nevertheless, since at times the shakers may touch the food or since one may have food residue on his hands when grasping the shaker, common practice is to use separate meat and dairy shakers. This is undoubtedly commendable in a household with children.

3) Tableware:
All flatware and dishes (and pots) used for meat food should be conspicuously different than those used for dairy. One using similar dishes for both is likely to mix the two and use meat dishes for dairy.[110] One may, however, use similar dishes if he clearly marks those that are dairy. This may be done with indelible paint or an indentation in the metal itself. Although marking the meat dishes instead is equally effective, one should nevertheless follow the custom of marking the dairy dishes. A guest may see the marked flatware, assume that it is dairy (as is the custom) and use it for dairy food.[111]

C. Foods used with one type

1) Bread remaining after meat or dairy meals:
Bread that was used in the course of a meat meal should not be used for a dairy meal.[112] Bread is often handled during a meal and perhaps some meat residue on someone's hands adhered to the challah. Thus, a housewife who makes a challah kugel from the leftover *Shabbos* challah must not use that kugel for a dairy meal. Similarly, the leftover challah may not be used for a dairy *se'udah shlishis*. This refers only to sliced challah. The challah loaf itself, however, is usually not touched by all those present. Thus, the remnant of the challah loaf may be used for a dairy meal.[113] Obviously, if children do in fact touch the loaf, it must be treated as sliced challah.

---

110. *Aruch HaShulchan* 89:16.

111. *Rema* 89:4. Actually, even one who uses different types of flatware should still be concerned that a guest may confuse the meat and dairy flatware. Perhaps it is inappropriate for a guest who finds two types of flatware to use either without inquiring as to which is dairy or meat. If, however, he finds a marking on one, he has the right to assume that it is dairy. Nevertheless, see *D.T.* §54 who cites an opinion that one should always mark the dairy utensils even if they differ from the meat utensils.

112. *Y.D.* 89:4.

113. *Igros Moshe: Y.D.* 1:38.

2) Other foods eaten with a meat meal:
Poskim advise that it is preferable not to eat any food remaining from a meat meal (e.g., salads) with a dairy meal.[114] Often the spoon used to serve the salad touches the meat and is subsequently replaced into the salad.

3) Ketchup and mustard:
Similarly, it is commendable to use separate ketchup and mustard containers for meat and dairy. One who wishes to use only one container should, at least, use squeeze type bottles.[115] Glass jars or the spoon used with them are more likely to touch the plate and thus the food.

D. The prohibition of dairy breads

These *halachos* are based on *Tur* and *Shulchan Aruch; Yoreh De'ah* 97.

Among the Talmudic[116] ordinances regarding *basar b'chalav* is the prohibition of dairy bread. One may not add milk to the dough of any bread regardless of whether one plans to eat it with dairy or alone.[117] Bread is the mainstay of all meals;[118] therefore, *Chazal* were concerned that dairy bread may inadvertently be eaten with a meat meal. Conversely, one may not knead a bread with meat gravy lest it be eaten with dairy.[119] As befitting a prohibition of this magnitude, *Chazal* ruled that a bread baked with milk or gravy may not be eaten even alone.[120] Since the basis of the prohibition is the concern that one may forget and eat the dairy bread with meat, the prohibition is confined to cases where that fear is warranted. Therefore, the following cases are exempt from the prohibition:

---

114. *Aruch HaShulchan* 89:15.

115. The fact that the flow of ketchup connects the bottle to the food is of no concern. Nevertheless, care must be taken that the nozzle of the plastic bottle should not touch the food or even the plate.

116. *Pesachim* 30a.

117. *Y.D.* 97:1. Initially, one should not add even a minute amount of milk that will become *batel b'shishim* (see *Kaf HaChaim* 97:6).

118. *S.D.* 97:1.

119. *Aruch HaShulchan* 97:3. See *S.D.* §1, who contends that one may not even knead a bread with goose fat (which is not Biblically prohibited with milk).

120. *Y.D.* ibid.

1) A small amount of bread:
   One may bake a small amount of dairy bread. A "small amount" is defined as the amount eaten in the course of that day.[121] One may bake even a large amount of dairy bread for many people if the bread will be eaten on the same day.[122]
2) Bread baked in a special form:
   One may bake even a large amount of dairy bread if he shapes it in an unusual manner.[123] The peculiar form of the bread will serve as a reminder that the bread is dairy.[124]

   These exemptions pertain only if they were in effect at the time of baking. If, however, one bakes a large amount of dairy bread to be eaten over a longer period of time and subsequently divides it among many families, the bread is forbidden. Similarly, one cannot put a mark on dairy bread after it is baked. In either case, the prohibition that was brought about at the time of baking remains in effect.[125]
3) Breads not to be eaten in the course of a meal:
   One may bake dairy breads if those breads are of a type that is

---

121. See *S.D.* 97:1, who notes that the *Shulchan Aruch* seems to imply that a "small amount" is that which is eaten at one time. He cites, however, the opinion of *Rema (Toras Chatas)* that anything eaten in the same day is considered a small amount. It seems from *S.D.* that the bread must be eaten before the following morning. However, *Aruch HaShulchan* 97:4, contends that one may bake an amount that will be eaten in the following twenty-four hours. He proves this from the ruling of the *Rema* that one may bake meat breads for the *Shabbos* meals. This proof is disputable, perhaps one can argue that since one does not eat dairy meals on *Shabbos* there is no reason to be concerned that the challah will be eaten with a dairy meal. On the contrary, *Yad Yehudah* §8a, contends that one who eats a dairy *Se'udah Shlishis* may bake challah only of the amount that will be consumed during the first two meals. This contradicts the contention of *Aruch HaShulchan*.

122. *Aruch HaShulchan* 97:4.

123. *Y.D.* 97:1. See *Pischei Teshuvah* §3 and *D.T.* §20 whether this applies to bread baked for public sale. Many authorities contend that since the consumers will not notice or not realize the purpose of the changed form, one may not bake dairy breads even for public sale. See footnote no. 132 below.

124. See *D.T.* §19, who speculates whether one must radically change the form or whether a minor change is adequate. See *Chochmas Adam* 50:3, who implies that a mere mark is sufficient. Nevertheless, it seems that the mark must last throughout the eating of the loaf. If, however, the mark is eaten first, nothing remains as a reminder that the bread is dairy.

125. *Pischei Teshuvah* 97:3 and *D.T.* §21. Conversely, if dairy came in contact with the bread after it had been baked, it may nevertheless be prohibited, see *D.T.* §7.

not eaten during a meal. Thus, muffins that are served as dessert may be baked with milk.[126] However, the muffins may not be eaten within six hours of meat.

4) Other foods that may be eaten with meat:
One should not add milk to any food or drink that may be eaten with meat or in the course of a meat meal unless it is a small amount that will be consumed that same day.[127]

5) Some practical applications of these *halachos:*
   a) One may bake a dairy loaf to be eaten during the dairy meal of the first day of *Shavuos*.[128]
   b) One may bake a challah with meat gravy if that challah is of the amount that will be consumed during the meat meals of *Shabbos*.[129]
   c) One may bake a dairy bread if it is baked in a unique form that will serve as a reminder that the loaf should not be eaten with meat.
   d) One may bake pastries and fruit danishes with milk since these are eaten only after a meal.
   e) One may certainly bake cheese cake or danishes since, in addition to the factor mentioned above, they are visibly dairy and will not be eaten with meat.[130]
   f) Similarly, meat pies or any bread that obviously contains meat or gravy may be baked and eaten.[131]
   g) One may not, however, bake pastries with a meat dough if the meat or gravy is not clearly visible. One may inadvertently eat these pastries as dessert with coffee.

---

126. *Pischei Teshuvah* §3, citing *Maharit, Chochmas Adam* 50:3. One need not be concerned that one may inadvertently eat them within six hours of eating meat. We are not empowered to add to the prohibition of *Chazal* which concerns only those breads eaten with meat (see *Sidei Chemed* vol 5, p. 289). See, however, *Yad Yehudah* 97:6a, 3k, cited in *D.T.* §14, who disagrees.

127. If the foods will be eaten only **after** the meat meal but during the six hours following the meal milk may be added *(D.T.* §1).

128. *Rema* 97:1. One may not, however, bake for both days of *Yom Tov (D.T.* §33).

129. *Rema* ibid. As noted above (footnote no. 121), if one eats a dairy *Se'udah Shlishis,* the challah must be of the amount that will be consumed during the first two meals (see *Yad Yehudah* §8a, *D.T.* §34).

130. *Aruch HaShulchan* 97:5.

131. *S.D.* 97:1.

h) One who errs and bakes a large dairy bread may not divide it among many households since it was not originally baked to be eaten in one day.

i) Similarly, one may not bake a dairy bread and affix a sticker or put it in a wrapper that identifies the bread as dairy.[132]

j) One should not bake bread while meat is being roasted in the same oven. One who bakes bread in this manner should consult a *moreh hora'ah* as to whether the bread may be eaten.[133]

CHART 14

THE PROHIBITION OF DAIRY BREADS

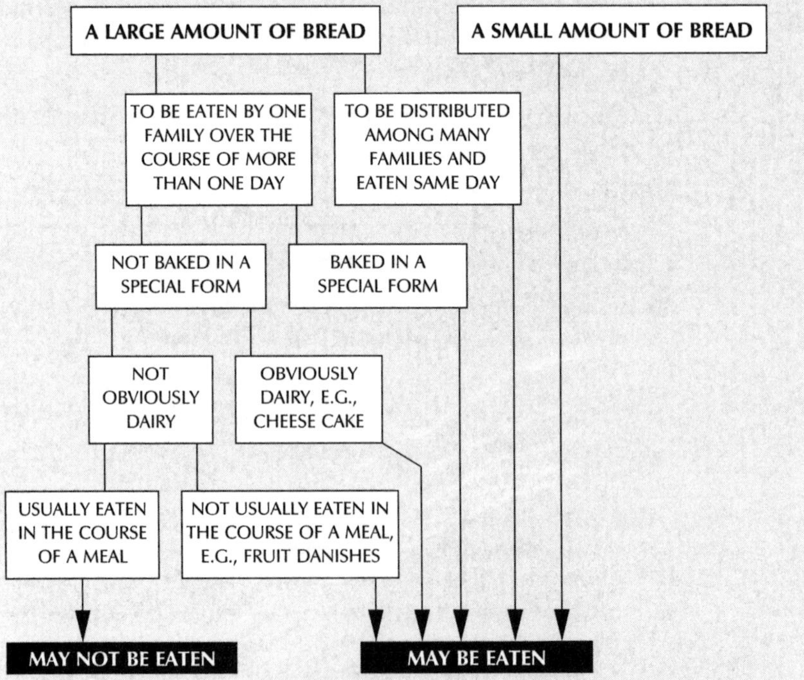

132. This leads one to question the propriety of marketing dairy breads. We noted above (footnote no. 123) the hesitation of *Poskim* to apply this rule to breads baked for public consumption. In addition, these breads are not baked in an unusual shape; rather, the wrapper identifies them as dairy. As mentioned above, this is insufficient. This being the case, one should not purchase dairy breads even if baked under kosher supervision.

133. See *Y.D.* 97:3, *Rema* 108:1, *Shach* 108:11.

k) One who warms the *Shabbos* challos by putting them in the oven or on the *blech* shortly before *Shabbos* should avoid putting them in a spot where they may come into contact with meat gravy. Challos that do come into contact with meat gravy may not be eaten.[134] A *moreh hora'ah* should be consulted.

E. Kashering utensils from meat to dairy use

Ashkenazic custom[135] prohibits *kashering* utensils from meat to dairy use or the reverse. *Poskim* were concerned that one may use one set of pots or tableware and regularly *kasher* it from one type to the other. One who does so will inevitably once forget to *kasher* and use dairy dishes for meat or the reverse.[136] The following cases are exceptions to this rule:

1) Dishes *kashered* for *Pesach*:
One who *kashers* dishes for *Pesach* use may then change them from one type to the other. The *kashering* is for *Pesach* purposes and not in violation of the custom.[137]

2) *Kashering treif* dishes:
Similarly, if a vessel becomes *treif*, it may be changed from one type to another once it is *kashered*. Indeed, one who wishes to *kasher* a vessel from meat to dairy may make the vessel *treif* so as to enable it to be *kashered* from meat to dairy.[138]

3) *Kashering* to *parve* status:
One may *kasher* a meat pot for *parve* use. After the pot has been used for a while as *parve*, one may decide to use it for dairy.[139]

---

134. *Rema* 97:1. See, however, *Aruch HaShulchan* 97:4, who contends that *Shabbos challos* are considered a "small amount" since they will be consumed within twenty-four hours. Although we questioned this ruling in footnote no. 121 above, a challah placed in the oven before the Friday night meal is usually consumed during that meal. Thus, perhaps the challah may be used.

135. *Sefardic* custom, however, permits *kashering* from one use to another, see *Kaf HaChaim: O.C.* 509:45.

136. *Magen Avraham* 509:11. See, however, *Pri Chadash* 97:1 who contends that we are not empowered to institute new regulations. See *D.T.* 121:59.

137. *Chasam Sofer: Y.D.* 110 (cited in *Mishnah B'rurah* 451:19).

138. *Pri Migadim: O.C., A.A.* 451:11, see also *D.T.* 121:59.

139. Responsa *Maharsham* 2:241, see *D.T.* ibid.

4) Utensils unused for a year:
   A pot unused for a year may be *kashered* from one type to another.[140]

5) *Kashering* with *libun:*
   One may *kasher* from meat to dairy using the *libun* process (*kashering* in direct fire until the vessel becomes red-hot).[141]

6) Selling or receiving a vessel:
   One selling a vessel may *kasher* from one type to another.[142] Similarly, one receiving a pot as a gift may *kasher* it from one use to another.[143]

7) One who is unaware of the custom:
   One who is unaware of the custom and *kashered* a meat pot and used it for dairy may eat the dairy food.[144]

While all the above exceptions may seem, at first glance, to be evasions of the custom, they are consistent with its logic. The purpose of the custom was to avoid repeated *kashering* from one type to the other; these cases do not lend themselves to repetition. Furthermore, since this rule is merely a custom, these variations are not contradictory to the basic custom.

Summary of Section III

- One should not cut either cheese with a meat knife or meat with a dairy knife. One may not even cut bread for a dairy meal with a meat knife (or the reverse) unless he does *ne'itzah* beforehand. Common custom is to cut bread for a dairy meal with a dairy knife only (and vice-versa). Punctilious individuals keep a separate *parve* bread knife.
- Cut bread that remains from a meat meal should not be used for a dairy meal. The remaining loaf may be used for a dairy meal providing that it was not touched by children during the course of the meal.
- One may not eat dairy on a tablecloth used for a meat meal (or

140. *Maharsham* ibid.

141. *Maharsham* ibid. citing *Shaar HaMelech*. See also *D.T.* 121:59, *Be'er Moshe* 3:105.

142. *Shelah* cited in *Maharsham* ibid. Apparently, one purchasing a vessel may *kasher* it as well.

143. *Be'er Moshe* 3:105.

144. *Maharsham* 2:241. Presumably, the pot may now be used for dairy.

the reverse). The tablecloth should be thoroughly washed between opposite uses. Some have the custom of using separate tablecloths for each type.

- ☙ It is preferable not to eat any food remaining from a meat meal (e.g., salads) with a dairy meal. Common practice is to use separate meat and dairy salt shakers. It is commendable to use separate ketchup and mustard containers for meat and dairy. All flatware and dishes (and pots) used for meat food should be conspicuously different than those used for dairy. If the utensils are similar, common custom is to place a differentiating mark on the dairy dishes.
- ☙ One may not add milk to the dough of any bread regardless of whether one plans to eat it with dairy or alone. Similarly, one may not knead a bread with meat gravy lest it be eaten with dairy. One may, however, bake a small amount of dairy bread that will be eaten in one day. One may also bake even a large amount of dairy bread if it is shaped in an unusual manner. Pastries that are served only as dessert, not with the meal itself, may be baked with milk.
- ☙ *Ashkenazic* custom prohibits *kashering* utensils from meat to dairy use or the reverse. One may *kasher* dishes for *Pesach* and then change them from one type to the other. Similarly, a *treif* vessel may be changed from one type to another once it is *kashered*. One may also *kasher* a meat pot for *parve* use. A pot unused for a year may be *kashered* from one type to another.

CHAPTER NINE

Avoiding Basar B'chalav Problems While Cooking

- □ Using one oven for both meat and dairy.
- □ Kashering an oven from one use to another.
- □ Microwave ovens.
- □ Use of a stove top for both meat and dairy.
- □ Use of a pot of one type for foods to be eaten with another.

I. Use of an oven and stove for both meat and dairy foods

One of the most common problems of *basar b'chalav* is use of one oven for both meat and dairy foods. Surely, one should make every effort to acquire two separate ovens for meat and dairy use if possible. Many individuals invest significant sums to modernize their kitchens and equip then with every modern convenience and gadget but omit this most worthwhile investment. Nevertheless, many families are limited to one oven that must be used for both meat and dairy foods. It is therefore imperative that the *halachos* pertaining to oven use be examined most carefully.

A. The problems of basar b'chalav encountered in oven use

Use of an oven for both meat and dairy presents three problems: a) The meat may come in direct contact with dairy. b) The issue of *reicha* — aroma. When two foods are baked or roasted simultaneously in an oven, they absorb aroma from one another. c) The problem of *zeiah* — steam. When liquid is cooked in an oven, steam is emitted. This steam carries the taste of the food to other foods and to the oven as well.

1) The problem of contact:
One may certainly not place meat and dairy foods in an oven so that they touch one another.[1] Two foods that touch while roasting absorb taste from one another. This may result in either the entire food or part thereof becoming prohibited.[2] In addition, the foods must not be placed in a manner that gravy or melted cheese reach food of the other type. Thus, they may not both be placed on the oven floor if gravy can spread from one to another.[3] It is definitely prohibited to place meat above dairy (or the reverse) while they bake in the oven if there is a possibility that they may drip onto one another. One must, in addition, place the foods in a manner that they not splatter onto one another. After all these precautions have been taken, we

1. *Y.D.* 108:1.

2. See *Y.D.* 105:4,5.

3. See *Rema* 97:1.

must yet contend with two additional serious problems.

2) The problem of *reicha*:

Cooking meat and dairy simultaneously in an oven causes the meat and dairy to emit aromas that are absorbed into one another.[4] The reader is referred to Chapter Five, Section II,C where the issue of *reicha* is discussed at length. To summarize: essentially the *halachah* follows the view that one should avoid any possibility of aroma being imparted from non-kosher to kosher or from meat to dairy foods. However, *bidieved* (ex-post-facto) — in the event that kosher foods are cooked simultaneously in an oven, we assume *reicha lav milsah* (aroma is insignificant) and the food may be eaten. We will highlight a few general rules as they apply to use of an oven for meat and dairy foods.

a) One may not cause meat and dairy to absorb aroma from one another. Thus, it is prohibited to roast meat and dairy concurrently in an oven even if they do not touch one another and there is no chance of the meat gravy reaching the dairy food. The aroma of the meat is nevertheless absorbed by the dairy food (and vice versa).[5]

b) In the event that meat was baked simultaneously in an oven with dairy food, they may both be eaten. A microwave oven, however, is completely closed and poses a serious problem of *reicha*[6] (besides the problem of *zeiah*, see below), and a *moreh hora'ah* should be consulted.

c) One who baked bread simultaneously with meat may not eat that bread with dairy. If, however, no other bread is available, one may eat the bread with dairy.[7]

d) One may bake meat and dairy foods simultaneously in the oven if one of the foods is in a covered pot.[8] However, the foods should not be placed above one another.

---

4. Although the *halachic* consensus is that one need not be concerned with aroma — *reicha lav milsah*, nevertheless, one should not initially cause a problem of *reicha*.

5. *Rema* 108:1.

6. See *Rema* 108:1.

7. *Rema* ibid. Providing that he is unable to eat the bread alone or that the dairy food cannot be eaten without bread (*Kreisi U'pleisi* §6). Otherwise the situation cannot be considered *bidieved*.

8. *S.D.* 108:10. The covering should be tight enough to prevent the aroma from spreading. Thus, although the cover need not be airtight, it should be a tight fitting cover.

It should be apparent that baking meat and dairy concurrently in an oven is fraught with potential kashrus problems and should be avoided. A more relevant concern is the permissibility of baking meat and dairy consecutively, which is our next subject of discussion.

3) Baking meat and dairy foods consecutively in an oven:
You will recall our discussion (Chapter Five, Section II,D) of the problem of *zeiah* — steam emitted from foods during cooking. Nevertheless, a review of the basic concepts may be worthwhile.

   a) All foods emit steam when cooked or baked. *Halachah* considers the steam of any liquid to have the status of that food. Thus, steam of milk that condenses into water is milk, while steam of meat gravy is meat.

   b) In the opinion of some authorities, this applies to liquids only. Most *Poskim* reject this view; thus, even steam emitted by foods (i.e., melted butter or gravy) has the *halachic* status of the particular food.[9]

   c) Solid foods produce a negligible amount of steam. Thus, one need not be concerned about *zeiah* when cooking solid food unless steam is visibly rising from the food.[10]

   d) Steam imparts its taste to any surface in its path. Thus, the steam rises and transfers its taste to the oven roof regardless of its distance.[11] In addition, there is the possibility of condensed steam falling back into the liquid. Some authorities[12] rule that usually one need not be concerned with this problem since, they contend, the steam usually escapes and dissipates. Nevertheless, if the cooking takes place in a confined area, we must assume that droplets of steam acquire taste from the surface and fall into the food.[13] *Poskim* assume that the common kitchen oven is a confined area that may cause condensed steam to fall back into the food.[14]

---

9. See *D.T.* 92:164, *Minchas Yitzchok* 5:20;10.

10. See *Minchas Yaakov: Toras Chatas* 35:21, *Igros Moshe*, *Y.D.* 1:40.

11. *Igros Moshe: Y.D.* 1:40.

12. See responsa *Beis Yaakov* cited in *Minchas Yitzchok* 5:20;8.

13. See *Imrei Baruch* cited in *D.T.* §165.

14. See *Igros Moshe: Y.D.* 1:40 and *Minchas Yitzchok* 5:20.

e) If a pot is covered in a manner that contains its steam, *zeiah* is of no concern.[15]

4) Lenient considerations:
The *zeiah* problem as pertaining to *basar b'chalav* is a serious matter. Whenever meat is cooked in the oven, steam is emitted which carries the taste of the meat and infuses it into the roof of the oven. When dairy is subsequently cooked in the oven, its steam rises, absorbs meat taste from the roof, condenses and falls back into the milk. The milk is now prohibited as *basar b'chalav*. Therefore, one who is able to keep separate meat and dairy ovens should surely do so.[16] There are, however, several lenient considerations as well.[17]

- ☐ Although our ovens are closed, they are vented. Thus the chance of the steam condensing may be minimal. *Poskim*, however, do not consider the vent significant.[18]
- ☐ It is far from certain that condensed steam ever drips from the oven top onto any food. In the event that droplets do fall, one may assume that the food contains sixty times their volume.[19]

In conclusion, use of an oven for consecutive meat and dairy use may present significant problems. It is therefore imperative that serious consideration be given to the proper manner in which to make use of one oven for both meat and dairy.[20]

---

15. *Rema* 92:8.

16. See responsa *Chelkas Yaakov* 2:136 who forbids use of one oven for both meat and dairy, even if one plans to heat and *kasher* the oven after each use.

17. Two additional considerations, albeit not accepted by the majority of *Poskim*, are: the doubt raised by *Rosh* himself (responsa 20:26) that perhaps the oven roof will not absorb any taste due to its extreme heat (see *Yad Yehudah* §55a, responsa *Beis Shlomo, Y.D.* 162 and *Minchas Yitzchok* 5:20;11). The opinion of responsa *Mishkanos Yaakov* 34, who disputes the assertion of the *Rosh* and maintains that steam cannot carry the taste of the food. However, as noted, *halachic* authorities do not rely on these views.

18. *Igros Moshe, Y.D.* 1:40.

19. *Igros Moshe: Y.D.* 1:40. See also responsa *Beis HaYotzer* cited in *Minchas Yitzchok* 5:20(13). In addition, the *Minchas Yitzchok* (ibid.;10) cites opinions that *zeiah* itself is a Rabbinical prohibition only.

20. See a thorough discussion of the various problems relating to oven use in *Badei HaShulchan* p. 211.

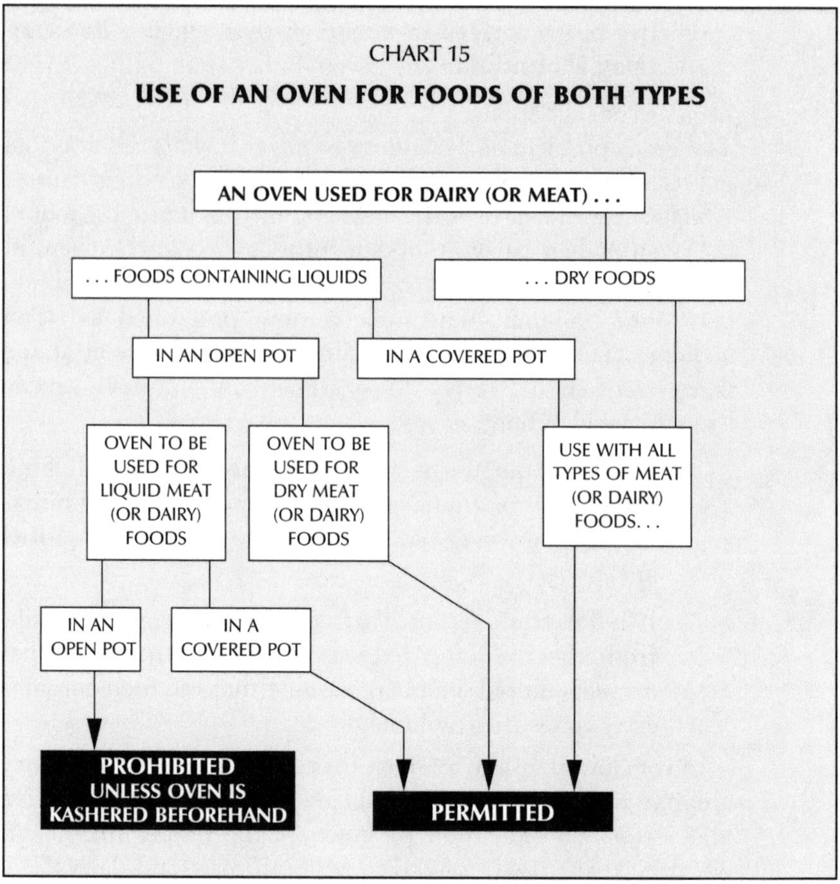

B. The proper use of an oven for both meat and dairy

Those who possess only one oven which must be used for both meat and dairy should observe the following guidelines based upon the principles set forth above.[21]

1) Determining the standard use:
One must determine which type of food is most frequently cooked in the oven. We are concerned with those foods containing liquids and cooked in an uncovered pot (dry foods or foods cooked in a covered pot present no *zeiah* problem and are of no concern). For example: one who roasts meat often in an open pot should consider meat foods as his standard use.

21. See *Igros Moshe: Y.D.* 1:59 and *Yabia Omer: Y.D.* 5:7.

One who frequently bakes cheese cakes or cheese lasagna in an open pan should assume his standard use as dairy. Once the standard use has been determined, whether meat or dairy, one may freely use the oven for both dry foods and liquids of that type, regardless of whether the pot is open or covered.

2) Use of the oven for the infrequent type:
Whenever one wishes to use the oven for a type other than that designated as the standard (or even for *parve* foods to be eaten with the other type), he must be mindful of two restrictions:
   a) The oven should be used for dry foods only. Thus, if the oven is considered dairy, one may not cook a meat roast with gravy in it.
   b) One may, however, bake challos immediately after roasting meat, providing that the oven surfaces are clean.
   c) In the event that one must cook liquid meat foods in the dairy oven, it should be done in a pot that is completely covered.

3) Broiling in the oven:
Many ovens have a broiling element at the top of the oven chamber itself. One may broil meats in the oven without being concerned about *zeiah*. Any steam produced while broiling is consumed by the flames.[22] The oven, however, must be cleaned of any meat splatters before being used for dairy. Nevertheless, it is advisable to wait twenty-four hours and *kasher* the oven in the manner described below.[23] Some ovens have a broiling chamber on bottom of the oven. This should not be used for both meat and dairy since it is extremely difficult to clean the broiler properly.

4) Use of the oven racks:
One may not place meat and dairy foods directly on the same oven shelf. The taste absorbed from one type will be transferred to the other. However, placing meat utensils on the same racks as dairy utensils poses no problem in itself. Taste cannot travel from utensil to utensil without the medium of liquid. Nevertheless, use of the same oven racks for meat and dairy pots can, at times, be problematic. Foods occasionally spill

---

22. See *Igros Moshe: Y.D.* 1:59.

23. At times, one broils foods on a lower shelf, not directly under the broiler, thus *zeiah* may travel to the oven sides.

from pots while cooking in an oven, soiling the rack. Thus, one should be concerned lest a dairy pot be placed over meat residue on the rack. Some contemporary authorities ruled that one may assume that any food residue on the rack has certainly dried and is no longer able to impart its taste to any pot placed upon it.[24] However, other authorities[25] contend that even if no meat residue is presently on the rack, dairy pots should not be placed on the rack. Contact of hot meat and dairy pots is to be avoided even when no liquid is present.[26] One who wishes to avoid any question should treat his oven racks as either meat or dairy and spread aluminum foil over the rack whenever cooking pots of the other type. Furthermore, it is advisable to spread aluminum foil under pots of all types, thereby avoiding much of the worry of food residue in the oven itself (see below).

5) Oven cleanliness:
Whenever one wishes to cook or bake in the oven, one must examine the oven to see if it is clean from any residue of the previous use. Any grease spots on the oven, even if they will not come into actual contact with dairy foods, can emit *reicha* — aroma. We noted above that meat aroma should be prevented from reaching dairy foods. One who follows our advice and spreads aluminum foil under all foods has avoided much, but not all, of the problem. Gravy may yet splatter on oven walls, and must be removed before cooking dairy foods.

6) A two chambered oven:
One who owns a two chambered oven should set aside one for meat and one for dairy. One may bake meat and dairy simultaneously in their respective ovens since the steam of one cannot travel to the other. The fact that the heat travels from one oven to another is irrelevant since the wall between the ovens is composed of two separate metal sheets. Taste cannot travel from one surface to another without a liquid medium.

---

24. See *Igros Moshe: Y.D.* 1:40.

25. *Minchas Yitzchok* 5:20.

26. See *Rema* 92:8 and *Taz* 97:3. See Chapter Eleven, Section D.

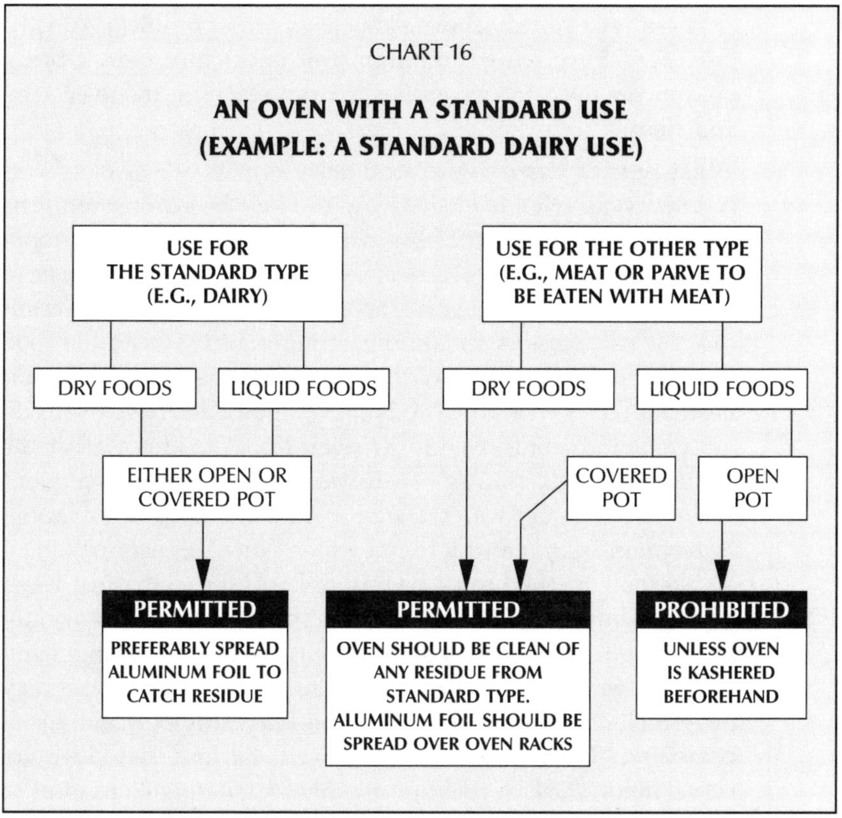

C. Kashering an oven from meat to dairy use

The procedure described above will avoid most of the potential problems for one who must cook meat and dairy in the same oven. There will be instances, however, where the procedure may be difficult to follow. For example, one whose standard oven use is for meat but wishes to bake a cheese cake. Cheese cake is normally baked in an open pan. According to the guidelines set above, the cheese cake cannot be baked in the oven. There are, however, opinions that permit the oven to be *kashered* from one use to the other. Nevertheless, there are several difficulties regarding the *kashering* of ovens.

1) Grease spots:
   We noted above that oven walls may be coated with grease and fat spots. One can neither bake in nor *kasher* an oven for dairy use so long as grease remains on the oven floor or sides. The oven must, therefore, first be thoroughly cleaned with a caustic

cleanser. As noted above, much of this problem can be prevented by placing aluminum foil under any utensil being used in the oven to prevent spills from reaching the oven rack and floor.

2) What type of *kashering* is required:
Normally, an oven is *kashered* with *libun* — heating until the metal becomes red hot. This is accomplished with a blow torch and is certainly not a practical solution for one who wishes to bake a cheese cake. However, actual *libun* is not required in our case for two reasons: a) *Libun* is required only where the food comes into direct contact with the surface to be *kashered* and is heated directly with fire. Foods cooked in modern day ovens do not come into contact with the oven floor or sides. Rather the contact is merely through steam reaching the oven top. Since steam is essentially water, the proper *kashering* process should be *hagalah* — immersing in hot water. Since this is impossible[27] an alternate method must be found. *Poskim* rule that the lesser level of *libun* known as *libun kal* is the equivalent of *hagalah*. b) Even if one must contend with grease drippings and splatterings as is common in an oven, the oven may nevertheless be *kashered* with *libun kal*. Although the grease comes into direct contact with the oven wall and should require actual *libun*, *Poskim* rule that a case of *kashering* from meat to dairy (or the reverse) is considered *heteira balah* (see above Chapter Seven, Section I,A), thus mere *hagalah*[28] or *libun kal*[29] is sufficient.

Accordingly, after the oven has been thoroughly cleaned with a caustic cleaner, it may be *kashered* with *libun kal*. *Libun kal* is accomplished by heating the vessel to be *kashered* until it

27. In actuality, a type of *hagalah* can be done. Since the taste was transferred by steam, it would suffice to replicate the very same process, i.e., to fill the oven with steam which will remove any taste absorbed in the oven roof. *Poskim* rule that a vessel that absorbed taste through steam can be *kashered* with steam (*M.Z.* 94:1, citing *Pri Chadash*). Nevertheless, even this solution is flawed. Besides the meat taste absorbed into the oven with steam, one must contend with taste absorbed by splattering as well. This must be removed through actual *hagalah* in boiling water, not mere steam. Nevertheless, see responsa *Minchas Yitzchok* 5:20(15), who advises that in addition to the *libun kal* one should, at the same time, place a bowl of water in the oven thereby *kashering* with steam as well.

28. *Shach* 121:8, and gloss of *R' Akiva Eger* (ibid.).

29. *O.C.* 509:4.

becomes hot enough to char a straw placed upon it. It is commonly accepted that heating an oven on its highest temperature for an hour accomplishes *libun kal*.

3) The objections to *kashering* ovens:
Several objections have been raised with regard to *kashering* an oven in the manner described above. a) Most ovens today are enamel coated. *Poskim* assume that enamel is a clay substance which cannot be kashered. b) *Libun* is effective only if the heat is applied to the surface through which the taste was absorbed into the vessel. Thus, since many ovens have the heat source in a chamber below the baking chamber, *libun* is ineffective.[30] c) We noted above that our custom is not to *kasher* from meat use to dairy and the reverse. The reason for this custom is to prevent one from using one vessel for both meat and dairy use through successive *kashering*. Authorities were concerned that one may forget to *kasher*. Using one oven by relying on regular *kashering* seems to be exactly what the custom tried to prevent.[31]

4) Self-cleaning ovens:
Many contemporary *morei hora'ah* sanction the use of a self-cleaning oven and its being repeatedly *kashered* from one type to another.[32] This view is, however, questioned by some authorities.[33] One who follows the lenient view is not required to clean the oven surface with a caustic cleanser since the heat of the self-cleaning cycle burns away any grease splatter.

One should note that this discussion pertains to self-cleaning ovens only. Continuous cleaning ovens are not *kashered* through normal use and may be impossible to *kasher*. A *moreh hora'ah* should be consulted.

5) In conclusion:
Many authorities advise that one should avoid *kashering* an

---

30. *Pri Migadim: O.C., A.A.* 451:44, *Beis Shlomo* 2:164.

31. The rationale to be lenient on this issue is because perhaps, since the transfer of taste is not certain (as explained above), one is not bound by the custom. In addition, the *kashering* process used is *libun* which is not party to the custom, see *Minchas Yitzchok* 5:20;16.

32. A self-cleaning oven has the heat source in the baking chamber itself. This is a definite advantage regarding the efficacy of *kashering*, see *Minchas Yitzchok* 5:20(14). In addition, the high heat generated by the oven may qualify as real *libun*, which is effective even for earthenware.

33. Although a self-cleaning oven reaches heat in excess of 1,000 degrees, it may not attain sufficient heat to qualify as actual *libun*.

oven. However, common custom is to rely on heating an oven in the manner described above.[34] One who uses one oven for meat and dairy should try to acquire a self-cleaning oven (even though some question its effectiveness as well). Nevertheless, one who has no self-cleaning oven and must cook both meat and dairy food that produce steam, in open pots, should follow the following procedure:[35]

a) The oven must be free of any splatters or grease spots. Lining the racks with aluminum foil while cooking, as recommended above, makes the later task of cleaning the oven easier.

b) One should wait twenty-four hours to ensure that the oven is no longer a *ben-yomo* from any absorbed taste.

c) The oven should be heated at the highest setting for a period of one hour to effect *libun kal*.

D. Microwave ovens

A microwave oven is essentially different than other ovens. Gas and electric ovens produce heat which is transmitted to the food. A microwave oven works in the reverse: the food is heated and in turn heats the area surrounding it. Despite this distinction, a microwave oven

---

34. A justification to ignore the porcelain problem may lie in the fact that *Poskim* have never definitely ruled that porcelain is clay, they merely questioned that it may be a clay type substance. According to information furnished to the author by Porcelain Industries of Nashville Tennessee, porcelain enameling used today is basically a glass substance (although it contains some clay as well) that is completely non-porous. Thus, although some question remains as to the status of this porcelain, since the transfer of taste is also not firmly established, perhaps one may take a more lenient position with regard to *kashering*. The objection to *kashering* with an outside heat source is also subject to dispute, see *Maharsham* 3:208 and *Yad Yehudah* 97:13a. See also *Minchas Yitzchok* 5:20(17). The objection to *kashering* from meat to dairy as being contrary to *Ashkenazic* custom may not apply to *kashering* through *libun* (see Chapter Eight, Section III,C). Thus, even *kashering* with *libun kal* may be acceptable (see *Maharsham* 2:241, who contends that the objection to *kashering* from meat to dairy is based on the concern that one may *kasher* even *ben-yomo* utensils. Thus, since one may *kasher ben-yomo* utensils with *libun* and *libun kal*, they should be exempt from the custom).

35. This is based upon the rulings of Rav Moshe Stern in appendix to *Pischei Halachah*. He requires the oven to be heated for a length of one and a half hours. However, it seems that since the oven is on a thermostat, the heat will not rise significantly with this additional time. Rav Stern is more lenient for one who wishes to cook *parve* after meat or dairy. He contends that either waiting twenty-four hours or heating the oven is sufficient.

shares the problems of other ovens. Foods may come in contact with residue of other foods if the oven surface is not clean. Two foods cooked simultaneously can absorb aroma *(reicha)* from one another. In addition, the most prevalent issue, a microwave may cause foods to absorb taste through steam — *zeiah*. Foods steam quite quickly in a microwave oven (indeed, the moisture in the foods is the first thing to heat). The steam rises and visibly condenses into droplets on the top of the oven. The concern that these droplets will subsequently fall onto the food is genuine. The question of whether a microwave oven effects actual *bishul* is moot for this purpose. Our concern is with *zeiah*, regardless of its source. One distinction, however, between a microwave and other ovens is the fact that the wall of the oven generates no heat; rather, all heat is derived from the food itself. Thus, the steam reaching the top of the oven is often no longer hot. Nevertheless, if food is heated for an extended period of time, even the oven top becomes hot from the vapor. In many aspects a microwave is worse than other ovens: a) The area is small and confined, thus, the steam is not vented and has no means of escape and is therefore prone to condense on the oven top.[36] b) The moisture in all foods steams very quickly, thus even solid foods emit *zeiah* (e.g., a potato baked in a microwave produces droplets of steam). c) Foods splatter on the oven top and sides quite frequently. Taking these facts into account, it is suggested that the following procedure be followed in using a microwave oven for both meat and dairy foods.

1) Cleanliness:
The oven must be kept clean from any food residue. As noted, foods cooked in a microwave oven splatter, boil over and drip. One must inspect the floor, walls and top of the oven before use to ascertain that no residue remains from previous use.

2) The foods should be covered:
All foods cooked in a microwave emit steam. Thus, meat or dairy foods placed in a microwave that is used for both should be covered. Perhaps *parve* solid foods (e.g., a potato) can be cooked without a covering.[37]

---

36. See *R' Akiva Eger*, gloss to 92:8 who notes that whenever the steam is in a confined area one must assume that it heats the upper surface.

37. Nevertheless, it may be advisable to cover lightly any food placed in the oven long enough to emit steam. Even if one covers the meat and dairy foods, some steam escapes and imparts its taste to the oven top. Thus, when one cooks a potato, the potato emits steam which condenses on the oven top. The steam may be hot and absorb *basar b'chalav* taste and fall back on the potato. One can avoid this problem by covering the potato with a paper plate.

3) The bottom surface:

One should not place meat and dairy dishes on the same surface. The microwave oven differs in this aspect from other ovens with regard to the following: Foods cooked in a microwave boil more quickly and tend to seep and spill. Thus, the bottom surface has absorbed taste from both meat and dairy. Other ovens generate heat which quickly dries any food residue on the hot oven grate. In addition, the pot is usually placed on a grate which does not permit liquid to collect. We noted earlier that taste cannot be transferred from vessel to vessel without the medium of liquid. In contrast, a microwave oven does not generate its own heat and the dish may rest on the flat oven bottom. As a result the oven bottom may become damp in the process of cooking. Placing a meat dish on this *treif* surface may cause *treif* taste to be absorbed into the dish. The proper method of avoiding this problem is to use one plate under meat dishes and another plate under milk dishes. If possible, glass plates are desirable.[38]

4) *Kashering* a microwave oven:

A microwave cannot be *kashered* in the manner of other ovens. Running the oven without food generates no heat to effect *libun kal*. Some permit *kashering* a microwave oven by means of first thoroughly wiping and cleaning all inside surfaces and then boiling a bowl of water in the oven until the oven fills with steam. The steam can *kasher* a surface that absorbed taste likewise through steam.[39]

E. Additional zeiah problems

1) Suspending utensils above a stove:

Another common *zeiah* problem is the issue of hanging spatulas, ladles or pans above a stove. As noted above, the steam produced

38. Glass may not absorb taste, thus the question of transfer of taste from the oven bottom to the plates is minimized. While some ovens are equipped with a glass tray, using separate trays for meat and dairy is recommended.

39. This requires further study. Hot food splatters onto the oven wall. This splatter may be considered *kli rishon* since it is continually heated by the microwaves as it splatters. Thus, it imparts its taste into the walls and cannot be *kashered* through steam. This may depend in the question of whether one is concerned only about the usual use of the vessel *(rov tashmisho)*. Therefore, since the main use of a microwave oven is not through direct contact with food, it may be *kashered* with steam. *Ashkenazic* custom, however, does not rely on *rov tashmisho*, see *Orach Chaim* 451:6.

CHART 17

INSTRUCTIONS FOR USE OF A MICROWAVE OVEN FOR MEAT AND DAIRY FOODS

1) The oven should always be clean from any food residue.
2) All foods cooked in the oven should be covered.
   Dry foods may be covered lightly (e.g. a paper plate).
3) Food dishes should be placed over separate plates, one for meat and one for dairy. Preferably glass plates should be used.

by foods as they boil retains the character of that food. The effect upon the utensils depends upon the distance between them and the boiling pot.

a) Utensils hanging near the pot:
   A ladle suspended in close proximity to a boiling pot of chicken soup comes in contact with hot steam and may no longer be used with dairy. Indeed, a dairy ladle in the path of hot meat steam becomes *treif.*
b) Utensils hanging a distance from the pot:
   If, however, the ladle is suspended a distance from the pot, the steam upon reaching the ladle is no longer hot *(yad soledes bo).* Thus, the ladle absorbs no meat taste and may be thoroughly washed[40] and used.[41] One should nevertheless not suspend any utensil above the cooking pot even if the steam is no longer hot. The steam reaches and dries upon the utensils, leaving them with meat taste on their surface. Although this may simply be washed away, one may forget to do so.[42]

2) Spice shakers:
   One must be concerned that steam from a cooking pot enters a spice shaker while spices are being added to the pot. It may be advisable to use separate spice shakers for meat and dairy foods.[43]

---

40. See *D.T.* 92:176,178.

41. See *Rema* 92:8.

42. See *Y.D.* 91:2.

43. See *Badei HaShulchan* 92:165.

3) The stove hood:
   A stove hood covering the cooking area of a stove top is similar to utensils suspended above the stove. If the steam reaching the hood is yet hot, the hood certainly absorbs its taste. Thus, the hood absorbs both meat and dairy tastes and must be considered *treif*. Nevertheless, this generally presents no kashrus problem since the area below the hood is open and the steam dissipates and will not condense upon the hood. One must, however, be conscious of the problem since, occasionally, one cooks foods in a large pot which may be in close proximity to a low hood, allowing droplets of condensed steam to fall from the hood into the food.[44]

4) Additional precautions:
   Pots cooking on the stove top should not be placed in a manner that steam from one type may reach a pot of another type. For example: a small pot of boiling milk should not be placed next to a large meat pot lest some of the milk steam impart its taste to the meat pot. One pouring hot water from an urn or an instant hot water faucet into a dairy cocoa mix, should be careful that hot steam from the mix does not rise to the spout or faucet, i.e., the spout should not be in or immediately above the cup.

F. Cooking on the stove top

One must be attentive to the following problems that may arise when cooking meat and dairy on a stove top as well.

1) Utensils touching one another:
   Meat and dairy pots cooking on a stove top must not touch one another. Although it has been noted previously that two dry vessels will not absorb taste from one another, nevertheless, it should be avoided.[45] In the event that the pots do touch, they and the food therein are permitted. If, however, the area of contact is damp the pot may become treif. A *moreh hora'ah* should be consulted.[46]

---

44. One who has an unusually low hood or uses very large pots should be particularly aware of this problem. He must also be careful that pots do not come into contact with the hood.

45. *Rema* 92:8. See *S.D.* 105:22.

46. See *Chavas Daas* 92:20, *Yad Yehudah* 92:56a and *D.T.* §183.

2) Splattering:
   One should not cook meat and dairy in open pots in close proximity since they may splatter onto one another as they boil.[47] In the event that the pots were placed near one another, one need not assume that any splattering occurred and, *bedieved*, the food is permitted.[48] If the pots are covered, one need not be concerned about splattering.[49] Some have the custom of placing a tin separation between meat and dairy pots. In the event that splattering did occur, see Chapter Eleven, Section H.

3) Stove grates:
   We noted earlier the problem of using the same oven racks for meat and dairy utensils. Stove grates present less of a problem since the flame reaches the grate and presumably burns away any food residue. Therefore, some authorities[50] permit use of the same grates for both meat and dairy. One who notices any meat residue on a grate should remove it before placing a dairy pot on that grate. Electric stove ranges are likewise permitted since the coils burn away any food residue. Other authorities[51] question this practice and advise that one keep separate grates for each type. Many follow this commendable custom.

Summary of Section I

☙ One should make every effort to acquire two separate ovens for meat and dairy use if possible. Use of an oven for both meat and dairy presents three problems: a) The meat may come in direct contact with dairy. b) When two foods are baked or roasted simultaneously in an oven, they absorb aroma *(reicha)* from one another. c) When liquid is cooked in an oven, steam *(zeiah)* is emitted which carries the taste of the foods to one another. One who must use the same oven for meat and dairy must be mindful of the following:

- ☐ It is prohibited to roast meat and dairy concurrently in an oven (in open pots) even if they do not touch one another

---

47. *Issur V'heter* 39:22, *Shach* 118:36 in interpretation of *Rema*. The *Taz* §12, however, disagrees with this interpretation. See *Yad Yehudah* 92:73k.

48. *Rema* 118:11.

49. *Shach* ibid.

50. *Igros Moshe: Y.D.* 1:59.

51. See *Minchas Yitzchok* 5:20.

and there is no chance of the meat gravy reaching the dairy food. In the event that meat was baked simultaneously in an oven with dairy food, they may both be eaten. Bread that was baked simultaneously with meat may not be eaten with dairy unless no other bread is available.

- One who wishes to use his oven for both meat and dairy foods baked consecutively should determine which type of food is most frequently cooked in the oven to set a standard use. Once the standard use has been determined, whether meat or dairy, he may freely use the oven for both dry foods and liquids of that type, regardless of whether the pot is open or covered.
- When one wishes to use the oven for the infrequent type, the oven should be used for dry foods or for foods in a covered pot only. In addition, the oven should be clean from any residue of the other type.
- One may not place meat and dairy foods directly on the same oven shelf. While some authorities permit meat utensils to be placed on the same racks that dairy utensils were previously placed, others disagree. Preferably, one should treat the oven racks as either meat or dairy and cover them with aluminum foil whenever cooking pots of the other type. It is advisable to spread aluminum foil under pots of all types.
- One who must use the oven for liquid foods of the infrequent type cooked in an open pot must *kasher* the oven beforehand. The oven must be thoroughly cleaned with a caustic cleaner. One should wait twenty-four hours and then heat the oven at the highest setting for a period of one hour. Many authorities raised strong reservations about the effectiveness of this process. A self-cleaning oven, however, may be repeatedly *kashered* from one type to another by running it through a self-cleaning cycle. Some authorities question the effectiveness of *kashering* even a self-cleaning oven.
- One may use a microwave oven for both meat and dairy foods. The oven must be clean from any residue of previous use. All foods should be covered. Meat and dairy dishes should not be placed on the same surface. A microwave oven may be *kashered* by thoroughly

cleaning all inside surfaces and boiling a bowl of water in the oven until the oven fills with steam.

- ☐ When cooking on a stove top, one must be careful that meat and dairy pots do not touch one another. If the pots do touch and the area of contact is damp, a *moreh hora'ah* should be consulted. Meat and dairy should not be cooked in open pots in close proximity lest they splatter onto one another. Some authorities permit use of the same stove grates for both meat and dairy if they are free of any food residue. Spatulas, ladles or pans should not be hung above the cooking surface of a stove.

II. Use of pots of one type for foods to be eaten with the other

Before proceeding to other *basar b'chalav* problems in the kitchen we must review a topic that was discussed at length in Chapter Six: the issue of *nat-bar-nat* — secondary infusions of taste. The reader is referred to that chapter for a more thorough examination of the many facets of this problem. We will limit our discussion in this chapter to the issues as they relate to *basar b'chalav*.

A. The theory

1) *Nat-bar-nat:*

Food fried in a pan infuses its taste into the pan. When another food is subsequently fried in that pan, the original taste is now transmitted to the second food. This secondary transfer (i.e., food to pot to food) is known as *nosen taam bar nosen taam* (lit. infused taste, the son of infused taste) or *nat-bar-nat* for short. Had the second food been boiled (not fried) in the pot, we would have an additional step, food to pot, to water and to food (three *"nats"*).

It should be noted, that our discussion involves use of a clean pot. A soiled pot is not subject to the principle of nat-bar-nat *since the food residue adhering to the pot is food itself, not mere taste. Nevertheless, any pot used for cooking is assumed to be clean unless known otherwise.*[52]

52. *Shach* 95:1.

In addition the reader should remember that throughout this section (unless noted otherwise) our subject is a ben-yomo *pot (i.e., a pot used for hot meat or dairy within the previous twenty-four hours).*

2) *Nat-bar-nat d'heteira:*

The practical application of the *nat-bar-nat* principle is limited to permitted foods — *nat-bar-nat d'heteira.* A taste that passes through two transfers and is *heteira* — permitted, becomes insignificant. However *nat-bar-nat d'isura* — a secondary taste that is forbidden — is considered a potent taste which may not be ignored. *Nat-bar-nat d'isura* is possible in one of two ways: a) either the taste is one that originated from forbidden foods or b) a taste that became forbidden in the process of the second transfer. The second example is of interest to us in our discussion of *basar b'chalav.* An example of *nat-bar-nat d'isura* as relating to *basar b'chalav* is:

Milk boiled in a meat pot becomes *basar b'chalav.* Although the meat taste was transferred twice (from meat to pot and then to milk), nevertheless, at the moment the second transfer is effected (i.e., the taste is absorbed into the milk), it immediately becomes *basar b'chalav.*

If, however, the *nat-bar-nat* remains permitted even after passing through the second transfer, it loses its power to be party to producing *basar b'chalav*. For example:

If *parve* food was cooked in a clean *ben-yomo* meat pot, the meat taste imparted from the pot is merely a secondary taste, i.e., it was transferred from the meat into the pot and from the pot into the food. Thus, when the food comes in contact with dairy, the meat taste is already negligible and cannot cause *basar b'chalav* to be produced.

B. The practical halachah

Poskim agree that initially *(lechatchilah)* one should not willfully cause *nat-bar-nat*. They also agree that in the event that *nat-bar-nat* did occur *(bidieved)*, the food may be eaten. They disagree, however, as to how far one must initially avoid *nat-bar-nat*. *Sefardic* custom regarding *nat-bar-nat* differs from *Ashkenazic* custom.

1) The *Shulchan Aruch*[53] rules that while one should not initially

53. Y.D. 95:1.

cook food in a meat vessel with the intention to eat it with dairy,[54] once it has been boiled or roasted in a meat pot or grill, it may be eaten with dairy. Similarly, he permits one to stuff chicken with eggs boiled in a dairy pot. *Sefardic* Jews follow this ruling.

2) *Ashkenazic* custom, however, follows a more stringent ruling:
   a) One may not boil food in a meat pot if it is to be eaten with dairy. Indeed, even if the food was already boiled in the meat pot, it may not be eaten with dairy.[55] The choice of eating the food with dairy constitutes a willful *(lechatchilah)* use of *nat-bar-nat.*
   b) Foods prepared in a meat pot may, however, be served in the course of a dairy meal, providing they are not actually eaten with dairy.[56]
   c) In the event that food cooked in a meat pot was erroneously mixed with dairy, it may be eaten.[57]
   d) If the *parve* food was not cooked in a meat utensil, but merely placed, while hot, on a cold meat dish (or placed, while cold, on a hot dish), it may be eaten with dairy.[58] However, one should not initially place hot food on a meat plate (or the reverse) if it is to be eaten with dairy.[59]
   e) These rules apply to food cooked in a *ben-yomo* pot. Food cooked in a non *ben-yomo* pot may be eaten with dairy.[60] Initially, however, one should not use even a non *ben-yomo* pot if another pot is available.[61]

---

54. *Shach* 95:3, see also *Kaf Hachaim* §1.

55. As opposed to the opinion of the *Shulchan Aruch* cited above who permits the fish to be eaten with dairy once it was already cooked.

56. See *Rema* 89:3. The basis of these prohibitions is the mixing of meat and dairy tastes. If the foods are not eaten with meat, no mixing of tastes occurs.

57. *Rema* 95:2. See *Shach* §3. See also *Shach* §4, who cites the opinion of the *Maharshal* that if the fish was fried in a meat pot, not boiled, and subsequently mixed with dairy food, it may not be eaten.

58. *Rema* ibid. See *Taz* §4. The basis for this difference is the fact that one surface is cold. Thus the transfer of taste is weaker, see Chapter Five, Section II,D. If, however, both the food and the dish are hot, it is the equivalent of cooking in the pot *(Taz* §3 and *Shach* §6, see *Aruch HaShulchan* §12 who disagrees).

59. *Taz* §4.

60. *Rema* 95:2.

61. *Chochmas Adam* 48:2. See, however, *Biur HaGra* 95:10 who seems to permit use of a non *ben-yomo* pot.

f) Although one may not eat food cooked in a meat pot with dairy, it may subsequently be placed, even while hot, on a dairy dish.[62] However, one should not initially cook food in a meat pot with the intention of placing it on a dairy dish while hot.[63]

g) All of the above applies to non-sharp foods. A sharp food, (a *davar charif*), when cooked in even a non *ben-yomo* meat pot and subsequently mixed with dairy food, may not be eaten.[64] We noted earlier (Chapter Three, Section II, B) that a *davar charif* negates the advantage of a non *ben-yomo* pot. The sharpness of the food revitalizes the stale taste. Likewise, the sharp taste of the food causes a transfer of primary meat taste, not merely a secondary taste.[65]

3) Some practical applications of these *halachos* are:

- ☐ Water boiled in a *ben-yomo* meat pot may not be used for coffee with milk.[66] In the event that one used the water for coffee with milk, he may drink it.
- ☐ Similarly, margarine melted in a *ben-yomo* dairy pot should not be used for challos served during a meat meal. In the event that it was mixed into the dough, the challos should not be served with meat. In this case, one has the option not to serve the challos with meat, whereas in the previous case, the milk was put into the coffee already.
- ☐ In either of these cases, if the pot was not *ben-yomo*, the water or margarine may be used. One should not, however, initially use a meat pot if a *parve* or dairy pot is available.
- ☐ Similarly, if hot gravy splattered on a hot coffee urn, it should not be used for coffee to be served with milk,

---

62. *Rema* 95:2. One should, however, not pour it directly into a dairy dish, see Chapter Eleven, Section F.

63. M.Z. §4,5. He notes, however, that the *Pri Chadash* disagrees.

64. *Rema* 95:2. If the pot is *ben-yomo* even the *Shulchan Aruch* concedes that the mixture may not be eaten (see *Y.D.* 96:3).

65. *Chochmas Adam* 49:1. This applies only to a *nat-bar-nat* absorbed by a *davar charif*. However, a *nat-bar-nat* taste originating from a *davar charif* is the equivalent of any *nat-bar-nat* (*Yad Yehudah* 95:1a, who notes that M.Z. is uncertain on this point).

66. A *Sefardic* Jew who follows the opinion of the *Shulchan Aruch* is permitted to use the water once it was boiled.

even when not a *ben-yomo,* unless no other urn is available. In the event that water was boiled in the urn when not a *ben-yomo,* it may be used for coffee with milk.[67]

- One should not boil water for coffee or tea in a *ben-yomo* meat pot, even for coffee or tea that is only to be served in a dairy cup without milk. In the event that the water was boiled already, it may be served in a dairy cup.[68]
- Some are of the opinion that while orange juice packaged by a dairy company may be used after eating meat it should not be used with meat.[69]
- One may not mix onions fried in a dairy pan with chopped liver, regardless of whether the pan was a *ben-yomo* or not. In the event that the onions were mixed with chopped liver, a *moreh hora'ah* should be consulted.[70]
- One should not store liquids in a dairy container (i.e. a container once used with hot dairy) for a period of twenty four hours if the liquids are to be used with meat. If no other suitable container is available, even a

---

67. Ibid. If it is difficult to *kasher* the urn, one may use it without *kashering* once twenty-four hours have passed. In the opinion of *Chochmas Adam* 45:3, any pot usually used for larger amounts of food that contain sixty times the splatter, may be used without *kashering*. See Chapter Eleven, Section H.

68. However, the water should not be poured directly from the meat pot into a dairy cup (since that is *iruy kli rishon* — see Chapter Eleven, Section F). It should first be poured into a meat cup and then into the dairy cup.

69. It seems reasonable to assume that the machinery was used for milk production within the previous twenty-four hours. However, even though the heat of the cleaning process required by law is not sufficient to effect *kashering,* some companies do clean the machinery with a heat of *yad soledes bo.* Thus, the possibility exists that the orange juice is not dairy at all. Thus, since, in the opinion of the *Shulchan Aruch, nat-bar-nat* is permitted, one may be lenient in a situation of doubt. In addition, when all the orange juice is combined it contains more that sixty times the milk that was absorbed into the machinery. Incidentally, one who considers non-Jewish milk to be actual *chalav Akum* prohibited by *Chazal* may not drink this juice at any time unless *kashering* was done. According to his tradition, this is *nat-bar-nat d'isura.*

70. See Chapter Twelve, Section II,C regarding cooked or fried onions and onions mixed with oil. See *Aruch HaShulchan* §15, who rules that if there is doubt as to whether the food is actually a *davar charif,* the mixture may be eaten.

ben-yomo dairy container may be used.[71] Sharp liquids should not be stored even in a non *ben-yomo* milk container, even for a short period of time, if they are to be eaten with meat.[72]

Summary of Section II.

- According to *Sefardic* custom, one should not cook food in a meat vessel with the intention to eat it with dairy. If the food was cooked in a clean meat pot, it may be eaten with dairy.
- According to *Ashkenazic* custom, even if the food was boiled already in a meat pot, it may not be eaten with dairy. The food may, however, be served in the course of a dairy meal, providing it is not actually eaten with meat. If the food was erroneously mixed with dairy, it may be eaten, unless the food was a *davar charif*.
- Food cooked in a non *ben-yomo* pot may be eaten with dairy, even according to *Ashkenazic* tradition. Nevertheless, one should not use even a non *ben-yomo* pot if another pot is available.
- Water boiled in a *ben-yomo* meat pot may not be used for coffee with milk. Margarine melted in a *ben-yomo* dairy pot should not be used for challos served during a meat meal. One should not boil water for coffee or tea in a *ben-yomo* meat pot, even for coffee or tea that is only to be served in a dairy cup without milk.

---

71. See *R' Akiva Eger* gloss to 95:2, who is uncertain whether *nat-bar-nat* applies to soaking — *kavush*. In addition, by the time the soaking can effect a transfer of taste (twenty-four hours) the vessel is no longer a *ben-yomo*. However, one may not put the *parve* liquid in the container immediately after the dairy use, see *R' Akiva Eger* ibid.

72. See Chapter Twelve, Section II,C that many sharp liquids have the status of a *davar charif* — sharp food, which revitalizes the non *ben-yomo* stale taste. See also Chapter Five, Section III,A, that soaking in sharp liquids can generate a taste transfer even in less than twenty-four hours.

CHAPTER TEN

Avoiding Basar B'chalav Problems While Washing Dishes

☐ Meat and dairy dishes washed together.

☐ Meat cutlery found among dairy cutlery.

☐ Use of one sink for both meat and dairy.

☐ Use of one dishwasher for both meat and dairy.

A. Meat and dairy utensils washed together

These *halachos* are based on *Tur* and *Shulchan Aruch; Yoreh De'ah* 95:3.

The problem of *nat-bar-nat* was discussed at length in Chapter Six and Chapter Nine, Section II. In order to avoid needless repetition, the reader is referred to those chapters for background information relating to the subject currently under discussion. The issue of *nat-bar-nat* is very relevant to the question of meat and dairy dishes that are washed together. When meat and dairy dishes are washed together, tastes from utensils of each type are absorbed into the utensils of the other type. The practical *halachah* depends upon the following variables: the heat of the water, whether the utensils are *ben-yomo* or not, the presence of soap or detergents in the water, whether all of the utensils are in the water at one time and the cleanliness of the utensils from any food residue. While all utensils are generally considered to be clean (with the exception of a knife, as noted in Chapter Twelve, Section I,B), dishes being washed are understandably assumed to be soiled. Thus, with regard to the following *halachos* of utensils being washed, we will assume that any utensil contains food residue unless one is certain that the residue has been removed.

1) *Ben-yomo* utensils — a definition:
In the context of our discussion, the term "*ben-yomo*" refers to a utensil that was: a) used as a *kli rishon*, b) within the previous twenty four hours, c) for food of its type (meat or dairy). If, however, the utensil was not used, or it was used only for water or *parve* food during that period, it is not considered *ben-yomo* (see Chapter Three and Chapter Nine, Section II). If the utensil was used only as a *kli sheni*, it is not considered *ben-yomo* and is exempt from the rules that follow.[1] One who is in doubt whether a utensil was indeed used during the previous twenty-four hours may assume that it was not used within the previous twenty four hours.[2] However, any utensil that was certainly used within the previous twenty four hours must be assumed to have been used as a *kli rishon* as well, unless one

---

1. *Rema* 95:3.

2. All utensils are considered non *ben-yomo* unless known otherwise (*Chavas Daas* 95:14c).

knows with certainty that it was used only as *kli sheni*.[3] In short: a utensil is assumed not to have been used during the previous twenty four hours unless one knows otherwise. If it was used, one must suspect that it may have been used as a *kli rishon*.

2) Clean *ben-yomo* utensils washed together:
When a clean *ben-yomo* dairy pan is washed in a clean *ben-yomo* meat pot that is a *kli rishon* (a pot originally over the fire) containing hot *(yad soledes bo)* water, one confronts the issue of *nat-bar-nat*. The meat taste that was absorbed into the pot (one *nat)* and infused into the water (second *nat)* has not yet combined with dairy taste and is still permitted *(heter)*. This is referred to as *nat-bar-nat d'heteira* (see Chapter Six). Similarly the dairy taste imparted into the water from the dairy pan is a secondary absorption *(nat-bar-nat d'heteira)*. Consequently, both pan and pot are unaffected and may be used for their original use. This is indeed the opinion of many *Rishonim* and the conclusion of the *Shulchan Aruch*.[4] However, *Ashkenazic* tradition follows a more stringent approach and requires that both the pot and pan be *kashered*. Two reasons are offered for this ruling: a) In the course of washing, the pan may have touched the pot and they may have absorbed taste directly from one another without the medium of water. If this is true, the taste is no longer *nat-bar-nat d'heteira* but *nat-bar-nat d'isura* since the second transfer (e.g., that of meat taste from meat pot to dairy pan) causes immediate formation of *basar b'chalav*. b) The meat and dairy taste meet one another directly in the water and immediately form *basar b'chalav*. Thus, the secondary transfer is not that of meat taste into water but that of meat taste directly into dairy taste. One who washes meat and dairy utensils together in a *parve* basin that is a *kli rishon* (subject to all the above conditions) confronts

3. *Shach* 95:13, see *Minchas Yaakov* 57:25 who disagrees. In addition, see *Chidushei HaGershuni* (gloss to *Y.D.* 122:7) who contends that the assumption that a utensil was unused during the previous twenty-four hours applies only if one is unaware of using any utensil during that period. If, however, a person used one of his utensils but cannot recall which was used, each one of them is suspect as the one that was used.

4. *Y.D.* 95:3. However, *Shulchan Aruch* concedes that initially one should not wash meat and dairy dishes together unless one type is not *ben-yomo (Shach* §9). See *Kaf HaChaim* §38, that it is meritorious for even a *Sefardic* Jew to follow the stringent opinion of *Rema* and *kasher* both pan and pot.

these very same problems. Therefore, if the meat and dairy utensils are *ben-yomo*, according to *Ashkenazic* tradition, the utensils and the *parve* basin must all be *kashered*.[5]

3) Non *ben-yomo* utensils washed together:
If either one of the utensils is not *ben-yomo*,[6] both utensils are unaffected. If, for example, the meat pot was not *ben-yomo*, the taste of meat imparted into either the water or into the dairy pan is stale and has no effect. The dairy taste, even if absorbed directly into the meat pot, cannot become *basar b'chalav* since it meets a stale meat taste and thus remains a permissible taste (*nat-bar-nat d'heteira*).[7] The water, however, may not be used with meat since it contains *ben-yomo* dairy taste. Common custom is to forbid any use of the water.[8]

4) Utensils not inspected for cleanliness:
If a meat pot and dairy pot that were washed together in a *kli rishon* were not inspected beforehand, they are assumed to contain food residue.[9] Thus, if, for example, the meat pot contained residue, the meat taste imparted by the residue is absorbed directly into the dairy pot which becomes *basar b'chalav*. Neither the principle of *nat-bar-nat* nor that of *nosen ta'am lifgam* can be applied in this case. The principle of *nat-bar-nat* cannot be applied since the residue is actual meat which infuses its primary taste directly into the pot. Similarly, the principle of *nosen ta'am lifgam* cannot be applied since it pertains only to taste absorbed into utensils, not actual meat

---

5. See *Shach* §15. It would seem that if the utensils were washed in a *kli sheni*, even *Rema* would concede that they do not require *kashering*.

6. See *Chochmas Adam* 48:14, who rules that since, in the view of *Shulchan Aruch*, the pots never need *kashering*, we may, regarding this case, rely upon the opinions that the passage of a full night gives a utensil the status of non *ben-yomo*. (We usually require the passage of a full twenty-four-hour period, as noted in Chapter Three, Section II,B.) Thus, if meat is cooked in a pot one afternoon and the pot is washed with clean, *ben-yomo* dairy dishes the following morning, neither of the utensils require *kashering*.

7. *Taz* §9, *Shach* §12.

8. *Rema* 95:3, see *Shach* §14. This applies to water only, since the loss of water is insignificant (*Taz* §10, even in a situation where the water was cooked specifically for drinking, M.Z. ibid.). See *D.T.* §54 who notes that even if both vessels are non *ben-yomo*, the water should not be used, while in 94:69 he cites opposing opinions.

9. Although utensils are generally assumed to be free of any residue, a pot being washed is presumably unclean (*Shach* §1). However, the basin in which the dishes are being washed is assumed to be clean (see *S.D.* §11, and *Minchas Yaakov* 57:17).

residue on utensils.[10] Both utensils (and the basin in which they were washed) absorbed *basar b'chalav* taste and must be *kashered.* This is true even if only one of the utensils had food residue. However, if the water contains sixty times the volume of the meat residue, the vessels need not be *kashered.*[11] If either of the utensils is not a *ben-yomo,* a *moreh hora'ah* should be consulted.[12]

5) Utensils washed successively:
If clean *ben-yomo* dishes are washed one after another in the same water, all *Poskim* agree that even the second utensil need not be *kashered.*[13] The taste imparted by the first utensil into the water is certainly *nat-bar-nat.* Thus, when the second utensil is placed into the water, it is unaffected.[14] If the utensils were not clean, a *moreh hora'ah* should be consulted.[15]

6) Utensils washed in a *kli sheni:*
If the utensils are washed in a *kli sheni* containing hot *(yad soledes bo)* water, *Poskim* disagree about the status of the utensils.[16] Many authorities rule that utensils washed in a *kli*

---

10. *Y.D.* 103:5.

11. *Y.D.* 95:3. The washing water is not assumed to contain the necessary volume for *bitul (S.D.* 95:1).

12. If, for example, the dairy pan was clean and not a *ben-yomo,* while the meat pot was soiled and *ben-yomo,* the dairy pan may not be used for either meat or dairy foods since it has absorbed primary (not secondary) meat taste from the meat residue. It may be used for hot *parve* foods *(Rema* 93:1). Nevertheless, common custom is to avoid using the dairy pan even for *parve* foods *(Shach* 93:3). The meat pot is unaffected since it absorbed only non *ben-yomo* taste from the dairy pot. If the soiled meat pot was not *ben-yomo,* but the clean dairy pot was *ben-yomo,* both pots must be *kashered.* The dairy pot absorbed primary meat taste from the meat residue and became *basar b'chalav,* and it then imparted its prohibited taste into the meat pot (see *Shach* §10).

13. *Rema* 95:3.

14. *Shach* §16. The water, however, may be used only with *parve,* not meat or dairy foods, according to *Ashkenazic* custom as cited above (2) *(M.Z.* §11).

15. See *S.D.* (beginning of §18) who rules that if the first utensil was unclean, the second utensil must be *kashered* since it absorbed primary taste. If, however, only the second utensil was unclean, neither utensil is affected. See *Chavas Daas* §8b who notes that according to the opinion of the *Shulchan Aruch* 94:5, the pot in which the utensils were washed must be *kashered.*

16. See *Issur V'heter* 34:22, who concludes that even soiled dishes are unaffected when washed in a *kli sheni.* This is based upon the premise that a *kli sheni* cannot effect *bishul.* Moreover, even if a *kli sheni* can effect *one* transfer of taste, it cannot effect *two* transfers (i.e., it may cause a vessel to impart its taste into the water but it cannot cause

sheni are unaffected even if they were soiled, while others disagree.[17] A *moreh hora'ah* should be consulted.

7) Utensils washed with *iruy kli rishon:*
If hot water is poured from a *kli rishon* onto meat and dairy dishes, the question is more serious since many *Poskim* believe that *iruy kli rishon* effects a taste transfer. Nevertheless, according to some opinions, the utensils are unaffected, even if they are soiled,[18] because even though *iruy* can cause a taste transfer into food, it cannot cause a taste transfer into a utensil.[19] Other *Poskim* rule that if the utensils are soiled, they must be *kashered*.[20] If one utensil is soiled and the other is clean, the clean utensil must certainly be *kashered*. The soiled utensil should be *kashered* unless serious financial loss is involved.[21] Authorities conclude that if hot water is poured over clean meat and dairy dishes, the dishes should be *kashered* unless serious financial loss is involved.[22]

8) Washing with detergents:
In the opinion of most *Poskim*, meat and dairy utensils washed together with detergents do not require *kashering*. The potent taste of detergents has an adverse effect on any taste imparted into the water and subsequently into the utensils. The reader will remember that any taste which is *nosen ta'am lifgam* (it affects the food into which it is imparted in an adverse manner) may be disregarded.[23] Thus, in the opinion of many *Poskim*, even if the utensils being washed were soiled, the taste of the food residue[24]

---

that taste to be infused into another vessel). See *Y.D.* 105:2 and *Shach* §5). This opinion is maintained by *Rema* 95:3. *Maharshal* (cited in *Taz* §12), however, contends that the food residue dissolves into the water and can be infused into the vessel. He argues that the dissolution of the residue is not considered a taste transfer. Thus, the infusion of residue taste into the vessel is considered a singular transfer which can be effected by a *kli sheni*.

17. See *Taz* §12, *Minchas Yaakov* 57:21 and *Chavas Daas* §9.

18. *Rema* 95:3.

19. *Shach* §20, in explanation of *Rema*.

20. *Maharshal* and *Shach* §20. It seems, however, from *Chochmas Adam* 48:12, that in a case of serious financial loss, one may be lenient.

21. *Shach* §20 and *Chochmas Adam* 48:12.

22. *S.D.* §20, even though *Shach* §20 permits the utensils if they were clean.

23. See Chapter Three, Section II,B.

24. One should note that the ability of detergents to ruin the taste of food is effective only before the taste is infused into the vessel. Once the taste is absorbed into the vessel, it cannot be neutralized by washing the utensil with detergents. The original food taste

is ruined by the detergents and cannot affect the utensils.[25]

9) Cutlery found among others of the opposite type:
A frequent occurrence in many homes is the mysterious appearance of dairy cutlery (e.g. a spoon or fork) among the meat cutlery, or the reverse. Should one *kasher* the suspect spoon or fork since it may have inadvertently been washed with the meat dishes? Perhaps one is required to *kasher* all the meat cutlery that may have been washed with the dairy spoon. *Poskim* rule that neither the spoon nor the cutlery requires *kashering.*[26] They base this ruling on the *s'fek sfeika* (multiple doubts) involved: a) The spoon may have been washed separately and merely placed in the wrong drawer. b) Even if it was washed with meat dishes, the meat dishes may have been clean of any meat residue and perhaps were not *ben-yomo,*[27] c) Even if there was meat residue, the water may not have been *yad soledes bo,* or d) there may have been sixty parts water to any amount of residue. Even if all of these

---

absorbed into the utensil remains potent (see *Chavas Daas* §13b, and *Chazon Ish:* Y.D. 23:1).

25. *Y.D.* 95:4, with regard to dishes washed with ash. Both *Taz* §15, and *Shach* §21, take strong exception to this ruling. See also *Yad Yehudah* 33a, who also expresses reservations about this ruling regarding utensils that were soiled. See *Chavas Daas* §21c, who rules that one may rely upon the ruling of *Shulchan Aruch* only in cases of severe loss. However, *Chochmas Adam* 48:15, and *Aruch HaShulchan* §24 accept *Shulchan Aruch's* ruling. Moreover, *Aruch HaShulchan* notes that this is the common custom among *morei hora'ah* (see *D.T.* §83, who takes strong exception to this). In addition, *Chazon Ish:* Y.D. 23:1, seems to accept the fact that detergents ruin any food taste. It is noteworthy that although *Taz* and *Shach* both question the *Shulchan Aruch's* sources, they offer no rationale why strong tasting additives do not ruin the food taste (unless their objections relate to ash only, which, they contend, does not ruin the food taste).

26. *Rema* 95:3.

27. *Taz* §14, citing *Issur V'heter* 34:25. In the opinion of *Shulchan Aruch* cited above (2), if no food residue is present, even a *ben-yomo* dish presents no problem.

28. See *Chavas Daas* §12b, and *Yad Yehudah* §36k, who rely upon this opinion. See, however, *D.T.* §81, who rules that if one can *kasher* the utensil without difficulty, one should do so (if the utensil cannot be *kashered,* one should wait twenty-four hours before using it). Nevertheless, in our modern kitchens, dishes are washed under a faucet (which is *iruy*) or in a basin (which is a *kli sheni*); thus, even one *safek* — doubt — (whether or not the dishes were washed together) is sufficient. See *Chavas Daas* (ibid.) and *Yad Yehudah* (ibid.) that in a case of *iruy* (and certainly *kli sheni*), one may be lenient in a case of one *safek*. In addition, see *Issur V'heter* 34:25, *Biur HaGra* §23, and *Yad Avraham* who note that one *safek* is always sufficient. They contend that since the spoon was found in the cutlery drawer, one is not required to assume that it was washed among the dishes.

arguments do not apply, e) it may be assumed that the dishes were washed with detergents which ruin any food taste that was present.[28]

One must be aware of the impropriety of permitting non-Jewish maids to wash dishes. We will enumerate in a following section the many problems relating to dish washing. Washing cutlery of one type with the other is only one of the many problems that may occur. A maid cannot be expected, much less trusted, to give this serious matter its proper attention.

10) Cutlery found in a dishwasher of the opposite type:
A milk spoon found in a meat dishwasher (or the reverse) should preferably be *kashered*. The spoon was certainly washed with meat dishes, the water was certainly *yad soledes bo* and there were certainly meat particles in the water which may have come in contact with the spoon before their taste was ruined by the detergent. In the event that the spoon was subsequently mixed with other dairy cutlery, a *moreh hora'ah* should be consulted.[29]

Summary of Section A

- If a clean *ben-yomo* dairy pan is washed in a clean *ben-yomo* meat pot that is a *kli rishon* containing hot water, or if both the meat and dairy utensils are washed together in a *kli rishon parve* basin, according to *Ashkenazic* custom, both the pot and pan must be *kashered.*
- If either of the clean utensils is not *ben-yomo,* both utensils are unaffected.
- If the utensils to be washed were not inspected beforehand, they are assumed to contain food residue. Thus, both utensils (and the basin in which they were washed) must be *kashered.* If either of the utensils was not a *ben-yomo,* a *moreh hora'ah* should be consulted.
- If clean *ben-yomo* dishes were washed one after another in the same water, all *Poskim* agree that even the second utensil need not be *kashered.* If the utensils were not clean, a *moreh hora'ah* should be consulted.
- If the utensils were washed in a *kli sheni,* a *moreh hora'ah* should be consulted.

---

29. See *Y.D.* 102:3.

- If the utensils were washed together with detergents, they do not require *kashering*.
- If a spoon of one type is found among cutlery of the other type, neither the spoon nor the cutlery require *kashering*.
- A milk spoon found in a meat dishwasher should preferably be *kashered*. If it was subsequently mixed with other dairy cutlery, a *moreh hora'ah* should be consulted.

B. Use of one sink for meat and dairy dishes

It should be apparent that use of one sink for both meat and dairy dishes is fraught with *kashrus* problems. It should be noted that no distinction should be made regarding these *halachos* between a *Sefardic* or *Ashkenazic* Jew.[30] Washing meat and dairy dishes in one sink involves the following factors: the hot water leaving the tap in most homes is *yad soledes bo*. Thus, the tap water has the status of *iruy kli rishon* since it flows in an uninterrupted manner from the boiler which is a *kli rishon*.[31] In the course of washing meat dishes, the sink comes in contact with meat residue which is absorbed into at least a *klipah* of the sink surface.[32] In the event that one subsequently washes dairy dishes in the same sink within a twenty-four-hour period, the sink may become *treif* with *basar b'chalav*.[33] Consequently, since we can no longer apply the *nat-bar-nat*

30. In the opinion of *Shulchan Aruch*, one would be permitted to wash clean dairy dishes in a meat sink. However, if the dishes are soiled, the rules of *nat-bar-nat* do not apply; thus, even *Shulchan Aruch* would concede that the sink becomes *basar b'chalav*.

31. See *Minchas Yitzchok* 2:100(2), who contends that this may be even a stronger form of *iruy kli rishon*, since the boiler may be actively heating the water while it flows from the tap (unlike common *iruy kli rishon* which refers to a vessel removed from the fire while it is being poured). In a post-script to this responsa, he notes that often one mixes cold water with hot water while using the sink; thus, the tap water may not be *yad soledes bo*. This is a significant factor to be considered with regard to any individual question pertaining to meat and dairy utensils in a sink. A *moreh hora'ah* must inquire whether or not the water was actually hot. Indeed, one usually does not wash dishes in water that is *yad soledes bo*. Nevertheless, it is difficult to use this as a lenient factor in our discussion since, at times, a sink is used with water that is *yad soledes bo*.

32. See *Minchas Yitzchok* ibid.(1).

33. In addition, hot meat and dairy liquids may have been poured directly into the sink from their pots (*Minchas Yitzchok* ibid.). See, however, *Igros Moshe: Y.D.* 1:42, who contends that a sink is not considered absolutely *treif*. He argues that when hot tap water is used to wash soiled meat dishes, the sink absorbs meat taste only if the water falls directly (or perhaps even when it falls in an uninterrupted indirect manner) onto meat residue sitting on the sink surface itself. Even then, the meat taste is absorbed only

principle, whenever one washes dishes in the sink, the dishes absorb *basar b'chalav* taste and become non-kosher.[34]

One with the financial and practical ability should acquire two kitchen sinks, one meat and one dairy. The ease of use and the prevention of numerous problems make this a worthwhile investment. However, we must consider the predicament of those living in rented premises or are otherwise unable to avail themselves of this luxury. Their options are as follows:

1) The safest, though least practical, solution is never to place any dishes or cutlery in the sink itself. All pots, dishes and cutlery should be washed while they are held in the hand.

2) One who finds the above solution impractical may wash both types of dishes in the sink, provided he insures that: a) no dishes or pots touch the sink bottom or side and that b) the dishes do not contact the water collected in the sink. This can be accomplished through one of two methods which reflect two opinions, one stringent and one lenient:

    a) The stringent opinion:
    In the opinion of some authorities,[35] dishes should never be put in the sink. Dishes should be washed only in metal or plastic basins inserted in the sink, one for meat dishes, one for dairy and one for *parve* (unless one

---

into a *klipah* of sink surface directly under the meat residue. In the event that within twenty-four hours, hot tap water is poured over dairy residue in the very same spot, the sink would indeed become *treif*. However, *Igros Moshe* considers this highly unlikely and beyond reasonable *halachic* assumption. He does not address the possibility that both hot meat gravy and dairy liquid were poured into the sink within twenty-four hours of one another. Apparently, he considers this unlikely as well. [A point of interest: If, in the opinion of *Minchas Yitzchok*, the sink is indeed *basar b'chalav*, how is one permitted to pour hot liquid into the sink? The hot liquid will effect *bishul* on a *klipah* of the sink surface and one will violate the prohibition against cooking *basar b'chalav*. See *Rema* 87:6, that according to some opinions, one may not light a flame under a non-Jew's pot since it is imbued with *basar b'chalav* taste. Apparently, we follow the opinion of most authorities that *iruy* can only effect a taste transfer but not actual *bishul*, as opposed to *Maharshal* cited in *Shach* 105:5, see Chapter Five, Section II,C,4.]

34. *Minchas Yitzchok* ibid. *Igros Moshe* (ibid.), however, disputes this contention as well. He argues that even if a dish is placed directly over a spot that did absorb *basar b'chalav* taste, the dish is unaffected since *iruy* cannot effect two transfers (into the sink and into the dish). In addition, the water volume presumably contains sixty times the *klipah* of sink surface. He concedes, however, that initially one should avoid this problem and not wash dishes directly in the sink.

35. *Minchas Yitzchok* 2:100.

washes *parve* utensils while they are held in the hand). The tap water should pour directly into the basin, not into the sink. One need not be concerned about any water subsequently flowing from the basin into the sink.[36] The basins themselves should preferably be placed on a rack or board, not directly on the sink surface.[37] The sink should be thoroughly washed between meat and dairy use so that no meat residue remains while dairy dishes are being washed (or the reverse). In addition, the drain should be kept free of any blockage so that the sink water should not gather in the sink and touch the dishes being washed.[38]

b) The lenient opinion:
Other authorities take a more lenient position.[39] They argue that although dishes should not come in contact with the sink bottom or sides while being washed,[40] one need not use a basin. Merely placing racks (one for meat, one for dairy and one for *parve)* on the sink to keep the dishes suspended above the water level and sink bottom is sufficient. One should, nevertheless, prevent sink water from rising and touching the dishes. In the event that the water does reach the dishes, they are unaffected.[41]

---

36. The water pouring into the basin is *iruy kli rishon.* After the water rests in the basin it becomes a *kli sheni.* Any water subsequently flowing over the side of the basin is *iruy kli sheni* and has no *halachic* effect. Thus, we are not concerned with contact between the basin and the bottom of the sink. If, however, one were to permit the water to flow directly to the bottom of the sink, the possibility of absorption of taste from the sink to the basin must be considered. One should preferably place racks under the basin, as noted in the text, to prevent any chance of absorption *(Minchas Yitzchok* ibid. §[3]).

37. This is mentioned as an additional precaution, but it is not imperative. The purpose is to prevent infusion of taste from the sink to the basin as noted in the previous footnote.

38. *Minchas Yitzchok* 2:100. Moreover, he advises that the sink be *kashered* between meat and dairy uses by running the tap water over all surfaces of the sink.

39. *Igros Moshe: Y.D.* I:42. When the previous stringent opinion was presented to R' Moshe, he responded, "This method is very tedious. The women involved will complain 'Rebbi! you have made it so difficult for me'."

40. See footnote 34 above, that in the opinion of *Igros Moshe*, even if the dishes do come in contact with the sink they do not need *kashering.*

41. *Igros Moshe: Y.D.* 1:42, *Minchas Yitzchok* 2:100.

3) Two adjacent sinks:
   One who has a meat sink and dairy sink adjacent to one another must prevent water containing food particles from splashing onto the dishes of one type while washing those of the other type. The most effective method is to place a cover over the sink not being used. Another common method is to construct a ridge separating the two sinks.

4) Attached sinks:
   Some double sinks are constructed of one sheet of metal that is formed into two sinks. Although, in effect, this constitutes one large vessel, half meat and half dairy, it presents no kashrus problem. The metal ridge connecting the two sinks never heats to the degree of *yad soledes bo*. Thus, no taste can be transferred between the two sinks.[42]

5) A common drain line:
   Adjacent sinks often share a common drain line with one drain trap. Although this is not the ideal situation since drain water may rise from one sink to another, it presents no serious kashrus problem. The water that may rise from the drain is generally not *yad soledes bo* and cannot affect the kashrus of the sink or the dishes therein. Nevertheless, the drain should always be kept clear to avoid this problem entirely. In the event that the water does rise from one sink to another, the dishes and the sink should be rinsed in cold or warm, but not hot, water.

6) Dishes or cutlery that fall into a sink:
   If a dish, spoon or fork falls into the sink while the hot water is running, if it was not directly under the water, it is unaffected. If, however, the utensil was directly under the water, a *moreh hora'ah* should be consulted.[43]

7) Additional precautions:
   When washing dishes, one must be mindful of the following:

---

42. See responsa of R' Moshe Stern no. 12, in appendix to Hebrew version of *Pischei Halachah, Kashrus* (1984). Moreover, even if the hot water of one sink could heat the other sink, it cannot cause a transfer of taste to it (see *Shach* 94:3).

43. See *Minchas Yitzchok* 2:100[4]. who suggests that, although *halachically* it is not mandated, the utensil should perhaps be *kashered*. However, according to the opinion of *Igros Moshe* cited above, the dish does not require *kashering* even if it was directly under the tap water (assuming that there was no food of the opposite type in the sink at the time). If detergents were used, perhaps all opinions would agree that the dish does not require *kashering*.

- ☐ One must keep separate sponges for meat, dairy and *parve* dishes, since actual food particles are absorbed into the sponges.
- ☐ Any steel wool used for dishes of one type should not be used for dishes of the other type or for *parve* dishes. If a sponge or steel wool used for one type was used on utensils of the other type, a *moreh hora'ah* should be consulted.
- ☐ One who wears plastic gloves while washing dishes should use separate gloves for meat and dairy use.
- ☐ One should avoid letting meat or dairy food remnants touch the hot water spout since they will impart their taste into the spout and affect the hot water as it passes through the spout.

Summary of Section B

⤜§ Ideally, one should acquire two kitchen sinks, one meat and one dairy. One who must use one sink for both meat and dairy should follow one of the following options:

1) Dishes and cutlery should never be placed in the sink itself, instead they should be washed while they are held in the hand.
2) Both types of dishes may be washed in the sink if they do not come in contact with the sink or the water collected in the sink. *Poskim* advise two procedures by which this can be accomplished:
   - ☐ The dishes should be washed only in basins inserted into the sink, one basin for meat dishes, one for dairy and one for *parve*. The tap water should pour directly into the basin, not into the sink. The basins should be placed on a rack or board. The sinks should be thoroughly washed between meat and dairy use. In addition, the drain should be kept free of any blockage.
   - ☐ A more lenient method: One may wash dishes on racks (one for meat, one for dairy and one for *parve)* placed on the sink bottom to keep the dishes suspended above the water level. One should prevent sink water from rising and touching the dishes.

- ◆§ Adjacent sinks (even if constructed of one sheet of metal) are permitted. However, one must prevent water containing food particles from splashing from one sink to the other.
- ◆§ Sinks that share a common drain line with one drain trap should always be kept clear to prevent water from rising from one sink into the other.
- ◆§ If a utensil falls into the sink while the hot water is running, it is permitted. If the utensil is directly under the water, a *moreh hora'ah* should be consulted.
- ◆§ One must keep separate sponges, steel wool and gloves for washing meat, dairy and *parve* dishes. In addition, one should avoid letting meat or dairy food remnants touch the hot water spout.

C. Use of a dishwasher for meat and dairy dishes

1) The operation of a dishwasher:
Use of a dishwasher for meat and dairy presents problems similar to those involved in washing dishes in the same sink, and then some. However, the reader must first understand the basic operation of a dishwasher:

- ☐ In many types of dishwashers, after hot water enters the dishwasher, it gathers on the bottom of the dishwasher where it is heated significantly by a heating element. Thus, the water should be considered a *kli rishon*.
- ☐ After the water has heated sufficiently, it is drawn by a revolving wand and sprayed upwards at the lower level of dishes. Another wand sprays hot tap water at the upper level of dishes. These sprays must be considered *iruy kli rishon*. However, since the stream of water is usually interrupted and not constant, it could be considered *iruy she'nifsak ha'kiluach* (an interrupted flow — see Chapter Five, Section II,B).
- ☐ A dishwasher dispenses detergents at different intervals of the washing cycle; thus, any food taste in the water is presumably ruined. Nevertheless, the final rinsing cycle is done without detergents, enabling potent taste to be emitted from the dishwasher into the water.[44]

---

44. We noted in Chapter Three that taste that is previously absorbed into a utensil *does* not become *pagum* (ruined) through contact with detergents. Another consideration is

- ☐ A dishwasher has a filtration system at its drain to prevent food particles from entering the mechanism of the pump. Some larger particles can be removed after each washing, but the finer filter cannot be cleaned completely; thus, residue of previous washes remains through every successive wash.

2) Use of one dishwasher for meat and dairy:
The *halachic* problems involved in using one dishwasher for meat and dairy are apparent and numerous:

a) The walls of the dishwasher:
When a dishwasher is used to wash soiled meat dishes, the spraying water carries with it meat particles and gravy to the washer sides. The taste of these may be absorbed into the washer walls. When, subsequently, dairy dishes are washed, dairy taste is absorbed into the walls as well. Thus, the walls contain *basar b'chalav* and the dishwasher is *treif*. Nevertheless, the following factors should be considered:

- ☐ Unlike a sink, which is actual *iruy kli rishon*, a dishwasher, as noted, is *iruy she'nifsak ha'kiluach* which is a lesser degree of *iruy*.[45]
- ☐ On the other hand, a sink has only a single flow which runs along a set pattern. A dishwasher sprays water over its entire surface thereby increasing the chance that meat and milk may be absorbed in the very same spot.
- ☐ Theoretically, one could avoid using the dishwasher for meat and dairy within the same twenty-four hour period, thus avoiding the creation of actual *basar b'chalav*. If one were to limit the use in this manner, the dishwasher would always be *nat-bar-nat d'heteira* and would not effect the dishes washed therein. The

---

the fact that in the very beginning of the washing cycle, the water may start spraying before it has been rendered *pagum* by the detergents. On the other hand, the water at the beginning of the cycle may not yet be hot.

45. See Chapter Five, footnote 46 for a discussion of the opinions regarding *iruy she'nifsak ha'kiluach*. They vary from those who contend that it cannot effect any transfer of taste to those who contend that it can effect one taste transfer. See M.Z. 68:9:4, who rules that an interrupted flow can only cause a Rabbinic prohibition; thus, in case of doubt, one may take a lenient position.

filter would nonetheless remain problematic, see below.

- □ Similarly, if one runs the dishwasher through an empty cycle between meat and dairy loads, the washer could perhaps[46] be *kashered*. Although dishes that become treif through heat of a *kli rishon* cannot be *kashered* through *iruy*, the washer itself, which became dairy through *iruy*, can also be *kashered* through *iruy*. The washer would thus never become *basar b'chalav* and *treif*. The fact that the washer is *ben-yomo* is irrelevant since any taste imparted into the water is *nat-bar-nat d'heteira*.[47]
- □ Even if the washer is considered *treif* through *basar b'chalav*, the washer is still not comparable to a kitchen sink. A sink which has absorbed *basar b'chalav* taste can possibly infuse that taste into dishes lying directly under the tap. A washer, however, cannot impart that taste into any dishes. The stream of water that hits the washer wall and absorbs the *treif* taste may be *iruy kli rishon*, but the moment it splashes off the wall, it becomes *iruy kli sheni* which is negligible (since it is an interrupted flow).

b) The racks holding the dishes and cutlery:
A more serious consideration is the racks or the cutlery holder upon which the dishes and cutlery are placed. These become soiled from meat and dairy residue and absorb both meat and dairy taste from the *iruy kli rishon*.[48] When dishes are subsequently placed directly upon the racks, they may absorb *basar b'chalav* taste from the racks. In addition, perhaps food residue remains on the racks. These problems could be avoided by using separate racks for meat and dairy dishes and cutlery.

---

46. Although the accepted custom is not to *kasher* utensils from meat to dairy use (or the reverse), perhaps one may do so in this case since it is questionable whether any *kashering* is required at all (see similar argument in *Minchas Yitzchok* 2:100 [8], although the cases are not alike).

47. In addition, one could put detergent into the water, although, as noted, this is unnecessary.

48. However, since the *iruy* is interrupted *(nifsak ha'kiluach)*, the problem may not be serious after all.

c) The filter:

Another serious problem is the filter found in many models which retains food residue from previous washes:

- □ Meat particles remain in the filter and may be sprayed on the dairy dishes washed in a subsequent load. Although one can remove much of the accumulated waste, perhaps one should be concerned that one may forget to do so.[49] In addition, it is practically impossible to remove all of the waste.[50]
- □ The washer bottom fills with hot water which is then heated further by an electrical element. In many models, the filter lies in this water. Thus, the water, which is a *kli rishon*, absorbs meat taste and is sprayed onto the dairy dishes and onto the dairy residue on the dishes, producing actual *basar b'chalav.*[51]
- □ A possible solution to this problem could be acquiring separate filters for meat and dairy washes.

In conclusion, it should be apparent that one should not use one dishwasher for both meat and dairy dishes. There are, however, lenient opinions.[52] One who finds it

---

49. See *Y.D.* 91:2.

50. Unless one may assume that any waste that cannot be manually removed will similarly not be removed in the process of washing and will not be sprayed on the dishes. This may vary from washer to washer, depending on the type of filter.

51. A possible consideration may be the fact that the water contains detergents which may ruin any taste imparted by the food residue. Nevertheless, one must still be concerned with the last rinse in which no detergents are present. However, the minute residue particles are perhaps completely ruined by the detergents and are rendered inedible and can therefore no longer effect the dishes. In addition, the water accumulated at the bottom of the dishwasher probably contains more than sixty times the volume of any food residue.

52. See *Igros Moshe: Y.D.* 2:28,29, *Y.D.* 3:10, who rules that one who uses two sets of racks may use one dishwasher for both meat and dairy (presumably, he requires separate cutlery holders as well). He advises that, in addition, one run an empty cycle between meat and dairy to *kasher* the washer. In addition, *Igros Moshe* requires separate dish racks because he contends that food residue may remain on the racks from one wash to another. This is difficult to understand. If the washer cleans the dishes upon which the residue dried and hardened, it certainly cleans the residue that came onto the rack during the washing process itself. Incidentally, he makes no mention of the filter problem. Perhaps, at the time, filters were not as common as they are today, or possibly he felt that the water certainly contained sixty parts the volume of the food residue in the filter.

necessary to use one dishwasher for both meat and dairy should consult with a competent *moreh hora'ah.*

3) Use of a meat or dairy dishwasher for *parve* dishes:
One who wishes to wash *parve* dishes in either a meat or dairy dishwasher must determine if his washer has a filter in the washing chamber. If no filter is present, one is permitted to wash *parve* dishes.[53] Nevertheless, scrupulous individuals would avoid using a meat or dairy dishwasher for even *parve* dishes.[54] Any meat taste absorbed in the walls or racks is *nat-bar-nat d'heteira* and poses no problem. If, however, the washer has a filter in the washing chamber, one must be concerned that meat remnants (or their taste), may be sprayed onto the *parve* dishes.

4) *Kashering* a *treif* dishwasher:
Poskim assume that a *treif* dishwasher cannot be *kashered.*[55] Nevertheless, one who faces a financial loss should consult a *moreh hora'ah.*

---

53. According to *Igros Moshe* (ibid.), who contends that food residue may remain on the rack, perhaps one should not use the dishwasher even for *parve* dishes. However, we noted above that this contention is difficult to understand.

54. Either out of concern that food residue may be on the racks or because of scrupulous avoidance of any chance of contact between meat and dairy tastes, however remote.

55. *Igros Moshe: Y.D.* 2:29. The reason given is that the walls of the dishwasher are made of porcelain, which cannot be *kashered.* It would follow that a dishwasher with metal sides can be *kashered.*

CHAPTER ELEVEN

Common Basar B'chalav Problems

- ☐ Meat cooked in a dairy pot.
- ☐ Milk soaked in a meat pot.
- ☐ A meat lid placed over a dairy pot.
- ☐ Hot pots that touch one another.
- ☐ Meat that falls into milk.
- ☐ Hot liquids poured from a dairy utensil into a meat utensil.
- ☐ A dairy ladle inserted into a meat pot.
- ☐ Meat splatterings on a dairy pot.
- ☐ A hot meat pot placed on milk.

Introduction

The objective of this chapter is to address many common problems that arise in the modern kitchen. Most of these relate to issues discussed in the earlier chapters of this work. We direct the reader to those pertinent sections so that he may better acquaint himself with the applicable principles.

Although the Biblical prohibition of *basar b'chalav* refers to meat actually cooked with milk, the prohibition applies to a mixture of meat and dairy tastes as well. We discussed in earlier chapters the concept of *ta'am k'ikar* — the taste is treated as the food itself. Thus, whenever meat and dairy tastes mingle, we encounter the possible creation of *basar b'chalav*. Therefore, one certainly may not use the same pot, dishes and flatware for meat and dairy foods. Use of the same utensils for hot foods involves transfer of taste from meat to the utensil and subsequently from the utensil to the dairy food. Use of the same utensil for cold food involves the question of whether the utensil has been thoroughly washed in between the two uses. Failure to wash the utensil properly will cause residue of the meat to mingle with the dairy.

The reader is reminded that the purpose of this work is neither to render *halachic* decisions nor to replace a *moreh hora'ah.* **This work should certainly not be used as a basis for reaching *halachic* conclusions.** All materials are cited solely for the purpose of alerting the reader as to what may constitute a *halachic* question and to familiarize him with the issues so that a question may be presented to a *moreh hora'ah* intelligently. This chapter can also serve as a review for one who has studied the primary sources.

A. Meat cooked in a dairy pot

It is understood even by the unlearned layman that one may not cook meat in a dairy pot (or the reverse). Passage of time in no way minimizes the dairy status of the pot. Although we noted in Chapter Three, Section II,B that any taste in a vessel loses its potency after twenty-four hours, *Chazal* were concerned that if one uses a non *ben-yomo* pot he may inadvertently use a *ben-yomo* pot as well. Therefore, a dairy pot may not be used for meat regardless of whether or not it is *ben-yomo.*

If meat was cooked in a clean[1] dairy pot or dairy was cooked in a

1. *Y.D.* 93:1. The dairy pot must be clean from prior use. If the pot was unwashed, the soup must contain sixty times the volume of that residue. *Poskim* assume that food

clean meat pot, the question is two-fold: a) may the food be eaten? and b) may one continue to use the pot? Although we will discuss the case of one who cooks meat soup in a dairy pot, the *halachah* is the same for one who cooks dairy in a meat pot.

1) The food:
Whether the meat and the soup may be eaten depends upon whether the pot was used for dairy[2] during the previous twenty four hours. A non *ben-yomo* dairy pot has no effect upon the kashrus of the soup. A *ben-yomo* pot, however, imparts its taste into the soup and creates *basar b'chalav*. Theoretically, if the soup contains sixty times the amount of the dairy taste, the soup is permitted.[3] We noted, however, in Chapter Four, Section II,E that since there is no way to determine the amount of dairy taste imparted into the soup, we must assume that the walls of the pot were saturated with dairy taste which was then completely transferred into the soup. Thus, the dairy taste cannot become *batel* unless the soup contains sixty times the volume of the metal in the pot body.[4] Since the volume of the food in a pot usually[5] does not equal sixty times the pot body,[6] the soup is prohibited. If, however, the pot was used during the

cooked in a pot contains sixty times the residue of any previous use (see *S.D.* 95:1). However, if the pot was presently used for only a small amount of food, it may not necessarily contain sixty times the residue. The *moreh hora'ah* to whom the question is presented must inquire about the amount of soup in the pot *(D.T.* §14).

2. We noted in Chapter Three, Section II,B and Chapter Seven, Section I,A that even if the dairy pot was used for *parve* foods in the previous twenty-four hours, it is not considered *ben-yomo*.

3. In the opinion of the *Shulchan Aruch* 93:1, one may let a non-Jew sample the soup to determine whether it tastes of dairy. *Rema* (92:1, 98:1), however, notes that common custom is not to rely on the sampling of a non-Jew (see *Shach* 93:1. See Chapter Four, Section I,B).

4. *Rema* 93:1.

5. See *Shach* §1, who notes that a wide pot with thin walls may contain sixty times the volume of the pot body.

6. Among the other assumptions regarding the ratio of food to the pot are: a) it is assumed (as noted in footnote (1) above) that the food in the pot contains sixty times the food residue on the pot surface from prior use *(Issur V'heter* 33:2, see also *S.D.* 95:1). b) It also is assumed that the food in a pot (as opposed to a flat plate) contains sixty times the volume of the *klipah* of the pot (see *Shach* 69:65). Thus, if the *klipah* of a pot absorbed dairy taste from hot cheese that was placed into the pot (as noted in Chapter Five, Section II,D, the pot will in this case absorb dairy taste only into its *klipah)*, any meat cooked in that pot (even while the pot is a *ben-yomo)* is unaffected, since we assume that the meat is sixty times the pot *klipah*.

previous twenty four hours for only a small amount of dairy, the meat soup is permitted if it contains sixty times that particular amount of dairy.[7]

2) The pot:

a) A *ben-yomo* dairy pot:
If the meat soup is cooked in a *ben-yomo* dairy pot, the pot as well as the food becomes *basar b'chalav*. The pot may not be used again unless it is *kashered*.

b) A non *ben-yomo* pot:
Even if the clean pot was non *ben-yomo* and the soup is permissible, the pot itself is forbidden to be used (even after twenty-four hours have transpired). The pot had previously absorbed dairy taste, albeit non *ben-yomo*, and has presently absorbed meat taste. Thus, although the pot is not *treif (basar b'chalav)*,[8] it cannot be used for dairy because of its absorbed meat taste or for meat because of its absorbed dairy taste.[9] In the opinion of the *Shulchan Aruch*,[10] although the pot may not be used for either meat or dairy before *kashering*, it may be used for *parve* foods. *Rema*, however, notes common *Ashkenazic* custom to treat the pot as *treif* until it is *kashered*.[11] If the pot is subsequently used for dairy within twenty-four hours of the meat use, the dairy food and the pot are *basar b'chalav*. The dairy food is discarded and all opinions agree that the pot must be *kashered*.[12]

c) Disposable aluminum pans:
One who cooks meat in a disposable aluminum pan that was previously used for dairy must be concerned that dairy residue may have remained in the crevices of the pan. A *moreh hora'ah* should be consulted.

---

7. See Chapter Four, Section II,E for a detailed discussion of these principles.

8. Since potent meat and dairy taste were not cooked together (the dairy taste was non-*ben-yomo*).

9. *Y.D.* 93:1.

10. *Y.D.* ibid.

11. *Rema* 94:5, see *Shach* 93:3.

12. *Shach* §3.

Summary of Section A

☙ The meat:

- ☐ If meat is cooked in a non *ben-yomo* dairy pot, the meat may be eaten.
- ☐ If meat is cooked in a *ben-yomo* dairy pot, the meat is prohibited.
- ☐ In the highly unlikely case that the soup contains sixty times the volume of the metal in the pot body, the meat is permitted.
- ☐ If the pot was used during the previous twenty-four hours for only a small amount of dairy, the meat is permitted if it contains sixty times that amount of dairy.

☙ The pot:

- ☐ If the meat is cooked in a *ben-yomo* dairy pot, the pot must be *kashered* before being used for any type of food.
- ☐ If the pot is not *ben-yomo,* it cannot be used for either dairy or meat. According to *Sefardic* custom, the pot may be used for even hot, *parve* foods. According to *Ashkenazic* custom, the pot is *treif* and must be *kashered*.

B. Milk soaked in a meat pot

In Chapter Five, Section II,A we noted the principle of *kavush k'mevushal* (soaking is the equivalent of boiling) by which foods soaked in liquids impart into and absorb taste from the liquids. In the opinion of some *Poskim,* this pertains only to foods, not utensils. Thus, in their opinion, liquid soaked in a pot cannot impart its taste into the walls of the pot. Others contend that the principle of *kavush k'mevushal* pertains to utensils as well.[13] There are many disagreements among *Poskim* as to how the principle of *kavush k'mevushal* applies to utensils:

1) *Poskim* disagree about which materials are affected by soaking, whether only earthenware and other porous materials or metals as well. See Chapter Five, Section II,A.

---

13. See *Toras Chatas* 85:1, *Taz* 93:2, 105:1 and *Shach* 98:13, 105:2.

2) In addition, there is a difference of opinion as to whether the taste is absorbed into the entire pot or merely into a *klipah* of the pot wall.[14]

3) We noted in Chapter Five, Section II,A that salt brine and vinegar have the ability to impart taste in a period of less than twenty-four hours. *Poskim* discuss whether their sharpness enhances the ability of liquids to impart their taste into a utensil.[15]

4) Another point of contention is whether the *kavush k'mevushal* principle is applicable to a permitted taste *(heter)*, e.g., if milk is soaked in a *parve* pot, does the pot become dairy?[16]

5) *Poskim* disagree whether liquid soaked in a non-kosher utensil is affected by the non-kosher taste. Essentially, any transfer of taste cannot take place before the *kavush* principle is activated, which is after twenty-four hours. Therefore, the liquid is basically unaffected, since by this time the non-kosher taste has become stale *(pagum)*.[17]

---

14. See *Toras Chatas* 85:1, who cites a contradiction in *Issur V'heter* (37:1 vs. 24:9) on this matter. *Toras Chatas* himself rules that the entire pot wall absorbs taste (*M.Z.* 105:1 concurs with this ruling). See also *Kaf HaChaim* 105:1. However, unlike boiling, which imparts taste to and from the entire vessel, soaking transfers taste only to the level that the liquid reached in the vessel (*Chochmas Adam* 57:11). See also *D.T.* §105:11.

15. See *M.Z.* 105:1, who notes that *Taz* 69:41 and *Shach* 69:68 appear to disagree on this question. *S.D.* 69:82, however, rules that salt brine does indeed impart its taste into a utensil quickly, but only to the depth of a *klipah*. The taste will not travel beyond the *klipah* before the end of twenty-four hours. See *S.D.* ibid. regarding earthenware utensils.

16. See *M.Z.* 87:1 who rules that the pot is regarded as a dairy pot and thus, if meat is cooked in it within twenty-four hours, the meat and the pot are prohibited. See, however, *Chavas Daas* 105:3c, who contends that since the milk is *heter*, the *kavush k'mevushal* principle does not apply. See *Yad Yehudah* 105:4k who disagrees, see also *D.T.* 105:5 who cites many opinions on this matter.

17. See *Issur V'heter* (30:9) who rules that milk which soaked in a meat pot becomes *basar b'chalav*. However, *Taz* 105:1 and *Shach* 105:2, 69:10, contend that the milk absorbs the meat taste only after twenty-four hours, by which time the meat taste is *pagum*. See *Pri Chadash* 105:1, who justifies the ruling of *Issur V'heter* in the case of milk that was put into a meat pot **immediately** after the hot meat was removed. He contends that the milk absorbs taste exactly at the end of twenty-four hours while the meat taste becomes *pagum* only **after** twenty-four hours. If, however, the milk was not poured into the pot immediately after the meat was removed, the milk is not affected (see *S.D.* 69:10, who supports this ruling). See *Shach* 69:68 who notes that even a salty brine soaked in a non-kosher utensil cannot cause a transfer of taste before twenty-four hours. *Shach* 105, end of 2, offers an additional argument that the kosher liquid is

Due to the complexity of these *halachos*, **a *moreh hora'ah* should be consulted** in any case of milk that soaked in a meat utensil (or vice versa).

Summary of Section B

Any question regarding milk which soaked in a meat utensil **should be presented to a *moreh hora'ah*.** There is a difference of opinion among *Poskim* whether the principle of *kavush k'mevushal* pertains to utensils. In addition, *Poskim* disagree over the following points: which materials are affected by soaking; whether the taste is absorbed into the entire pot or merely into a *klipah* of the pot wall; whether sharp liquids impart their taste into a utensil more quickly; whether the *kavush k'mevushal* principle pertains to a permitted taste; and whether liquid soaked in a non-kosher utensil is affected by the non-kosher taste that has been previously absorbed in the utensil.

C. A meat lid placed on a dairy pot

If a meat lid is placed on a dairy pot (or the reverse),[18] it is possible that the milk steamed up to the surface of the lid and absorbed meat taste. The status of the milk, pot and lid will depend upon whether the lid is *ben-yomo* from meat use. We will assume that the lid is *ben-yomo*.[19] The *halachah* will also depend upon whether the lid, pot or both were hot at the time and whether or not the milk in the pot was boiling. The reader is cautioned: since these *halachos* have many variables, **any**

---

unaffected. He notes that, in the opinion of some *Poskim, kavush k'mevushal* is effective only after three days, while an absorbed taste, in the opinion of some *Poskim* becomes stale after passage of only one night. See *Chavas Daas* 105:3c who differentiates between bland and sharp liquids. A similar ruling to that of *Chavas Daas* is found in *Yad Yehudah* 105:4k and *Binas Adam* 59(77). Two reasons are offered for this variation: a) sharp liquids revive non *ben-yomo* tastes; thus, if a sharp liquid is soaked in a non kosher utensil, the non kosher taste will still be potent after twenty-four hours when the soaking becomes effective. b) Sharp liquids may effect *kavush k'mevushal* sooner than twenty-four hours (as noted in Chapter Five, Section II,A), thus, the transfer of taste may occur before the taste becomes stale. In any case, the pot must be *kashered* since it absorbed both meat and dairy taste. See Chapter Five note 126.

18. We will discuss the status of a meat lid placed on a dairy pot since that is the case mentioned in the primary sources. The *halachah* is similar regarding a dairy lid placed on a meat pot.

19. We will also assume that the food in the pot does not contain sixty times the volume of the lid. If in fact it does, the *halachah* may vary (see *Issur V'heter* 31:19).

question of a lid placed on a pot of another type should be presented to a *moreh hora'ah.*

1) A hot lid placed on a cool pot:
   If a hot meat lid is placed on a dairy pot on the stove that has not yet become *yad soledes bo,* and is removed before the pot boils, the lid is permitted. The status of the pot and milk are as follows:

   a) The pot:
      If the lid was dry at the time it was placed on the milk pot, the pot, lid and milk are permitted.[20] However, since the lid was taken directly from a steaming meat pot, it is assumed to contain condensed moisture on its underside. *Poskim* disagree as to whether the moisture affects the pot. Some *Poskim* contend that any moisture that may have come on the pot rim is considered *kli sheni* and cannot affect the pot. The pot rim may be wiped immediately from any moisture before the milk pot becomes hot.[21] Others argue that the heat of the cover enables the moisture to impart its taste into the pot. Thus, in their opinion, the pot and perhaps the lid[22] must be *kashered*.[23] Authorities follow this stringent ruling unless financial loss is involved.[24] In the event that the pot cannot be *kashered,* **a *moreh hora'ah* should be consulted.**[25]

   b) The milk:
      The milk is permitted since it had not yet boiled and reached the lid. We need not be concerned with any droplet that may have fallen from the hot meat lid into the milk since one may assume that the milk contains sixty times the volume of any droplets.[26] If solid dairy food is in the pot, the rule of *tatai gavar* applies, since hot droplets may have fallen onto cool food[27] (see Chapter

20. *Rema* 93:1.

21. *Issur V'heter* 31:18 and *Rema* ibid.

22. See *Aruch HaShulchan* §18, who contends that the lid must also be *kashered*. See *Badei HaShulchan* s.v. *"veim hakisuy"* for a discussion of this point.

23. *Shach* 93:6.

24. *Chochmas Adam* 46:5.

25. See *Chochmas Adam* ibid.

26. *Yad Avraham* gloss to 93:1. *Yad Yehudah* §11k.

27. See *Y.D.* 91:4.

Five, Section II,D). Thus, a *klipah* of that food would have to be removed. If for any reason the *klipah* cannot be removed, a ***moreh hora'ah* should be consulted.**[28]

2) A cool lid placed on a boiling pot:
The question of a lid placed on a boiling pot is far more serious. The boiling milk steams up to the lid and absorbs and imparts taste. Nevertheless, if the lid is removed immediately while it is still dry, neither the milk nor the pot and lid are affected.[29] If, however, the lid is not removed immediately and the milk steams up to the lid, the milk, pot and lid may be prohibited.[30] The *halachah* would then depend upon whether the meat lid was *ben-yomo* from meat use or not:

   a) A *ben-yomo* lid:
   If the lid is *ben-yomo* from meat use, the milk, pot and lid are prohibited. The milk is discarded and the pot and lid are *kashered*.[31]

   b) a non *ben-yomo* lid:
   If the lid is not *ben-yomo* from meat use, the milk and pot are permitted since the taste absorbed by the milk and pot is *pagum*. The lid, however, must be *kashered* since it absorbed both meat and milk taste.[32]

3) A hot lid placed on a boiling pot:
If the lid was removed from a boiling meat pot and placed on a boiling[33] dairy pot, the pot, lid and milk are prohibited.[34] Even if the dairy pot was empty, the pot rim absorbs meat taste from

---

28. *Rema* 93:1, permits use of the food. See, however, *Taz* 91:7 and *Shach* §8. *Chochmas Adam* 46:5 and 42:10, permits the food only in a case of serious financial loss.

29. *Issur V'heter* 31:19.

30. *Rema* 93:1. See *Shach* §5 who contends that this is only if the steam that rose to the lid is *yad soledes bo*. If the lid remained on the pot for a while, we must certainly assume that the steam rose to the lid (see *Issur V'heter* ibid.).

31. *Rema* 93:1.

32. *Issur V'heter* 31:20.

33. It is assumed that a boiling pot steams up to its lid, as opposed to the earlier case of the cold lid where we are concerned only if we know that the steam rose to the lid and was *yad soledes bo* (*Yad Yehudah* 93:7k). However, if the lid was removed immediately from the dairy pot and was free of any moisture, the utensils and the milk are permitted according to some opinions, even though both utensils were hot (*D.T.* §27. Apparently, these *Poskim* assume that since the lid is dry at the moment it is removed from the dairy pot, it was also dry when it was removed from the meat pot).

34. *Rema* 93:1.

the moisture assumed to be on the lid and must be *kashered*.[35] If the lid was removed from a hot meat pot in which *parve* foods had been boiled and was placed over a dairy pot in which *parve* foods are boiling, the situation is similar to that of a dairy ladle inserted into a meat pot (see section G,1,e below). If both pot and lid are *ben-yomo*, the pot, lid and food are prohibited according to *Ashkenazic* tradition.[36] If either the pot or lid[37] are not *ben-yomo*, the non *ben-yomo* utensil is *kashered* and the *parve* food in the dairy pot is not eaten with either meat or dairy.[38] Sefardic tradition permits use of the utensils and food without restriction.

Summary of Section C

- If a dairy pot is cooking on the stove but has not yet come to a boil, and a hot meat lid is placed on the pot, the lid is permitted if it was removed before the pot came to a boil. The pot is permitted if the lid is dry. However, since the lid is assumed to contain condensed moisture on its underside, the pot must be *kashered*. If the pot cannot be *kashered*, a *moreh hora'ah* should be consulted. The milk that was cooking in the pot is permitted. If solid dairy food was in the pot, a *klipah* of the food must be removed. If the *klipah* cannot be removed, a *moreh hora'ah* should be consulted.
- If a cool meat lid is placed on a boiling dairy pot and removed immediately while still dry, the milk, pot and lid are unaffected. If the lid was not removed immediately and the lid was *ben-yomo* from meat use, the milk must be discarded and the pot and lid must be *kashered*. If the lid was not *ben-yomo* from meat use, the milk and pot are permitted but the lid must be *kashered*.
- If a lid is removed from a boiling meat pot and placed on a boiling dairy pot, the pot, lid and milk are prohibited. If both the meat pot and the dairy pot contain only *parve* foods but are

35. See *R' Akiva Eger* gloss to 93:1. See *Badei HaShulchan* s.v. *"veim lokchu"*, regarding the status of the lid in this case.

36. *Rema* 95:3.

37. See *Rema* 93:1 who notes a custom to treat even a non *ben-yomo* lid as if it were *ben-yomo*. See *Taz* §2 and *Shach* §4 who try to find justification for this custom.

38. See Section G,1,e below, for a more comprehensive discussion of the various opinions.

both *ben-yomo*, the pot, lid and food are prohibited according to *Ashkenazic* tradition. *Sefardic* tradition permits use of the utensils and food. If either the pot or lid was not *ben-yomo*, according to *Ashkenazic* tradition, the non *ben-yomo* utensil is *kashered* and the *parve* food is not eaten with either meat or dairy. *Sefardic* tradition places no restriction cn use of either the food or the utensils.

CHART 18

A MEAT LID PLACED OVER A DAIRY POT

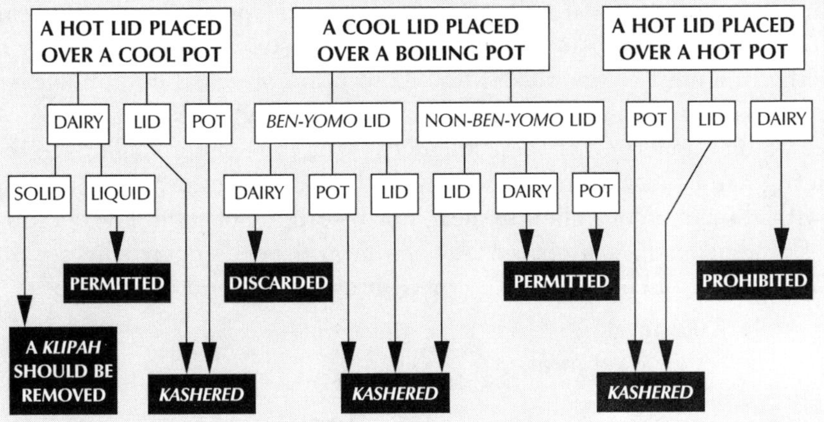

D. Hot pots that touch one another

One should always be careful never to allow a meat pot and dairy pot to touch one another when they are hot.[39] A meat pot should not even be placed near a cooking dairy pot (or the reverse) since food may splatter onto the meat pot.[40] When a hot meat pot touches a hot dairy pot, if both surfaces that came in contact are dry, the pots are not affected. However, if either of the pots are moist at the point of contact, *Poskim* disagree as to their status. Some *Poskim* rule that the moisture on the side of a pot is not significant enough to permit a taste transfer from one pot to

39. *Rema* 92:8. See *S.D.* 97:3, citing *Toras Chatas* 35:10, that this is based upon the concern lest some liquid drip outside one of the pots.

40. *Yad Yehudah* 92:73k.

another.[41] Others contend that the moisture does transfer taste; thus, the pots must be *kashered*.[42] **A *moreh hora'ah* should be consulted.**

E. Meat that falls into milk or milk that spills over meat

These *halachos* are based upon Talmud: *Chullin* 112a, *Tur* and *Shulchan Aruch; Yoreh De'ah* 91:7 (see footnote).[43]

If meat falls into milk or milk spills over meat, the problem should be presented to a *moreh hora'ah*. What follows is a discussion of the issues involved. When meat comes in contact with milk, we are concerned with two factors: a) whether taste *(ta'am)* of milk was absorbed into the meat and b) whether actual milk *(chalav b'en)* was absorbed into the meat. The reader remembers that an infusion of taste can take place only if either the meat or the milk is hot. Absorption of actual milk, however, may occur under specific circumstances, even when both are cold. A common application of these *halachos* is the problem of spillings in the refrigerator. Since the meat and milk are both cold, we are concerned only with absorption of milk into meat, not absorption of taste. The question of whether milk is absorbed into the meat depends upon whether the meat is raw or cooked, smooth or with crevices, bland or spiced:

1) Cold meat:
   a) Raw meat:

---

41. *Chavas Daas* 92:20b. *D.T.* §183 contends that *M.Z.* §29 agrees with *Chavas Daas*. This is less than apparent from *M.Z.'s* words.

42. Responsa *Maharsham* 3:236, who concedes that one may rely upon the lenient opinions with regard to the food in the pot. See also *D.T.* §183, who cites other authorities who disagree with *Chavas Daas*.

43. The Talmud relates a story of a fowl that fell into jug of *kutach* (a dressing popular at the time that contained whey and salt). *Rav Chininah* the son of *Rava* of Pashrunia permitted the fowl since the salt in the *kutach* was of an insufficient amount to cause a taste transfer. The Talmud, however, notes several conditions: a) only a raw *(chai)* fowl is permitted; had the fowl been roasted *(tzli)* it would have absorbed *kutach* into its *klipah*. b) If the fowl had crevices or c) if the fowl were seasoned with spices, it would have absorbed *kutach* and been totally prohibited. *Rishonim* disagree in their interpretation of the terms *"chai"* and *"tzli"* used in this verse. In the opinion of *Rashi*: *"chai"* is defined as "cold", while *"tzli"* is defined "a hot roast". *Rosh*, however, contends that *"chai"* denotes "raw", while *"tzli"* denotes even cold roasted meat. In addition, *Rishonim* disagree as to whether the discussion of crevices and seasoning refers to hot roasted, cold roasted or, in the opinion of *Sefer HaTerumah*, even raw meat. The various *halachos* and opinions that follow reflect these different views.

If cold, raw meat falls into cold milk, the meat is merely rinsed of any milk residue and is permitted. The milk is also permitted since any meat residue is *batel*. In the opinion of some *Poskim*, raw meat does not absorb milk, even if it has crevices. Thus, if raw meat falls into milk or if milk spills over raw meat, the meat may be rinsed, cooked and eaten.[44] It should, however, be soaked, thoroughly rinsed and squeezed to remove any milk that may be absorbed in the crevices.[45] Other authorities maintain that milk is absorbed in the crevices and cannot be removed.[46] **A *moreh hora'ah* should be consulted.**[47] If the raw meat has no crevices, it may certainly be rinsed thoroughly and cooked.

b) Boiled, baked or roasted meat (without crevices):
Meat that has been boiled, baked, roasted or fried etc.[48] softens considerably and is more readily absorbent. Therefore, merely rinsing the meat of its milk residue is inadequate. A *klipah* of the meat surface must be removed.[49] The remainder of the meat may be eaten if it has no crevices.

c) Cooked meat with crevices:
If the cooked meat has crevices,[50] the meat may not be eaten since the milk penetrates throughout the meat.[51]

---

44. Following the opinion of *Issur V'heter* cited in *Beis Yosef* 91, and *Shach* §21. As opposed to the opinion of *Sefer HaTerumah* cited below.

45. *D.T.* 91:87.

46. *Sefer HaTerumah* cited in *Beis Yosef* and *Shach* 91:21. See *Biur HaGra* §18 who follows the opinion of *Sefer HaTerumah*.

47. See *Chochmas Adam* 42:6 who contends that one should follow the latter opinion. See note no. 62 below, regarding if the meat contains sixty times the absorbed milk.

48. At least a third or half of a full cooking *(k'maachal ben drusai)*. Otherwise, the meat is considered raw and rinsing it suffices *(Chavas Daas* 91:16b).

49. In the opinion of *Rashba* as followed in *Shulchan Aruch* 91:7, only cooked meat that is *yad soledes bo* absorbs taste when immersed in cold milk. *Rema* (ibid.), however, follows the opinion of *Issur V'heter* who rules that even cold, cooked meat absorbs milk into a *klipah* of its surface.

50. Cooked meat usually has crevices *(Aruch HaShulchan* §37).

51. *Rema* 91:7. In the opinion of *Shulchan Aruch*, this refers to hot meat only. *Rema* concedes to *Shulchan Aruch* in a case of substantial loss. See *Taz* §12 and *Shach* §25 as to whether one should follow the stricter opinions even in a case of substantial loss, see also *Aruch HaShulchan* §37.

d) Spiced meat:
Cooked, spiced[52] meat[53] is more absorbent than plain, cooked meat. Therefore, if cooked, spiced meat falls into milk, it absorbs milk throughout, even if it has no crevices and therefore it may not be eaten.[54]

e) Use of the meat:
In all of the cases above when meat or its *klipah* may not be eaten, one may nevertheless derive benefit from the meat. Since the meat and milk were not cooked together, the prohibition of *basar b'chalav* is only Rabbinic; thus, as in all cases of Rabbinic *basar b'chalav*, one may derive benefit from them.[55] Nevertheless, the meat may not be cooked since the absorbed milk will combine with the meat to produce *basar b'chalav* prohibited by Torah law.[56]

f) The status of the milk:
In all the cases cited above, the milk is permitted since even spiced, cold meat can only absorb milk but not infuse its taste into the milk.[57] Any meat residue in the milk is *batel b'shishim*.

g) A case of serious financial loss:
If any of the rules mentioned above cause serious financial loss, a *moreh hora'ah* must judge the individual circumstances.[58]

---

52. Salty meat, however, is governed by different rules, see Chapter Five, Section III,B.

53. *Poskim* disagree as to the amount of spicing required to give the meat this status. In the opinion of *Chavas Daas* §15b, and *Chochmas Adam* 42:6, the spicing must be so strong as to make the meat inedible unless washed beforehand. *Yad Yehudah* §35a, however, argues that spices cooked with the food are not washed off but eaten with the food. Thus, when *Poskim* speak of cooked meat, they refer to normally spiced meat.

54. *Rema* 91:7. See conditions noted in note no. 51, since they apply here as well. See *Chavas Daas* §16b, who contends that hot spiced meat absorbs taste even from a dry substance. Thus, if hot, cooked, spiced meat comes in contact with cheese, the entire piece of meat is forbidden. See, however, *Yad Yehudah* §48k, who disagrees. In his opinion, the *halachah* of spiced foods refers only to a solid soaked in a liquid.

55. *Y.D.* 91:8.

56. *Kaf HaChaim* §73. Thus, the cooking itself is prohibited.

57. *Shach* §25.

58. *Rema* 91:7, permits the cold meat if serious loss is incurred. In these cases, he relies upon the opinion of *Rashba* that only hot meat absorbs milk through its crevices or if spiced. See, however, *Chochmas Adam* 42:6, who is uncertain whether one should rely on the lenient opinions, even in a case of serious loss.

2) Hot meat:

If hot, raw meat falls into cold milk, in addition to the problem of absorption of milk, we confront the issue of *tatai gavar* (the bottom overpowers, see Chapter Five, Section II,D).[59] A *klipah* of the meat must certainly be removed and the meat must be thoroughly rinsed.[60] If the hot[61] meat has crevices or if it is spiced, the entire meat[62] is prohibited (as in c) and d) above).[63] **A *moreh hora'ah* should be consulted.**

Summary of Section E

- If cold, raw meat falls into cold milk, the milk is permitted and the meat is thoroughly rinsed of any milk residue. If the meat has crevices, a *moreh hora'ah* should be consulted.
- If the meat was cooked in any manner, a *klipah* of the meat surface must be removed. The remainder of the meat may be eaten if it has no crevices. However, if the cooked meat has crevices, the meat may not be eaten.
- If spiced meat falls into milk, the meat may not be eaten.
- In all of the above cases when the meat may not be eaten, the milk is permitted. In addition, one may derive benefit from the meat. In case of serious financial loss, a *moreh hora'ah* must judge the individual circumstances.
- If hot, raw meat falls into cold milk, even if the meat is uncooked, a *moreh hora'ah* should be consulted.

F. Liquid poured from a hot utensil — iruy

In Chapter Five, Section II,C we discussed *iruy kli rishon* — pouring hot liquid from the original boiling pot. We noted that *iruy* can cause a

59. Although the meat is submerged in and is covered by milk, the milk is nevertheless considered *tatai* (*Rashba* cited in *Beis Yosef* and *Shach* §23). See, however, *Chavas Daas* §13b, who contends that, in the opinion of some *Rishonim*, the submerged meat becomes *tatai* vis-a-vis the milk.

60. *R' Akiva Eger* gloss to *Y.D.* 91:4.

61. See *D.T.* §87, citing *Yad Yehudah*, that even if the meat was from a *kli sheni*, if it was *yad soledes bo*, it must be treated as hot meat if it has crevices.

62. See *Chavas Daas* §14b, who contends that even if the meat contained sixty times the absorbed milk, it may not be eaten, while *Yad Yehudah* §34, disagrees.

63. See *Shach* 91:21.

transfer of taste to a *klipah* of the surface upon which it is poured. The pouring water retains only enough of its original heat to heat the surface upon which it falls. If the water continues to flow in an uninterrupted manner onto other surfaces, *Poskim* disagree as to whether it can cause a taste transfer into those surfaces.[64] The question of *iruy* is relevant to our discussion of contact between meat and dairy utensils:

1) Hot milk poured into a meat dish:
Hot milk poured from a *kli rishon* into a *ben-yomo* meat dish (or meat gravy poured into a dairy dish) infuses its taste into a *klipah* of the dish and absorbs meat taste from the dish. The milk (or gravy) must be discarded and the dish must be *kashered*.[65]

2) Water poured from a non-kosher pot:
If hot water is poured from a *ben-yomo* non-kosher[66] pot into a kosher cup, the non-kosher taste is infused into a *klipah* of the cup surface. The water is discarded and the cup must be *kashered* before use.[67]

3) Water poured from a clean utensil of one type into a utensil of the other type:
If, for example, one pours hot water from a meat pot into a dairy mug (both *ben-yomo)*, some *Poskim* contend that the mug should be *kashered*.[68] Many authorities disagree.[69] Authorities

64. See *Chavas Daas* 95:18c and 92:23b, who contends that if the water flows from the second utensil to a third utensil, the third vessel is unaffected. However, *S.D.* §18, contends that if the flow is uninterrupted, the water retains its heat and the ability to infuse taste into the third vessel. See *Igros Moshe: Y.D.* 1:42, who resolves the apparent contradictory rulings of *Rema* 92:7 and 95:3, in this matter.

65. See *Rema* 95:3.

66. Regardless of whether it was used for non-kosher foods or for cooking meat and milk within twenty-four hours of one another (see *Rema* 103:7 regarding when a full night passed between the meat and dairy use).

67. *Chochmas Adam* 48:13, see also *Shach* 95:18.

68. *Rema* 95:3. Apparently *Rema* compares this to the case of meat and dairy dishes washed together. In this case, although the mug cannot affect the kashrus of the meat pot *(M.Z.* §13), it nevertheless absorbs meat taste.

69. *Shach* §5, *Pri Chadash* §17. There are two reasons to require *kashering* for meat and dairy utensils washed together: a) there is a possibility that the vessels may touch and absorb primary taste from one another. This reason is certainly not applicable in our case since the vessels do not come in actual contact. b) The possibility that the meat and dairy tastes absorb one another immediately upon being infused into the water. This argument cannot be applied in our case either since the water absorbed meat taste first

conclude that the mug should preferably be *kashered*.[70] If, however, this will cause a significant loss (i.e., the mug cannot be *kashered)*, the mug may be used as is[71] after waiting a twenty-four-hour period.[72] If the pot or the mug is not *ben-yomo*, the mug need not be *kashered*.[73]

4) Water poured from, or into, a soiled meat or dairy utensil:
If hot water is poured from a soiled meat pot into a clean dairy mug, the mug must be *kashered*.[74] If water is poured from a clean *ben-yomo* meat pot into a soiled dairy mug, the mug should be *kashered*, if possible.[75]

5) Water poured from a *parve* pot onto meat and dairy dishes:
If hot water is poured from a *parve* (or non *ben-yomo)* pot onto meat and dairy dishes sitting together, they should be *kashered* regardless of whether the dishes are clean or not.

6) Pouring *parve* liquid into hot meat or dairy:
One should not pour liquid from a utensil into hot non-kosher food that is in a *kli rishon* if the liquid remaining in the utensil is to be used.[76] Some authorities, maintain that this applies only to cold liquids. Hot kosher liquids may be poured into hot non-kosher food in a *kli rishon*.[77] Other authorities disagree.[78] In

---

and only afterward absorbed dairy taste. Thus, the meat taste in the boiled water is *nat-bar-nat d'heteirah*. See *Taz* §13 who attempts to justify *Rema*'s ruling. However, this too, is rejected by later authorities (see *Minchas Yaakov* 57:24 and *Aruch HaShulchan* 95:22).

70. *Aruch HaShulchan* §22.

71. *Toras Chatas* 57:12. *Poskim* assume that this ruling of *Rema* is merely a restrictive custom, since the objections cited above are logically correct.

72. *Aruch HaShulchan* §22.

73. Even in the case of utensils washed together, the utensils are permitted if one was not *ben-yomo*.

74. See *Toras Chatas* 57:12.

75. See *Issur V'heter* 34:18, who rules that the mug is unaffected, even if the pot was *ben-yomo*, since the clean water from the meat pot is *nat-bar-nat d'heteira*. However, according to the opinion of *Rema* (cited in 3 above) that even if both utensils are clean the bottom utensil must be *kashered*, this case certainly requires *kashering*.

76. See *Rema* 105:3. Several theories have been offered in explanation of this *halachah*, see *Taz* §6, *Shach* §11 and *M.Z.* §6. Essentially, they explain that the steam or heat of the bottom food creates a connection between the two utensils and imparts its taste into the liquid in the top utensil.

77. *Kreisi U'pleisi* 105:8 and *Chochmas Adam* 59:5. The rationale behind the distinction between hot and cold liquids lies in the theory of *tatai gavar*. When cold is poured into

the event that one did pour even cold kosher liquid into non-kosher food in a *kli rishon,* the remaining food in the kosher utensil is permitted.[79] It should follow that one should not pour from a *parve* utensil into hot meat or dairy that is in a *kli rishon*[80] if the remaining water is to be used with food of the other type. One who wishes to add water to a *chulent* pot on *Shabbos,* should preferably not pour water directly from the parve kettle into the *chulent* pot if the remaining water in the kettle will be used for coffee and milk. The water should first be poured into a cup and then into the *chulent*.[81] In the event that one poured directly from the kettle into the *chulent* the water and kettle are unaffected. One should certainly avoid holding the kettle directly in the steam of the *chulent*. If the hot steam did reach the kettle a *moreh hora'ah* should be consulted.[82]

7) Pouring water from a *parve* pot into a clean meat or dairy utensil:

One may pour hot water from a *parve* kettle into a clean (even *ben-yomo*) meat or dairy cup, the water in the kettle is unaffected even though a stream of hot water connects the two utensils.

Summary of Section F

☙ If hot milk is poured from a *kli rishon* into a *ben-yomo* meat

---

hot, the hot overpowers the cold to heat it and, in the process, imparts its taste into the upper liquid. However, when hot is poured into hot, *tatai gavar* does not apply and the upper liquid is unaffected.

78. See *D.T.* 105:96 citing *Kanfei Yonah.* See also *Yad Yehudah* §31k and 19a. *M.Z.* §6 seems to be undecided on the matter.

79. *Rema* 105:3.

80. See *Badei HaShulchan* 92:180 for an in depth analysis of these issues.

81. This is based upon a ruling of Rav Y.S. Eliashiv (through a third party). He said that initially one should avoid pouring even hot liquid into hot meat or dairy. When questioned about the permissibility of pouring the water in the *kli sheni* into the *kli rishon* on *Shabbos,* he responded that, according to *Ashkenazic* custom, it is only a minor problem. See *Shaar Hatziyun: O.C.* 253:47. Although initially it may be advisable to pour the hot water into a meat cup as opposed to a dairy or parve cup, one may use a dairy cup as well. Any connection between the two utensils affects only the liquid, not the cup. The problem with pouring from the kettle itself is because the remaining water in the kettle may be used for coffee with milk. See also responsa *Emek Hateshuvah* (Jerusalem 1975, *Rav Y. Roth)* no. 119.

82. This creates a problem of *zeiah,* see Chapter Five, Section III,D.

dish (or the reverse), the liquid must be discarded and the dish must be *kashered*.

- ◆§ If hot water is poured from a *ben-yomo*, non-kosher pot into a kosher cup, the water must be discarded and the cup must be *kashered*.
- ◆§ If hot water is poured from a clean meat pot into a clean dairy mug (both *ben-yomo)*, the mug should preferably be *kashered*. If the mug cannot be *kashered*, it may be used as is after waiting twenty-four hours. If either the pot or the mug are not *ben-yomo*, the mug may be used without *kashering*.
- ◆§ If hot water is poured from a soiled meat pot into a clean dairy mug (or the reverse), the mug must be *kashered*. If water is poured from a clean *ben-yomo* meat pot into a soiled dairy mug (or the reverse), the mug should be *kashered* if possible.
- ◆§ If hot water is poured from a *parve* (or non *ben-yomo)* pot onto meat and dairy dishes sitting together, they should be *kashered* regardless of whether the dishes are clean or not.
- ◆§ One should preferably not pour water from a *parve* utensil into a hot *kli rishon* of meat or dairy.
- ◆§ One may pour hot water from a *parve* kettle into a clean (even *ben-yomo*) meat or dairy cup.

CHART 19

LIQUID POURED FROM A HOT UTENSIL

HOT WATER POURED FROM A	ONTO A MEAT DISH	ONTO A DAIRY DISH	ONTO MEAT AND DAIRY DISHES
BEN-YOMO NON-KOSHER POT	MUST BE *KASHERED*	MUST BE *KASHERED*	MUST BE *KASHERED*
BEN-YOMO CLEAN MEAT POT	OK	PREFERABLY *KASHERED*	MUST BE *KASHERED*
BEN-YOMO CLEAN DAIRY POT	PREFERABLY *KASHERED*	OK	MUST BE *KASHERED*
SOILED MEAT POT	OK	MUST BE *KASHERED*	MUST BE *KASHERED*
SOILED DAIRY POT	MUST BE *KASHERED*	OK	MUST BE *KASHERED*
PARVE POT	OK	OK	MUST BE *KASHERED*

G. Utensils inserted into hot food

These *halachos* are based on *Tur* and *Shulchan Aruch; Yoreh De'ah* 94:1-5

1) A ladle of one type inserted into food of the other type. When a ladle used for one type of food is inserted into a pot of hot (*yad soledes bo*[83] in a *kli rishon*[84]) food of the other type (even for a second[85]), taste may be infused from the ladle to the food and from the food to the ladle. We will discuss the case of a clean[86] dairy ladle inserted into meat food since that is the case discussed in *Shulchan Aruch;* however, the *halachah* is identical in the reverse case.[87] Determining the status of a dairy ladle[88] inserted into meat foods hinges upon several variables: a) the amount of dairy taste absorbed into the ladle, b) the depth to which the ladle was inserted, c) the ratio of the volume of the meat (and other foods in the pot) to the volume of the ladle, and d) whether or not the ladle is a *ben-yomo.* Since these *halachos* are complex, **a question of this nature should always be presented to a *moreh hora'ah.***

   a) The amount of dairy taste imparted by the ladle: Theoretically, one need be concerned only with the amount of dairy taste imparted by the ladle into the meat. However, since it is impossible to measure the amount of taste imparted,[89] one must assume that all of the dairy taste absorbed into the ladle was infused into the meat. Moreover, since it is impossible to calculate the amount of dairy taste absorbed into the ladle, one must

---

83. See *M.Z.* 94:1 who discusses the case of one who is uncertain whether the meat pot was *yad soledes bo.*

84. See *Taz* 105:4, *Shach* 105:5, *Chochmas Adam* 59:6, regarding a *kli sheni* (see note 97 below). A *moreh hora'ah* should be consulted.

85. See *P.T.* 105:8 and *D.T.* 105:65. If serious financial loss is involved and the ladle was inserted only momentarily, a *moreh hora'ah* should be consulted.

86. Regardless of whether it is hot or cold (*Chochmas Adam* 46:6).

87. Or in the case of one who inserts a *treif* ladle into kosher food.

88. See *D.T.* 94:1 regarding one who is uncertain whether the ladle was meat or dairy (i.e., one who has both a meat and a dairy ladle and is uncertain which of the two was inserted into the meat pot).

89. The only way to measure whether any taste was imparted is by having a non-Jew sample the meat. However, as noted in Chapter Four, Section I,B, our custom is not to rely on sampling.

assume that the ladle was permeated with dairy taste. We therefore require a ratio of sixty parts meat to the entire volume of that part of the ladle inserted in the pot (see below).[90] If one can ascertain the maximum amount of dairy taste in the ladle, i.e., the ladle was used only once for a small amount of dairy,[91] we require only the ratio of sixty parts meat to that small amount.[92] See Chapter Four, Section II,E.

b) The depth to which the ladle was inserted:
The ladle can impart its absorbed dairy taste only from its parts that were submerged into the meat,[93] regardless of whether the ladle is made of metal or any other material.[94] Thus, if only the cup of the ladle was inserted into the meat, we require *bitul* only to the volume of the cup. One may rely on the testimony of the one who inserted the ladle in order to determine the depth of the insertion.[95] In case of doubt, it may be assumed that the

---

90. See *Shach* §1 and *Y.D.* 98:4. See *M.Z.* §1, that even if the ladle was used for foods that cause only a Rabbinic prohibition (i.e., fowl meat), one may not attempt to calculate the amount of taste imparted by the ladle but one must assume that all of the ladle imparts taste.

91. And thus any taste imparted by the ladle is no more than that small amount.

92. *Beis Yosef* 94, *Shulchan Aruch* 98:5. See *Gilyon Maharsha* 94:1, regarding a ladle that was used originally for a mixture containing dairy, not actual dairy.

93. In the opinion of some *Poskim*, the heat or steam rising from the boiling food causes taste to be imparted from all of the ladle that is within the pot. Thus, even the parts of the handle that did not touch the meat itself (but were in the pot) impart their taste (*Kreisi U'pleisi* 94:10 and *Chavas Daas* 94:2c, see also *M.Z.* §1). Other authorities disagree (*Chochmas Adam* 46:6, responsa *Chasam Sofer* Y.D. 82, see also *Yad Yehudah* §2a). See also *Pischei Teshuvah* §1.

94. See *Y.D.* 94:1, who cites an opinion that since metal transmits heat, it transmits taste as well. Thus, if the handle of the ladle that was not inserted into the meat becomes hot (*yad soledes bo*), it transmits its taste into the meat (see explanation to this in *Yad Yehudah* 92:36a s.v. "*henei*"). Consequently, one requires a ratio of sixty parts meat to the entire ladle. The *Shulchan Aruch* rejects that opinion (*Shach* §3, see, however, *Kaf HaChaim* §16, who contends that, in the opinion of *Shulchan Aruch*, one should follow the stringent opinion unless serious financial loss is involved) as does the *Rema* who notes that common custom is not to differentiate between metal and other materials. Although heat is certainly transmitted to the entire handle of a metal ladle, the taste previously absorbed into the ladle is imparted only from that part of the ladle actually in the meat (*Beis Yosef* ibid.). See *M.Z.* end of §1, who notes that if metal is heated in actual fire (not merely boiled in water), the heat is conducted and the taste is imparted from all of the utensil.

95. *P.T.* §1. See, however, a dissenting opinion in *Yad Yehudah* §1a.

ladle was inserted no further than its cup.[96] For the sake of brevity, we will assume that only the cup of the ladle was submerged into the meat. It should be noted that this applies to a ladle used to serve the food. A ladle or spoon that is used to stir the food is usually inserted deeper than the cup itself.

c) Whether the ladle was *ben-yomo:*

□ A non-*ben-yomo* ladle:

If the clean ladle was not used for hot[97] dairy[98] during the previous twenty-four hours, the ladle cannot affect the meat or the meat pot. The ladle also does not become *basar b'chalav* since the dairy taste was not *ben-yomo.* However, it may not be used for any food[99] since it absorbed both dairy and meat taste. If the ladle was subsequently (within the following twenty-four hours) inserted into dairy food, it will impart potent meat taste and produce *basar b'chalav.*[100] The ladle would then also become *basar b'chalav* since it absorbed both tastes within twenty-four hours. If it was inserted into meat, the meat is unaffected since the dairy taste in the spoon is non-*ben-yomo.*[101]

□ A *ben-yomo* ladle:

If the ladle was used for hot dairy during the previous

---

96. *Shach* §1, citing *Maharshal.*

97. Hot is defined as *yad soledes bo* in a *kli rishon* (*Y.D.* 94:1). If hot dairy from a *kli rishon* was poured over the ladle, only a *klipah* of the ladle is considered dairy. Thus, we require a ratio of sixty to only the *klipah* of the ladle (see *Taz* §1 and *Nekudas HaKesef* ibid.). One may, however, assume that the food contains sixty times the volume of the spoon's *klipah* (*M.Z.* §1). If the ladle was previously used only with a *kli sheni,* a *moreh hora'ah* should be consulted. See *Darcei Moshe* 94:1, however, many *Poskim* oppose *Darcei Moshe's* view (see note 84 above).

98. If the ladle was used for hot dairy thirty-six hours earlier and subsequently used for water twenty hours before it was inserted into the meat pot, the ladle is considered non-*ben-yomo.* However, if the ladle was non-kosher it would be considered *ben-yomo* (*Shach* §2). See Chapter Three, Section II,B and Chapter Seven, Section I,A,3.

99. *Y.D.* 94:4. *Halachically,* the ladle may be used for *parve* foods (*Shach* §13). Although the ladle contains both meat and dairy taste, they have not combined into *basar b'chalav* since the dairy taste was not *ben-yomo.* Thus, each taste is a permitted taste. Nevertheless, *Rema* 94:5, notes that common custom is to avoid using the ladle for any food (see *S.D.* §9,13). *Sefardic* Jews do not follow this custom (*Kaf HaChaim* 93:16).

100. *Taz* 94:5, *Shach* §14.

101. *Y.D.* 94:4.

twenty-four hours, it is *ben-yomo* and subject to all the rules below.

d) The ratio of the food to the ladle:
Since we assume that the cup of the *ben-yomo* ladle is permeated with dairy taste, we must also assume that all of its taste may be imparted into the food. Accordingly, we require a suitable amount[102] of food to nullify any dairy taste imparted by the cup of the ladle.[103]

□ A sixty to one ratio:
If the food contains sixty times the volume of the cup, the food and the pot are permitted. Any dairy taste infused into the food is *batel*, even if the ladle was *ben-yomo*. The *ben-yomo* ladle, however, must be *kashered* since it absorbed meat taste and became *basar b'chalav*. The ladle may not be used with any[104] hot food until it is *kashered*.[105] If the ladle is subsequently (within the following twenty-four hours)[106] put into either meat, dairy or *parve*[107] hot food, the food absorbs *basar b'chalav* taste and must be discarded.[108]

---

102. In the opinion of the *Shulchan Aruch* 94:2, if the ladle was inserted twice before anyone realized that it was a dairy ladle, a ratio of one hundred and twenty to one is required for *bitul*. *Rema* (ibid.) rejects this view. *Ashkenazic* custom follows *Rema's* opinion.

103. The volume of the cup is measured by its displacement of water. The ladle cup must be inserted into the displacement container at an angle so that only its actual body displaces water, not the empty space of the cup.

104. Although *Shulchan Aruch: Y.D.* 94:3 mentions only that it may not be used for meat or dairy foods, *Shach* §9 and *Biur HaGra* §12 note (and *Shulchan Aruch* agrees, *S.D.* ibid.) that it may not be used for any food.

105. Even when it is no longer a *ben-yomo (Shach* §10).

106. Even though more than twenty-four hours have passed since the ladle was used for dairy *(Shach* §10. See *S.D.* and *R' Akiva Eger* ibid. regarding the opposing view of *Bach)*. If, however, more than twenty-four hours have passed between the original dairy use and the subsequent meat use, the food is unaffected since the ladle never became *basar b'chalav*. Similarly, if the meat use and dairy use were within the same twenty-four hour period but the subsequent use was twenty-four hours after the meat use, the food is permitted since the ladle was not *ben-yomo* at the time of its subsequent use with other foods.

107. If the ladle was used for *parve* foods, they may not be eaten but they may be sold to a non-Jew *(S.D.* §9).

108. *Y.D.* 94:3. This assumes that it was animal meat; fowl meat cooked with milk is merely prohibited from being eaten *(assur b'achilah)*, but may be used *(mutar b'hanoah)*.

☐ A ratio of less than sixty:
If the food does not contain a volume of sixty times the *ben-yomo* cup, the food, pot and ladle are prohibited. The food must be discarded in the manner of all *basar b'chalav.*[109] The pot and ladle must be *kashered.* However, they may be used for cold, dry[110] foods[111] on a temporary basis.[112]

e) If no meat is in the pot:
If the meat pot contains only *parve* food but is *ben-yomo* from meat use, *Rema*[113] contends that the food and the pot are nevertheless subject to all of the rules cited above. Thus:

☐ Both utensils are *ben-yomo*:
If the ladle is *ben-yomo,* the food in the pot is considered *basar b'chalav* according to *Ashkenazic* tradition and the pot and ladle must both be *kashered.*[114]

☐ One utensil is not *ben-yomo*:
If either the pot or the ladle is not *ben-yomo,*[115] the food and utensils are essentially unaffected. However, the food should be treated as the same type as the *ben-yomo* utensil.[116] Common custom is to avoid eating the food with either meat or dairy foods[117] if possi-

109. *Issur V'heter* 35:6, *Taz* §4.

110. See *Shach* 94:12, 91:3 and *Taz* 91:3 regarding use with cold liquids. *Aruch HaShulchan* 94:14 rules that it should not be used with liquids. See *Kaf HaChaim* §39 who notes that the reason it may not be used with liquids is out of concern that the liquids may remain in the utensil for twenty-four hours and present a *kavush* problem. *Kaf HaChaim* implies that while initially one should not use the utensil with liquids, it is *halachically* permissible to do so.

111. *Y.D.* 94:3. See *Taz* §4, that it may be used with hot liquids for non-food purposes. *Aruch HaShulchan* §14 concurs with this ruling.

112. *S.D.* §12.

113. 94:5.

114. *Shach* 94:8,16 and *Taz* 95:8. However, according to *Sefardic* tradition, the pot and ladle do not need *kashering.* See Chapter Ten, Section A.

115. See *Chochmas Adam* 48:14, who rules that in the event that either of the utensils was unused the entire previous night, one may, in this case, rely upon those opinions who consider it non-*ben-yomo*, see Chapter Three, Section II,B.

116. *Rema* 94:5. This is in accordance with the opinion of *Rema* regarding *nat-bar-nat* as explained in Chapter Six, Section II (see *Shach* §18). If water was boiled in the pot, it should be discarded (*Shach* §19).

117. *Rema: Toras Chatas,* cited in *Shach* §18. Although *Shach* questions this ruling,

ble,[118] and to avoid even placing the hot food on a dish of the type of the non *ben-yomo* vessel.[119] In addition, the utensil that is non-*ben-yomo* is customarily *kashered* since it absorbed taste from the *ben-yomo* utensil.[120] For example: A non *ben-yomo* dairy ladle was put into a *ben-yomo* meat pot containing *parve* food. The food should essentially be treated as meat food and should not be eaten with dairy. By custom, the *parve* food should not even be eaten with meat if possible and not placed, while hot, on a dairy dish. In addition, the dairy ladle is customarily *kashered*. If these customs cause hardship, a *moreh hora'ah* should be consulted.[121]

□ *Bitul b'shishim*:
If the food in the pot contains sixty times the volume of the cup of the dairy ladle, the food may be eaten with *parve* food or with meat food, since the dairy taste is *batel b'shishim* (nullified in sixty times its volume).[122]

In the opinion of the *Shulchan Aruch* the *parve* food, pot and ladle may be used without restriction, even if the pot was *ben-yomo* from meat use. *Ashkenazic* Jews follow the former opinion while *Sefardic* Jews follow the latter.

2) A ladle of either type inserted into a *parve* pot.
If a meat or dairy ladle (or spoon) is inserted into food cooking in a *parve* pot, the status of the food and the pot depends upon whether the ladle is *ben-yomo* or not.

a) A *ben-yomo* ladle:
If the ladle was used for hot meat during the previous twenty-four hours, the *parve* food should not be eaten

---

Chavas Daas §16c, follows *Rema's* opinion. See *Chochmas Adam* 48:11, who rules that, if possible, one should follow *Rema's* opinion.

118. If, however, one finds it difficult to eat the food without meat or dairy, it may be eaten with food of the same type as the *ben-yomo* vessel (*Chochmas Adam* 48:11).

119. *Rema* 94:5. See *Shach* §18, who has difficulty finding a basis for *Rema's* ruling.

120. *Rema* ibid. If the pot was used for other foods before it was *kashered*, the food may be eaten (*Chochmas Adam* ibid.).

121. See *Yad Yehudah* §35k.

122. *Rema* 94:5. See *Shach* §8, *R, Akiva Eger*, *Gilyon Maharsha* ibid. and *Chavas Daas* §17c, and 10b, as to whether the custom of *kashering* the vessel applies in this case. See *S.D.* ibid. who contends that this should depend upon the two reasons given for the custom (see Chapter Ten, Section A,2). If the meat pot was not *ben-yomo*, the food may be eaten with dairy as well (*M.Z.* end of §7).

with dairy.[123] In addition, the pot should initially be used for *parve* or meat foods only.[124] If the *parve* food contains sixty times the volume of the part of the ladle that was inserted, both the food and the pot are unaffected. This ruling follows *Ashkenazic* custom, as explained in Chapter Six, Section II,B. According to *Sefardic* custom, *nat-bar-nat* is permissible; thus, the food and pot are unaffected (even if the *parve* food does not contain sixty times that part of the ladle).

b) A non-*ben-yomo* ladle:
If the meat ladle is not *ben-yomo*, the food and pot remain *parve*. If one desires, one may, in the future, even designate the pot as a dairy pot. [125]

3) A *parve* pot into which both a meat and dairy ladle are inserted:
If a *ben-yomo* meat ladle is inserted into *parve* food cooking in a *parve* pot and subsequently, a *ben-yomo* dairy ladle is inserted into another *parve* food cooking in that pot,[126] the taste imparted by both ladles is *nat-bar-nat* and cannot affect either the second food or the pot. Nevertheless, some authorities rule that the pot should not be used with either meat or dairy foods.[127] Other authorities disagree. They contend that the *nat-bar-nat* tastes cannot make the pot *treif*.[128] However, since the last taste (of the dairy ladle) has a more lasting effect, they rule that the pot should be considered dairy and initially used for either *parve* or

---

123. *Rema* 94:5.

124. *Issur V'heter* 35:11. Essentially, the pot remains *parve* even according to the more stringent opinion regarding *nat-bar-nat* as explained in Chapter Six, Section II,B. *Shach* 94:15 explains that since one will designate the pot as either meat or dairy, one should choose the same use as the type of the *ben-yomo* ladle. It would seem that one who wishes to keep the pot *parve*, may do so (heard in the name of R' Moshe Feinstein).

125. *Issur V'heter* 35:14.

126. While we followed the case cited in *Shulchan Aruch*, the *halachah* would be the same if the second ladle is inserted into the same food.

127. *Y.D.* 94:5, *Rema* (ibid.) and *Taz: Daf Acharon*. They argue that all opinions agree that the pot should have been set aside for meat after the *ben-yomo* meat ladle was inserted, as noted above (this itself is a *chumrah* since a *nat-bar-nat* taste cannot essentially affect the pot). Thus, they argue, the insertion of the dairy ladle cannot alter that status. On the contrary, the insertion of the dairy ladle determines that the pot should not be used for meat. Accordingly, the pot may not be used for either meat or dairy but may be used for *parve* (*Taz, Daf Acharon*).

128. *Issur V'heter* 35:11, *Shach* 94:15, *Gra* 94:16 and *Chochmas Adam* 48:3.

dairy foods.[129] *Poskim* conclude that although the second opinion is *halachically* correct, one should follow the first and more stringent opinion. In case of serious financial loss, a *moreh hora'ah* should be consulted.[130]

- □ If either meat or dairy is subsequently cooked in the pot, it may be eaten.[131]
- □ If the two *ben-yomo* ladles (of different types) are not inserted within twenty-four hours of one another, the pot may be used with the type of the second ladle.[132]

It should be apparent that any question regarding a ladle that was inserted into a pot should be presented to a *moreh hora'ah*. **A layman should not attempt to resolve these questions based upon the information provided in this work.**

Summary of Section G

⇛§ When a clean dairy ladle is inserted into a pot of hot meat, taste is infused from the ladle to the food and from the food to the ladle. We require a ratio of sixty to the entire volume of that part of the ladle inserted into the meat, unless the ladle was used only once for a small amount of dairy. Some additional considerations:

- □ If the clean ladle is not *ben-yomo*, the meat is not affected. The ladle, however, may not be used for either dairy or meat. According to *Ashkenazic* tradition the ladle should be *kashered*.
- □ If the ladle is *ben-yomo*, the meat, pot and ladle are prohibited. If the meat contains sixty times the volume of the cup, the meat and the pot are permitted. The ladle may not be used with any hot food.
- □ According to *Ashkenazic* tradition, even if the meat pot contains no meat, but both ladle and pot are *ben-yomo*, the pot and ladle are prohibited. If either of the utensils are not *ben-yomo*, the food should not be eaten with either meat or dairy foods (and should be served hot only in a dish of the type of the *ben-yomo* utensil). The utensil that is not *ben-yomo* should be *kashered*. According to

---

129. *Issur V'heter* 35:11, *Shach* 94:15.

130. See *Minchas Yaakov* 85:24,25, *S.D.* §21 and *Yad Yehudah* §25k.

131. *Rema* 94:5.

132. *Yad Yehudah* §25k.

Sefardic tradition, the food, pot and ladle may be used without restriction.

- If a *ben-yomo* meat ladle is inserted into food cooking in a *parve* pot, the *parve* food should not be eaten with dairy and the pot should initially be used for *parve* or meat foods only. The result is similar if the ladle is dairy. In that case, the food should not

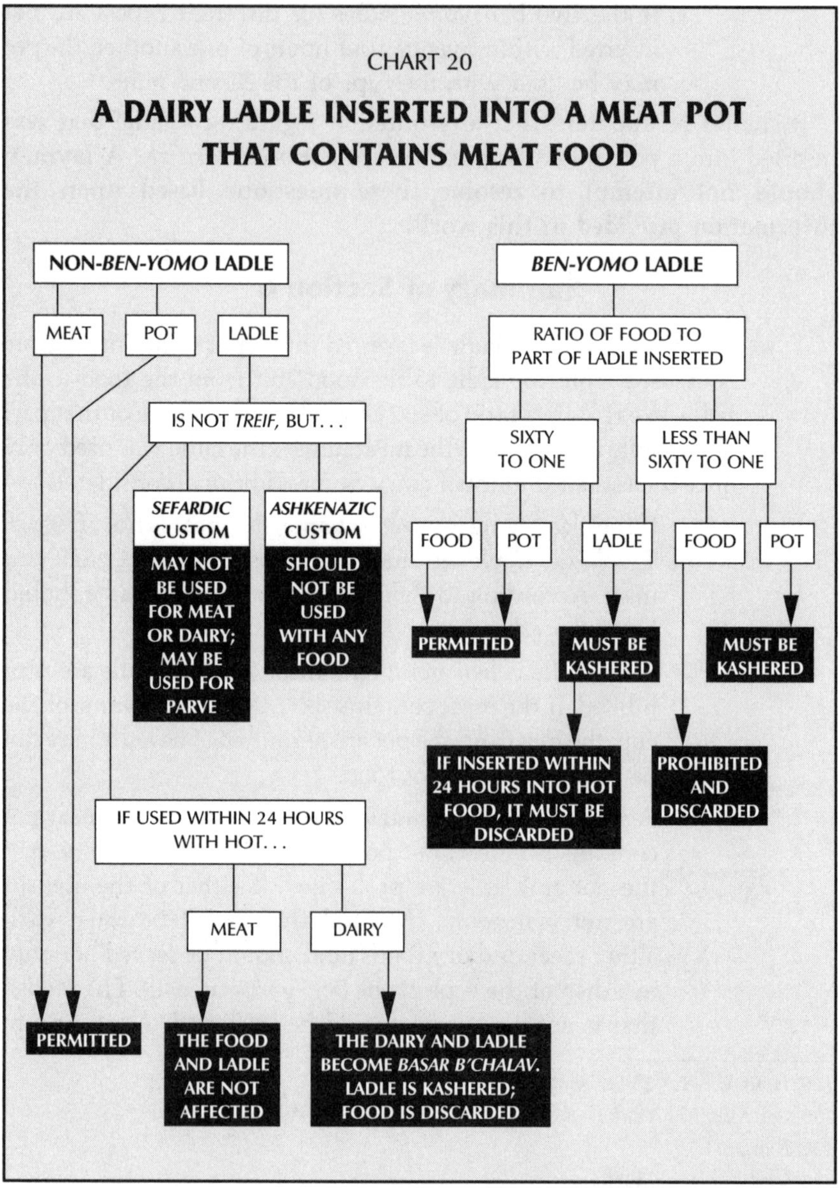

be eaten with meat and the pot should initially be used for *parve* or dairy foods only. According to *Sefardic* custom, the food and

CHART 21

A DAIRY LADLE INSERTED INTO A MEAT POT THAT CONTAINS PARVE FOOD

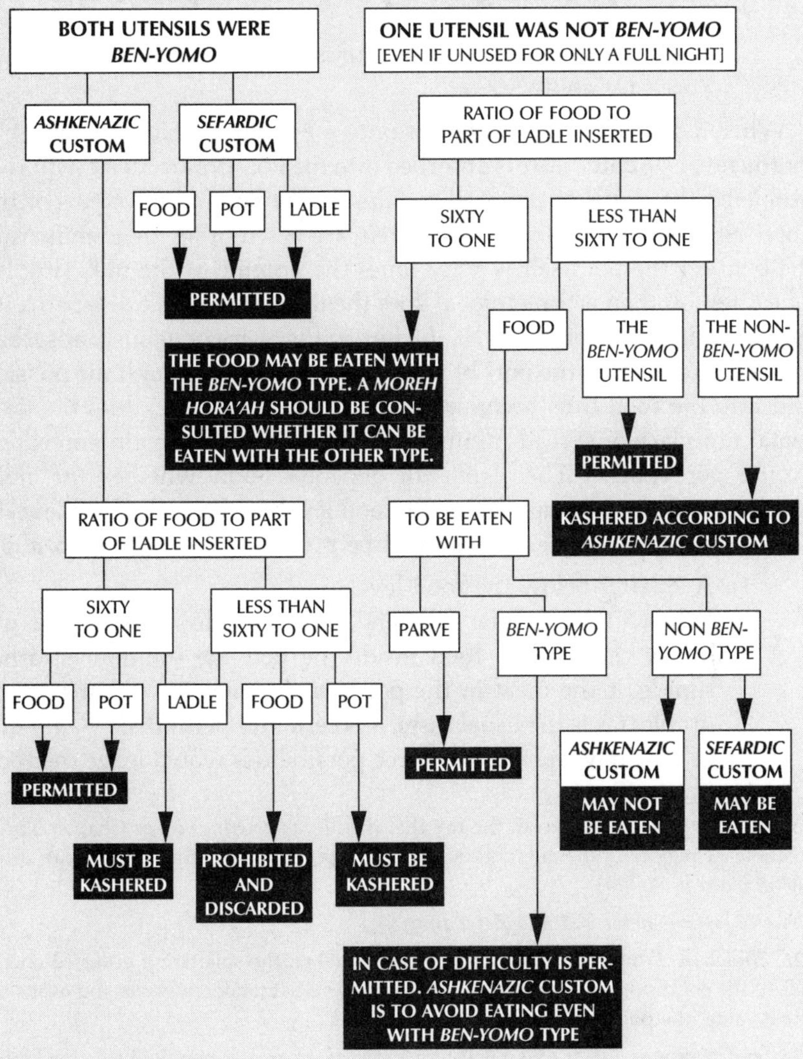

pot are unaffected. If the ladle is not *ben-yomo* the food and pot remain *parve*.

§ If both a *ben-yomo* meat and *ben-yomo* dairy ladle are successively inserted into *parve* foods cooking in a *parve* pot, the pot should not be used with either meat or dairy foods. If either of the ladles is not *ben-yomo*, the pot assumes the status of whichever utensil is *ben-yomo*.

H. Food splattering on a pot of the opposite type

These *halachos* are based on *Tur* and *Shulchan Aruch; Yoreh De'ah* 92:5-7

When a droplet of milk splatters onto a meat pot which is cooking[133] (or the reverse), dairy taste is absorbed into the pot. We are faced with two problems: the status of the food cooking in the pot and the status of the pot itself. The *halachos* discussed herein are based upon the premise that the body of the pot itself is sixty times the volume of the milk droplet. The question then is threefold: a) does the taste of the milk dissipate into the pot wall and become *batel b'shishim* in the tastes previously absorbed in the entire body of the pot? b) Does the taste travel through the pot side and into the food thus becoming *batel* in the food, or c) does the taste remain in place or spread minimally but nonetheless remain embedded in the pot wall?[134] The *halachah* depends upon whether the milk splattered on the pot wall below the food level or above the food level.[135] This question is complex and should be presented to a *moreh hora'ah*.

1) A splatter below the food level:
When a milk droplet splatters on the outside surface of the pot below the level of food inside the pot, the solution is rather simple. If the meat in the pot is sixty times the volume of the droplet (as is the usual case), it is certainly permitted.[136] Any one of the above mentioned three possibilities would leave the food

---

133. Or on a pot removed from the fire that is still *yad soledes bo* (see Chapter Three, footnote 31 regarding the question of whether a pot removed from the fire can cause *bishul basar b'chalav*).

134. See *Issur V'heter* 31:1 and *Zer Zahav* §1.

135. *Shulchan Aruch* 92:6, discusses the case of when the splattering occurred on the side of the pot facing the fire. We omitted this case since in modern stoves and ovens the fire is under the pot; thus, this is a rare occurrence.

136. See *Chochmas Adam* 45:3, regarding a case of when one is in doubt as to whether the pot contained sixty times the volume of the droplet.

unaffected. Either a) the dairy taste dissipated throughout the pot wall and became *batel b'shishim* in tastes previously absorbed in the pot wall. Or, b) the taste traveled through the pot wall and into the food and became *batel b'shishim* in the food.[137] Or, c) if the taste remained embedded in the pot wall. In all of these case the food is unaffected and therefore permitted.[138] The pot needs *kashering* since the taste may not have traveled into the food nor dissipated throughout the pot wall but rather may have remained in place embedded in the pot wall.[139] Thus, in effect, we have kosher food in a non-kosher pot. Accordingly, the food should immediately[140] be emptied from the pot by pouring it, without interruption[141] over the side opposite the splatter.[142] If the pot was used for other food prior to *kashering*, a *moreh hora'ah* should be consulted.[143]

2) A splatter above the food level:
If the milk droplet splattered above the food level of an

---

137. *Smak* as explained by *Shach* 92:18, and *Biur HaGra* §26.

138. *Rema* 92:6 as explained in *Taz* 92:19 and *Shach* §27, while *Maharshal* (cited in *Taz* ibid.) permits use of the pot. *Taz* follows the opinion of *Maharshal*.

139. *Taz* §17.

140. So that the dairy taste should not spread further in the pot and affect the food.

141. *D.T.* §111.

142. *Rema* 92:6.

143. *Taz* §17, cites, and agrees with, *Maharshal* who states that *halachically* the pot is not *treif*. He argues that if the milk taste was imparted into the food, it became *batel* and thus the pot is kosher as well. The only reason to question the *kashrus* of the pot is because we are uncertain if the taste actually left the pot. If this is so, argues *Maharshal*, the taste will not leave the pot during any subsequent cooking either. On the other hand, if we are to be concerned that the taste will be imparted into any food subsequently cooked, the taste was also imparted into the first food and has since become *batel*. Accordingly, *Maharshal* contends, the requirement to *kasher* the pot is merely a *chumrah*, not *halachah*. Other authorities reject *Maharshal's* contention, see M.Z. §17. *Shach* §27 agrees with *Rema*, while *Chazon Ish* 17:6 agrees with *Maharshal*. Thus, if another food is subsequently cooked in the pot, its status would depend upon the disagreement of *Rema* 92:6, who forbids the food and *Maharshal* who permits it. A *moreh hora'ah* must weigh these opinions with any additional factors in the particular case. See *Chochmas Adam* 45:3, and *Minchas Yaakov* 55:5, who contend that if the pot is usually used for larger amounts of food that contain sixty times the volume of the splattered milk, it may be used without *kashering*. Thus, a small splatter on a full size pot would not make the pot *treif*. However, in *Binas Adam* 41(58), the *Chochmas Adam* writes that one should wait twenty-four hours before using the pot, if possible.

uncovered pot,[144] we are concerned about a fourth possibility. The taste may indeed have spread in the pot wall but not to an area sixty times its volume;[145] thus, the taste is not *batel*, but remains potent. In addition, the taste may have spread towards, but does not actually reach, the food level. This being the case, any meat taste in the pot wall absorbs dairy taste and becomes *basar b'chalav*. The status of the food and the pot are as follows:

a) The pot:
The area around the milk splatter is considered *basar b'chalav;* thus, the pot must be kashered before any further use.[146]

b) The food:
Common custom is to forbid using the food.[147] At times, a more lenient position is followed.[148] A *moreh hora'ah* must be consulted.[149]

3) A splatter on the pot lid:
If milk splatters on the lid of meat pot which is cooking, the

144. See *Pri Chadash* §23, and *Pri Toar* §14, who contend that if the pot was covered and steaming at the time that the milk splattered, we do not differentiate between a splatter above the food level or below. In either case, the droplet is absorbed into the food and *batel b'shishim*. The reason for this is because the cover causes the food to boil and steam to the top of the pot. Thus, the entire pot is considered below the food level. See also *Rema* end of 92:7.

145. Had it spread to sixty times its volume, it would be *batel b'shishim* in the previously absorbed tastes.

146. In this case, even if the pot contains *parve* food, nevertheless, if the pot was used for meat in the previous twenty-four hours, it must be *kashered (Issur V'heter* 31:2, see ibid. §3 regarding when the milk splattered below the food level).

147. *Y.D.* 92:6.

148. *Y.D.* 92:7.

149. Essentially, according to *halachah*, the meat in the pot is unaffected since even if any dairy taste reached the food, it is certainly *batel b'shishim*. Nevertheless, one cannot pour the food out of the pot since the food may pass over the *basar b'chalav* area of the pot and absorb *treif* taste. Although we assume that the food contains more than sixty times the milk droplet, we now require a ratio of approximately thirty-six hundred times the droplet. The reason for this is the possibility that the dairy taste spread to an area of the pot wall containing tastes that are just under sixty times its volume as noted above. Accordingly, we must now contend with an area of *basar b'chalav* sixty times the milk drop (the drop itself and fifty-nine times its area in the pot wall, see *Shach* 92:20 regarding computation of the exact amount required for *bitul*). Thus, in order for the food being poured over that surface not be affected by the *basar b'chalav* taste, it must contain sixty times that area. See *Shach* §20 and *D.T.* §89 who contend that even if the

halachah depends upon whether the food in the pot was boiling or not.

a) A boiling pot:
The food in a covered boiling pot is assumed to steam up and rise to the top of the pot, bringing the food in contact with the pot cover.[150] Thus, a splatter on the pot lid can be compared to a splatter below the food level of the pot side.[151] Therefore, if the food contains sixty times the volume of the splatter, the food may be eaten.[152] The lid, however, must be removed immediately[153]

---

food contains that amount, it should nevertheless not be poured before it cools. Pouring the food through the opposite side of the pot is not a viable solution since even moving the pot may cause the food to shake and touch the *treif* side of the pot (*Taz* §19 and *Shach* §21). Indeed, *Poskim* advise that the pot should not be touched at all but left to cool before removing the food (*Y.D.* 92:5). They were concerned that the milk taste reached until just above the food level. Thus, any movement of the pot may cause the food to come in contact with that non-kosher area (see *Taz* end of §19). All that has been said heretofore regarding the kashrus of the food is the basic *halachah*. However, the *Shulchan Aruch* notes the common custom which forbids using the food in any case. *Poskim* (*Issur V'heter* cited in *Taz* §20 and *Shach* §25) were concerned that some of the food may boil up and touch the *treif* area of the pot and absorb *basar b'chalav* taste. Although *Shach* §24, questions the authenticity of this custom, as does *Biur HaGra*, nevertheless *S.D.* §24 notes that common custom follows the ruling of *Shulchan Aruch* as opposed to *Shach*. See, however, *Shach* §25, who contends that if the pot was previously unused or was not *ben-yomo* from previous meat use, or if the food contained approximately thirty-six hundred times the droplet, the food may be used even according to the strict ruling of the *Shulchan Aruch*. In addition, *Aruch HaShulchan* §43, cites the custom to permit the food if it contained sixty times the volume of the droplet. According to *Shulchan Aruch* 92:7 even if the food contains sixty times the droplet it may not be eaten unless one needs the food for Shabbos or guests, or in an instance of serious loss (*Taz* §22, *Shach* §29). See *Rema* §5, who differentiates between a new or used pot. See *Shach* §22, regarding a non *ben-yomo* pot and §23 regarding a pot not previously used for meat. If the food was poured before it cooled, a *moreh hora'ah* should be consulted.

150. See *D.T.* §158, concerning a lid that was not covering the pot tightly.

151. *Rema* 92:7.

152. *M.Z.* §28. See *Taz* §28, who cites and agrees with *Maharshal* that the food may not be eaten unless it contains sixty times the volume of the pot lid. He contends that the food may not immediately be boiling to the degree to reach the pot lid, thus the lid absorbs the milk taste into its meat taste and produces *basar b'chalav*. Accordingly, when the food does rise to the lid, we require sixty times the volume of the lid. Later *Poskim*, however, support the opinion of *Rema*. See *Pri Chadash* §33, and *Chochmas Adam* 45:9.

153. *Maadanei HaShulchan* §148.

and *kashered*.[154]

b) A non boiling pot:
If the pot was not boiling at the time of the splatter, the food is unaffected even if it contains less that sixty times the splatter. The pot lid should be removed immediately and requires *kashering* if it was hot at the time. If the lid was removed before it became *yad soledes bo*, it may be merely washed of any milk residue.[155] If the lid remained on the pot until the food started steaming, the lid requires *kashering* and the food may not be eaten.[156]

4) A splatter on a pot handle:
If splattering occurs on a hot meat pot handle, a *moreh hora'ah* should be consulted.[157]

5) A milk or meat splatter on a *parve* pot:
If a *small amount* of meat gravy or milk splatters on a *parve* pot, e.g., if gravy splatters on a hot water urn, the urn may continue to be used as *parve*. The urn contains no previous dairy taste, thus the absorbed meat taste cannot produce *basar b'chalav*. Similarly, the meat taste cannot impart its status to any taste absorbed in the urn since *chatichah na'asis neveilah* does not apply to *parve* foods that absorbed meat or dairy taste.[158] Consequently, we must merely contend with the meat or dairy taste itself. Since the urn is certainly used for sixty times the volume of the droplet, it does not require *kashering*.[159] If, as is the common case, the water presently in the urn is sixty times the volume of the droplet, even the water in the urn at the time of the splatter may be used with dairy.

6) A hot splatter on a cold pot:
Until now we discussed the question of a cold splatter on a hot pot. In that case the hot pot heats the droplet and absorbs its

---

154. *Taz* 92:28 and *Chochmas Adam* 45:9.

155. See *Chochmas Adam* 45:9.

156. Unless the food contains approximately thirty-six hundred times the volume of the splatter (*M.Z.* §28).

157. The issues involved are: was the handle *yad soledes bo*, did the food in the pot reach the level of the handle and was the handle part of the actual pot body or merely attached to it? See *Badei HaShulchan* 92:5 s.v. "*im*" for a discussion of the issues.

158. See Chapter Seven, Section I,A.

159. However, one should wait twenty-four hours before using the urn, *Binas Adam* 41(58).

taste. If, however, hot milk splatters on a cold meat pot (or the reverse), the hot milk is considered an interrupted *iruy kli rishon* (see Chapter Five, Section II,C). Therefore, the food in the pot is certainly unaffected. A *moreh hora'ah* should be consulted regarding the pot.[160]

Summary of Section H

- A food splatter on the pot side:
  - ☐ If milk splatters on the outside surface of a hot meat pot below the level of food inside the pot, the food is permitted if the meat in the pot is sixty times the volume of the droplet. The pot needs *kashering*.
  - ☐ If the milk splattered above the food level of an uncovered pot, the pot must be *kashered*. Common custom is to forbid using the food as well. In case of difficulty a *moreh hora'ah* should be consulted.
- A splatter on the pot lid:
  - ☐ If milk splatters on the lid of a steaming meat pot, the food may be eaten if it contains sixty times the volume of the splatter. The lid must be removed immediately and *kashered*.
  - ☐ If the pot was not boiling at the time, the food is not affected. The pot lid should be removed immediately and *kashered*, if the lid was hot at the time. If the lid was not hot, it may simply be washed of any milk residue. If, however, the lid remained on the pot until the food started steaming, the lid requires *kashering* and the food may not be eaten.
- If milk splatters on a hot meat pot handle, a *moreh hora'ah* should be consulted.
- A splatter on a *parve* pot:
  If a small amount of milk splatters on a *parve* pot that is usually used for larger amounts of food, the pot remains *parve*.
- A hot splatter on a cold pot:

---

160. See M.Z. 92:26 who notes that essentially even an interrupted *iruy* can cause a transfer of taste into a *klipah* of the pot (unless it flows over a surface). Nevertheless, if the splatter is no more than a small drop, it cannot retain its heat and does not affect the pot.

If hot milk splatters on a cold meat pot, the food in the pot is unaffected. The pot, however, must be *kashered*.

I. A pot of one type that is placed on liquid of another

At times, milk or soup spills on a surface and flows towards and under a pot of the opposite type or a pot is placed over the spill. We will alternate our discussion between these two cases since their *halachos* are similar. The following factors must be considered: a) whether the surface upon which the liquid spilled is hot or cold, b) whether the pot is hot or cold, c) whether the soup itself is hot or cold.

1) A spill onto a cold surface:

   a) Both pot and liquid are hot:
   If, for example, hot chicken soup spills onto a dairy counter top and flows under a hot dairy pot, the pot must be *kashered* and the counter top must be *kashered* by pouring boiling water over the area of the spill. In the opinion of some *Poskim*, the food in the pot is unaffected.[161] Others contend that the food must be discarded (unless it contains sixty times the soup spillage).[162] A *moreh hora'ah* should be consulted.

   b) A hot pot over cold liquid:
   Even if the spilled soup is cold, the pot may not be used without *kashering* beforehand. In this case we use the principle of *tatai gavar*, thus even though the food in the pot is not affected, taste is imparted into a *klipah* of the pot.[163]

---

161. *Rema* 92:7. The hot soup is considered a *kli sheni* even if it is *yad soledes bo*. Thus, following the principle of *tatai gavar* (see Chapter Five, Section II,D) only a *klipah* is affected. In this case the pot itself is the *klipah*.

162. *Chavas Daas* §22b, who notes that according to *Taz* 105:4, a *kli sheni* causes an infusion of taste into a *klipah* and, in this case, since the pot itself is hot, even the food must be discarded. See, however, *Yad Yehudah* §43a, who contends that a small amount of liquid poured over a cold flat surface cannot retain even the heat of a *kli sheni* and cannot cause a taste transfer to the food. As noted, *Chavas Daas* disagrees. In addition, we must contend with those *Poskim* who hold that the rule of *tatai gavar* refers to hot placed over cold not a *kli rishon* placed over a *kli sheni*. Although a *kli sheni* cannot impart taste it is still *yad soledes bo* and will not cool the *kli rishon* placed above it (see *Minchas Yaakov* 51:1, 56:21 and *M.Z.* 92:25, who disagree on this point, see also *Chochmas Adam* 45:19).

163. The only reason that some *Poskim* prohibited the food in the previous case is because it was a *kli sheni* that was *yad soledes bo*. In the current case the liquid is cold,

c) A cold pot on hot liquid:
If a cold[164] dairy pot is placed on hot chicken soup that spilled onto a counter top, in the opinion of some *Poskim*,[165] even the pot is unaffected and may be used after being thoroughly cleaned of any meat residue.[166] However, since other authorities disagree,[167] a *moreh hora'ah* should be consulted.

2) A spill onto a hot surface:
If the liquid spilled onto a hot surface over or near a source of heat (e.g., a *Shabbos blech* over the fire) the problem is more serious. The liquid is being heated even after it has spilled and must be considered a *kli rishon*.[168] Thus, it may infuse taste even into the dairy food in the pot.

a) Both pot and liquid are hot:
The pot must be *kashered* and the dairy food must be discarded.[169] If the pot contains sixty times the volume of the spilled soup, a *moreh hora'ah* should be consulted.[170]

b) A cold pot over hot soup:
Even if a cold pot is placed over the hot spilled soup on the *blech*, the pot must be *kashered* and the food must be discarded.[171] In case of difficulty, a *moreh hora'ah* should

---

therefore this is a simple case of *cham l'toch tzonan* (hot onto cold) which affects only a *klipah* (see *Biur HaGra* §35). If, however, the hot pot was next to the fire, even the food becomes prohibited (see *Taz* §25 and *Shach* §33).

164 Even if the pot was warm but not *yad soledes bo* (*Chochmas Adam* 45:11).

165. *Rema* 92:7, see also *Shach* §31.

166. *Chochmas Adam* 45:19.

167. As above, in the opinion of *Chavas Daas* §22b, the pot must be *kashered*, while in the opinion of *Yad Yehudah* §43a, *kashering* is unnecessary. In this case, the additional objection raised in footnote 162 does not apply.

168. Indeed, in this case, the spilled soup may be even more severe than a *kli rishon* since it is being actively heated (see *Shach* §32 and *S.D.* ibid.).

169. *Shach* §32.

170. See *Taz* §25 who rules that we require only sixty times the liquid actually under the pot, not the remainder of the spillage. See *Chavas Daas* §20, who notes that this is due to the fact that the soup residue is merely a dampness but nothing of substance. See *D.T.* §129, who cites conflicting opinions on this question. See also *Igros Moshe: Y.D.* 1:41, who contends that one needs only sixty times the amount actually absorbed into the pot.

171. *Shach* §32.

be consulted.[172]

c) A hot pot over cold liquid:
If the pot on the cold liquid is hot and heated by a fire. For example, if cold milk spills on a *blech* and flows under the chulent pot, the case is comparable to a hot pot placed over hot liquid.[173] The chulent must be discarded unless it contains sixty times the volume of the milk. The pot must be *kashered* in any case, and the *blech* must not be used again unless it is *kashered*.

Incidentally, since foods often spill onto a *blech*, every *blech* should be considered a meat utensil. The *blech* may contain food residue and certainly absorbs meat taste from these spillings. Therefore, one should not place any dairy utensil on a hot *blech* since meat and dairy utensils should not be permitted to touch one another.[174] Thus, one should not warm dairy pots on the *blech* in preparation for the dairy meal of *Shavuos*. A *parve* utensil (e.g., a kettle) may be placed on any clean area of the *blech*.[175] Any food that is to be eaten with dairy should not be warmed directly on the *blech*.

172. See *Chavas Daas* §21 and gloss *Imrei Baruch*. See also *Yad Yehudah* §44a, who takes strong exception to this ruling.

173. See *Toras Chatas* 23:4 and M.Z. §25. In this case the soup is perhaps immediately heated by the *blech* and becomes *yad soledes bo*.

174. *Rema* 92:8.

175. This is the common custom. Even *Rema* would concede that this is permitted since any possible transfer of taste is *nat-bar-nat*.

CHAPTER TWELVE

The Kashrus of a Knife

- ☐ The principle of *duchka d'sakina.*
- ☐ The residue on a knife surface.
- ☐ Fruits and vegetables cut with a non-kosher knife.
- ☐ Purchasing kosher fish in a non-kosher store.
- ☐ Bread cut with a meat or dairy knife.
- ☐ Cheese cut with a meat knife.
- ☐ The principle of *davar charif.*
- ☐ The *halachos* of a grater, grinder and food processor.
- ☐ Kashering a knife.
- ☐ The method of *ne'itzah.*

I. General principles

A knife is unique among utensils in so far as the laws of kashrus are concerned. It differs from other utensils in three aspects of the *halachah:* A) The circumstances under which it transmits or absorbs taste. B) Its nature to retain fatty residue. C) The method by which it is *kashered.*

It should be noted that in this section the term "knife" applies to any utensil that cuts or grinds food, i.e., a slicer, chopper, grater,[1] *pestle,*[2] *shredder or even a fork.*[3]

A. Transmission or absorption of taste

Chazal consider a knife capable of transmitting and absorbing taste in ways unlike any other utensil. This special status is based upon two considerations:

1) *Duchka d'sakina* — the pressure of a knife:
A knife, unlike other utensils, comes into contact with food under conditions of pressure. This pressure is known as *"duchka d'sakina"* (lit. the pressure of a knife). This pressure increases the ability of the knife to absorb taste from a food or to infuse some of its previously absorbed taste into the food. Although *duchka d'sakina* alone cannot bring about the absorption or transfer of taste, it enhances the absorption in the following ways:

    a) The degree of the taste penetration:
    Although heat can transmit taste from one food to another or from food to a vessel without the aid of *duchka d'sakina*, the degree of the penetration of taste is greatly enhanced by *duchka d'sakina*. We noted in Chapter Five, Section I that ordinarily, two dry hot foods that touch one another cannot transmit taste beyond *k'dei netilah* (the thickness of approximately one inch). Only liquids (or foods immersed in liquids) or oily fatty foods can (in conjunction with heat) generate a transmis-

1. M.Z. 96:3, see also *Chochmas Adam* 47:4.

2. Y.D. 96:3.

3. D.T. 94:101.

sion of taste throughout the food.[4] Nevertheless, when hot food is cut with a knife,[5] the combination of *duchka d'sakina* and heat may cause taste transfer throughout the food even without a liquid or fatty medium.[6]

b) The degree of heat required:
It is one of the axiomatic principles in *hilchos kashrus* that only heat (or its equivalents, e.g. salt) can cause a transfer of taste from one object to another. We noted in Chapter Five, Section II,A that heat is *halachically* defined as *yad soledes bo.* Any degree of heat less than *yad soledes bo* cannot effect a transfer of taste. (Liquids soaking in a utensil for a twenty-four-hour period are an exception and can effect a transfer of taste — *kavush k'mevushal* — see Chapter Five, Section III,A.) Thus, if a spoon is put in a non-kosher liquid which is cooler than *yad soledes bo,* the spoon is merely washed well, *kashering* is not required. Similarly, a knife used to cut

---

4. *Y.D.* 105:4,5.

5. There is an additional unique aspect of *duchka d'sakina* pertaining to a knife held under the meat and used to cut it in an upward manner. We noted in Chapter Five, Section II,D that whenever hot milk spills on cool meat, the outside surface of the meat must be removed and discarded. The remainder of the meat, however, may be eaten. The hot milk is unable to affect the meat beyond its outside surface. The Talmud: *Pesachim* 76a, bases this upon the concept of *tatai gavar* (the bottom item overpowers the top item; i.e., the cooling effect of the meat on the milk is more powerful than the heating effect of the milk on the meat, since the meat is beneath the milk). Although upon initial contact, the milk heats and penetrates the outer surface of the meat, the meat cools the milk sufficiently to prevent it from affecting the meat beyond the outer surface. (If both the meat and milk were hot, the milk and the entire piece of meat would have to be discarded. Indeed, following the principle of *tatai gavar*, when cold milk spills on hot meat the entire mixture must be discarded, *Y.D.* 91:4.) Similarly if hot meat is placed on a cold dairy plate, the meat surface touching the plate must be discarded but the remainder of the meat may be eaten. The rules of a knife, however, are at variance with this principle. The pressure of the knife — *duchka d'sakina* — counters the effect of *tatai gavar*. Consequently, if a cold dairy knife is used to cut hot meat the entire piece of meat may be forbidden even if the knife was held under the meat and cut in an upwards manner. *Duchka d'sakina* increases the ability of the "upper" hot meat to absorb taste from the "lower" cold dairy knife *(Shach* 94:25).

6. *Tur* end of 94, as explained in *Issur V'heter* 36:7 and *Shach* 94:27, see also *S.D.* 10: end of §22. See below Section II,B. Another explanation of this *halachah* is based upon the fact that a knife is assumed to retain fatty residue which, as all fatty foods, is able to spread the taste throughout the food *(Shach* ibid. and *S.D.* ibid.) According to this second explanation, this *halachah* is not dependant upon *duchka d'sakina*. See *Shach* ibid. for a third explanation.

cool, non-kosher meat must be scrubbed well but need not be *kashered*.[7] However, a knife that was used to cut warm non-kosher food heated to less than *yad soledes bo*, must be *kashered* with a process called *ne'itzah* (described below Section III). The warmth of the food combined with *duchka d'sakina* transfers taste from the food to the knife as well as from the knife to the food even though the heat is less than *yad soledes bo*.[8] For practical applications of this principle see below (Section II,B,2).

c) The ability to absorb without heat:
A knife used to cut even cold sharp foods *(davar charif)* is effective in causing a transfer of taste as a utensil that comes in contact with hot non-sharp foods. The combination of the sharp taste of these foods and the *duchka d'sakina* creates a transfer of taste from the food to the knife and from the knife to the food even though both knife and food are cold. For practical applications of this principle, see below (Section II,C).

B. The retention of residue on the knife surface

A knife, unlike other utensils,[9] retains unnoticeable fatty residue on its surface.[10] This residue adheres to or may be absorbed into any food subsequently cut by that knife. Consequently, the food may require scrubbing to remove the residue[11] or may possibly even require the removal of the surface that was cut by the knife (as will be explained below).[12] It should be noted that regarding this *halachah* even a knife that was not used in the previous twenty-four hours can affect the food that it cuts.[13]

---

7. *Chochmas Adam* 47:4. See, however, below, Section II,A, that under certain circumstances even a knife used to cut cold foods may require *ne'itzah*.

8. See *Biur HaGra* 94:27 and *Yad Yehudah* §39a.

9. See *Shach* 95:1 and *Aruch HaShulchan* 95:8.

10. See *Rashi: Chullin* 8b, s.v. "*tzonan*" and 112a, s.v. "*kishus*," *Taz* 94:13 and *Shach* §29.

11. See *Chavas Daas* 91:1.

12. As in *Rema* 94:7. Some of the residue may have been absorbed into the meat surface through *duchka d'sakina*.

13. Although absorbed taste becomes stale *(pagum)* after a twenty-four-hour period and can no longer affect other foods and utensils, actual food (or residue thereof) is

Although other utensils may be presumed clean,[14] a knife is normally assumed to retain residue on its surface.[15] Some authorities differentiate between a knife found on the counter top and a knife found in a drawer: the former may have been used and not washed as yet, while the latter presumably has been washed and cleaned.[16] One should, however, take note of the following:

- □ Our discussion in this chapter pertains only to the *ex-post-facto (bidieved)* situation of a non-kosher knife used to cut kosher food. One may not, however, knowingly *(lechatchilah)* use a non-kosher knife to cut kosher food[17] or a meat knife to cut dairy food[18] unless one *kashers* it in the prescribed method, as will be explained below.
- □ This discussion relates only to a knife being used to cut cold foods or a knife originally used to cut cold food only. If, however, the knife was previously used to cut hot or sharp foods, one who wishes to continue to use it to cut hot or sharp foods must contend with the taste absorbed into the knife as well. Thus, even if the knife is completely clean, its use with hot or sharp foods may affect the food being cut (as will be discussed in Section II,B and C below).

C. The method by which a knife is kashered

In addition to the usual methods of *kashering* utensils, *Chazal* mandated that under certain conditions a knife may be *kashered* in a

---

unaffected by this passage of time. See *Y.D.* 96:1, see also *Y.D.* 103:5 for a dissenting opinion. See note no. 67 below.

14. See *Shach* 95:1.

15. It seems from the *Shulchan Aruch* 96:1 that if the knife is thoroughly wiped clean it is considered free of any residue. See *Issur V'heter* 36:8 who implies that the knife must be wiped clean with specific intent to clean it. See *D.T.* 96:4 citing responsa *Chut Hashoni*. The wording of *Shach* 10:6 implies that a mere visual inspection of the knife is sufficient to determine if it is clean of residue. See *R' Akiva Eger* (gloss to *Shach* 96:3) who cites a method for determining the cleanliness of the knife. A similar method is mentioned in *Issur V'heter* 58:4. In gloss to 94:7, *R' Akiva Eger* notes that a clean knife is not subject to these rules. In gloss to *Shach* 96:3 he cites *Tevuas Shor* 10:18 who contends that merely rinsing the knife without wiping it clean is insufficient.

16. See *D.T.* 96:4 who cites an opinion that most knives today are kept clean when not in use and may be assumed to be free of residue. *D.T.* seems to accept this view insofar as he suggests that one inquire into the particular circumstances of each case.

17. *Y.D.* 121:7.

18. *Y.D.* 89:4.

unique manner. This method is known as *ne'itzah* — thrusting (into the ground). Essentially, this is done by thrusting the knife into hard earth ten times. The procedure, its effect and its limitations are discussed in Section III below.

Summary of Section I

- A knife, slicer, chopper, grater, pestle, shredder or even a fork comes into contact with food in a situation of pressure *(duchka d'sakina)*. This pressure increases the ability of the knife to transfer or absorb taste to and from the food being cut in the following ways:
  - The taste may be absorbed into the entire food even in the absence of a liquid medium.
  - The taste may be absorbed even if the food was not hot to the degree of *yad soledes bo.*
  - If the food was a *davar charif,* the taste is absorbed even without heat.
- A knife, unlike other utensils, is considered to retain unnoticeable food residue on its blade.
- A knife may, in certain circumstances, require *ne'itzah* — thrusting into the ground ten times.

II. Practical kashrus situations

The circumstances under which use of a knife presents a *kashrus* problem are complex and subject to many considerations. Thus, they rightfully belong within the realm of those questions to be addressed to a *moreh hora'ah* who will evaluate each specific case. Given the scope of this *sefer,* we cannot possibly describe and address all the possible factors *vis-a-vis* the use of a knife with regard to *hilchos kashrus.* We will therefore, limit our discussion to those questions to which *Poskim* have rendered clear-cut decisions. Those situations that require evaluation must be referred to a *moreh hora'ah*. The following topics will be covered: a) knife used to cut cold foods. b) A knife used to cut warm foods. c) A knife used to cut sharp foods.

A. A knife used to cut cold foods

[Note: this section deals with non-sharp foods. Sharp foods will be discussed in Section C.]

These *halachos* are based on the Talmud *Chullin* 112a, *Tur* and *Shulchan Aruch; Yoreh De'ah* end of 89 and end of 96.

Whenever a knife is used to cut cold non-sharp foods, the taste contained in the knife cannot be imparted to the food. As noted above, one must, nevertheless contend with the food residue assumed to remain on the knife blade. Meat, dairy or non-kosher fatty residues on the blade may adhere to the food it cuts. If, however, the knife was certainly clean, the food is not affected[19] (see Section I above). Our discussion in this section pertains to a knife that cannot with certainty be assumed to be clean.

1) A dairy knife used for meat (or a meat knife used for cheese):

One should note that the rules discussed in this section apply to one who ***inadvertently*** *used a knife of one type to cut food of another type.* ***Under no circumstances*** *may one intentionally use a dairy knife to cut even cold meat (or a meat knife to cut cold cheese). Indeed, one may not even cut bread for a dairy meal with a meat knife unless one does* ne'itzah *beforehand (see 2-d below).*[20]

a) Firm — not hard[21] — food (e.g., meat or cheese[22]): When a dairy knife is used to cut meat (or a meat knife is used to cut cheese), the *duchka d'sakina* is minimal. Meat is not generally hard, thus minimal pressure is applied in the cutting. In addition, since the meat was cold, no transfer of taste occurred. The *halachic* consequences are as follows:

---

19. Authorities, however, recommend that, in any case, the food should be rinsed, see no. 23 below.

20. *Y.D.* 89:4. See *Taz* §6 who rules that after *ne'itzah* one may even use a meat knife to cut cheese. In §7, however, he notes that common custom forbids doing so. The wording of the *Shach*, §22, although ambiguous, seems to imply that *ne'itzah* is acceptable only for use to cut bread for a dairy meal, not to cut cheese itself *(S.D.* ibid). See Chapter Eight, Section III,A, that common custom is not to rely upon *ne'itzah* to cut bread with a meat or dairy knife.

21. I.e., food that is neither extremely soft nor extremely hard. Extremely soft foods do not cause *duchka d'sakina* since they offer little resistance to the blade, while extremely hard foods cause excessive *duchka d'sakina* and are governed by more stringent rules, as in (b) below. *Poskim* refer to a knife used to cut meat in their discussions of *duchka d'sakina*.

22. E.g., perhaps American or Muenster cheese. Soft cheeses such as cheese spread or cream cheese cause no *duchka d'sakina*.

□ The food:

Both cut surfaces of the meat (or cheese) should be scrubbed well in cool water (hot water will cause the dairy residue to be absorbed into the meat) in order to remove any dairy residue that may have adhered to the meat.[23] Preferably, one should discard a sliver of both cut surfaces *(k'dei klipah)* of the meat (or cheese).[24]

□ The knife:

The knife must be cleaned and scrubbed thoroughly in cool water to remove any meat (or cheese) residue.[25] One who has no access to water may wipe the blade thoroughly with a thick cloth.[26] If the knife was not cleaned immediately after use, the residue is assumed to have dried onto the knife surface.[27] Simple scrubbing will no longer do, rather the knife requires *ne'itzah*.[28]

---

23. *Chochmas Adam* 47:3. See *Chavas Daas* 91:1 for a detailed discussion as to when scrubbing is necessary and when rinsing suffices.

24. *Issur V'heter* 36:8, *Chochmas Adam* 47:3. However, if the knife was clean this is not necessary (see *Issur V'heter*, ibid.). See discussion above (I-B), as to whether a knife may be assumed to be clean. The knife used to cut away these surfaces should be of the same type as the food being cut (e.g., a dairy knife should be used to cut away the cheese surface). One need not be concerned that the knife will be affected by the minute residue on the meat surface.

25. See *Shach* 94:31 who implies that a knife used to cut meat does not require *ne'itzah*. Apparently he assumes that typical meat is not as hard as hard cheese. This is implied in *Yad Yehudah* 94:46k as well. See, however, *Maharshal* cited in *Shach* 89:22 who seems to maintain that if a dairy knife is used to cut meat *ne'itzah* is required. See *Chochmas Adam* 47:4 who rules that if a knife is used for cold foods it may be merely washed, while in 47:3 he rules that a knife used to cut cold meat requires *ne'itzah*.

26. *Chullin* 8b.

27. *Yad Yehudah* 94:46k based on *Rema* 69:20.

28. We find no such concern regarding a dairy pot used with cold meat even if the meat residue dried on its surface. Apparently, *Poskim* were concerned only with the minute residue adhering to a knife which may become absorbed into the outside surface of the food through *duchka d'sakina*. A pot, however, presents no such problem since any minute quantity of meat residue remaining on the pot is certainly diluted in any food subsequently cooked in the pot and nullified *(batel b'shishim)*. A knife, however, leaves its residue only on (or in) the outside surface of the food (not mixed into the food) and hence the residue is not nullified.

b) Hard food (e.g., hard cheese[29]):
When a meat knife is used to cut hard cheese, significant pressure is exerted and the *duchka d'sakina* is more effective.

□ The food:
Both cut surfaces of the cheese should preferably be removed and discarded.[30] If the knife was certainly clean and not *ben-yomo*, the entire cheese may be eaten after it is rinsed.

□ The knife:
The knife requires *ne'itzah* before it may be used with meat.[31]

2) A dairy or meat knife used to cut *parve* foods
Or a non-kosher knife used to cut kosher food:

[Note: In this section, we are obviously concerned only with the effect of the knife on the food, not the reverse.]

a) Root[32] vegetables:
A meat knife (even unwashed)[33] used to cut a cold, non-sharp root vegetable (e.g., carrots,[34] turnips, parsnips[35]) cannot impart its meat taste to the vegetable. *Duchka d'sakina* alone, without the combination of

---

29. I.e., very hard Swiss cheese.

30. See *Issur V'heter* 58:4 who rules that in this case *ne'itzah* is required for the knife. In 58:8 he contends that in any case that the knife needs *ne'itzah* the food needs *klipah*. If, however, financial loss will be incurred *klipah* is not required (see *Chochmas Adam* 47:4).

31. *Shach* 94:31 and *Chochmas Adam* 47:4 in reference to hard cheese. Apparently, *Poskim* were referring to very hard cheese as opposed to typical cheese which is not considered hard (see *Shach* 94:31) Presumably, a very hard meat is governed by rules similar to those of hard cheese (see *Chochmas Adam* 47:4 who implies that hard cheese is used only as an example but the *halachah* would be the same with any hard food).

32. This general category is based on the Talmudic *(Chullin* 112a) law pertaining to *lefes* (turnip). *Poskim* assume that all vegetables of this type are included in this category *(Chochmas Adam* 49:9). The essential criteria for this category is a food that is similar to a turnip in that it can be washed well. A soft juicy food, however, if washed, may absorb even more of the residue on its surface, thus it cannot be cleansed by washing; it must be scraped to remove any residue on its surface, as in (b) below.

33. The *Shulchan Aruch* in the entire Chapter 96 is referring to an unwashed knife since any knife is assumed to be unwashed (see section 1,B).

34. In Yiddish - *"mehren"*, *Chochmas Adam* 49:9.

35. In Yiddish — *"reebin"*, *Shach* 96:22, possibly also kohlrabi.

either heat or a sharp food, cannot transfer taste. We did, however, note that a knife is assumed to retain food residue on its surface. Therefore, the cut surfaces of any root vegetable cut with a meat knife must be rinsed well before being eaten with dairy food.[36]

b) Fruits or vegetables:[37]
A fruit[38] or juicy vegetable (an orange, watermelon,[39] cucumber, cabbage, tomato, pumpkin, beet or lettuce[40]) cut with a meat knife cannot be cleaned by merely rinsing in water. The water, instead of removing the meat residue, may cause the residue to become further absorbed into the food.[41] Rather, both cut surfaces of the foods must be scraped with a *parve* knife to remove the outside surface of the food. This scraping is called *g'reidah* or *g'reirah*.[42] If the knife was certainly clean, some authorities permit the food to be washed[43] and eaten with dairy food,[44] while others

---

36. Y.*D.* 96:5. See *Yad Yehudah* 96:34a and §35k (cited in *Kaf HaChaim* §59 and *Darcei Teshuvah* §78) who rules that if the knife was certainly clean, the food need not be washed. *D.T.* ibid. quotes *Yad Yehudah* as initially requiring *g'reidah* even if the knife is clean. However, *Yad Yehudah* seems to require this only for mildly sharp vegetables not for root vegetables.

37. This general category is based on the Talmudic *(Chullin* 112a) law pertaining to a *kishus* (cucumber). *Poskim* assume that the essential criteria is a juicy moist vegetable that, if washed, may absorb even more of the non-kosher surface residue.

38. See *Chochmas Adam* 49:9 who implies that all fruits should be included in this category.

39. Perhaps this is *"avatiach"* mentioned in *Rambam* 9:24 (see *Tiferes Yisrael: Maasros* 1:37, although he contradicts himself in *Kilayim* 1:65). In addition, a watermelon certainly is a juicy vegetable and belongs in this category.

40. See *Aruch HaShulchan* 96:21 who includes cucumbers, pumpkins, beets, cabbage and all green vegetables *(yerakos)* in this category.

41. *Shach* 96:21.

42. Y.*D.* 96:5. See *Taz* §14, *Shach* §21, who explain that *g'reidah* differs from *klipah*. Whereas *klipah* requires removal of a sliver of food of sufficient thickness to be removed as one piece, *g'reidah* is the removal of merely the thinnest surface and can be accomplished through scraping.

43. See *Maadanei HaShulchan* 96:72 who explains that this washing is necessary to remove any minute amount of residue that may have remained on the knife.

44. See *Yad Yehudah* 96:34a, 35k (cited in *Darcei Teshuvah* §78) who assumes that according to the opinion of the *Toras Chatas* (cited in *Shach* §21) one cannot differentiate between the use of a washed or unwashed knife (both require *g'reidah)*.

disagree.[45] If, in addition to being clean, the knife was not used to cut hot food during the previous twenty-four hours, the food may be used without any preparation.[46]

□ A vegetable salad in a non-kosher restaurant:
One may not eat a vegetable salad in a non-kosher restaurant even if the salad contains no onions (if the salad contains onions or any sharp food, one certainly cannot eat the salad, as will be explained in Section C below). A restaurant may use the same knife to cut non-kosher foods (e.g., a meat sandwich) without thoroughly washing the knife in between. One may, nevertheless, purchase cut watermelon in a fruit store or supermarket since presumably they keep separate knives to cut the melons.[47]

---

45. See *S.D.* §21. It seems that the more stringent opinion is based upon the understanding that a *kishus* (assumed to be a cucumber) is a bit sharp. Thus, this stringency applies only to those vegetables which are likewise a bit sharp. We have no basis to extend it to all the above mentioned vegetables which are not at all sharp. Indeed, since our cucumbers have no bitter taste, it is possible that the Talmud is referring to a species of cucumber unlike those eaten today. Although perhaps, one should follow the stringent opinion regarding a cucumber itself since *Chazal* referred to it directly, we have no reason to include other vegetables into this category (see footnote 93 below).

46. See *S.D.* ibid. and *Kaf HaChaim* §59.

47. See *Rema* 96:2. Furthermore, if a non-kosher knife was used to cut watermelons, it was certainly cleaned well beforehand, both out of hygienic concern and concern not to ruin the taste of the watermelon (see *Rashba: Chullin* 8b). See, however, *Maadanei HaShulchan* 96:72, who notes that although *halachically* one may purchase a cut watermelon, there is a rationale to avoid doing so since we do not rely upon the assumption that separate knives are used (unless there are additional considerations, see *Yad Yehudah* 96:26a). Nevertheless, see *Rema: Toras Chatas* 61:8, that even when a non-kosher knife is used to cut sharp foods the sharp foods may be eaten since the taste is transferred to the first and second cuts only. The subsequent cuts are not affected since, by then, the knife has been sufficiently cleaned through the cutting itself. Thus, even in the unlikely event that a knife was brought from the meat department of the supermarket it was certainly used to cut many watermelons and was thus cleaned in the process. The first cuts of watermelon that may have become prohibited are *batel* in the others. Thus even the objection of the *Maadanei HaShulchan* should not apply. When this question was asked of *Rav Y.S. Eliashiv* (through a third party), he responded that one may assume that a separate knife or at least a clean knife is used for cutting watermelons. One who wishes to eat salads from a salad bar in a restaurant should consult a *moreh hora'ah*. Although a salad bar that is separate from the non-kosher part of the restaurant may be similar in principle to a watermelon, several serious problems must be considered: salad bars use many types of salad dressings, most of which contain

c) Fish:

In the opinion of some authorities, fish cut with a meat knife may be eaten with a dairy meal if the cut surfaces are thoroughly washed and scrubbed beforehand. Similarly, a fish cut with a non-kosher knife may be thoroughly washed and scrubbed. Although fish (being juicy and moist) is similar to juicy vegetables that require *g'reidah*, nevertheless, since fish cannot be scraped, a thorough washing may suffice. Preferably, the cut edges should be scraped lightly with a knife edge.[48] Others[49] are uncertain whether washing is sufficient. Presumably, if the knife was clean, one may follow the lenient opinion.

□ Purchasing fish from a non-kosher store:

Since the matter is controversial, one should not purchase cut fish from a store that sells non-kosher fish,[50]

---

non-kosher ingredients. Even if one requests salad without dressing, the serving utensils may have been used for dressings and may contain non-kosher residue. Also, many vegetables must be checked for insects. It is impossible to check cut-up vegetables that are served on a plate. Third, even if one finds a salad free of any kashrus problem, one should be concerned with *maris ayin*, i.e., people who see one eating a salad in the restaurant may suspect that the salad is non-kosher (since most salads do have kashrus problems) or, worse yet, they may erroneously conclude that it is permissible to eat salads at that salad bar. If the vegetables are not cut with a knife but with a shredder, one must also determine whether the shredder is used for anything non-kosher e.g., cheese. *Poskim* note that it is extremely difficult to clean a shredder properly. If the salad contains radishes or onions, the problem becomes more difficult since a radish or an onion is a *davar charif*. (See *Shach* and *S.D.* 96:12 and *Pischei Teshuvah* §2. Although *Aruch HaShulchan* §17 takes a lenient position regarding cut radishes unless they were certainly cut with a *ben-yomo* non-kosher knife. It is questionable if he would advise that one initially *(lechatchilah)* rely on his position.) In short, one must consult with a *moreh hora'ah* who is well acquainted with the nature of the particular circumstances before eating salads in a restaurant.

48. Responsa *Chavos Ya'ir* 179 who recommends that the cut edge be scraped lightly. This light scraping, as opposed to *g'reidah*, is done by merely pressing and scraping the knife blade across the cut surface without actually removing any of the surface. See also *Toras Chatas* 61:9, cited in *Shach* 96:16, who notes that unsalted fish cut with a non-kosher knife may be merely washed clean.

49. See *Yad Yehudah* 96:34a.

50. See *Yad Yehudah* (ibid.) who relies on washing and scrubbing the fish only on the assumption that the knife is presumably clean and has not been used in the previous twenty-four hours. While this may be the case with a knife used at home, it is an improbable assumption pertaining to a fish store. However, *Chavos Ya'ir* himself permits the fish even if it is cut with a *ben-yomo* knife.

even though the fins and scales of the kosher fish are recognizable (skinless fish or fillets may, in fact, be non-kosher). Since the proprietor cannot be believed that the knife is used exclusively for kosher fish[51] we must be concerned that the knife may have had non-kosher residue. In the event that one has no alternative to purchasing cut fish from a non-kosher store, the fish should be thoroughly washed and the cut surfaces lightly scraped with a knife edge.[52] If the store sells only kosher fish, one may purchase cut fish (if the scales are recognizable) although one has no assurance that the knife is kosher.[53]

□ One may not purchase pickled or salted fish without proper Rabbinical supervision, even if the fins and scales are recognizable. Indeed, one may not purchase a pickled or salted fish even with Rabbinical supervision if it was cut with a non-kosher knife. Pickled or salted fish is considered a *davar charif* and subject to all the rules discussed in section C below.[54]

d) Bread:

One should not use a meat knife to cut bread for a dairy meal (or vice-versa).[55] One who must use a meat knife to cut bread for a dairy meal should do *ne'itzah*[56] beforehand if possible. Otherwise, one should wash the knife well with soap and steel wool.[57] In the event that a meat knife was used without *ne'itzah,* the cut surfaces of the bread should be scraped. In this respect, bread is

51. See *Darcei Moshe* 96:5, *Taz* 96:12 and *Minchas Yaakov* 61:35.

52. As advised in *Chavos Ya'ir* 179. Perhaps, in a situation of hardship one may rely on the *Chavos Ya'ir,* whose opinion is cited by many authorities (see *Pischei Teshuvah* 96:5).

53. Even in the remote possibility that the knife was brought from a private home, it was certainly used to cut many fish in the interim (see *D.T.* 96:36).

54. *S.D.* 96:15.

55. *Y.D.* 89:4.

56. *Shach* 89:22, *R' Akiva Eger* ibid. The *Aruch HaShulchan* §16, and the *Chochmas Adam* 40:14, however, follow the opinion of the *Taz* 89:6, that wiping the knife thoroughly is sufficient.

57. Relying on the *Taz* (ibid.); in addition, washing with steel wool is perhaps the equivalent of *ne'itzah.* See section III below.

similar to fruits since bread cannot be washed.[58] If, however, the knife was definitely clean and not used to cut hot meat during the previous twenty-four hours, the bread may be eaten without any preparation.[59] *Poskim* relate that the common custom is not to rely on *ne'itzah* but to cut bread for a dairy meal with a dairy knife only (and vice-versa).[60] *Poskim* commend the custom of punctilious individuals who keep a separate *parve* bread knife.[61]

e) A worm found while cutting a vegetable:
One who cut a worm while cutting a vegetable should wash the cut surface of the vegetable and scrub the knife well.[62] A fruit in which a worm was found should be scraped on its cut surfaces.[63]

Summary of Section A

When cold food is cut with a knife of the other type (or with a non-kosher knife), one need not be concerned about the taste absorbed into the knife. However, unless the knife was certainly clean one must contend with the food residue assumed to be on the knife blade. The effect on the food and on the knife is dependent upon the type of food that was cut.

☙ A dairy knife used for meat or the reverse:

- ☐ Soft food (meat or cheese): Both the cut surfaces of the food and the knife must be scrubbed well in cool water. Preferably, a sliver of the cut surfaces should be removed. If the knife was not scrubbed immediately, it requires *ne'itzah*.
- ☐ Hard food (e.g., hard cheese): The cut surfaces of the food should preferably be removed. The knife requires *ne'itzah*.

---

58. *M.Z.* 96:14. If, however, meat merely touched the crust of the bread, the crust need only be washed (*Pischei Teshuvah* 91:4).

59. See *Yad Yehudah* 96:35k, as in (b) above.

60. *Rema* 89:4.

61. *D.T.* 89:53.

62. See *Taz* 96:13 and *Yad Yehudah* §34k.

63. As in II A. (b) above.

ॐ A dairy, meat or non-kosher knife used to cut *parve*, kosher food:

- ☐ Non-sharp root vegetables (e.g., carrots, turnips or parsnips): The food should be rinsed well to remove any meat, dairy or non-kosher residue.
- ☐ Fruits and juicy vegetables (e.g., orange, watermelon, cucumber, pumpkin, beets and all green vegetables): The cut surfaces should be scraped clean *(g'reidah)* unless the knife was clean *and* not a *ben-yomo*.
- ☐ One should not eat a vegetable salad in a non-kosher restaurant.
- ☐ Cut watermelon may be purchased in a supermarket.
- ☐ One who cuts fish with a clean meat, dairy, or non-kosher knife should thoroughly wash the cut surfaces. If the knife was not positively clean, the cut surfaces should preferably be scraped lightly.
- ☐ One should not purchase fish from a store that sells non-kosher fish. One who must purchase kosher fish (with recognizable fins and scales) from a non-kosher store, should scrub and scrape the cut surfaces. If the store sells kosher fish only, one may purchase cut fish with recognizable fins and scales. Pickled or salted fish should not be purchased without a Rabbinical supervision.
- ☐ Ideally, bread should be cut only with a *parve* knife or a knife of the same type as the food to be eaten with the bread. If the only knife available is of the other type, the knife requires *ne'itzah* beforehand. If *ne'itzah* was not done, the bread should be scraped (similar to fruits).

B. A knife used to cut hot or warm foods

These *halachos* are based on the Talmud *Chullin* 8b, *Tur* and *Shulchan Aruch, Yoreh De'ah* end of 94.

[Note: A hot knife used to cut cold meat is governed by similar rules.]

Whenever a knife is used to cut hot foods, in addition to the residue on the knife surface one must also contend with the taste that has been previously absorbed into the knife. Therefore, even if the knife was clean, its absorbed taste may have been imparted into the food. If, in addition to being certainly clean, the knife was never used for hot foods[64] or was not used for hot foods within the previous twenty-four hours (i.e., it is not a *ben-yomo*),[65] it cannot transfer taste even when used to cut hot foods. A utensil is assumed not to be a *ben-yomo* unless it is known to have been used with hot food in the previous twenty-four hours.[66] Accordingly, the rules specified below apply only to a knife known to have been used for hot food in the previous twenty-four hours.

> It should be noted that our discussion relates to a clean knife only. If the knife was not clean, its residue is absorbed into any food it cuts, regardless of whether or not it was used within the previous twenty-four hours. The twenty-four-hour respite affects only absorbed taste, not actual food residue.[67]

1) A dairy knife used to cut hot meat (or vice-versa):
   If one uses a dairy knife to cut hot (i.e., *yad soledes bo*) meat that was in a *kli rishon* (the original vessel that was over the fire even though it has since been removed), a significant infusion of taste occurs. Although, heat cannot transfer taste beyond a *k'dei klipah* (a sliver, the thinnest surface that is removable in one slice) without a liquid medium, when that heat is combined with *duchka d'sakina,* its power is intensified. Therefore, the taste absorbed in the knife is infused into the entire food.[68]

---

64. See *Aruch HaShulchan* 94:35, who notes that ordinarily a dairy knife is used solely to cut butter and cheese, not hot foods, and is thus not governed by these rules (if it was certainly clean). He advises any *moreh hora'ah* faced with a *halachic* question, to inquire as to whether the dairy knife was used for hot dairy or washed with dairy during the previous twenty-four hours (see Chapter Ten, regarding dishes washed with dairy). Although *Aruch HaShulchan* is certainly correct, we nevertheless used the example of a dairy knife in our discussion since that is the example used by the *Shulchan Aruch.*

65. If the knife in question is a meat or dairy (not non-kosher) knife, it is considered a *ben-yomo* only if it was used to cut hot meat or dairy during the previous twenty-four hours. If the knife was used during the previous twenty-four hours only with hot (and certainly cold) *parve* food it is not considered a *ben-yomo.* A non-kosher knife, however, is considered a *ben-yomo* if it was used for *any* (even kosher) hot foods during the previous twenty-four hour period (*Shach* 94:2,22). See Chapters Three, Section II,B.

66. *Y.D.* 94:7, 122:7.

67. See *Y.D.* 96:1 and *Aruch HaShulchan* 94:30. See, however, a dissenting opinion in *Y.D.* 103:5.

68. See *Shach* 94:27 *S.D.* 10.22 s.v. *"din chadash"* and Section I above.

□ The food:
Depending upon the size of the meat in relation to the size of the knife blade, and depending upon whether the knife was a *ben-yomo*, the entire piece of meat may be forbidden (even to derive benefit thereof). A *moreh hora'ah* should be consulted.[69] We noted above that if the knife was certainly clean and was not a *ben-yomo*, the entire meat may be eaten after being rinsed.[70]

□ The knife:
Requires *hagalah*.[71]

If the meat was hot but transferred to a *kli sheni*, *Poskim* disagree about the status of the meat. Some require only *klipah* (removal of the cut surface).[72] Other *Poskim* rule that the entire piece of meat may be forbidden. In their opinion the meat (or any solid food) is not affected by a transfer to a *kli sheni*[73] and thus retains the status of a *kli rishon*.[74] The status of the knife is likewise subject to this dispute among *Poskim*. In the opinion of some, it requires *hagalah*; others contend that *ne'itzah* is sufficient.[76] A *moreh hora'ah* should be consulted.

□ If the knife did not cut, but was merely placed on the meat, only a *k'dei klipah* must be removed.[77]

2) A dairy knife used to cut warm meat:
If a dairy knife is used to cut warm, but not hot meat (i.e., not *yad soledes bo)* (or a meat knife is used to cut warm cheese), the knife imparts its taste to the meat. Although, generally, heat less than *yad soledes bo* cannot effect a transfer of taste, in this

---

69. See Y.D. 94:7.

70. See *Aruch HaShulchan* 94:30. In this case we do not have to be concerned with either the residue or the absorbed taste.

71. *Rema* 94:7, see *Badei HaShulchan* 94:96.

72. *Rema* (ibid). Although, in the opinion of *Rema* 105:3 a *kli sheni* cannot impart taste even to a *klipah* of the food, in this case the *duchka d'sakina* combines with the heat of the *kli sheni* to transfer taste to a *klipah* of the food (see *Biur HaGra* 94:27).

73. Or even a *kli shlishi*, see *Aruch HaShulchan* 94:32.

74. The source of this opinion is the *Issur V'heter* 36:7 and *Maharshal (Yam Shel Shlomo: Chullin* 7:44) cited in *Taz* 94:14 and *Shach* 94:30. *Taz* (ibid.) follows the opinion of *Maharshal* only in a case of *duchka d'sakina*. See also *Aruch HaShulchan* 94:32.

75. *Shach* 94:30.

76. *Rema* 94:7.

77. *Gilyon Maharsha* 94:7. See also *Shach* 105:23.

case, the warmth of the food combines with *duchka d'sakina* to effect a partial infusion of taste from the knife to the food[78] resulting in the following ruling:

- □ The food:
  Both cut surfaces of the meat *(klipah)* should be removed and discarded.[79] If the knife was certainly clean and not *ben-yomo,* the entire meat may be eaten after it is rinsed.
- □ The knife:
  Requires *ne'itzah.*[80]

3) A dairy knife used to cut hot *parve* food:
If a dairy knife was used to cut hot (or perhaps even warm) *parve* food (e.g., fish), the food should not be eaten with meat. Similarly, if hot bread is cut with a dairy knife, the entire bread may not be eaten with meat.[81] In the event that the food was mixed into meat, a *moreh hora'ah* should be consulted.[82]

Summary of Section B

When a meat, dairy or non-kosher knife is used to cut warm foods, one must contend with both the taste previously absorbed into the knife and with the food residue assumed to have remained on the knife blade.

☙ If a dairy knife was used to cut hot *(yad soledes bo)* meat in a

---

78. Although the heat, in itself, is insufficient to effect a transfer of taste, when combined with *duchka d'sakina,* its power is enhanced. (See *Biur HaGra, Y.D.* 94:27 and *Yad Yehudah* 94:39a, based on the Talmud: *Chullin* 8b, and the second opinion in *Tosfos* (ibid) s.v. *"agav".)*

79. *Yad Yehudah* §47k. Indeed, see *Chochmas Adam* 47:3 who advises that even when cold meat is cut, the cut surface should preferably be removed.

80. *Rema* 94:7. All authorities agree that since the meat was not *yad soledes bo* the knife requires only *ne'itzah.* Apparently, just as the *duchka d'sakina* and the partial heat effect a transfer of taste from the knife to the meat, so, too, they effect a transfer in the reverse; thus the knife absorbs taste from the meat. This being so, it seems odd that *ne'itzah* should be adequate. Evidently, *ne'itzah* removes some of the knife's surface (see *Shach* 10:6) or removes the taste absorbed into the knife surface (see *R' Akiva Eger* 96:1 on *Shach* §9).

81. *S.D.* 10: end of 22.

82. See *Kaf HaChaim* 96:15. Although this is a situation of *nat-bar-nat* (a secondary infusion of taste, see Chapters Six and Section C below), nevertheless, the *duchka d'sakina* may effect a transfer of primary taste in the manner of a *davar charif.* See M.Z. 96:3.

kli rishon, the entire meat may be forbidden — a *moreh hora'ah* should be consulted. The knife certainly requires *hagalah.*

- If the meat was hot but transferred to a *kli sheni*, the status of both the meat and the knife is subject to dispute — a *moreh hora'ah* should be consulted.
- If the meat was warm but not hot (not *yad soledes bo),* both cut meat surfaces should be discarded. The knife requires *ne'itzah.*
- If a dairy knife is used to cut hot *parve* food, the food should not be eaten with meat. If the food was mixed into a meat dish, a *moreh hora'ah* should be consulted.

  Note: if the knife was certainly clean and not a *ben-yomo* (i.e., it was not used to cut hot foods of that type during previous twenty-four hours), these rules do not apply.

C. A knife used to cut sharp foods – davar charif

These *halachos* are based on the Talmud *Chullin* 112a, *Tur* and *Shulchan Aruch, Yoreh De'ah* 96.

We are already acquainted with the special ability of *duchka d'sakina* to facilitate the transmission of taste. We have also noted several times in this work, the unique ability of a *davar charif* — a sharp food — to absorb and to transmit *taste* in a manner unlike that of any other food. In this section, we will examine the distinctive *halachos* that govern the combination of these two unique factors (i.e., *duchka d'sakina* and *davar charif).* A *davar charif* interacts with the *duchka d'sakina* of a knife in three ways, one which is unique to a knife and two which are due to the general properties of a *davar charif:*

- ☐ A *davar charif* as a substitute to heat:

  Under normal circumstances, *taam* (taste) is transmitted or absorbed only through the medium of heat. As explained in Chapter Five, Section I, ordinarily, neither *duchka d'sakina* alone nor the sharpness of a *davar charif* alone can cause a transfer of taste. Thus, sharp foods placed in a non-kosher dish retain their kosher status.[83] If, however, a non-kosher knife is

83. *Taz* 96:3, see also *Toras Chatas* 17:2. However, in the opinion of many *Poskim* a damp *davar charif* placed on a dish may effect a transfer of taste, see *D.T.* 96:15, *Kaf HaChaim* 96:13 and 3-g below.

used to cut a kosher *davar charif*, the combination of *duchka d'sakina* and sharpness cause non-kosher taste to be absorbed into the food. Correspondingly, if a kosher knife is used to cut a non-kosher sharp food, the two factors combine to cause the knife to absorb non-kosher taste from the food.[84]

[The following two aspects are general characteristics of a davar charif *and although not unique to a knife, they apply to a knife as well.]*

☐ *Davar charif* in a situation of *nat-bar-nat:*

The *halachos* of kashrus differentiate between a primary infusion of taste *(nosen taam)* and a secondary infusion of taste *(nosen taam bar nosen taam* — "infused taste the 'son' of infused taste" — commonly referred to by the acronym "*nat-bar-nat.*" See Chapter Six and appendix for a detailed discussion of this concept). A taste directly absorbed by one food from another is considered a primary infusion of taste. A taste absorbed from food into a vessel and subsequently imparted by the vessel into another food is considered a secondary infusion of taste. When dealing with the taste of forbidden foods infused into kosher foods, *halachah* does not distinguish between a primary taste and a secondary taste. The taste of a permitted foods, however, loses its identity when it is transferred twice *(nat-bar-nat d'heteira)* and cannot affect another permitted food. Therefore, potatoes boiled in a meat pot and subsequently mixed with butter may be eaten.[85] A *davar charif*, however, has the ability to elevate a secondary infusion of taste and make it equivalent to a primary infusion. Thus, a radish cut with a meat knife is considered as if it absorbed the primary taste of the meat itself[86] *(nosen taam),*

---

84. Notwithstanding the above, a *davar charif* is not the complete equivalent of boiling. For example, a *davar charif*, in the absence of heat, perhaps absorbs taste only to the depth of *k'dei netilah*, while boiling causes an absorption throughout the entire food (see *Shach* 94:27 and discussion in note 126 below).

85. Nevertheless, according to *Ashkenazic* custom one should not mix the potatoes with butter or eat them with milk, see Chapter Six, Section II.

86. See *Rashi: Chullin* 112a, *Shach* 96:2. A *davar charif* cooked in a pot is similar in this respect to a *davar charif* cut with a knife. In either case we do not use the principle of *nat-bar-nat (Rema* 95:2). See also *D.T.* 96:3 for a discussion as to whether this principle continues to apply to additional transfers of taste (i.e., *nat-bar-nat-bar-nat*, e.g., the radish was boiled with another food and the other food is subsequently mixed with milk).

not merely a secondary meat taste *(nat-bar-nat)*, and consequently, if the radish was mixed into cheese salad the salad may not be eaten.

- A *davar charif* in conjunction with *aino ben-yomo:*
  It is an axiom of kashrus that a taste absorbed into a vessel for a twenty-four-hour period loses its potency and its ability to transfer its non-kosher status *(nosen taam lifgam* — see Chapter Three). Thus, food cooked in a non-kosher pot that was not used for hot food during the previous twenty-four hours may be eaten. A *davar charif,* however, revitalizes the absorbed taste in the vessel and endows it with the strength to permeate into the food.[87] Thus, an onion cooked in a non-*ben-yomo* non-kosher pot may not be eaten.[88] This principle applies to a knife as well. If a non-kosher knife is used to cut a sharp food, the food may be prohibited despite the fact that the knife was not used for the previous twenty-four hours.[89]

In this section, we will discuss the following: i) What foods are considered *davar charif?* ii) Is there a distinction between a clean knife and a soiled knife as affecting a *davar charif?* iii) Practical *halachos* pertaining to sharp foods cut with a dairy, meat or non-kosher knife.

In order to facilitate discussion of this difficult subject, we will use the example cited in the Shulchan

87. See *Darcei Teshuvah* 96:11 and *Aruch HaShulchan* §12, for a discussion as to whether this rule is Biblical or Rabbinic in origin. See also *Daas Torah* 96:1 p. 259, for a fascinating discussion as to how the absorbed taste which has lost its potency and its status as an *issur* (forbidden food) is able to regain its status of *issur*. Normally, a forbidden food that became permissible cannot revert to its original status of *issur*. See also *Badei HaShulchan* 96:1 s.v. *"lechatcham"* citing *R' Akiva Eger* regarding the question of a non-sharp food cooked in an *aino ben-yomo* pot and subsequently changed into a *davar charif*. For example; Eggs that were cooked in an *aino ben-yomo* pot and subsequently mixed into fresh onions. See M.Z. 96:13 who notes that a *davar charif* can only revitalize an edible taste that became stale. It cannot improve a taste that was never edible.

88. Y.D. 103:6. Nor can an onion cooked in a non-*ben-yomo* meat or dairy pot be eaten with foods of the other type *(Rema* 95:2).

89. This is subject to a dispute among the *Rishonim* cited in *Tur* ch. 96. *Shulchan Aruch* 96:1 cites both opinions without issuing a ruling. *Shach* §6, however, rules that one follow the stringent opinion. See *R' Akiva Eger* (gloss to *Taz* 96:10) who notes that although in the case of a knife *Shulchan Aruch* does not issue a ruling, in the case of a *davar charif* cooked in a vessel, he follows the stringent opinion as is apparent in Y.D. 103:6.

Aruch: *if a meat knife was used to cut a radish, may the radish subsequently be eaten with milk or cheese?*

1) What is considered a *davar charif?*
In discussing the *halachos* of *davar charif*, the Talmud uses the example of a *"tz'non"* — radish.[90] Several issues require clarification: a) What does the Talmud mean by the word *"tz'non?"* Are all radishes (i.e., white, black or red), regardless of their level of sharpness, considered a *davar charif?* Should one assume that the Talmud specified a radish as the *only* instance of a *davar charif*, or should one assume that a radish was mentioned merely as an example of the general category of sharp foods which includes onions, garlic and any sharp food? b) If a radish (or other sharp food) is cooked, is it still considered a *davar charif?* Perhaps cooking diminishes the sharpness of a radish and it can no longer qualify as a *davar charif*. c) What is the status of a food consisting of a mixture of sharp and bland ingredients?

a) Radishes and other sharp foods:
Although there are differing opinions,[91] *halachic* consensus rules that all radishes[92] and all sharp foods[93] (and spices[94]) are included in the category of *davar charif*.

---

90. See *D.T.* 96:1 who questions why *Chazal* chose the example of a radish rather than a horseradish which is sharper yet.

91. See *Beis Yosef*, 96, who contends that in the opinion of *Rashba* other sharp foods should not be compared to radishes, while in the opinion of *Rambam* and other *Rishonim* all sharp foods are considered *davar charif*.

92. *D.T.* 96:1, as opposed to *Aruch HaShulchan* 96:13 who cites an opinion that only black radishes are considered a *davar charif*, not white (or, presumably, red) radishes. The *Aruch HaShulchan* accepts this opinion in a case of financial loss. Further support for this view may be found in the opinions cited in *Daas Torah* 96:2 p. 264, that any food eaten without bread (i.e., a food that can be eaten alone) is not considered a *davar charif*. As noted, *D.T.* opposes this view and rules that no distinction be made between different types of radishes. See, however, *Beis Yosef* 96 s.v. *"u mashe'kasav v'im chatach"* who implies that a sweet radish *(tz'non masuk)* does not have the *halachah* of a *davar charif*. Certainly, even *D.T.* would agree that a radish without any sharp taste cannot be considered a *davar charif*. See *Rema* 96:1 who notes that only the root of a radish is a *davar charif* not its leafy top.

93. See *D.T.* 96:39, who cites an opinion that although any food which appears to be sharp must be considered a *davar charif* even though it is not mentioned in Rabbinic sources, the reverse is not true. A food cited in the Talmud or Rabbinic literature as a *davar charif* must be considered as such, regardless of whether or not it appears to be sharp. See note 45 above.

94. See *Shach* 96:19 regarding pepper, and 96:17 for a discussion as to whether ginger is considered a *davar charif*.

Thus, garlic, onions,[95] leek,[96] horseradish,[97] olives,[98] sour fruits or vegetables (lemons,[99] esrog,[100] sour apples[101] or sour plums[102]), pickled fruits or vegetables (perhaps pickled cucumbers[103] or sauerkraut)[104] and salted herring[105] are each considered a *davar charif*.[106] Certain liquids (although they do not pertain to our discussion) are considered a *davar charif* as well, e.g., very salty water (brine), strong vinegar,[107] perhaps even whiskey,[108] olive oil[109] and wine.[110]

b) Cooked sharp foods:
There is considerable controversy among *halachic*

95. See *Pischei Teshuvah* 96:3 whether small onions (scallions?) are considered a *davar charif*.

96. *Y.D.* 96:2. *k'rishin* is generally translated as leek.

97. *Rema* 96:2.

98. Either fresh or completely pickled (*M.B.* 447:89). See *Shach* 96:20 who is uncertain about the exact level of the sharpness of olives, whether they are as sharp as radishes or even milder than the sharpness of lemons.

99. *Y.D.* 96:4. See *Shach* §20 who discusses the level of sharpness of lemons.

100. *Magen Avraham* 447:33.

101. See *Taz* 96:9, as to whether sour apples are considered a *davar charif*. If the sour fruits are not very sour, *Poskim* permit their use with meat when cut with a clean, *non-ben-yomo* dairy knife (*Chochmas Adam* 49:7). It would appear that those fruits that are edible raw are not considered *charif* (see *Yad Yehudah* 96:22k).

102. *Issur V'heter* 38:14.

103. *Daas Torah* 96:2 p. 264, cites conflicting opinions whether sour pickles are considered a *davar charif*. Indeed, he cites opinions that perhaps any food which is eaten without bread (i.e., eaten alone) is not considered a *davar charif*. *Poskim* rely on their opinions in combination with other considerations or in a case of financial loss. See, however, *Aruch HaShulchan* 96:13, who assumes that pickles and sauerkraut are not considered a *davar charif*.

104. See *Taz* 96:12, the *Aruch HaShulchan* 96:13, as noted above however, disagrees.

105. *Shach* 96:16 assumes that *Shulchan Aruch* 96:2 refers to extremely salty fish. See *Badei HaShulchan* 96:48. See *D.T.* 96:54, for a discussion as to whether salt itself is considered a *davar charif*. See also *Yad Yehudah* 96:2a, who notes that salt unlike any other *davar charif* has the ability to act upon other foods (as does heat) and cause them to transmit their taste. Other sharp foods can only absorb the moisture on the surface of another food, not cause it to transmit their taste.

106. *Y.D.* 96:2.

107. *Magen Avraham* 447:28.

108. *Taz; O.C.* 442:4, *D.T.* 96:40, however, cites opposing opinions.

109. See *D.T.* 96:65 who cites conflicting opinions regarding olive oil.

110. See *D.T.* 96:42. Presumably, this discussion pertains only to very dry sour wines.

authorities as to the status of a cooked (i.e., boiled) *davar charif.*[111] Some authorities contend that its sharpness has dissipated, while others disagree.[112] *Poskim* avoid giving a clear ruling on the matter, leaving the judgment dependent upon the individual circumstances (i.e., the amount of water, the duration of the period of boiling and whether the status of the food as a *davar charif* is certain).[113] Boiled or fried onions or garlic are assumed to have lost their sharpness.[114]

c) A mixture:
Sharp foods mixed into other foods may cause the entire mixture to assume the characteristic of a *davar charif* if the sharpness is strongly tasted in the mixture. If the sharp taste is not very noticeable, the mixture is not considered a *davar charif*. This would depend upon the sharpness of the original *davar charif,* its ratio in the mixture and the strength of taste of the other ingredients in the mixture.[115]

2) A clean knife as opposed to a soiled knife:
Whenever a decision is made regarding a radish cut with a meat knife, the initial consideration should be whether that knife was clean.[116] A greasy knife presents the problem of the

---

111. This discussion pertains only to a situation where the *davar charif* was boiled prior to its contact with the vessel in question, e.g., a *davar charif* that was cooked first and subsequently cut with a knife. If, however, the *davar charif* was boiled in a non-*ben-yomo* meat pot (i.e., it was placed in the pot before the water boiled), according to some opinions, it must be considered a *davar charif* since at the beginning of the cooking process it still retained its sharpness (*D.T.* 96:20).

112. See *Pischei Teshuvah* 96:4, *D.T.* 96:20,45, 108:29.

113. Ibid. *Kaf HaChaim* 96:12. See also *Pischei Teshuvah* (ibid.) who contends that boiled horseradish or spices retains their sharpness.

114. *Pischei Teshuvah* (ibid.), *D.T.* 96:45. See *Aruch HaShulchan* 96:20, who rules that even raw onions mixed with oil no longer have the status of *davar charif*, *D.T.* 96:20, however, disagrees. *Aruch HaShulchan* (ibid.) contends that even a soaked *davar charif* loses its potency. In addition, *D.T.* 96:1, cites an opinion that a salted radish is no longer considered a *davar charif;* other *Poskim,* however, dismiss this view (ibid.).

115. See *Rema* 95:2 and *Yad Yehudah* 95:22k. It is questionable whether one can apply this principle to a chopper used in preparing eggs or liver with onions, since the chopper cuts pieces of onion before they lose their sharpness in the mixture (see *Yad Yehudah* 95:21k, see also *D.T.* 96:56,59).

116. Earlier in this chapter (Section I-B) we discussed the question of whether a knife should be assumed clean or not.

meat residue on its surface,[117] while a clean knife presents only the problem of the meat taste absorbed into the blade. It would follow that if a clean knife was not used in the previous twenty-four hours it will not impart its taste to the radish.[118] Practically speaking this distinction is of minor significance. *Halachic* consensus generally does not differentiate between a clean or a greasy knife. The sharpness of the radish revitalizes the taste absorbed in a non *ben-yomo* knife and gives it a status of a *ben-yomo*.[119] Thus, merely scrubbing the knife is insufficient to permit its use with sharp food.[120] If, however, the knife was *kashered* by *ne'itzah* (thrusting into the ground, as will be explained below), even a non-kosher knife may be used on a temporary basis to cut sharp foods and is thus not subject to these rules.[121] If the knife was *kashered* with *hagalah*, it is no longer considered a non-kosher, meat or dairy knife and is certainly not subject to these deliberations. In addition, one must note that when discussing a meat knife or dairy knife, we are referring to a knife that was used to cut hot meat or hot dairy food. A knife used to cut cold foods exclusively is not considered a meat or dairy knife; Thus if it is used to cut a radish, the cut surface of the radish may be thoroughly washed and used with food of the other type.[122] *Poskim* disagree whether a knife that is used primarily for cold meat but occasionally for hot meat is considered a meat knife.[123]

3) Practical *halachos* concerning sharp foods:

a) A radish cut with a meat knife:

A radish cut, peeled or scraped[124] with a meat knife may

---

117. Accordingly, there is no distinction between a greasy knife used for meat in the previous twenty-four hours or one that was used prior to twenty-four hours. See notes 13 and 67 above.

118. This is the first opinion of *Shulchan Aruch* 96:1.

119. The second opinion ibid., see *Shach* ibid. no 6.

120. *Yad Yehudah* 96:3k.

121. *Y.D.* 121:7. See *R' Akiva Eger* gloss to *Shach* 96:3, *Yad Yehudah* 96:3k. See, however, *Pischei Teshuvah* 96:10, who cites opinions that one should not rely on *ne'itzah* to use a knife to cut a *davar charif*.

122. *Kaf HaChaim* 96:48 based on the *Beis Yosef* 96.

123. See *Daas Torah* 96:1 p. 260. See footnote no. 133. Although the knife may have been washed with meat dishes in hot water or a dishwasher, it is not necessarily considered a meat knife. See Chapter Ten, Section A.

124. *Yad Yehudah* 96:27.

not be eaten with dairy food according to *Ashkenazic* custom.[125] According to *Sefardic* custom one may eat the radish with dairy food after merely cutting away the cut surface of the radish to the depth of approximately one inch — *k'dei netilah*.[126] This is true regardless of whether or not the knife was clean[127] and regardless of whether or not the knife was used in the previous twenty-four hours to cut hot meat.[128] If the radish is subsequently mixed or cooked with dairy food,[129] a *moreh hora'ah* should be consulted.[130] A radish cut with

125. *Rema* 96:1, *Shach* ibid. §10 (following the opinion of *Rashba* cited in *Tur* 96).

126. See *Kaf HaChaim* 96:27 that *Sefardic* tradition follows the lenient opinion of the *Shulchan Aruch*. A *davar charif* differs in this respect, in the opinion of *Shulchan Aruch*, from hot food. Although hot food cut with a knife is affected in its entirety by the taste absorbed in the knife, a cold *davar charif* is affected to the depth of an inch only (see *Shach* 96:4 and *P.M.* ibid.). Even if the knife is coated with a greasy residue (which ordinarily, as any fatty substance, has the ability to cause taste to be absorbed throughout the food — see *Y.D.* 105:5), nevertheless, in the absence of heat, the taste is not absorbed further than a *k'dei netilah* (ibid). see note 84 above.

127. A *davar charif* has the ability to cause the knife to infuse its absorbed taste into the radish. Furthermore, the conventional rule of *nat-bar-nat d'heteirah* (a secondary taste of a permitted food — see introduction to this section above) is not applicable. The radish, as a *davar charif*, has the power to effect a primary transfer of taste (*Shach* 96:2).

128. This is subject to a dispute between the author of *Sefer HaTerumos* and *Maharam M'Rottenburg* cited in *Tur* 96. *Shulchan Aruch* 96:1, cites both opinions. *Shach* 96:6,19, rules that the stringent opinion of *Sefer HaTerumos* must be followed even if the knife was clean (although we have two independent factors which favor leniency, i.e., the knife was both clean and unused for twenty-four hours). There are lenient opinions who contend that this applies only to an onion, while other sharp foods, e.g., an onion, may be treated more leniently, see *D.T.* 96:62. The radish may be kept to be eaten with meat. We need not be concerned with the possibility that one may forget and eat it with dairy foods (*D.T.* 96:6).

129. Or even cooked in a clean dairy pot. The fact of whether the pot was a *ben-yomo* must, however, be considered. See *Yad Yehudah* 96:10.

130. See *Shach* 96:9,10 that one may eat the mixture if it contains a ratio of sixty parts dairy food (and radish) to the volume of the knife blade (if one is certain that only part of the blade came in contact with the radish, we may require only sixty times that part, see *Taz* §4 and *Shach* §8 who disagree on this point) or to the volume of the *k'dei netilah* if it is less than the knife blade. If the amount of dairy food equals this ratio one may eat the entire radish without removing the cut surface. See *Taz* 96:5. and *Shach* 94:23 citing *Maharam Lublin*. See an opposing opinion in *S.D.* 94:23, 96:8. See, however, *Badei HaShulchan* 96:26 citing *R' Akiva Eger* who questions this ruling. See also *Badei HaShulchan* 96:56 as to whether the stringent ruling of the *Rema* not to differentiate between a *ben-yomo* and a non-*ben-yomo* knife, applies to sharp foods other than a radish. In the event that the radish was cut with a non-kosher knife see *Maadanei HaShulchan* 96:24.

a meat knife and subsequently cut with a dairy knife contains taste of both meat and dairy. A *moreh hora'ah* should be consulted.[131]

b) A radish cut with a dairy knife:
Similarly, a radish cut with even a clean dairy knife should not be eaten with meat. Often a dairy knife is used exclusively for cold dairy foods, and has thus never absorbed dairy taste.[132] In such a case, the radish may be eaten with meat if the cut surface is thoroughly washed.[133]

c) A radish cut on a dairy plate:
In the opinion of some authorities, the concept of *duchka d'sakina* applies even to the plate upon which the radish is cut. They contend that since the radish is pressed against the plate it absorbs taste from the plate. Thus, a radish cut with a *parve* knife onto a dairy plate may not be eaten with meat and vice versa. Similarly, a radish cut on a non-kosher plate may not be eaten. One faced with either of these situations should consult a *moreh hora'ah*.[134] *[Note: A radish or horseradish grated onto a dairy plate may not be subject to this question, as will be discussed in (j) below.]*

d) A radish cut with a non-kosher knife:
In the opinion of some authorities, a radish cut with a non-kosher knife should not be eaten.[135] Other authori-

---

131. If both knives were used on the same side of the radish, the area that was affected by both knives (i.e., it was within a *k'dei netilah* of both cuts) should be discarded, the remainder of the radish may be eaten with *parve* food (see *Rema* 96:1 and d below). See *Pri Migadim: O.C.* 447:13, and *D.T.* 96:3,5, as to whether the dairy knife needs to be *kashered*. Perhaps it does not require *kashering* since the radish cannot transmit into the second knife a taste infused into it without a liquid medium. See also *Chavas Daas* 96:6b.

132. See *Aruch HaShulchan* 94:35.

133. *Kaf HaChaim* 96:48. If, however, the knife is used on occasion with hot dairy food, there is considerable doubt as to whether one may base the status of the knife on the majority use and ignore the occasional use with hot foods. This question is subject to a dispute among *Poskim* (see *Daas Torah* 96:1 p. 260). See also *Beis Meir* 96:3 regarding an onion that was cut with a milk knife primarily used for cold foods, see *D.T.* 96:62 as to when one may rely on the *Beis Meir's* ruling.

134. See *Chochmas Adam* 56:2, *Darcei Teshuvah* 96:37, *Daas Torah* 96:1 p. 260. See *Matamei HaShulchan* 96:9, that in the event a radish was cut with a meat knife on a dairy plate (or vice-versa), the plate should be *kashered* if possible.

135. *Shach* 96:10.

ties follow a more lenient view and rule that even if other radishes are available, the radish may be eaten after an inch of both cut surfaces *(k'dei netilah)* is removed.[136] Even so, one should not initially purchase a cut radish from a non-Jew. In the event that no other radish is available, one may purchase a cut radish from a non-Jew, remove a *k'dei netilah* of the cut surface and eat the remainder.[137] In either of these cases, if the radish was cooked without removing the cut surface, a *moreh hora'ah* should be consulted.

e) A situation of doubt:
One who is in doubt whether a radish was cut with a non-kosher knife may use the radish.[138]

f) A pickle jar:
We noted above that a pickle may be considered a *davar charif*. Thus, a pickle cut with a meat knife should not be eaten with a dairy meal. Furthermore, we noted that any instrument that pierces food is the equivalent of a knife. Accordingly, one should be careful when removing a pickle from a pickle jar not to create a problem of *basar b'chalav*. Often one inserts a meat fork or knife into the jar in an attempt to remove a pickle and is unable to extricate the pickle from the jar. The pickle thus remains in the jar pierced in many spots by a meat fork. Subsequently, someone else may remove the pickle and eat it during a dairy meal or someone may remove the pickle using a dairy knife. The pickle has thus absorbed both meat and milk and perhaps may not be eaten.[139]

---

136. See *R' Akiva Eger* on *Shach* ibid. citing *Minchas Yaakov*.

137. *Rema* 96:1. This is true even if the non-Jew's knife was used for non-kosher food in the previous twenty-four hours *(Aruch HaShulchan* 96:17).

138. *Rema* 96:1. The doubt, however, must be reasonable. Thus, if it is to be assumed that a non-kosher knife was indeed used, one cannot follow this lenient ruling (see *Shach* 96 end of §20). This lenient ruling is based on the fact that even if a non-kosher knife was used, the knife may not have been a *ben-yomo* and thus, in the opinion of some authorities, unable to transfer taste. If, however, the non-kosher knife that may have been used was certainly used in the previous twenty-four hours, this lenient ruling may not be applicable *(Shach* 96:12, see, however, dissenting opinions in *Kaf HaChaim* §31). If a *ben-yomo* knife was used to cut any other sharp food besides a radish (e.g., an onion or horseradish), a *moreh hora'ah* should be consulted (see *D.T.* 96:32).

139. One must, however, consider the following lenient considerations: the status of a pickle as a *davar charif* is not definitely established (see note 103 above). Also a pickle

One should preferably avoid this problem by removing from the jar any pickle that was pierced by a meat or dairy fork.

g) A horseradish jar:
We noted above that a *davar charif* causes a transfer of taste only in a situation of *duchka d'sakina.* Merely placing a *davar charif* onto a plate creates no *kashrus* problem.[140] Thus, one should be permitted to use a clean meat or dairy spoon (or fork) to remove horseradish or sauerkraut from a jar regardless of whether it is to be used with a meat or dairy meal. The spoon or fork is used neither to pierce nor to cut; thus, no *duchka d'sakina* takes place and consequently no transfer of taste occurs. Indeed, many are accustomed to using a meat or dairy spoon without discretion. In the opinion of many authorities, however, a moist *davar charif* has the ability to effect a transfer of taste even without *duchka*

---

may be soft and not require much pressure from the knife. Perhaps the rule of *duchka d'sakina* does not apply where minimum pressure is required. In addition, a fork (unlike a knife) may be assumed to be clean. Even if one used a knife, it, too, may be considered clean (see Section I,B above). In addition, the fork or knife may not usually be used with hot foods; thus, their status as a meat or dairy fork is questionable, see notes 64 and 133 above. Also, the fork may have not been used during the previous twenty-four hours, in which case it poses no problem according to the first opinion cited in *Y.D.* 96:1. Since the status of a pickle as a *davar charif* is questionable, one may follow that lenient opinion. In addition, the volume of meat taste to be contended with is no more than the volume of the fork tips; thus, the complete pickle should not be prohibited since one may assume that even the pierced pickle alone contained sixty times the volume of the fork tips (see *Y.D.* 96:1, *Shach* §9. The pierced area, however, must be considered meat food even though the pickle itself contains a volume of sixty times that of the fork tips, as in *Y.D.* 105:9.) Therefore, one may eat the pickle if the pierced section is cut away. In this case we probably can rely upon the opinion of *Minchas Yaakov* (cited in footnote no. 136) as opposed to *Rema* since we have the additional considerations mentioned above. If the pierced pickle was submerged in the pickle juice, one may further assume that the entire contents of the pickle jar contributes to the sixty to one ratio to nullify the meat taste in the punctured pickle, followings the principle of *kavush k'mevushal*. See Chapter Five, Section II,A, as to the length of time required for *kavush.* Whether eighteen minutes since the juice itself contains vinegar and may be a *davar charif* according to the opinion of *Shulchan Aruch* 105:1 or twenty-four hours according to *Shach* 105:2. One may therefore eat even the pierced part of the pickle with any food (see *Taz* 96:5 and *Shach* 94:23 citing *Maharam Lublin*). Nevertheless, one should certainly avoid this problem entirely and not allow a pickle to remain in the jar after piercing it with a meat or dairy knife.

140. *Toras Chatas* 17:2, *Taz* 96:3.

d'sakina.[141] It would, therefore, be preferable to refrain from using a dairy or meat spoon to remove horseradish from a jar if the removed or remaining horseradish is to be eaten with food of the other type.[142] One should certainly not allow a meat or dairy spoon to remain in the horseradish or sauerkraut jar for an extended period of time (a utensil or food soaked in a vinegar solution for an eighteen [or perhaps even ten] minute span may cause a transfer of taste).[143]

h) A grinder, blender or food processor:
A grinder is the equivalent of a knife since it also presses against the food while cutting. Similarly, a blender or food processor is, in essence, a knife. Thus, one who grinds hot[144] *(yad soledes bo)* meat in a grinder has rendered the grinder a meat utensil. If onions or horseradish are subsequently ground in the grinder they become meat food and may not be eaten with dairy foods.[145] *[Note: a fried onion has lost its sharp taste, and is no longer considered a* davar charif; *see 1-b above.]* Similarly, a grinder in which livers and fresh onions are ground may become a meat utensil.[146] An onion or

---

141. See *M.Z.* 96:3, *D.T.* 96:15, *Kaf HaChaim* 96:13 *Maadanei HaShulchan* 96:12, *Badei HaShulchan* 95:103.

142. One who finds it difficult to set aside a *parve* spoon for horseradish, should use a meat teaspoon. A meat teaspoon is generally not used for hot meat foods; thus, it cannot be classified as a meat utensil, as noted above. Even if the spoon was washed with meat dishes it may not have become a meat utensil, see Chapter Ten.

143. *D.T.* 105:42. See *M.Z.* 105:1, *Chochmas Adam* 57:10, as to whether this rule applies to utensils as well as food. Another lenient consideration in this case is the question of whether or not *kavush k'mevushal* applies to kosher tastes, see *D.T.* 105:5. Further consideration must be given to the fact that in the opinion of some *Poskim* vinegar is no different than other liquids and requires twenty-four hours to effect *kavush k'mevushal*, see Chapter Five, Section II,A.

144. See Chapter Five that in the opinion of many *Poskim* a solid retains the status of *kli rishon* even after being placed into a *kli sheni.*

145. In addition, some grinders and most blenders may be difficult to clean and should be assumed to contain meat particles.

146. This would depend upon the ratio of onions to meat. See *Binas Adam* 49(67) who rules that if the onions are only few they cannot effect a chopper. This *Binas Adam* is quoted in *D.T.* 96:56. However in §59, *D.T.* cites a seemingly contradictory ruling. In addition the onions were probably cut with a meat knife, thus in the opinion of *Chochmas Adam* 49:10 the grinder becomes a meat utensil, see following note.

horseradish cut with a dairy knife should not be ground in that grinder.[147] If, subsequently, one uses that grinder to grind dairy food with onions, a *moreh hora'ah* should be consulted.[148] However, one who grinds a non-sharp food, i.e., potatoes or eggs in a meat grinder may use that food with a dairy meal providing that the grinder was cleaned properly beforehand.[149] Nevertheless, since a blender and a grinder may be difficult to clean, perhaps one should not grind foods for a dairy meal in a meat grinder.

i) A chopper:
A chopper is the equivalent of a knife. Thus, one who chops livers and fresh onions[150] and subsequently uses the chopper to chop eggs and onions may perhaps not eat the chopped eggs with dairy foods. A *moreh hora'ah* should be consulted (as in (h) above).

j) A grater:
In the opinion of some authorities, if an onion or horseradish is cut with a dairy knife and subsequently grated, the grater has become a dairy grater and may not be used for meat.[151] Indeed, one may not even use the grater to grate bread for a meat meal since it is very difficult to clean a grater of onion remnants properly.[152] Some *Poskim* contend that the dish onto which the grated horseradish falls does not affect the status of the

---

147. An onion cut with a dairy knife and subsequently ground in a *parve* grinder may render the grinder dairy. See *Chochmas Adam* 49:10, *Binas Adam* cited above and *Chavas Daas* 96:6b. See *D.T.* 96:61 for a discussion of the differing opinions on this matter. See also *Badei HaShulchan* 96:56.

148. See *D.T.* 96:3 and end of 62. It should be noted that this pertains to an onion cut with a meat or dairy knife. An onion cut with a non-kosher knife presents a more serious problem and may render the grinder *treif*.

149. *D.T.* 96:55. Presumably, this applies only if one specifically cleans the grinder for this purpose, otherwise, it is questionable if one may assume that it is clean. See *R' Akiva Eger* cited in note 15 that even a knife may not be assumed clean based on mere visual inspection.

150. See notes 115, 146 and 147 above.

151. As in 146 above.

152. *Chochmas Adam* 49:11, *D.T.* 96:14. Certainly one who grates cheese may not use that grater for foods to be eaten with a meat meal.

horseradish.[153] Other authorities rule that one should not use a dairy plate when grating horseradish to be eaten with a meat meal (or the reverse).[154]

k) Preparing salads:
One who wishes to prepare salads for use with both meat and dairy meals must use a *parve* knife if the salads contain radishes or onions.

l) A worm found while cutting a radish:
One who cuts a worm while slicing a radish should cut away the cut surface of the radish *(k'dei klipah)*. The knife requires *ne'itzah.*[155]

[Note: One who eats a radish cut with a clean meat knife need not wait six hours before eating dairy foods.[156] *In the opinion of some* Poskim, *one who ate meat should wait six hours before eating a radish cut with a dairy knife.*][157]

Summary of Section C

⊷§ A sharp food *(davar charif)* differs from a regular food in the following manner:

- □ The sharpness of the food combines with the *duchka d'sakina* to effect a transfer of taste even though both the knife and the food are cold.
- □ Sharp food absorbs a primary taste from a vessel, not merely a secondary taste *(nat-bar-nat)*.
- □ Sharp food enhances an *aino ben-yomo* taste absorbed in a vessel enabling it to affect the food.

⊷§ Included in *davar charif* are the following foods:

---

153. *Taz* 96:3 and *Chochmas Adam* ibid.

154. See *D.T.* 96:15, *Kaf HaChaim* 96:13.

155. *Yad Yehudah* 96:34k. See also *Taz* and *M.Z.* 96:13 and gloss of *R' Akiva Eger* on *Taz* ibid. If one cut a sharp food other than a radish, *Yad Yehudah* requires a mere scraping away of the cut surface. One who cuts other fruits is required to merely wash them.

156. See *R' Akiva Eger* gloss to *Shach* 89:19 and *D.T.* 89:42. If the knife was not clean the *halachah* may be different, see *D.T.* ibid.

157. See *Pri Migadim: O.C., A.A.* 494:6, cited in *D.T.* 89:42. See *Yad Yehudah* end of 89:5a who contends that if the dairy knife was not *ben-yomo* one may eat the radish.

- ☐ All radishes, sharp spices (e.g., pepper), garlic, onions, leek, horseradish, olives, lemons, esrog, very sour apples and plums, salted herring and perhaps pickles and sauerkraut.
- ☐ Depending upon the circumstances, cooked sharp foods may no longer be considered *davar charif*. Boiled or fried onions are not considered *davar charif*.

☙ A meat (or dairy) knife has the ability to infuse its absorbed taste into a *davar charif* regardless of whether or not the knife is clean and regardless of whether or not the knife is a *ben-yomo*. Unless:

- ☐ the knife was never used to cut hot or sharp meat (or dairy) foods.
- ☐ the knife was *kashered* with *hagalah* or even *ne'itzah* prior to cutting the sharp food.

☙ Some practical rules concerning sharp foods:

a) A radish cut with a knife:

- ☐ A radish cut with a meat or dairy knife should not be eaten with foods of the other type according to *Ashkenazic* tradition. In the event that it was mixed with the other type, a *moreh hora'ah* should be consulted.
- ☐ If a radish is cut with both a meat and dairy knife, a *moreh hora'ah* should be consulted.
- ☐ A radish cut with a non-kosher knife should not be eaten according to some authorities. One should not purchase a cut radish from a non-Jew. If no other radish is available, the radish may be eaten after removal of both cut surfaces to the depth of an inch.

b) A pickle or horseradish jar:

- ☐ If one pierces a pickle in a jar with a knife or fork, the pickle should preferably be removed from the jar and eaten only with foods of the same category as the knife.
- ☐ One should preferably not remove horseradish from a jar with a meat or dairy spoon if the removed or remaining horseradish is to be eaten with foods of the

other type. The spoon should certainly not remain in the jar for ten minutes or more.

c) A grinder, grater, chopper or food processor:

- ☐ A grinder etc. is considered a meat utensil if it was used for hot meat or perhaps even for meat with onions.
- ☐ A *davar charif* ground in a meat grinder etc. may not be eaten with dairy foods.
- ☐ A *davar charif* cut with a dairy knife should not be ground in a meat grinder etc. One who did so should consult a *moreh hora'ah.*
- ☐ One should not chop a *davar charif* with a meat chopper onto a dairy plate or vice versa. One who did so should consult a *moreh hora'ah.*
- ☐ Non-sharp foods (e.g., potatoes or eggs) ground in a clean meat grinder may be eaten with dairy foods. The grinder must be thoroughly scrubbed beforehand.
- ☐ A meat grater should not be used even for non-sharp foods to be eaten with a dairy meal since it is difficult to clean a grater properly.

CHART 22

FOODS CUT WITH A COLD MEAT KNIFE

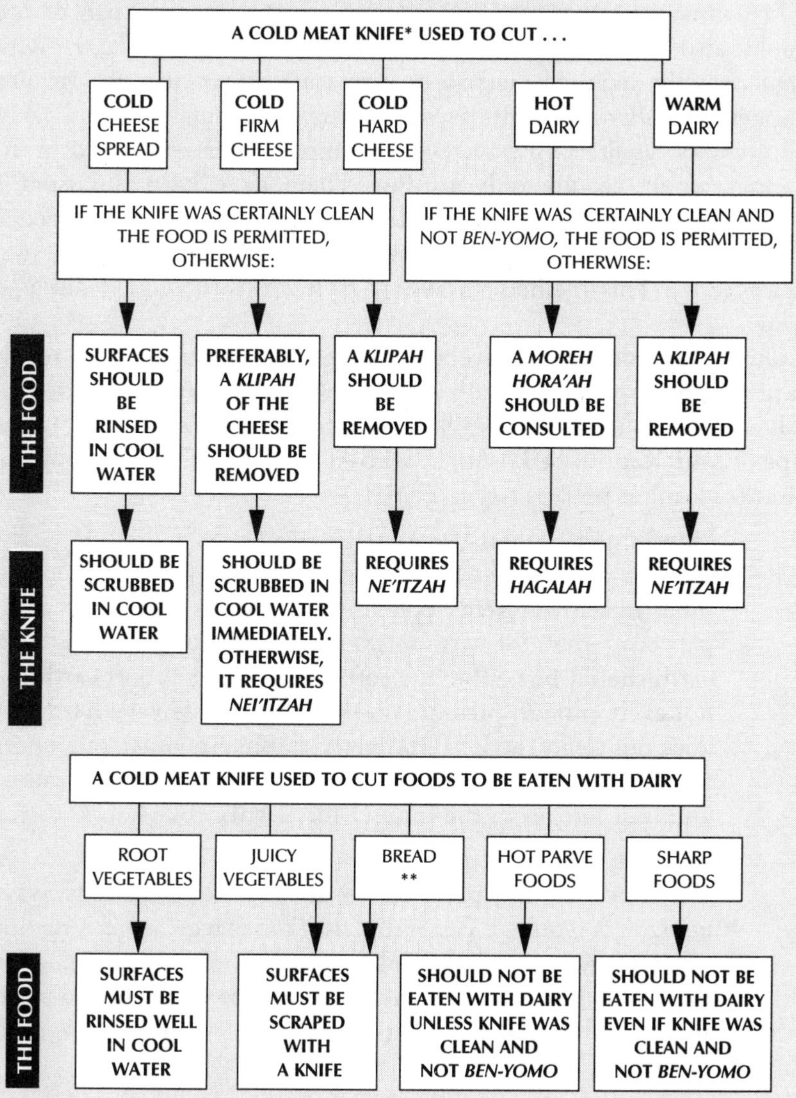

* A meat knife is assumed to retain food residue on its surface even if unused for the previous 24 hours.

** One should not use a meat knife to cut bread for a dairy meal unless *ne'itzah* is done beforehand. Common custom is to not rely even on *ne'izah* to cut bread for a dairy meal with a meat knife.

III. Kashering a knife — A unique method

All methods of *kashering* utensils apply to a knife as well. Thus, circumstances that require *libun* in order to *kasher* a pan or fork would also require *libun* for *kashering* a knife. Similarly, when *hagalah* is the required method of *kashering* a fork, it is the required manner of *kashering* a knife as well. There are circumstances in which a knife may require *kashering* even though another vessel used in that manner would require only rinsing. These have been discussed in Section I above. In addition, *Chazal* mandated a specific method in which a knife (unlike other utensils), under certain circumstances, must be *kashered*. This method known as *ne'itzah* (thrusting) is discussed below.

Our discussion in this section focuses on six issues that require clarification: i) How is *ne'itzah* done? ii) When is *ne'itzah* required? iii) When is *ne'itzah* ineffective? iv) What is the effect of *ne'itzah?* v) What type of knife cannot be *kashered* with *ne'itzah?* vi) Can one substitute another cleaning process for *ne'itzah?*

1) How is *ne'itzah* done?
A knife requiring *ne'itzah* must be thrust into the ground ten times in ten different spots (once the knife was thrust into a particular spot, the earth in that spot is no longer hard).[158] The earth should be neither too soft nor too hard.[159] Soft earth does not exert enough pressure on the knife, while very hard earth does not clean the knife properly. Despite popular misconception, there is no *halachic* basis for *kashering* a knife by merely letting it remain in the ground for twenty-four hours.

2) When is *ne'itzah* required?
We noted in the previous section several situations where *ne'itzah* is required. Generally, *ne'itzah* is required in situations where other utensils would not require *kashering* i.e., when there is no heat involved. *Ne'itzah* may be performed to permit the use of a knife on food for which it would otherwise be unsuitable. For example:

- ☐ One who wishes to cut bread for a dairy meal with a meat knife (or the reverse) must do *ne'itzah* before-

158. *Y.D.* 121:7.

159. *Tosfos: Avoda Zara* 76b, *S.D.* 10:22.

hand.[160] We noted earlier,[161] that common custom is to cut bread for a dairy meal with a dairy knife only (and vice-versa) rather than to rely on *ne'itzah*.[162] We noted too that *Poskim* commend the custom of purchasing a separate *parve* bread knife. One who has no other knife may use any knife to cut bread providing *ne'itzah* is done beforehand.[163]

- ☐ If a dairy knife was inadvertently used to cut cold meat and was not cleaned immediately after use, the residue dries onto the knife surface and is removable only with *ne'itzah*.[164]
- ☐ A knife used to cut very hard food (e.g., a meat knife inadvertently used to cut hard cheese) requires *ne'itzah* before it may be used for its original use.[165]
- ☐ If a dairy knife was inadvertently used to cut warm, but not hot, meat (or a meat knife was used to cut warm cheese), the knife requires *ne'itzah.*[166]
- ☐ One who cuts a worm while slicing a *davar charif* must *kasher* the knife with *ne'itzah.*[167]
- ☐ After *ne'itzah* was done one may use a non-kosher knife on a temporary basis to cut cold foods. In the opinion of some *Poskim*, one may then cut even sharp foods.[168]

3) When is *ne'itzah* ineffective?

- ☐ It should be noted that **at no time may *ne'itzah* be substituted for another method of *kashering.*** A knife requiring *libun* or *hagalah* cannot be *kashered* with

---

160. *Shach* 89:22, *R' Akiva Eger* on *Shach* (ibid). *Aruch HaShulchan* §16, and *Chochmas Adam* 40:14, however, follow the opinion of *Taz* 89:6, that wiping the knife thoroughly is sufficient.

161. Section I A, 2-d.

162. *Rema* 89:4.

163. *Shach* 89:22.

164. *Yad Yehudah* cited in *D.T.* 94:102 based on *Rema* 69:20.

165. *Shach* 94:31 and *Chochmas Adam* 47:4.

166. *Rema* 94:7. See Section I, B-2 above.

167. *Yad Yehudah* 96:34k.

168. *Y.D.* 121:7. See *R' Akiva Eger* gloss to *Shach* 96:3, *Yad Yehudah* 96:3k. See, however, *D.T.* 121:80 who cites opinions that one may not rely on *ne'itzah* to use a knife to cut a *davar charif*.

ne'itzah. Popular misconception has it that any *treif* knife can be *kashered* with *ne'itzah;* this is erroneous. A non-kosher knife (whether a knife of a non-Jew or a knife of a Jew that became *treif)* may be used **temporarily** for **cold** foods after *ne'itzah*, never for hot foods.[169]

☐ A meat knife should not be used to cut cheese even if *ne'itzah* is done beforehand.[170]

4) The effect of *ne'itzah:*
In the opinion of most authorities, *ne'itzah* is essentially a cleaning process. The rubbing against the hard earth wipes the knife clean of all grease and residue of non-kosher food.[171]

5) What type of knife cannot be *kashered* with *ne'itzah?*
Ne'itzah is effective only on a smooth blade. A knife with grooves and crevices cannot be *kashered* with *ne'itzah* since the non-kosher food remains embedded in the crevices would not be removed. A knife of this type must be *kashered* with *libun*.[172]

6) Substituting another cleaning process for *ne'itzah:*
Simply washing, scrubbing or wiping a knife cannot be substituted for *ne'itzah.*[173] Perhaps, scrubbing a knife well with detergent and steel wool may be equally effective, nevertheless

---

169. See *Y.D.* 121:7.

170. See *Taz* 89:6 who rules that after *ne'itzah* one may even use a meat knife to cut cheese. In §7, however, he notes that common custom forbids doing so. The wording of *Shach* 89:22, though ambiguous, implies that *ne'itzah* is acceptable only for use to cut bread to be eaten with a milk meal, not to cut cheese itself *(S.D.* ibid). See Chapter Eight, Section III,A, that common custom is not to rely upon *ne'itzah* to cut bread with a meat or dairy knife.

171. *Darcei Moshe* 105:5, *Toras Chatas* 23:7 and 61:13 explains that *ne'itzah* removes the residue of the food on the knife. See, however, *Shach* 10:6, who contends that *ne'itzah* removes the thin outer surface of the knife blade (although *S.D.* (ibid.) interprets the words of the *Shach* to imply that *ne'itzah* only causes the taste absorbed within the knife surface to be purged, *Yad Yehudah* 10:3a interprets the *Shach* that the *ne'itzah* removes a bit of the blade surface). See also *R' Akiva Eger* (gloss to *Shach* 96:9) who seems to assume that *ne'itzah* removes the taste absorbed in the surface of the knife blade (this is the opinion of *Yad Yehudah* (ibid.) himself as well). See *Yad Yehudah* ibid. for a comprehensive discussion of the issue.

172. *Y.D.* 121:7. Perhaps, even a scalloped edged knife should not be *kashered* with *ne'itzah* since the earth does not clean the crevices.

173. *Tosfos: Avodah Zarah* 76b.

ne'itzah is the preferred method and should be employed when possible.[174] One living in an urban surrounding without accessibility to hard earth should do *ne'itzah* in a flower pot.[175]

---

174. See *R' Akiva Eger* (gloss to *Shach* 96:3) as to whether washing a knife is sufficient in an *ex post facto* situation. *R' Akiva Eger* notes that one should not initially use the knife without *ne'itzah* even if it was wiped clean with a hard substance (see also *Badei HaShulchan* 96:1 s.v. *"o she'aino")*. Although logically, steel wool is no less effective than *ne'itzah*, perhaps *Chazal* specifically mandated *ne'itzah*. Indeed, according to the contention of *Shach* 10:6 that *ne'itzah* scrapes away the outside surface of the knife, perhaps one cannot substitute any other cleaning process (unless we assume that steel wool duplicates that process). It is difficult to offer a definitive ruling on this matter since different contemporary authorities have ruled differently on this subject.

175. This ruling was given by Rav S.Z. Auerbach (through a third party). The earth in the pot must be as hard as natural earth. If a flower pot is unavailable, one may *kasher* the knife in boiling water after cleaning it with steel wool and detergent, or perhaps rely on the steel wool cleaning itself. In the opinion of some authorities, one may clean the knife with sand paper since sand paper is essentially earth (heard in the name of Rav Yosef Breuer *z"l)*. One may also place the knife momentarily in a flame as this will burn off any residue and *kasher* the knife surface.

CHAPTER THIRTEEN

A Kosher Kitchen

□ A utensil by utensil overview of the kitchen to assist the reader in avoiding *basar b'chalav* problems.

Introduction

This chapter relates to most utensils found in the modern kosher kitchen. Since non-kosher foods are generally not found in a kosher kitchen, our discussion will deal primarily with problems relating to meat, milk and *parve* utensils. However, in no way does this imply that these are the only kashrus difficulties that may arise in the home. One must be attentive to meat and fish deliveries to the home by a non-Jew to ensure that they were sealed properly. One must be aware of the many difficulties relating to non-Jewish help in the home. A non-Jewish maid is not permitted to cook. Permitting a maid to wash dishes may be problematic. Indeed, even leaving a maid in the home alone for an extended period of time is questionable. Rabbinic guidance should be sought regarding these problems.

Before proceeding with our discussion, a note of caution is appropriate. The kitchen is the domain of the Jewish housewife. While women throughout the generations have not mastered the intricate *halachos* of *basar b'chalav*, they had and have a tradition of what is proper and what is improper in regard to *basar b'chalav*. Thus, a discussion such as ours is certain to strike many as not in accordance with their custom. In reality, it is impossible to set guidelines that will conform with everyone's tradition. Therefore, the proper perspective for every housewife is to do "as Bubby did". Our grandmothers lived and breathed kashrus. The kashrus of "their" kitchen was central to their lives. The pride and achievement that we find in other mundane matters, they found in their flawless separation of meat from dairy. Many things were "just not done" even if they were *halachically* permitted. The story is told of the wife of a great *talmid chacham* who upon finding her husband in the kitchen doing something not within her standards, shouted at him "get out of my kitchen before you make it *treif*".

Accordingly, this chapter should be viewed as a minimum standard. This chapter is intended to alert the reader to possible problems of which they were unaware. In addition, a family that has no previous tradition may follow these guidelines in keeping a kosher kitchen. However, those with stricter traditions should not loosen their standards based on anything written herein.

❧ Barbecue

A barbecue used for grilling meat may certainly not be used for any dairy food or for anything to be served with dairy. (The grid should also not be used for grilling fish). The barbecue grid is difficult to clean and assumed to contain meat or gravy residue. Even if the grid were properly cleaned of all meat residue it should nevertheless not be used for food to be eaten with dairy. Even using separate dairy and meat grids may be problematic depending upon the type of grill, and one should seek Rabbinic guidance. A closed grill should certainly not be used for meat and *parve* foods intended to be eaten with dairy since meat splatterings on the cover may fall into the *parve* food in the course of grilling.

◆§ Blender

A blender is essentially a knife and is thus subject to the *halachos* noted below regarding a knife. A *parve* blender should not be used with onions cut with a meat or dairy knife. One should not use either a meat blender for even cold dairy or a *parve* blender for even cold meat or dairy since its blades are difficult to clean properly.

◆§ Bread

Bread that was used in the course of a meat meal should not be used for a dairy meal. Bread is often handled during a meal and perhaps some meat residue on someone's hands adhered to the challah. Thus, a housewife who makes a challah kugel from the leftover *Shabbos* challah must not use that kugel for a dairy meal. Similarly, the leftover challah may not be used for a dairy *se'udah shlishis*. This refers only to sliced challah. The challah loaf itself is usually not touched by those present. Thus, the remnant of the challah loaf may be used for a dairy meal. Obviously, if children do in fact touch the loaf, it must be treated as sliced challah.[1]

◆§ Bread Board

One may slice bread on a bread board regardless of whether it is to be used with a meat or dairy meal. One should not butter a slice of bread or cut a salami or cream cheese sandwich on a *parve* bread board.

◆§ Bread Box

One may store bread in a bread box regardless of whether it is to be used with a meat or dairy meal. Bread that came into contact with meat or dairy should not be returned to a *parve* bread box.

◆§ Bread Knife

One may not cut bread with a meat knife if he plans to eat that bread with a dairy meal. Conversely, one may not cut bread with a

1. For a discussion of these *halachos* see Chapter Eight, Section III,3.

dairy knife for use with a meat meal. No distinction is made between a *ben-yomo* or non-*ben-yomo* knife.[2] One who must use a meat knife to cut bread for a dairy meal should do *ne'itzah* (thrusting into the ground) beforehand if possible. The process of *ne'itzah* is discussed in detail in Chapter Twelve, Section III as are many other relevant *halachos*. If one cannot do *ne'itzah* the knife should be thoroughly cleaned of any grease residue. In the event that a meat knife was used without cleaning, the cut surfaces of the bread should be scraped. *Poskim* relate that the common custom is not to rely on *ne'itzah* but to cut bread for a dairy meal with a dairy knife only (and vice-versa). *Poskim* commend the custom of punctilious individuals who keep a separate *parve* bread knife.

◆§ Broiler

Some ovens have a broiling chamber on bottom of the oven. This broiler is extremely difficult to clean properly and should be used for either meat or dairy exclusively, not for both. Many ovens have a broiling element in the oven chamber itself. These may be used for both meat and dairy, if necessary, providing that the oven is cleaned of any splatters between uses. In addition, one should wait twenty-four hours and *kasher* the oven between uses by heating it on its highest setting for approximately an hour.[3]

◆§ Broom

One may sweep remnants of both meat and dairy meals with one broom. We are not concerned with any mixture of meat and dairy in the broom since it does not come into contact with food.

◆§ Cabinets

Common custom is to store meat and dairy utensils in separate cabinets to prevent them from being mixed. Some have the custom to label their cabinets "meat" and "dairy" so that guests will not come to mix dishes.

◆§ Can Opener

Most canned goods are *parve*. Thus it is not necessary to keep a separate opener for canned foods to be used with meat and for foods eaten with dairy. However, one who uses canned meat or canned dairy should use a different can opener for each type since it is difficult to clean a can opener properly.

---

2. These *halachos* are discussed in Chapter Eight, Section III,2.

3. See Chapter Nine, Section I,C.

◈ Chicken

One who purchases chickens from a kosher supplier cannot assume that each chicken was inspected for broken limbs by the *shochet* or *bodek*. One is not required to check each chicken since we assume that the chicken is free of blemishes. However, one who notices any abnormality should consult a *moreh hora'ah*. A broken wing or leg or a discolored drumstick may render the chicken *treif* depending on the type of break or discoloration. At times this may merely be a result of the processing and have no effect on the *kashrus* of chicken.

◈ Chopper

A chopper is the equivalent of a knife. Thus, one who chops livers and fresh onions (or any sharp food) and subsequently uses the chopper to chop eggs and onions may perhaps not eat the chopped eggs with dairy foods. A *moreh hora'ah* should be consulted.

◈ Chulent Pot

One who wishes to add water to a *chulent* pot on *Shabbos,* should preferably not pour water directly from the parve kettle into the *chulent* pot since the remaining water in the kettle absorbs meat taste and may not be used for coffee and milk. The water should first be poured into a cup and then into the *chulent*. If one did pour into the *chulent* the water and kettle are unaffected. One should certainly avoid holding the kettle directly in the steam of the *chulent*. If the hot steam did reach the kettle a *moreh hora'ah* should be consulted.

◈ Coffee Maker

A coffee maker may be used to brew coffee for both meat and dairy meals. However, a coffee maker used for dairy grinds should not be used for coffee to be served in a meat cup or during a meat meal.

◈ Colander

A colander may be used in preparing *parve* foods for both meat and dairy meals.

◈ Containers

One should not store even cold liquids in a dairy container for a period of twenty-four hours if the liquids are to be used with meat. If no other suitable container is available, one may store the liquids even in a *ben-yomo* dairy container even if they are to be used with meat. One should not store meat or dairy liquids in a *parve* container for twenty-four hours.

◆§ Cookie press

A *parve* cookie press (a tube filled with dough that is pressed out through assorted forms to shape different types of cookies) should not be used for dairy dough since it is difficult to clean.

◆§ Cookie Shaper

One may use a *parve* cookie shaper (a mold pressed into the dough to shape cookies) to shape dairy dough providing that the shaper is thoroughly cleaned afterwards. Some individuals would avoid using a *parve* shaper for dairy dough.

◆§ Cork

A cork used to seal a bottle of milk should not be used with liquids to be served at a meat meal. A cork cannot be properly cleaned from absorbed milk.

◆§ Counter Top

One should set aside separate counter tops for use with meat and dairy foods. At times a hot pot or hot foods are placed on the counter top causing it to absorb meat and dairy taste. Cold empty dairy pots may be placed on a meat counter top (or the reverse). One may place a meat hot-plate or crock pot on a dairy counter if necessary. However, one should avoid serving from a meat crock pot over a dairy counter since food may drip onto the counter.

◆§ Cutting Board

One may cut foods (e.g., vegetables) on one cutting board for both meat and dairy meals. A meat cutting board should not be used to cut foods for a dairy meal.

◆§ Dairy Bread

One may not add milk to the dough of any bread regardless of whether one plans to eat it with dairy, or alone. Similarly, one may not knead a bread with meat gravy lest it be eaten with dairy. Bread baked with milk or gravy may not be eaten even alone.[4] The exceptions to this rule:

- ☐ One may bake an amount of dairy bread that will be eaten during that day either by the person himself or his family or guests.
- ☐ One may bake even a large amount of dairy bread if he shapes it in an unusual manner to serve as a reminder that the bread is dairy.

---

4. These *halachos* are discussed at length in Chapter Eight, Section III,B.

- □ One may bake dairy cakes of the type that is not eaten during a meal. For example, muffins that are served as dessert (with tea) but are never eaten in the course of the meal itself, may be baked with milk. Similarly, one may bake pastries and fruit danishes with milk since these are eaten only after a meal.
- □ One may certainly bake cheese cake or danishes since, in addition to the factor mentioned above, they are visibly dairy and will not be eaten with meat. Similarly, one may bake meat pies or any bread that obviously contains meat or gravy. One should not bake pastries containing meat or gravy that is not clearly visible since they may inadvertently be eaten as dessert with coffee and milk.
- □ One may bake a dairy loaf to be eaten at the dairy meal of the first day of *Shavuos* since one will not forget in the short time span that the loaf is dairy. Similarly, one may bake a challah with meat gravy if that challah is of the amount that will be consumed during the meat meals of *Shabbos*. If one eats a dairy *Se'udah Shlishis* the challah must be of the amount that will be consumed during the first two *Shabbos* meals.
- □ One should not bake bread while meat is being roasted in the oven. One who bakes a bread in this manner should consult a *moreh hora'ah* as to whether the bread may be eaten.
- □ One who warms the *Shabbos* challos by putting them in the oven or on the *blech* shortly before *Shabbos* should avoid putting them in a spot that they may come into contact with meat gravy. If the challos do come into contact with meat gravy a *moreh hora'ah* should be consulted.

Decanter

See "Pitcher".

Dentures

One who uses dentures may treat them as regular teeth. They may be used for both meat and dairy meals. Children that wear braces on their teeth must be particularly careful to clean their mouth between dairy and meat.

Dishcloth

One should preferably use separate dish cloths for washing meat and dairy dishes. The cloth comes in contact with actual meat or dairy and is used with hot water, thus it absorbs both particles and taste. *Halachically*, one may launder the cloth in hot water and detergent to change it from one use to another.

◆§ Dish Drainer

It is customary to use separate dish drainers for meat and dairy dishes.

◆§ Dishtowel

One should not use a dish towel for meat and dairy dishes without laundering it in between.[5] Some have the custom to keep separate meat and dairy dish towels.

◆§ Dishwasher

The problem of using one dishwasher for both meat and dairy is discussed at length in Chapter Ten. Initially one should not use one dishwasher for both meat and dairy dishes. There are, however, lenient opinions. One who finds it necessary to use one dishwasher for both meat and dairy should consult a *moreh hora'ah*. One who wishes to wash *parve* dishes in either a meat or dairy dishwasher must determine if his washer has a filter in the washing chamber. If no filter is present, one may be permitted to wash *parve* dishes. Nevertheless, scrupulous individuals would avoid using a meat or dairy dishwasher for even *parve* dishes. If, however, the washer has a filter in the washing chamber, one must be concerned that meat remnants may be sprayed onto the *parve* dishes.

Poskim assume that a *treif* dishwasher cannot be *kashered*. Nevertheless, one who faces a financial loss should consult a *moreh hora'ah*.

◆§ Drinking Glasses

There are authorities who contend that glass does not absorb taste from foods. In their opinion, one may use the same drinking glasses for meat and dairy meals. In previous times when glasses were costly this was the accepted custom. Indeed, some retain this custom today. Nevertheless, it is advisable that one purchase separate drinking glasses for each type.

◆§ Egg Slicer

One may use a *parve* egg slicer to slice eggs for both meat and dairy meals even if the eggs were boiled in meat or dairy pots.

◆§ Egg Cups

A *parve* egg cup may be used for eggs regardless of whether they

---

5. A dishtowel is not used directly with hot water and does not generally come in contact with meat or dairy thus it differs from a dishcloth.

were cooked in a meat or dairy pot, providing that no meat or dairy was cooked with the eggs.

❧ Fish

One may drink milk while eating fish or even fry fish in butter. There is a view, however, that one should not cook fish in dairy products. Although most authorities reject this view, many have the custom to refrain from eating fish with dairy. One may not eat fish with meat or grill fish on a meat barbecue. In addition one should eat some food and drink a liquid between eating fish and meat (or the reverse). Fish may, however, be cooked in a clean meat pot.

❧ Fish Store

Purchasing fish from a store not owned by an observant Jew or under Rabbinical supervision is fraught with difficulties.[6] Some guidelines:

- ☐ Fillet fish:
  One may not purchase any fish from a store without supervision if the fins and scales are not recognizable.
- ☐ Salted fish:
  One may not purchase pickled or salted fish without a proper Rabbinical supervision, even if the fins and scales are recognizable. Indeed, one may not purchase loose pickled or salted fish produced under Rabbinical supervision if it is being sold in an unsupervised store. One may not rely on the proprietor that the fish is indeed produced under supervision. Furthermore, he may cut the fish with a non-kosher knife.
- ☐ A store that sells non-kosher fish as well:
  One may not purchase cut fish from a store that sells non-kosher fish, even though the fins and scales of the kosher fish are recognizable. The knife used may have residue from a non-kosher fish and the proprietor cannot be believed that the knife is used exclusively for kosher fish. If the fins and scales are not recognizable the fish pieces may be from non-kosher fish. One who has no alternative to purchasing cut fish from a non-kosher store should purchase only whole fish, have the fish cut in his presence or purchase only pieces that have recognizable scales. If the fish was cut in the store, the cut pieces should be thoroughly washed and the cut surfaces lightly scraped with a knife edge.

---

6. See Chapter Twelve, Section II,A,2.

□ An unsupervised store that sells only kosher fish:
If the store sells only kosher fish, one may, if necessary, purchase cut fish (if the scales are recognizable) although one has no assurance that the knife is kosher.

◆§ Flatware

All flatware (and dishes and pots) used for meat food should be conspicuously different than those used for dairy. One using similar flatware for both is likely to mix the two and use meat utensils for dairy (or vice versa). One may, however, use similar utensils if he clearly marks those that are dairy. This may be done with indelible paint or a indentation in the metal itself. Although marking the meat flatware instead is equally effective the accepted custom is to mark the dairy flatware.

If a spoon (or any piece of flatware, or dish) became *treif* and subsequently mixed with other spoons one should not use any of the spoons until a twenty-four-hour period has elapsed since the non-kosher use. Preferably, one should remove one spoon to be *kashered*.[7]

One who finds a dairy spoon among the meat cutlery (or vice versa) may return it to its proper place. Neither the dairy spoon nor the meat cutlery is affected.[8] A milk spoon found in a meat dishwasher should preferably be *kashered*. In the event that the spoon was subsequently mixed with other dairy cutlery a *moreh hora'ah* should be consulted.

◆§ Food Processor

A food processor is, in essence, a knife. Thus, one who grinds hot meat or cold meat with onions in a food processor has rendered the utensil a meat utensil. The processor should not be used for any sharp food that is to be eaten with dairy. One should not grind an onion cut with a meat knife in a *parve* food processor.

◆§ Fork

A fork used to pierce foods is governed by the same rules as a knife. See below regarding a fork used to remove pickles from a jar.

◆§ Frying Pan

See "pot".

---

7. See Chapter Two, Section II,D.

8. See Chapter Ten, Section A,8.

◆§ Gloves

One who wears plastic or rubber gloves while washing dishes should use separate gloves (preferably of different colors) for meat and dairy use.

◆§ Grate, Grill

It is very difficult to clean a grate properly. Therefore, a grate used to broil meat may not be used for any food to be eaten with dairy or used to broil fish. A grate used to broil livers should not be used to broil meat unless it is *kashered*.

◆§ Grater

If an onion or horseradish is cut with a dairy knife and subsequently grated, the grater may have become a dairy grater and should not be used for meat (a *moreh hora'ah* should be consulted). One may not even use the grater to grate food for a meat meal since it is very difficult to clean a grater properly. One certainly may not grate food for a meat meal on a grater used to grate cheese.

One who uses a *parve* grater to grate horseradish should preferably not use a dairy plate if the horseradish is to be eaten with a meat meal (or the reverse).[9]

◆§ Grinder

A grinder in which hot meat or even cold livers and fresh onions was ground becomes a meat utensil. One who grinds a non-sharp food (e.g., potatoes or eggs) in a meat grinder may use that food with a dairy meal if the grinder was thoroughly cleaned beforehand. Some would avoid doing so since the grinder may not have been cleaned properly from meat residue. Onions or horseradish ground in a meat grinder becomes meat food and may not be eaten with dairy foods. If they are mixed with dairy foods or if one grinds dairy food with onions in the same grinder a *moreh hora'ah* should be consulted. An onion or horseradish cut with a dairy knife should not be ground in a meat grinder.[10]

◆§ Hard Cheese

One who eats "hard" cheese must wait six hours before eating meat. "Hard" cheese is defined as cheese that has aged for six months. Most commercial cheeses produced in this country do not fall into this category. However, one who eats the type of cheese commonly called

---

9. See Chapter Twelve, Section II,C,3,c.

10. See Chapter Twelve, Section II,C,3,h.

"Swiss cheese" or the equivalent (which is usually aged), must wait six hours before eating meat. One who eats "hard" cheese that has been melted into food (e.g., lasagna) need not wait six hours.

◈ Horseradish Jar

Many are accustomed to using a clean meat or dairy spoon (or fork) to remove horseradish or sauerkraut from a jar regardless of whether it (or the remaining horseradish) is to be used with a meat or dairy meal. It may be advisable, however, to avoid doing so. One should certainly not allow a meat or dairy spoon to remain in the horseradish or sauerkraut jar for an extended period of time.[11]

◈ Hot-plate

One should not use a hot-plate for both meat and dairy foods. One may warm dairy foods on a meat hot-plate if the hot-plate is cleaned and covered with a sheet of aluminum foil.

◈ Ice Cream Scooper

An ice cream scooper should not be used to serve chopped liver unless it is reserved for meat use. Since the scooper is difficult to clean, one must be concerned that it will not be cleaned properly between uses.

◈ Juicer

A juicer may be used to squeeze juices for both meat and dairy meals.

◈ Ketchup and Mustard

It is commendable to use separate ketchup and mustard containers for meat and dairy meals. One who wishes to use only one container should, at least, use squeeze type bottles. Glass jars or the spoon used with them are more likely to touch the plate and thus the food.

◈ Kettle

One may not use a dairy kettle to boil water to be used with meat or boil water in a meat kettle if the water is to be used for coffee with milk. If gravy splattered on a hot *parve* kettle or coffee urn, the kettle should not be used for coffee to be served with milk.[12] If no other kettle is available it may be used after twenty-four hours have passed.[13] Preferably, one should nevertheless pour boiling water over the area

---

11. See Chapter Twelve, Section II,C,3,g.

12. One should not boil the water in a *ben-yomo* meat pot even for coffee or tea that is only to be served in a dairy cup without milk. In the event that the water was boiled already, it may be served in a dairy cup.

13. See Chapter Eleven, Section H.

of the splatter. See "chulent pot" regarding pouring water from a kettle into a *chulent* pot.

◆§ Kiddush Cup

A *kiddush* cup may be used for *kiddush* in both meat and dairy meals. One must be careful not to wash the cup with dishes of both types.

◆§ Knife

One may not use a dairy knife to cut even cold meat (or a meat knife to cut cheese). Indeed, one may not even cut bread for a dairy meal with a meat knife unless one does *ne'itzah* beforehand.[14] In the event that the knife was used without *ne'itzah* the cut surfaces of the bread should be scraped. If a dairy knife was used to cut root vegetables they may be eaten with a meat meal after being thoroughly washed. A fruit or juicy vegetable (e.g., an orange, watermelon, cucumber, cabbage, tomato, pumpkin, beet or lettuce) that was cut with a meat knife must be scraped with a *parve* knife to remove the outside surface of the food before it may be eaten with dairy. If, however, the knife was certainly clean, the food is merely washed and may be eaten with dairy food afterwards.

Any sharp food cut, peeled or scraped with a meat knife may not be eaten with dairy (and the reverse). Sharp foods include: radish, garlic, onions, leek, horseradish, fresh olives, sour fruits or vegetables (lemons, esrog, sour apples or sour plums), pickled fruits or vegetables (perhaps pickled cucumbers or sauerkraut) and salted herring. This is true regardless of whether or not the knife was clean and regardless of whether or not the knife was used in the previous twenty-four hours to cut hot meat. If the sharp food is subsequently mixed or cooked with dairy food, a *moreh hora'ah* should be consulted. A sharp food cut with a meat knife and subsequently cut with a dairy knife contains taste of both meat and dairy. A *moreh hora'ah* should be consulted.

There is a popular misconception that any *treif* knife can be *kashered* by thrusting it in the ground. This is untrue; a knife, as any other utensil, must be *kashered* with *libun* or *hagalah*. There is, however, a method of *cleaning* a knife by inserting it in hard earth ten times. This method, described at length in Chapter Five, Section III, is known as "*ne'itzah*". Only a smooth knife, not a serrated knife can be "*kashered*" with *ne'itzah*. We will note some of the instances where *ne'itzah* is effective or required.

---

14. See Chapter Eight, Section III,A,2 and Chapter Twelve, Section II A,2,d.

- ☐ A non-kosher knife (whether a knife of a non-Jew or a knife of a Jew that became *treif)* may be used *temporarily* for cold foods after *ne'itzah*. It cannot, however, be used for hot foods.
- ☐ One who has only a meat knife and wishes to cut bread for a dairy meal (or the reverse) may do so providing *ne'itzah* is done beforehand.
- ☐ If a dairy knife was inadvertently used to cut cold meat and was not cleaned immediately after use, the residue dries onto the knife surface and is removable only with *ne'itzah*.
- ☐ A knife used to cut very hard food (e.g., a meat knife inadvertently used to cut hard cheese) requires *ne'itzah* before it may revert to its original status.
- ☐ If a dairy knife is inadvertently used to cut warm, but not hot, meat or a meat knife is used to cut warm cheese, the knife requires *ne'itzah*.
- ☐ One who cuts a worm while slicing a sharp food must *kasher* the knife with *ne'itzah*.

Where *ne'itzah* is required, simply washing, scrubbing or wiping a knife will not do. Although scrubbing a knife well with detergent and steel wool may perhaps be equally effective, *ne'itzah* is nevertheless the preferred method and should be employed when possible. One living in an urban area without accessibility to hard earth should do *ne'itzah* using a flower pot that contains hard earth.

◆§ Knife Sharpener

One may sharpen both meat and dairy knives on a sharpener[15] providing that they were thoroughly cleaned (preferably with steel wool) beforehand. Some have the custom of using separate sharpeners for meat and dairy.

◆§ Ladle

Meat and dairy ladles should not be similar. In the event that they are similar the dairy ladle should be marked to differentiate it from the meat ladle. If a ladle of one type is inserted into a pot of the other type a *moreh hora'ah* should be consulted.

One should not use a meat ladle to serve *parve* soup cooked in a dairy pot. In the event that this is done a *moreh hora'ah* should be consulted. One should not use a meat ladle to serve into a dairy bowl *parve* soup that was cooked in a *parve* pot (or the reverse).

---

15. See *Mordechai* cited in *Beis Yosef*, end of 122.

◆§ Measuring Spoon or Cup

One may use a *parve* measuring spoon or cup to measure cold milk. Some scrupulous individuals would refrain from doing so.

◆§ Microwave Oven

A microwave oven presents problems similar to other ovens (see below "oven"). One who wishes to use a microwave oven for both meat and dairy must follow the following precautions: The oven must be kept clean from any food residue. Foods cooked in a microwave oven splatter, boil over and drip. One must inspect the floor, walls and top of the oven before use to ascertain that no residue remains from previous use.

All foods cooked in a microwave should be covered. *Parve* solid foods (e.g., a potato) should be covered lightly with a paper plate.

One should not place meat and dairy dishes on the same surface. One should put separate plates (preferably glass) under meat and dairy dishes.

One should never cook meat and dairy concurrently in a microwave oven. In the event that this was done a *moreh hora'ah* should be consulted.

Some permit *kashering* a microwave oven by thoroughly wiping and cleaning all inside surfaces and then boiling a bowl of water in the oven until the oven fills with steam.

◆§ Milk Bottle

Milk bottles may be refilled with juice and used with a meat meal if the bottles are thoroughly washed beforehand.

◆§ Milk Cartons

One should not place milk cartons in a refrigerator above meat foods. Milk often drips from milk cartons to the food below.

◆§ Mixer

A mixer may be used for *parve*, meat and dairy foods. A set of beaters and bowls should be used only for either *parve*, meat or dairy. *Parve* beaters should not be used for hot meat or dairy. *Halachically*, one may use *parve* beaters for cold meat or dairy foods. Thus, one is permitted to whip cream with a *parve* mixer. Some are more scrupulous and refrain from this practice lest one not clean the beaters properly afterwards.

◆§ Onion Chopper

An onion chopper should be kept *parve* and used to chop onions for both meat and dairy foods. One should cut the onions to be used in the chopper with a *parve* knife only.

◆§ Oven

Ideally, one should try to acquire two separate ovens or an oven with two chambers, one set aside for meat and one for dairy use. One may bake meat and dairy simultaneously in their respective chambers. Those who possess only one oven which must be used for both meat and dairy should determine which type of food is most frequently cooked in the oven in liquid form in an open pot (only those foods containing liquids and cooked in an uncovered pot present a problem, not dry foods or foods cooked in a covered pot). For example; one who roasts meat often in an open pot should consider meat foods as his standard use. One who frequently bakes cheese cakes or cheese lasagna in an open pan should assume his standard use as dairy.

Once the standard use has been determined, whether meat or dairy, one may freely use the oven for both dry foods and liquids of that type, regardless of whether the pot is open or covered.

Whenever one wishes to use the oven for a type other than that designated as the standard, one must examine the oven to see if it is clean from any residue of the previous use. Any spots on the oven must be removed. (It is highly recommended to always spread aluminum foil under all foods being cooked in the oven to minimize the amount of spillage in the oven.) In addition, the food being cooked must either be dry or must be cooked in a covered pot. For example:

- ☐ If the oven is considered dairy, one may not cook in it an open meat roast with gravy.
- ☐ One may, however, bake challos immediately after roasting meat, providing that the oven surfaces are clean.
- ☐ In the event that one must cook liquid meat foods in the dairy oven, it should be done in a pot that is completely covered.

Sometimes one cannot follow these guidelines, for example, one whose standard oven use is for meat but wishes to bake a cheese cake. Cheese cake is normally baked in an open pan and cannot be covered. According to the guidelines set above, the cheese cake cannot be baked in the oven. The proper procedure in this case is to clean the oven thoroughly with a caustic cleaner, to wait twenty-four hours and then to heat the oven on its highest temperature for approximately an hour. Many authorities question the effectiveness of this process. However, common custom is to rely on heating an oven in the manner described above. One with the ability should acquire separate ovens for meat and dairy or a self-cleaning oven. A self-cleaning oven heats to an extremely high temperature. Some *Poskim* consider a cleaning cycle sufficient to *kasher* the oven from meat to dairy use (or the reverse). A continuous cleaning oven should not be confused with a self-cleaning oven. It cannot be *kashered* from one use to another. A *moreh hora'ah* should be consulted as to whether it can be used for meat and dairy.

One should never place meat and dairy foods directly on the same oven shelf. One may, however, place meat utensils on the same shelves as dairy utensils. Nevertheless, one should be concerned about foods that may have spilled on the racks. For example, a dairy pot may be placed over meat residue on the rack. Some authorities rule that one may assume that any food residue on the rack has certainly dried and poses no problem, while other authorities disagree. One who wishes to avoid any question should treat his oven racks as either meat or dairy and spread aluminum foil over the rack whenever cooking foods of the other type. Furthermore, as noted above, it is advisable to spread aluminum foil under foods of all types.

Baking meat and dairy concurrently in an oven:

It is prohibited to roast meat and dairy in open pots concurrently in an oven even if they do not touch one another and there is no chance of the meat gravy reaching the dairy food. In the event that meat was nevertheless baked simultaneously in an oven with dairy food, they may both be eaten. In the event that bread was baked simultaneously with meat it may not be eaten with dairy unless no other bread is available.

◈ Pastry Brush

One should not use a *parve* pastry brush to brush dairy cakes.

◈ Peeler

A peeler shares the same *halachos* as a knife. A peeler may be kept *parve* and used to peel vegetables for both meat and dairy meals. A *parve* peeler should not be washed with either meat or dairy dishes. One may keep two peelers, one meat and one dairy. The dairy peeler should be marked in a way to distinguish it from the meat peeler. One should not use a dairy peeler to peel sharp foods for use with meat (or the reverse).

◆§ Pet Food

One may not feed *basar b'chalav* to pets. Thus one must ascertain that any dog food does not contain any *basar b'chalav* that is Biblically prohibited (i.e., the meat and dairy are both from kosher species of animals, excluding e.g., horse meat or pork). If, however, the meat (or milk) is from a non-kosher animal the food may be used even though it contains both meat and milk. One who erroneously purchased *basar b'chalav* dog food should consult a *moreh hora'ah* as to whether they may return it for a refund or exchange.

◆§ Pickle Jar

When removing a pickle from a pickle jar one often inserts a meat fork or knife into the jar to remove the pickle. The pickle is pierced in many spots by a meat fork and thus absorbs meat taste. Frequently, one is unable to extricate the pickle from the jar and the pickle remains in the jar. Someone else may subsequently remove the pickle and eat it with dairy or someone may remove the pickle using a dairy knife or fork. This may be problematic since the pickle has absorbed both meat and milk taste. One should avoid the problem and remove any pickle that was pierced with a meat or dairy utensil.[16]

◆§ Pitcher

One may use a single pitcher for both meat and dairy meals, provided that one prevents meat and dairy from coming in contact with the pitcher. In addition the pitcher handle should be wiped clean of any food residue after each meal. Some have the custom of using separate pitchers for meat and dairy.

◆§ Place Mat

Common custom is to keep separate and distinct looking place mats for meat and dairy meals.

◆§ Pot

- ☐ Foods cooked in a meat or dairy pot:
  Dairy foods should not be eaten together with *parve* foods that were cooked in a *ben-yomo* meat pot (or the reverse) even if the meat pot was thoroughly washed. One may, however, put the food on a dairy dish even while hot. Thus, if water was boiled in a *ben-yomo* meat pot it may not be used for coffee with milk. In the event that one used the water for coffee with milk, he may drink it. Some contend that orange juice packaged by a dairy company should not be used with meat unless the

16. See Chapter Twelve, Section II,C.

machinery is *kashered* between milk and dairy runs. One may, however, drink the juice after eating meat. Similarly, margarine melted in a *ben-yomo* dairy pot should not be used for challos served during a meat meal. In the event that it was mixed into the dough, the challos should not be served with meat since one has the option not to serve the challos with meat, whereas in the previous case the milk was put into the coffee already. If, however, the meat pot was not used for hot meat in the previous twenty four hours, one may eat the *parve* food (e.g., the water or margarine) with dairy unless the *parve* food was sharp.

- ☐ Cooking *parve* foods in a meat or dairy pot:
  One may not cook *parve* food in a meat pot if the food is to be eaten with dairy (or the reverse). If one has no suitable *parve* or dairy pot a non-*ben-yomo* meat pot may be used for *parve* non-sharp foods.

⇜§ Pot Lid

One must never cover a cooking dairy pot with a meat lid (or the reverse or a *parve* lid on either a meat or dairy pot). In the event that a cooking pot was covered by a lid of the other type the pot and lid may require *kashering* and the food may be prohibited. A *moreh hora'ah* must be consulted.

⇜§ Refrigerator

One is not required to keep separate shelves in the refrigerator for meat and dairy foods. However, one should be careful that meat or dairy spills should be wiped away before foods are placed on the shelves. One should not place meat or dairy in a place from which they can drip upon one another. Since spillings are common one should keep meat and dairy foods on separate sides of the refrigerator.

⇜§ Restaurant

One may not eat a vegetable salad in a non-kosher restaurant even if the salad contains no onions. The knife may have been used for non-kosher foods and not thoroughly washed in-between.[17] One may purchase a cold kosher drink from a non-Jewish restaurant even if it is served in a glass (if the establishment is owned by a Jew, this may be problematic since presumably he did not perform *tevilas keilim*). A hot drink (e.g., black coffee) may be purchased only if it is served in a disposable cup.

17. See Chapter Twelve, Section II,A,2,b.

⚘ Rolling Pin

A *parve* rolling pin may be used to roll a dairy dough providing that it is thoroughly washed afterwards. Some would refrain from this practice especially since the rolling pin may be difficult to clean.

⚘ Salad

When preparing a salad for use with a meat meal one may not use a dairy knife, peeler or shredder to cut, peel or shred any vegetables for that salad. One who wishes to prepare a salad for use with both a meat and dairy meal should use a *parve* knife, peeler and shredder only. It is preferable not to eat any salads remaining from a meat meal with a dairy meal. Often the spoon used to serve the salad touches the meat and is subsequently replaced into the salad.

⚘ Salad Bowl and Spoon

One may use the same salad bowl and spoon for meat and dairy meals provided that they are washed well in between. It is nevertheless commendable to use separate spoons since they come in contact with both meat and dairy.

⚘ Salt Shaker

Before the advent of salt shakers, salt was placed on the table in a dish into which the food was dipped. Therefore, one could not use the same salt dish for both meat and dairy. Today when salt shakers are used, this reason no longer applies. Nevertheless, since at times the shakers may touch the food or since one may have food residue on his hands when grasping the shaker, common practice is to use separate meat and dairy salt shakers. This is undoubtedly commendable in a household with children.

⚘ Scale

One may weigh both meat and dairy foods on one scale if the scale is of a type that is always washed after use. Nevertheless, it is preferable to place the foods in a plastic bag before placing them on the scale.

⚘ Self-cleaning Oven

In the opinion of many contemporary authorities a self-cleaning oven is exempt from many of the restrictions relating to regular ovens. Thus one who runs a full self-cleaning cycle between meat and dairy use may use the oven for both. Waiting twenty-four hours and cleaning the oven surface with a caustic cleaner between uses is not necessary. This is the commonly accepted view although some authorities question the effectiveness of a self-cleaning cycle. A continuous cleaning oven should not be confused with a self-cleaning oven. There is serious doubt whether it can be *kashered*. One who wishes to use it for both meat and dairy should consult a *moreh hora'ah*.

☙ Serving Tray

A tray used exclusively for *parve* foods (e.g., drinks) may be used for both meat and dairy meals. However, since one often spills hot foods on a tray, a tray should not be used to serve both meat and dairy foods. One should purchase two distinct trays, one meat and one dairy.

☙ Sharp Foods

Sharp foods include: radish, garlic, onions, leek, horseradish, fresh olives, sour fruits or vegetables (lemons, esrog, sour apples or sour plums), pickled fruits or vegetables (perhaps pickled cucumbers or sauerkraut) and salted herring.

☙ Sharpener

See "knife sharpener".

☙ Shears

Parve shears may be used to cut food (e.g., vegetables) for both meat and dairy meals. Chicken shears, however, should not be used for foods to be eaten with a dairy meal even if they are washed beforehand.

☙ Shopping Bag

One should preferably not put meat and dairy foods in one shopping bag. Meat and dairy foods may drip on one another. The wrappers of packaged meats may be fatty and touch other foods. Cottage cheese and yogurt containers may open and spill.

☙ Silverware

See "Flatware."

☙ Sink

One with the ability should certainly acquire two kitchen sinks, one meat and one dairy. The ease of use and the prevention of numerous problems make this a worthwhile investment. One who has only one kitchen sink has the following options:

a) The safest solution is never to place any dishes or cutlery in the sink itself. All pots, dishes and cutlery should be washed while they are held in the hand.

b) One who finds this difficult may wash both types of dishes in the sink, provided he insures that no dishes or pots touch the sink bottom or side and that the dishes do not contact the water collected in the sink. *Poskim* offer two methods by which this can be accomplished:

- □ In the opinion of some authorities, dishes should never be put in the sink. Dishes should be washed only in basins inserted in the sink, one for meat dishes and one for dairy (and one for *parve*, if necessary). The tap water should pour directly into the basin, not into the sink. One need not be concerned about any water subsequently flowing from the basin into the sink. The basins themselves should preferably be placed on a rack or board, not directly on the sink surface. The sinks should be thoroughly washed between meat and dairy use so that no meat residue remain while dairy dishes are being washed (or the reverse). In addition, the drain should be kept free of any blockage so that the sink water should not gather in the sink and touch the dishes being washed.
- □ A more lenient position is offered by other authorities. One may merely place racks (one meat, one dairy and one parve) on the sink to keep the dishes suspended above the water level and sink bottom. One should nevertheless prevent sink water from rising and touching the dishes. In the event, however, that the water does reach the dishes, they are nevertheless unaffected.

One who has a meat sink and dairy sink adjoining one another must prevent water containing food particles from splashing onto the dishes of one type while washing those of the other type. The most effective method is to place a cover over the sink not being used. Another common method is to construct a ridge separating the two sinks.

Some double sinks are constructed of one sheet of metal that is formed into two sinks. Although, in effect, this constitutes one large vessel, half meat and half dairy, it presents no kashrus problem.

Adjoining sinks often share a common drain line with one drain trap. Although this is not the ideal situation since drain water may rise from one sink to another, it presents no serious kashrus problem. Nevertheless, the drain should always be kept clear to avoid this problem entirely.

In the event that a dish, spoon or fork falls into the sink while the hot water is running, if it was not directly under the water, it is unaffected. If, however, the utensil was directly under the water a *moreh hora'ah* should be consulted.

When washing dishes, one must be mindful of the following:

- One must keep separate sponges for meat, dairy and *parve* dishes since actual food particles are absorbed into the sponges.
- Any steel wool used for dishes of one type should not be used for dishes of the other type or for *parve* dishes. In the event that a sponge or steel wool used for one type was used on utensils of the other type, a *moreh hora'ah* should be consulted.
- One who wears plastic or rubber gloves while washing dishes should use separate gloves for meat, dairy and *parve* use.
- One should avoid letting meat or dairy food remnants touch the hot water spout since they will impart their taste into the spout and effect the hot water as it passes through the spout.

Spatula

One may not use a meat spatula while frying *parve* food in a dairy pan (or the reverse). In the event that this was done a *moreh hora'ah* should be consulted.

Sponge

One must keep separate sponges for meat, dairy and *parve* dishes since actual food particles are absorbed into the sponges. It is customary to use differently colored sponges for each type. In the event that a sponge of one type was used on utensils of the other type, a *moreh hora'ah* should be consulted.

Steel Wool

Steel wool used for dishes of one type should not be used for dishes of the other type or for *parve* dishes. One who uses one sink for both meat and dairy should never put the steel wool on the sink bottom or in the water gathered at the sink bottom. It is advisable to discard the steel wool after each use. In the event that steel wool used for one type was used on utensils of the other type, a *moreh hora'ah* should be consulted. Reusable washing pads should preferably be marked as meat and dairy (by using different types or colors).

◆§ Stove Top

Cooking meat and dairy on one stove top requires attention to the possible *basar b'chalav* problems that may arise:

- ☐ Meat and dairy pots cooking on a stove top must not touch one another. In the event that the pots do touch a *moreh hora'ah* should be consulted.

  ☐One should not cook meat and dairy in open pots in close proximity since they may splatter to one another as they boil. In the event that open pots were placed near one another the food is permitted since we do not assume that any splattering occurred. When meat and dairy pots are cooking near one another they should be covered to avoid any splattering. Some have the custom of placing a separation between meat and dairy pots. In the event that splattering did occur a *moreh hora'ah* should be consulted.
- ☐ Some authorities permit use of the same burner grates for both meat and dairy since presumably the flame burns away any food residue. One who notices any meat residue on a grate should remove it before placing a dairy pot on that grate. Electric stove ranges are likewise permitted since the coils burn away any food residue. Some have the commendable custom to use separate grates for dairy and for meat.

One should not suspend utensils above the stove top (e.g., spatulas, ladles or pans) since they are affected by the steam from meat and dairy pots cooking on the stove. For example, a ladle suspended in close proximity to a boiling pot of chicken soup comes into contact with hot steam and may no longer be used with dairy. Similarly, a dairy ladle in the path of hot meat steam becomes *treif*. Even if the ladle is not close enough to the pot for the steam to impart its taste, the steam may dry on the ladle.

A stove hood covering the cooking area of a stove top generally presents no kashrus problem since the area below the hood is open and allows the steam to dissipate and not condense upon the hood. One must, however, be conscious of the problem since, occasionally, cooking is done in large pots which may be in close proximity to a low hood allowing droplets of condensed steam to fall from the hood into the food.

Most stoves have a useable area between the left and right burners. Hot foods of both types commonly splatter and spill on this area thus it absorbs both meat and dairy tastes and should be considered *treif*. Hot foods and utensils should therefore not be placed on this area. One should avoid placing even cold foods and utensils on that area since it may become hot while the oven is in use. One may purchase two distinct covers to cover the area, one for meat use and one for dairy (and a third for *parve* if necessary).

◆§ Strainer

A *parve* strainer may be used for foods to be served at either meat or dairy meals. A dairy strainer should never be used for foods to be served at a meat meal (or the reverse) since it is impossible to clean a strainer properly.

◆§ Sugar Dish

One should use a separate sugar dish for meat and dairy meals since the spoon may touch the food into which it is added. A sugar shaker may be used commonly for meat and dairy meals, even though it is advisable to purchase separate shakers for meat and dairy.

◆§ Table Top

One eating meat may not share a table with one eating dairy. *Chazal* were concerned that if two people eat at one table, one meat and one dairy, they may share their food and transgress the prohibition of *basar b'chalav*. This prohibition applies only to two people that are on friendly terms and would feel comfortable partaking of one another's food. Strangers may share a table even if one eats meat and one dairy. Even acquaintances may share a table if they put a sign or mark that will remind them not to share food. For example:

- □ They may place a separate tablecloth for each individual or one of the parties may use a tablecloth while the other eats on the table itself.
- □ If they normally do not use place mats they can each eat on a separate place mat or one uses a place mat while the other places his plate on the table itself.
- □ One may place an object that is usually not placed on the table to serve as a separation and reminder between the two. This object must be of sufficient size to be noticeable.

If the two are sitting apart and are not within hands-reach of one another (i.e., the food of one is not within reach of the other), they may eat together.

One may not even place meat upon the table at which dairy is being eaten (or the reverse) since one may absent-mindedly eat some of the meat. If, however, the table is large and the meat is not within hands-reach this is permitted.

Although *halachically* one is permitted to eat directly on the table both meat and dairy cold meals providing that one wipes the table clean, common custom is not to eat meat and dairy on the same surface. The table may be uncovered for dairy meals and covered during meat meals (or the reverse).

◆§ Tablecloth

One may not eat dairy on a tablecloth used for a meat meal (or the reverse) since meat residue remaining on the cloth may touch the dairy food. Most authorities do not differentiate between foods eaten directly on the cloth and those eaten only on plates. One need not, however, keep separate tablecloths for meat and dairy. A tablecloth used for meat may be thoroughly washed and subsequently used for dairy. Nevertheless some have the custom of using separate tablecloths for each type. A plastic tablecloth may be wiped and cleaned of any residue and reused for dairy. Nevertheless, common custom is not to eat meat and dairy on the same surface.

◆§ Teapot

A teapot may be used to brew tea for both meat and dairy meals. Even a teapot that is used to serve tea at the table may be used for both meals since it does not come in contact with meat and dairy. One must be careful not to wash the pot with the meat or dairy dishes.

◆§ Thermos Bottle

One should not use a thermos bottle for both meat and dairy liquids. A dairy thermos should not even be used for *parve* foods to be served at a meat meal since it is difficult to ascertain that the bottle has been properly cleaned of any dairy residue.

◆§ Toaster

One may use a toaster to toast *parve* breads for both a meat and dairy meal provided that any bread that came in contact with meat or dairy is not placed in the toaster.

◆§ Toaster Oven

A toaster oven is extremely difficult to clean and *kasher*, thus it should not be used for both meat and dairy foods. Bread that was toasted in a dairy toaster oven may not be eaten with a meat meal.

◆§ Towels

See "Dish towels."

◆§ Tray

See "Serving tray."

◆§ Warming Drawer

A warming drawer reaches temperatures that are considered *yad soledes bo.* Thus, using one drawer for meat and dairy poses a *basar b'chalav* problem. Foods often drip on the surface and their taste is absorbed into the drawer bottom. Manufacturers claim that lining the drawer with foil may damage the mechanism. Thus the only possible method to use the drawer for both types is to place the dishes on a separate rack for meat, dairy and *parve* use. Steaming foods should be kept covered since the steam may transfer taste between the foods and the drawer. It is advisable to keep all foods covered lest one forget and put in steaming foods without covering them beforehand.

◆§ Water Urn

One may use the same water urn for both meat and dairy meals. One should be careful that milk does not splatter on the outside surface or the spout of the urn.

◆§ Watermelon

One may purchase cut watermelon in a fruit store or supermarket since they presumably keep separate knives to cut the melons. Although it is not *halachically* required, some advise that the cut surfaces be washed.

◆§ Wok

One may use a single *parve* wok to stir fry vegetables for both meat and dairy meals. Preferably, only *parve* utensils should be used when stirring the food.

CHAPTER FOURTEEN

Glossary of Halachic Terms Used in Kashrus

- An encyclopedic reference for topics and terms used in this work.

This chapter contains encyclopedic definitions of kashrus terms used in this work and in classic *halachic* literature. Many items listed here may be found in the various chapters of this work as well. Generally, we attempted to include in this section additional information that may better define the concepts and theories involved with these terms. On the other hand, the practical *halachah* is elaborated upon more thoroughly in the text itself.

◆§ *Achilah,* אֲכִילָה — Eating:

In Biblical law the act of eating is considered *"achilah"* only if one eats a *kizayis* (a half egg's volume — somewhat more than one fluid ounce) of that food or one drinks a *riviyis* (somewhat more than three fluid ounces) of the forbidden liquid. [There is a disagreement among *Poskim* whether the size of our olives (or eggs) corresponds to the size of the olives (or eggs) of Biblical times (see *Tzlach: Pesachim* 116b, *Shaarei Teshuvah: O.C.* 486, *Mishnah B'rurah* 486:1 and *Biur Halachah* 271:13).] The *kizayis* is measured exclusive of what may remain between one's teeth. Thus, one who eats an exact *kizayis* is not liable for punishment (see *Chullin* 103b and *Rambam* 14:3). However, any food remaining in one's gums *(bein ha'chanichim)* is included in the measurement of the *kizayis* (ibid.). Even eating less than a *kizayis* or *riviyis* may be Biblically prohibited, see *"Chatzi shiur"*. The *kizayis* must be eaten in a span of time that constitutes one eating act. This is defined as the amount of time necessary to eat wheat bread in the volume of three (or four) eggs *(Rambam* 14:8), while sitting in the most comfortable manner *(B'rachos* 41a). This is called *"k'dei achilas pras." Halachic* authorities assume this to be approximately four (or perhaps nine) minutes. Similarly, drinking a *riviyis* must be completed in the time span normally required to drink a *riviyis (Rambam: Hilchos Ma'achalos Asuros* 14:9, *Hilchos Terumos* 10:3. See, however, *Raavad: Hilchos Terumos* ibid. who contends that the time span for drinking is *k'dei achilas pras*, see *Sidei Chemed* vol. 4 p. 396). There is disagreement among *Poskim* whether the time span of drinking a *riviyis* is uniform to all drinks or whether each drink has a particular time span in accordance with the drinking custom of that drink. See *Mishneh L'melech: Hilchos B'rachos* 3:12 and responsa *Maharam Shick: O.C.* 86. The act of eating must be done in a normal manner. One who eats a prohibited food in an unnatural manner has not transgressed Biblical law. For example: swallowing hot, scalding food *(Rambam* 14:11), eating foods into which repugnant matter has been added, causing it to become inedible, and gluttonous eating. Thus, one who has overeaten and feels a revulsion towards food and subsequently eats non-kosher food has not transgressed a Biblical prohibition *(Yoma* 80b). If, however, he is merely satiated but feels no revulsion towards the food, any subsequent eating is considered a natural act of eating *(Tosfos: Pesachim* 107b s.v. *"dilma")*. Swallowing food without chewing is considered natural eating *(Nodah b'Yehudah* I: *Y.D.* 35, *Chelkas Yoav: Y.D.* 9, as opposed to *Toras Chaim: Chullin* 120b. See, however, *Beis Ha'otzar* 153, citing *Mizrachi: Shemos* 34:26, who seems to support the view of *Toras Chaim)*. Authorities disagree whether eating raw meat constitutes a natural eating act (see *Minchas Chinuch* 7 and *Reshash: Menachos* 100a).

See also *"aino ra'uy l'achilah"*, *"chatzi shiur"*.

This topic is discussed at length in Chapter One, Section II,A and in introduction to Chapter Three.

◆§ *Ain m'vatlin issur lechatchilah,* אֵין מְבַטְלִין אִיסוּר לְכַתְּחִילָּה — One may not initially nullify forbidden foods:

In the opinion of some *Rishonim*, this is a Biblical prohibition. See *Chasam Sofer*, gloss to *Y.D.* 319, who argues that if it were permitted to nullify prohibited foods, the Torah would not have ordered that a *treifah* be thrown to the dogs since they may be eaten after *bitul*. In the opinion of responsa *Nodah B'Yehudah* II *Y.D.* 45, while one is Biblically prohibited from nullifying prohibited food by actually mixing it with kosher food, one may nullify its taste. Other *Rishonim* contend that it is Rabbinic in origin (see *Beis Yosef* 99, *Shach* 99:7, *Chochmas Adam* 52:6). Thus, one may not intentionally mix a non-kosher piece of meat with two pieces of kosher meat (unless the intention of the mixing is for some other purpose which cannot be accomplished in another manner, see *Taz* 99:7). Similarly, one may not blend a non-kosher ingredient into kosher food sixty times its volume (*Y.D.* 99:5). Even in the event that non-kosher food falls into an amount of kosher food that is insufficient to effect *bitul*, one may not add kosher food to increase the ratio *(Y.D.* 99:5) even if he plans to remove the non-kosher food itself *(Aruch HaShulchan* 99:21). *Sefardic* custom permits the addition of kosher food to a mixture containing non-kosher food that is prohibited by Rabbinic prohibition only, while *Ashkenazic* custom does not differentiate between Biblical and Rabbinic prohibitions (see *Rema* 99:6, *Kaf HaChaim*

99:68). One who intentionally causes a *bitul* of non-kosher food may neither partake of that food (*Y.D.* 99:5) nor sell it to another Jew or in any way derive benefit from his transgression (*Rashba* cited in *Beis Yosef* 99). Others, however, may eat from the mixture, unless it was specifically nullified for their sake (*Y.D.* 99:5). In the event that they were unaware of the *bitul* being done, some *Poskim* permit their eating the food (see *Taz* 99:10, see, however *Yad Yehudah* 99:23k). Among the exceptions to this rule: One who intentionally nullified non-kosher food without realizing that it is forbidden to do so may eat the mixture (*Y.D.* 99:5, see *Taz* §7).

See responsa *R' Akiva Eger* 207, as to whether this prohibition applies to mixing meat and dairy. He argues that perhaps *basar b'chalav* is never created since the milk immediately becomes nullified in the meat.

There is a difference of opinion among *Poskim* if one may nullify a food that is still permitted so that it will not become prohibited later. For example: may one nullify bread before *Pesach* so that it may be eaten on *Pesach* or may one nullify milk so that it may be cooked with meat? See *Magen Avraham* 447:42,45, *Taz* §18, *Graz: Kuntres Acharon* 442:3, *S.D.: Y.D.* 99:22, *M.Z.: O.C.* 447:8 and *Sidei Chemed* vol. 1 p. 7.

These *halachos* are discussed in Chapter Two, Section V.

◆§ *Aino ra'uy l'achilah,* אֵינוֹ רָאוּי לַאֲכִילָה — Literally, unfit to eat:

Any forbidden food, whether of Biblical or Rabbinic origin, which becomes unfit to eat, loses its status as a forbidden food. It is most important to note that this *halachic* exclusion of *foods*, "unfit to eat" differs in a most significant manner from the *halachah* excluding unnatural *eating* from the prohibition of eating non-kosher foods (see "*achilah*" above). While the exclusion of eating in an unnatural manner relates to the act or the person ("*gavra*" in Talmudic terminology), the exclusion of inedible foods relates to the food or object ("*cheftza*"). The contrast between the two is profound. 1) Eating foods that are inedible is not considered an "eating" act; however, this applies only to items that the Torah prohibited with use of the word "*achilah*" — (eating). There are other items whose consumption is prohibited with use of other terms in the Torah. Since the term "*achilah*" is not utilized in regard to those prohibitions, they would not be excluded from the prohibition merely by reason of their inedibility. The *halachah* presently under discussion teaches us that *any* item completely inedible is excluded from the Torah prohibition, not merely because the eating act is not considered "eating" but because the matter is excluded from the prohibition (see *Shaagas Aryeh* 75). 2) If we were to exclude inedible foods merely because the eating act is not considered "eating", it would apply only to the prohibition of eating. One may still be prohibited from deriving benefit from the item if it is an item which is *assur b'hana'ah* (prohibited from deriving benefit). If, on the other hand, inedible items are excluded from the prohibition, as *Chazal* derived from the verse pertaining to *neveilah,* it may be that the item was removed entirely from the realm of prohibited foods. One may therefore be permitted to derive benefit from it as well. [This is, however, quite less than certain. Although the prohibited food is inedible and thus excluded from the prohibition of eating, it may nevertheless retain its status as pertaining to other *halachos*. For example, although a *neveilah* loses its prohibited status once it is unfit for human consumption, it retains the status of *neveilah* regarding the *halachah* of *tumah* (spiritual defilement) see *Rambam: Hilchos Avos Hatumos* 1:13 who rules that the *neveilah* retains its status as far as *tumah* is concerned until it has become unfit for even a dog's consumption. Therefore, the question remains, should we compare the prohibition of benefit to that of eating or that of *tumah?* See *Mishneh L'Melech: Hilchos Avel* 14:21, and *Chidushei HaGrach* on *Rambam* 14:11. See also *Yad Yehudah* 103:8a for a most comprehensive discussion of this and related topics. *Yad Yehudah* presents a convincing proof that the prohibition of benefit remains. He cites the Talmud *(Temurah* 34a) that the ashes of most forbidden foods retain their prohibition of benefit. Ashes are certainly inedible, and yet they retain their prohibition.] See also responsa *Nodah B'Yehudah* I *Y.D.* 26 and *Achiezer* 2:11, 3:5 regarding the difference between foods unfit for human consumption and those unfit for even canine consumption. 3) A prohibited food which became spoiled and inedible and thereby lost its prohibition perhaps will not regain that status even if it was somehow made edible again. Were it merely a matter of an unnatural eating, once the food is made edible, it returns to its prohibited status (see *Chavas Daas* 103:1, *Yad Yehudah* 103:11a citing *Re'ah* in *Bedek HaBayis)*. For further study, see *Nodah B'Yehudah* I *Y.D.* 26, *Kreisi U'pleisi* 87:15, *Chidushei HaGrach* on *Rambam* (ibid.), Responsa *Chasam Sofer (Y.D.* 98), and *Chavas Daas* (103:1).

Hence, any prohibited food which putrefied or, for any reason became completely unfit to eat (even if only because it assumed a repulsive odor [*Yad Yehudah* 103:2k]), loses its status as a forbidden food. (See *Chavas Daas* 103:1 and *Yad Yehudah* 103:8a, 11a who make a distinction between food which spoiled on its own as opposed to food which was spoiled through addition of foreign matter.) If, however, it is somewhat edible, albeit with difficulty, it retains its non-kosher status.

Rabbinic law prohibits eating even inedible non-kosher foods unless they became mixed with kosher food (*Y.D.* 103:2. See also *Minchas Kohen* 1:9 and *M.Z.* 103:1). See *Yad Yehudah* 103:8a who explains this Rabbinic prohibition on the basis of the fact that one who eats even inedible foods has accorded them the status of food (*ach'shevei*) (a source for this explanation may be found in *Rosh: Pesachim* 2:1).

⁂ *Ben yomo*, בֶּן יוֹמוֹ — Literally, "of the day":

Food taste that has been absorbed in a vessel for a period of time becomes stale and cannot affect food subsequently cooked in that pot (see *nosen taam lifgam*). *Poskim* disagree as to the length of time required for the taste to become stale. While some contend that the passage of a complete night (from sundown to dawn) is sufficient (*Rashi*, as interpreted in *Tosfos: Avodah Zarah* 76a, and *Ran*, cited in *Tur* 103. See also *Chochmas Adam* 55:4 and *S.D.* 103:19), others require the passage of a twenty-four-hour period (*Rashbam* cited in *Tur* 103). This second, more stringent opinion is most widely accepted by *Poskim* (*Y.D.* 103:5). Thus, the term "*ben yomo*" is used to describe a vessel that was used during the previous twenty-four hours. The taste absorbed in a *ben yomo* vessel is fresh, not stale and therefore must be *halachically* reckoned with. If the pot was used for cooking kosher foods (e.g., water) during those twenty-four hours *Poskim* disagree as to whether it is considered *ben-yomo* from non-kosher use (see Y.D. 103:7 *Shach* §20). A meat or dairy vessel is certainly considered *aino ben-yomo* once twenty-four hours have passed from the original cooking of the meat or milk, regardless of any *parve* food or water cooked in between (*Tur* 94, 103, see *Issur V'heter* 34:7).The twenty-four-hour respite is determined from the time that the non-kosher food stopped infusing its taste into the vessel. Therefore, if upon completion of the cooking the non-kosher food was not immediately removed from the vessel, one must determine the twenty-four hours from the time that the food was no longer *yad soledes bo* (*D.T.* 103:76). In addition, if a non-kosher liquid remained in the vessel for twenty-four hours or more, the vessel is considered *ben-yomo* until twenty-four hours after the liquid was removed (*Yad Yehudah* 103:29k).

See also "*nosen taam lifgam*".

See Chapter Three, Section II,B for further discussion of this topic.

Bishul, בִּישׁוּל — Cooking:

The *halachic* term of "*bishul*" (cooking) should not be confused with the term "heating". Although similar, they are not synonymous. "Heating" is a broad term that applies to many forms of warmth, while "*bishul*" is a term more restricted in its definition and application. Many forms of heat can effect a transfer of taste often regardless of the source of heat. However, in regard to certain *halachos* actual *bishul* is required, mere transfer of taste is not sufficient. For example: One is forbidden to do an act of *bishul* (cooking) on *Shabbos*. Merely warming food to the degree of *yad soledes bo* does not necessarily violate *Shabbos* even though it may cause a transfer of taste. This would depend on the source of the heat that brought about the warmth. For example: One may warm food in direct sunlight on *Shabbos* even if it attains the degree of *yad soledes bo*. Similarly, one who warms food in a *kli sheni* (a vessel into which the original boiling pot was emptied) has not, in the opinion of many *Poskim*, violated the *Shabbos* even if the food attains the heat of *yad soledes bo*. Similarly, one is forbidden to perform the act of *bishul* on meat and milk together. This too, depends upon the source of the heat. Solar cooking or even cooking in a natural hot spring may not violate the Biblical prohibition of cooking *basar b'chalav*. Even though either of these forms of cooking may bring about a transfer of taste from meat to dairy (or the reverse). *Bishul* can take place when food is placed in a *kli rishon* (even after it has been removed from the fire) containing liquid that is *yad soledes bo*. *Poskim* disagree as to whether or not *iruy* or *kli sheni* can effect *bishul*. See also Chapter Five, Section II,B.

See also "*kli rishon*", "*kli sheni*" and "*iruy*".

Bishul achar bishul, בִּישׁוּל אַחַר בִּישׁוּל — Literally, "cooking after cooking":

The question of whether or not one who recooks foods that were previously cooked is performing an act of "*bishul*". This pertains to the prohibition of cooking on *Shabbos* and the prohibition of cooking *basar b'chalav*. The issue of *bishul achar bishul* regarding *Shabbos* is discussed in *Orach Chaim* 318:4,5. The question of *bishul achar bishul* in regard to *basar b'chalav* is discussed in the later *Poskim*. The *halachic* consensus is that if meat and milk were first cooked separately and then subsequently cooked together, the Biblical prohibition of cooking *basar b'chalav* has been violated (responsa *Chasam Sofer: Y.D.* 82). If, however, the meat and milk were initially cooked together, many *Poskim* contend that recooking them violates no additional Biblical prohibition *(R' Akiva Eger* and *Gilyon Maharsha* gloss to 87:1. See also *D.T.* 87:4 and *Sidei Chemed* vol. 1 page 184), while others disagree *(S.D.* 87:18, and 99:11, rules that the prohibition applies in all cases. However, in *O.C., A.A.* 673:1 he contradicts this ruling and in *M.Z.* 105:2, seems to be uncertain).

ⓢ *Bitul b'rov,* בִּיטוּל בְּרוֹב — Literally, "nullified in a majority":
Whenever two similar tasting foods become mixed, the non-kosher food may become *batel* in a simple majority of kosher food. This is true even if the non-kosher food remains intact but is unrecognizable among the pieces of kosher food. The foods need not even be mixed together or even close to one another. Indeed, even three unrecognizable pieces of meat in three different rooms or stories of a house are *batel b'rov (M.Z.* 109:1, *D.T.* 109:4). *Chazal* derived the principle of *bitul b'rov* from the rule that one must follow the majority opinion in a *Beis Din*. For an in-depth analysis of the relationship of these two concepts, see *Shaarei Yosher* 3:4. Classic *halachic* sources describe *bitul b'rov* as *"chad bitrei"* one (piece mixed) into two (pieces). This seems to imply that a ratio of two-to-one is required for *bitul b'rov.* Indeed, this is the opinion of some authorities. Many *Poskim,* however, rule that a simple majority is sufficient (see *Shach* 109:6, *Chochmas Adam* 51:4 and *Pischei Teshuvah* 109:1). See also *D.T.* 109:22, who cites opinions that in regard to a Biblical prohibition, a ratio of two-to-one is required whereas regarding a Rabbinic prohibition, a mere majority is adequate. *Poskim* note that *bitul* becomes effective only after the mixture becomes known, i.e., someone noticed the fact that non-kosher food fell into kosher food. Thus, if non-kosher food fell into kosher food in two stages without being noticed in between, we require one act of *bitul,* not two. Hence, we require *rov* the entire non-kosher food, not *rov* against the two individual parts. *(Shach* 109:12 implies that this restriction is Biblical in origin see, however, *D.T.* 99:97.)

Rishonim disagree about the underlying principle of *bitul b'rov*. In the opinion of *Rashba (Toras HaBayis* 4:1 and *Ran* cited in *Beis Yosef* 109), *bitul b'rov* is based on the logical premise that when any part of the mixture is removed, we may assume that it has come from the majority. Thus, each piece, as eaten, is assumed to be from the permitted majority. Indeed, even the last piece may be eaten by the same person since, we may assume that it is from the majority as well and is now assumed to be kosher. One who is punctilious would avoid eating, or even giving another Jew, the last piece (see *Beis Yosef* 109 citing *Maharam*). *Rashba* does concede, however, that one may not eat the entire mixture at once. To do so would leave no alternative other than to assume that non-kosher food is now being eaten. This prohibition, however, is Rabbinic in origin (*Taz* 109:1, see *M.Z.* See a dissenting view in *Tosfos Rid; Bava Basra* 31b). Even *Rashba* concedes that according to Torah law each piece actually becomes permitted (see *Pri Migadim* in his introduction to *Hilchos Taaruvos* 1:3).

In the opinion of *Smag* I:141 and *Tosfos* (*Chullin* 100a s.v. "*beriah*") cited in *Beis Yosef* 109 *one person* may not eat the entire mixture even if he were to eat each piece individually. He may eat the mixture only if he leaves uneaten a piece equal in size to the original non-kosher food. This piece may, however, be eaten by another Jew.

In the opinion of *Rashi* (*Avodah Zarah* 74a, cited in *Rema* 109:1) the last piece is certainly the non-kosher piece itself and should not be eaten by *anyone*, it must be discarded or sold to a non-Jew.

Rosh (*Chullin* 7:37 and *Smak* and *Maharam Rotenburg* cited in *Beis Yosef* 109; see also *Bedek HaBayis* 4:1) takes a radically different view of *bitul b'rov*. In their opinion, *bitul b'rov* does not entail an assumption that any part removed from the mixture is from the majority. Rather, *bitul b'rov* brings about the complete transformation of the non-kosher food into kosher food. The non-kosher food has been nullified and has completely lost its identity. Therefore, the entire mixture may be eaten by one person even at once.

Rishonim (see *Ran: Nedarim* 59b) note that only prohibited matter can become nullified, permitted matter cannot become nullified. Thus if kosher food falls into a majority of non-kosher food, the kosher food is prohibited because of the non-kosher food in the mixture but the kosher food itself is not transformed into non-kosher food (unless the principle of *chatichah na'asis neveilah* can be applied). Some explain this in the following manner: *bitul* is the means by which something loses its status; *bitul* cannot create a status. All matter is permitted unless it possesses a prohibited status. Therefore, prohibited matter can become *batel* since once its prohibited status is revoked, it becomes permitted. Permitted matter cannot become *batel* since its permitted status is merely the absence of any status (see responsa *Oneg*

Yom-Tov: O.C. 4 and *Or Sameiach: Ma'achalos Asuros* 15:10). There is a dissenting opinion among *Rishonim* that contends that even permitted matter can become *batel* (see *Ran* ibid.).

In the opinion of most *Poskim* (with the exception of *Issur V'heter* 57:15), when a non-kosher food becomes *batel*, the mixture may be eaten even by the most scrupulous (see *D.T.* 116:109 who cites opposing views on this).

The *halachic* ramifications of these opinions are discussed in Chapter Two, Section I.

⁂ *Bitul b'shishim*, בִּיטוּל בְּשִׁשִּׁים — Literally, "nullified in sixty":

Bitul b'shishim differs from *bitul b'rov* in that while *bitul b'rov* nullifies the non-kosher food itself, *bitul b'shishim* nullifies its taste as well. The necessity of *bitul b'shishim* is based on the principle of *taam k'ikar*. According to Torah law, *bitul b'shishim* is required only when these *two* features are combined: a) the foods are dissimilar in taste *(min b'sheaino mino)*. If, however, the foods are similar tasting, the taste of one is not noticeable in the other; thus, *bitul b'rov* suffices. b) the foods are either liquids or solids that are blended or cooked together. If, however, the foods are solids that are neither blended nor cooked together, they do not impart taste to one another; thus, *bitul b'rov* is adequate. If *either* of these two factors is missing, *bitul b'shishim* is not mandated by Torah law. *Chazal*, however, extended the requirement of *bitul b'shishim* to cases that resemble the primary Biblical case in some aspect. *Chazal* were concerned that one may confuse the rules pertaining to similar tasting foods with those of dissimilar ones and transgress a Biblical prohibition. (See *Shach*, 109:9, and *D.T.* 109:47, as to whether or not this applies to Rabbinic prohibitions as well.) Therefore *Chazal* extended the requirement of *bitul b'shishim* to any case which resembles the Torah requirement of *bitul b'shishim*. Thus, since the Torah requires *bitul b'shishim* in a case of *taam k'ikar* — dissimilar mixtures cooked or blended together, *Chazal* extended this requirement to similar mixtures blended or cooked together and to dissimilar mixtures which are neither cooked nor blended, since each of these resembles the Torah requirement in one aspect. If, however, the mixture is neither similar nor blended together, *Chazal* left *bitul b'rov* intact since no resemblance exists to the Torah requirement *(Minchas Kohen* II;2:1). Hence, similar tasting foods that are blended or cooked together *(Y.D.* 109:2) or uncooked, dissimilar tasting foods *(Rema* 109:1) require *bitul b'shishim*. This represents the opinion of the majority of

Rishonim. Beis Yosef 109, however, cites the opinions of *Rashi, Raavad* and *Rambam* (15:4) who contend that even uncooked, similar tasting foods require *bitul b'shishim.* See *Chavas Daas* 109:3,5, who notes that in a case of *bitul b'shishim,* when the mixture is blended together, even *Rashba* would concede that one may eat the entire mixture at once (even though *Rashba* contends that when *bitul b'rov* is employed one may not eat the entire mixture at once). See *Pri Migadim* (introduction to *Hilchos Taaruvos* 3:5) for an analysis of the distinction between *bitul b'rov* and *bitul b'shishim.* He explains that the prohibition of eating the entire mixture is based on the idea that had the mixture been of dissimilar tasting foods, the non-kosher food would have spread its taste throughout the mixture. In a case of *bitul b'shishim,* however, even if the mixture would have been of dissimilar tasting foods, the non-kosher taste would have been completely diluted. Therefore, *Chazal* did not deem it necessary to prohibit eating the entire mixture at once. (See *Shaarei Yosher* 3:9 for further discussion of this topic.)

Even a mixture of dry, similar tasting foods that had previously become *batel b'rov* may lose the status of *bitul* if it is subsequently cooked together. *Bitul b'rov* is not, in the opinion of most Rishonim, the actual transformation of the non-kosher food into kosher food. The non-kosher food retains its status. We merely assume that any part (or perhaps all parts) removed from the mixture is of the permitted majority. Thus, if the mixture is cooked and the non-kosher taste is spread throughout, the entire mixture may be prohibited (*Rashba* cited in *Beis Yosef, Y.D.* 109:2. See *Rema* 109:2, regarding *Ashkenazic* custom and *Kaf HaChaim* 109:40, regarding *Sefardic* custom.

These *halachos* are discussed at length in Chapter Two, Section II and Chapter Four, Section II.

§ *Beriah,* בְּרִיָּה — Literally, a complete creature:

A complete creature such as an insect, an egg that contains an unhatched bird (see *Shach* 100:2) or even a complete limb torn from a living animal cannot become *batel.* The ramifications of this *halachah* are explained in *Shulchan Aruch* (*Y.D.* 100).

§ *Chamira sakanta me'isura,* חֲמִירָא סַכַּנְתָּא מֵאִיסּוּרָא — One must be stricter regarding a *sakana* (a hazard) than regarding a prohibition (*Chullin* 10a, *O.C.* 173:2, *Rema* 116:5):

Among the questions raised based upon this principle are: Do the rules of *bitul b'shishim* apply to those foods that are forbidden because of *sakana?* For example, if a piece of fish fell into a pot of meat will it be *batel b'shishim?* See *Taz* 116:2, citing *Darcei Moshe* and *Maharil,* who rules that *bitul b'shishim* does not apply, while *Shach* in *Nekudas Hakesef* rules that pertaining to *bitul,* a *sakana* is no more severe than a prohibition. Most *Poskim* follow the opinion of *Shach* (see responsa *Chelkas Yaakov* 2:10 and *Yabia Omer* I, *Y.D.* 7). See *Shach* 116:1 who cites *B'er Sheva* that meat and fish baked in an oven simultaneously are prohibited even in an ex-post-facto situation.

⤛§ *Chaticha ha'ruyah l'hischabed,* חֲתִיכָה הָרְאוּיָה לְהִתְכַּבֵּד — Literally, "a piece fit to serve":

A piece of meat of a size and condition fit to serve to company cannot become *batel.* A piece of meat can only be considered *chatichah ha'ruyah l'hischabed* if it is prohibited on its own. A permitted piece of meat which absorbed non-kosher taste is not subject to this *halachah. Poskim* disagree whether or not raw meat is considered *chatichah ha'ruyah l'hischabed* (see *Y.D.* 101:3, *Rema* and *Taz* §5). The criterion of whether something is fit to serve depends upon the custom of the time and place *(B'er Heitev* 101:12).

⤛§ *Chatichah na'asis neveilah,* חֲתִיכָה נַעֲשִׂית נְבֵילָה — Literally, "the piece become prohibited like a carcass":

Chatichah na'asis neveilah is predicated on the principle of *efshar l'sochto assur* — a non-kosher taste cannot be extracted from a mixture in which it was infused. *Chatichah na'asis neveilah* goes a step further; it declares that if non-kosher taste is mixed into kosher food in a ratio that it cannot become *batel* the entire mixture becomes a prohibited entity that generates non-kosher taste of its own. Thus if one ounce of meat is cooked in thirty ounces of milk the entire mixture is viewed as prohibited matter which requires *bitul*. Consequently, we require eighteen hundred and sixty ounces of kosher food to nullify the original thirty one ounces of *basar b'chalav*. Most *Rishonim* (excluding *Raavad* and apparently, *Rif,* cited in *Beis Yosef 92)* rule that in meat and milk mixtures *(basar b'chalav),* we assume the mixture to be a prohibited entity of its own *("chatichah na'asis neveilah")*. This is the theory attributed to *Rabeinu Efraim* (cited in *Tosfos: Chullin* 100a). The difference between *basar b'chalav* and other non-kosher foods is explained in Chapter Seven, Section I,A (see *Taz* 92:9 and *Shach* 92:10). Accordingly, we require a ratio of sixty against the meat and milk mixture. *Rishonim* disagree as to whether or not *chatichah na'asis neveilah* applies to mixtures of other non-kosher foods. The *Shulchan*

Aruch (*Y.D.* 92:4) follows the opinion that *chatichah na'asis neveilah* applies to *basar b'chalav* only. Therefore, in mixtures of other non-kosher foods, while the original mixture retains its prohibition, it combines with any additional kosher food to dilute the original non-kosher taste. *Sefardic* Jews follow this opinion (*Kaf HaChaim* 92:16). *Rema* 92:4, however, follows the opinion that *chatichah na'asis neveilah* applies to all non-kosher mixtures, albeit by Rabbinic law only (*Taz* 92:11, *Shach* 92:12). *Ashkenazic* custom follows this ruling. *Poskim* discuss the question of whether or not *chatichah na'asis neveilah* pertains to utensils that absorbed non-kosher taste. See *Y.D.* 98:5 and *Rema* 92:4. See Chapter Four, footnotes 30, 34-36.

See also "*efshar l'sochto*".

See Chapter Two, Section IV,B and Chapter Seven, Section I,A.

Chatzi shiur, חֲצִי שִׁיעוּר — Literally, "half the required amount":

One who eats non-kosher foods is Biblically liable for punishment only if he eats a *shiur* (the minimum amount; usually a *kizayis* the size of an olive) within a specific time span —*k'dei achilas pras* (approximately four minutes). The Talmud (*Yoma* 74a) cites a dispute debating whether or not one is Biblically prohibited from eating less than a *shiur*. The *halachic* ruling follows the stringent opinion. This is known as "*chatzi shiur assur min haTorah*". Thus, even one who eats a minute amount of non-kosher food has transgressed a Biblical prohibition even though he is not liable for punishment (*Rambam; M.A.* 14:2). Similarly, one who does not conclude eating the non-kosher food within the prescribed time, has violated the prohibition of *chatzi shiur*.

See also "*achilah*".

Chozer veniyur, חוֹזֵר וְנֵיעוֹר — Literally, "it is reawakened":

If additional non-kosher food is added to a mixture after *bitul* has taken effect, the *bitul* must be re-evaluated. If the kosher food no longer contains enough to nullify the non-kosher food, the original *bitul* is no longer valid (*Rema* 99:6). *Chazal* name this phenomenon *chozer veniyur* — a reawakening (of the original non-kosher food). Although the non-kosher food has already become *batel*, the mixture must now be judged in accordance with the new circumstances. This is the opinion of the majority of *halachic* authorities. A minority of *Poskim* contend that since the non-kosher food has become *batel*, it is no longer considered non-kosher. Therefore, it cannot combine with any non-kosher food subsequently added (see the minority opinions cited in *Shach* 99:21). In the opinion of *Rema* this applies to mixtures of similar tasting foods as well. See *Shach* (ibid.) who contends that the concept of *chozer veniyur* applies only to dissimilar tasting foods. Thus he rules that if the foods are similar tasting and the mixture was noticed before the additional food fell in, one may eat the mixture in a situation of serious monetary loss. Other authorities follow the opinion of *Rema* (see *D.T.* 99:95).

See Chapter Two, Section IV.

⁂ *Davar chashuv,* דָּבָר חָשׁוּב — Literally, "something prominent":

Certain foods cannot become *batel* due to their prominent nature. This rule is a Rabbinic decree *(Rambam* 16:9). *Davar she'biminyan* is one type of *davar chashuv*. Others that are listed in *Shulchan Aruch (Y.D.* 110:1) include: certain species of walnuts, pomgrenates, cabbages and gourds, large sealed wine barrels and certain loaves of bread. If, after becoming mixed with permitted foods, the *davar chashuv* loses its prominence, it becomes *batel* (*Y.D.* 101:6). However, one may not intentionally make it lose its prominence after it became mixed (see *"ain mivatlin issur l'chatchilah"*).

⁂ *Davar charif,* דָּבָר חֲרִיף — A sharp food:

A sharp food has the unique ability to affect the absorption and transmission of *taam* in a manner unlike that of any other food. Although sharpness alone cannot effect a taste transfer (e.g.,sharp foods placed in a non-kosher dish retain their kosher status, *Taz* 96:3), it can enhance the taste transfer in several ways: a) *duchka d'sakina* — when a knife is used to cut a *davar charif*, the combination of *duchka d'sakina* (the pressure of the knife) and sharpness cause taste to be absorbed to a *k'dei netilah* (approximately one inch) of the food *(Rema* 96:1). b) *Nat-bar-nat — halachah* usually differentiates between a primary infusion of taste and a secondary infusion of taste *(nosen taam bar nosen taam — "nat-bar-nat")* regarding permitted foods *(nat-bar-nat d'heteira)*, see Chapter Six. A *davar charif*, however, has the ability to elevate a secondary infusion of taste and make it equivalent to a primary infusion. Thus, a radish cut with a meat knife is considered as if it absorbed the primary taste of the meat itself *(Rema* 95:2). c) *Nosen taam lifgam* — a non-kosher taste absorbed into a vessel for a twenty-four-hour period loses its potency and its ability to transfer its non-kosher status to a food cooked in the pot (see Chapter Three). A *davar charif*, however, revitalizes the absorbed taste in the vessel and endows it with the strength to impart its taste into the food. Thus, an onion cooked in a non-*ben-yomo* non-kosher pot may not be eaten (*Y.D.* 103:6).

What is considered a *davar charif?*

Although there are differing opinions, *halachic* consensus rules that all sharp foods are included in the category of *davar charif*. (See *D.T.* 96:39, who cites an opinion that although any food which appears to be sharp must be considered a *davar charif* even though it is not mentioned in Rabbinic sources, the reverse is not true. A food cited in the Talmud or Rabbinic literature as a *davar charif* must be considered as such, regardless of whether or not it appears to be sharp.) This includes: garlic, onions (see *Pischei Teshuvah* 96:3 whether scallions are considered a *davar charif*), leek (*Y.D.* 96:2), horseradish (*Rema* 96:2), olives (either raw or completely pickled, see *M.B.* 447:89, see also *Shach* 96:20), sour fruits or vegetables, e.g., lemons (*Y.D.* 96:4), esrog (*Magen Avraham* 447:33), sour apples (see *Taz* 96:9) or sour plums (*Issur V'heter* 38:14), pickled fruits or vegetables (see *Daas Torah* 96:2 p. 264 regarding sour pickles), sauerkraut (see *Taz* 96:12 as opposed to *Aruch HaShulchan* 96:13), salted herring (see *Shach* 96:16), certain spices (see *Shach* 96:19 regarding pepper, and 96:17 regarding ginger), and liquids e.g., very salty water (brine), strong vinegar (*Magen Avraham* 447:28) whiskey (*Taz; O.C.* 442:4, *D.T.* 96:40, however, cites opposing opinions), olive oil (*D.T.* 96:65), and wine (*D.T.* 96:42).

See also "*duchka d'sakina*", "*nat-bar-nat*" and "*nosen taam lifgam*".

◈ *Davar gush,* דָּבָר גּוּשׁ — Literally, "a thing of substance", a solid object:

In the opinion of some *Poskim* (*Issur V'heter* 36:7 and *Maharshal: Chullin* 7:44, cited in *Taz* 94:14 and *Shach* 94:30, 105:9. See also *A.H.* 94:32) only a liquid is affected by its transferral from a *kli rishon* to a *kli sheni* since the walls of the vessel cool the liquid. A solid, however, retains its form and does not come in contact with the walls of the vessel and is therefore unaffected by the walls of the vessel, it therefore retains the status of a *kli rishon* even after it is placed in a *kli sheni*. Other *Poskim* do not differentiate between liquids and solids (*Rema* 94:7). *Halachic* authorities follow the more stringent view unless significant loss is involved (*Chochmas Adam* 60:12, *Aruch HaShulchan* 105:20). All opinions agree that a solid food that was roasted over the fire retains its status as a *kli rishon* even after it has been removed from the fire. However, if the roasted food is placed on a cool surface after its intense heat has dissipated some no longer consider it a *kli rishon* even though it is *yad soledes bo* (see *Aruch HaShulchan* 105:26, in his interpretation of *Rema* 105:3). In the opinion of the *Maharshal*, however, the food retains the status of *kli rishon* even after it has lost its intense heat (see *Darcei Moshe* 105:4). *Poskim* disagree as to whether or not, in the opinion of *Maharshal*, a *davar gush* is considered *kli rishon* even in terms of effecting actual *bishul*. *Chavas Daas* 91:5 and 92:23 cites *Minchas Yaakov* 61:45, who contends that even *Maharshal* concedes that a *davar gush* cannot effect *bishul* (i.e., regarding the *halachos* of *Shabbos* and *basar b'chalav*). However, *Magen Avraham* 318:45 (cited in *Mishnah B'rurah* 318:118) rules that, in the opinion of *Maharshal*, a *davar gush* effects actual *bishul*. See also *Binas Adam* 48(66).

See also "*kli sheni*".

◆ *Davar hama'amid*, דָּבָר הַמַּעֲמִיד — Something that causes solidification:

A non-kosher food which solidifies or jells the food with which it combines cannot become *batel*. In the opinion of most *Poskim* this rule is Rabbinic in origin (see *Chok Yaakov* 442:16). For example, cheese that was curdled with non-kosher rennet may not be eaten although the amount of rennet used is minimal and its taste is unnoticeable (*Rambam* 16:26). The effect of the non-kosher rennet on the cheese is noticeable and prevents its *bitul* (see *Avodah Zarah* 35a). However, *davar hama'amid* applies only to prohibited foods, not foods which, when combined, will produce prohibited food (e.g., meat and milk). Thus, kosher rennet (produced from the stomach lining of a properly slaughtered cow) may be used in the cheese-making process and presents no *basar b'chalav* problem (*Y.D.* 87:11).

◆ *Davar she'biminyan*, דָּבָר שֶׁבְּמִינְיָן — Literally, "a thing that is counted":

An object that is sold solely by unit is considered "prominent" and cannot become *batel*. For example: a whole egg of a non-kosher bird that became mixed into other kosher eggs is not *batel b'rov* since eggs are sold by number (a dozen). The ramifications of this *halachah* are found in *Shulchan Aruch* (*Y.D.* 110:1).

◆ *Davar sheyesh lo matirim*, דָּבָר שֶׁיֵּשׁ לוֹ מַתִּירִים — Literally, "a thing that will be permitted":

A food that will, in time, become permitted or a thing that can easily be made permitted (as opposed to something that will be permitted only through much effort or expense, see *Y.D.* 102:2,3), cannot become *batel* in another food similar in type. For example, *chadash* (any of the five types of grain [wheat, barley, oats, spelt and rye] that took root after the sixteenth of *Nissan* until the following sixteenth of *Nissan* — see Chapter One I,A,13) cannot become *batel* since it will become permitted on the following sixteenth of *Nissan* (*Rambam* 15:10). It can, however, become *batel b'shishim* when mixed with food of a different type (ibid. §12 *Y.D.* 102:1. See *Rema* for dissenting opinions). Here, similarity of foods is determined by name not by taste (*Shach* 102:3, as opposed to *Taz* §10) while usually it is determined by taste (*Shach* 98:6). Other examples of *davar sheyesh lo matirim* are: *tevel,* since it will be permitted after the proper shares are removed, and an egg that was laid on *Yom Tov,* since it will be permitted the following day. This restriction is Rabbinic in origin (*Taz* 102:1). A complete discussion of the principle of *davar sheyesh lo matirim* is found in *Shulchan Aruch* (*Y.D.* 102).

◆§ *Duchka d'sakina,* דּוּחְקָא דְסַכִּינָא — Literally, "the pressure of a knife":

A knife, unlike other utensils, comes into contact with food under conditions of pressure. This pressure increases the ability of the knife to absorb taste from a food or to infuse some of its previously absorbed taste into the food. Although *duchka d'sakina* alone cannot bring about the absorption or transfer of taste, it enhances the absorption in the following ways:

a) The degree of absorption: Although heat can transmit taste from one food to another or from food to a vessel without the aid of *duchka d'sakina*, the degree of the penetration of taste is greatly enhanced by *duchka d'sakina*. We noted in Chapter Five, Section I that ordinarily, two dry hot foods that touch one another cannot transmit taste beyond *k'dei netilah* (the thickness of approximately one inch). Only liquids (or foods immersed in liquids) or oily fatty foods can (in conjunction with heat) generate a transmission of taste throughout the food (*Y.D.* 105:4). Nevertheless, when hot food is cut with a knife, the combination of *duchka d'sakina* and heat may cause taste transfer throughout the food even without a liquid or fatty medium (*Tur* end of 94, as explained in *Issur V'heter* 36:7 and *Shach* 94:27, see also *S.D.* 10: end of §22). Another explanation of this rule is based upon the fact that a knife is assumed to retain fatty residue which, as all fatty foods, is able to spread the taste throughout the food (*Shach* ibid. and *S.D.* ibid.)

b) The degree of heat required: Normally, any degree of heat less than *yad soledes bo* cannot effect a transfer of taste (Liquids soaking in a utensil for a twenty-four-hour period are an exception and can effect a transfer of taste — *kavush k'mevushal* — see Chapter Five, Section III,A.) Thus, if a spoon is put in a non-kosher liquid which is cooler than *yad soledes bo*, the spoon is merely to be washed well, *kashering* is not required. Similarly, a knife used to cut cool, non-kosher meat must be scrubbed well but need not be *kashered (Chochmas Adam* 47:4). However, a knife that was used to cut warm non-kosher food heated to less than *yad soledes bo*, must be *kashered* with a process called *ne'itzah* (trusting into the ground). The warmth of the food combined with *duchka d'sakina* transfers taste from the food to the knife as well as from the knife to the food even though the heat is less than *yad soledes bo* (see *Biur HaGra* 94:27). For practical applications of this principle see Chapter Twelve, Section II,B,2).

c) The ability to absorb without heat: A knife used to cut sharp foods *(davar charif)* is the equivalent of any utensil coming into contact with hot foods. The combination of the sharp taste of these foods and the *duchka d'sakina* creates a transfer of taste from the food to the knife and from the knife to the food even though both knife and food are cold.

See also *"davar charif"* and *"ne'itzah"*.

The practical *halachos* are explained in Chapter Twelve.

◆§ *Efshar l'sochto,* אֶפְשָׁר לְסוֹחְטוֹ — Literally, "(is it) possible to extract it":

Efshar l'sochto is the question of whether a food that absorbed non-kosher taste can be purged of that taste when cooked with additional kosher food. The Talmud *(Chullin* 108a) cites a difference of opinion on this issue. For example: if one fluid ounce of milk fell into a pot of thirty fluid ounces of meat, the entire mixture becomes *basar b'chalav*. If, subsequently, the original mixture becomes combined and is cooked with another thirty ounces of meat, we are confronted with the question of *efshar l'sochto*. Should we assume that the original milk now becomes diluted into the total sixty ounces of meat and becomes *batel ("efshar l'sochto mutar")?* Or perhaps the milk remains in the original thirty ounces of meat to a degree that the meat retains its non-kosher status *("efshar l'sochto assur"). Poskim* rule that the milk cannot be extracted from the original mixture.

Therefore, the first thirty ounces of meat remain forbidden. Indeed, the second thirty ounces of meat became forbidden since they absorbed taste from the original mixture which became a prohibited entity of its own *(chatichah na'asis neveilah)*. Even if the original mixture is cooked with sixty times the original mixture (1,860 ounces), the original thirty ounces of meat retain their prohibited status *(efshar l'sochto assur)*. *(Y.D.* 92:2,3). In the opinion of prevailing *Poskim* the rule of *efshar l'sochto assur* applies to *all* prohibited foods as well as to *basar b'chalav (Y.D.* 106:1, *Poskim* are troubled by the apparent contradiction in the ruling of the *Shulchan Aruch* (92:4). See *Shach* 92:11 and *P.M.* ibid). *Efshar l'sochto,* however, does not apply to permitted foods. For example: onions that were cooked with meat and subsequently cooked with *parve* food in a dairy pot require *bitul b'shishim* in ratio to the absorbed meat only, not the onions (see *Beis Yosef* 94, citing *Smak, Shach* 94:23 and *Taz* 96:5).

See also *"chatichah na'asis neveilah"*.

See Chapter Two, Section IV,B and Chapter Seven, Section I,A.

☙ *Hefsed merubah,* הֶפְסֵד מְרוּבָּה — A substantial loss:

At times a lenient position is taken or lenient opinions are followed where otherwise, a substantial loss of money will be incurred. *Poskim* will occasionally be lenient in a particular case when *any* loss is involved — *b'makom hefsed.* At times they will be permissive only in a case of substantial loss — *hefsed merubah.* Although some *Poskim* defined *hefsed merubah* in terms of amounts or ratios, most *Poskim* rule that *hefsed merubah* is determined by the financial status of the particular owner (see *Soles L'mimchah* (gloss to *Minchas Yaakov* 38:2), *Pischei Teshuvah Y.D.* 31:2, *D.T.* § 11 and *Sidei Chemed* vol. 2 p. 187,214. See *D.T.* ibid. regarding a loss of food belonging to two partners that is not significant to either of the two but which is, in total, a significant loss. See *D.T.* ibid. as to whether others may purchase something that was permitted to its owner because of *hefsed merubah.*

☙ *Heteirah balah,* הֶיתֵּרָא בָּלַע — Literally, "a permitted taste was absorbed":

One may *kasher* a vessel with a more lenient method if the absorbed taste is presently a permitted taste. A common application of this principle pertains to *basar b'chalav*. The taste of either meat or dairy prior to their combination is a permitted taste. Therefore, we apply a lenient standard to *kashering* a vessel from meat or dairy use. Normally, a vessel used in direct contact with fire (without a liquid medium) requires the *kashering* method of *libun* (heating in fire) as ruled in O.C. 451:4. Nevertheless, when *kashering* a kosher meat grill to dairy use, one need not use the method of *libun*. The meat taste, which is *heter*, can be purged merely with *hagalah* (scalding with water, see *Shach* 121:8, and gloss of *R' Akiva Eger* ibid.) or with *libun kal* (O.C. 509:4). See Chapter Eight, Section III,C as to when it is permitted to *kasher* from meat to dairy or the reverse.

☙ *Iruy*, עירוי — Pouring:

Liquid that is being poured from a *kli rishon* is no longer considered *kli rishon* (since it is no longer being warmed by the original vessel) nor is it considered *kli sheni* (since it is not yet cooled by the second vessel). *Rishonim* disagree as to the exact status of the liquid. In the opinion of *Rashbam* (cited in *Tosfos: Shabbos* 42b, *Zevachim* 95b), *iruy* is considered a *kli sheni* and cannot actually cook *(bishul)*; it can, however, generate either a discharge or absorption of taste (not both concurrently — *"maflit u'mavliah k'echad")* into the thickness of a *klipah*. In the opinion of *Rabbeinu Tam* (ibid.) *iruy* is considered a *kli rishon* and even though it cannot cause absorption of taste into the entire food it can effect actual *bishul* to the thickness of a *klipah* *(Shach* 105:5 cites opinions that *iruy* causes actual *bishul* throughout the food). Although this dispute has little significance in regard to transfer of taste since we usually (except in a case of loss) follow the stringent opinion that even a *kli sheni* capable of transferring taste, it does have much relevance to the prohibition of *bishul* on *Shabbos* and to the prohibition of *bishul* of *basar b'chalav*. In contrast, *Maharshal* (cited in *Shach* 105:5) contends that according to *Rabbeinu Tam, iruy* effects *bishul* on the entire food, see also M.Z. 68:9:3. *Poskim* rule that if hot non-kosher liquid is poured over cold kosher food, the taste of non-kosher liquid is absorbed into a *klipah* of the food). See, however, *Shach* 105:5, *S.D.* (ibid.), M.Z. 68:9:3, and *Chochmas Adam* 59:2 who differentiate between an uninterrupted flow i.e., the poured liquid is still connected to the *kli rishon (lo nifsak ha'kiluach)* and an interrupted flow *(nifsak ha'kiluach)*. In the former case, they contend, the *iruy* is considered *kli rishon* and effects actual *bishul* to the thickness of a *klipah*. In the latter case the *iruy* is considered *kli sheni* and merely causes *one* transfer of taste to the thickness of a *klipah* but cannot effect *bishul* or two taste transfers *(maflit u'mavliah k'echad)*. See M.Z. 68:9:4, who rules that in regard to an interrupted flow, the prohibition of the *klipah* is only Rabbinic. Thus, in a case of doubt, one may disregard the problem. See *Chazon Ish*

Y.D. 9:5, who contends that an interrupted *iruy* effects no transfer of taste at all. Most authorities, however, disagree, see *Badei HaShulchan* 91:20). *Iruy* cannot, however, effect *two* transfers, e.g., if hot water was poured over a kosher and non-kosher food placed side by side, the kosher food is unaffected. If the liquid was not poured directly over the food but reached the food only after flowing over a surface, a *klipah* must be discarded if the flow was uninterrupted (see *Shach* 95:18 who seems to contradict himself, see *S.D.* ibid. See also *Chavas Daas* 92:23 who notes that an indirect *iruy* causes only a taste transfer but cannot effect *bishul*). If the flow was interrupted it cannot affect even a *klipah* of the food (See *Biur HaGra* 92:36, in explanation of *Rema* 92:7, and *Chochmas Adam* ibid). A utensil that became *treif* through *iruy* may be *kashered* through *iruy* as well (*O.C.* 451:5).

See also *"bishul"*.

See Chapter Five, Section II,C and Chapter Eleven, Section F.

◆§ *Kavush k'mevushal,* כָּבוּשׁ כִּמְבוּשָּׁל — Literally, "soaking is the equivalent of boiling":

Any food that has soaked in a liquid effects the same transfer of taste that occurs when the two are cooked together. This is known as *"kavush k'mevushal"*. Thus, if a non-kosher food soaked in a kosher liquid or a kosher food soaked in a non-kosher liquid, the kosher liquid or food absorbs non-kosher taste. A kosher food that soaked in a liquid in which a non-kosher food previously soaked or is presently soaking, is likewise affected by the non-kosher taste (*D.T.* 105:2 citing *Minchas Yaakov*). Similarly, if a non-kosher liquid is contained in a kosher vessel for a twenty-four-hour period, the vessel absorbs non-kosher taste. See *D.T.* 105:11, regarding which types of vessels absorb through *kavush k'mevushal*.

Most *Rishonim* (see *Beis Yosef* Y.D. 105) agree that a soaking of twenty-four hours effects a transfer of taste. The twenty-four-hour soaking must be consecutive. If, however, the food is removed from the liquid, even momentarily, and then returned, no transfer of taste occurs even if the total soaking time was twenty-four hours. Although *Chavas Daas* 105:2c, *R' Akiva Eger* 105:1 and *Pischei Teshuvah* 69:33 follow the lenient ruling (see also *D.T.* 105:8) *M.Z.* 105:1, relies on it only in a case of serious financial loss. See *Yad Yehudah* 105:2k,1a, who contends that if the interruption was short, the *kavush k'mevushal* process is not interrupted. *Yad Yehudah* perceives *kavush k'mevushal* to depend entirely on the softening of the solid matter, thus a momentary interruption of the soaking does not interfere with the process. It is for this reason too, that *Yad Yehudah* argues that flowing water can effect *kavush k'mevushal*. He also contends that if meat soaked in a vessel for twenty-four hours and only then milk falls in, the *kavush k'mevushal* effect is immediate since the meat was previously soaked and softened. Other *Poskim* rule that if the food is soaked in running water, it is not considered *kavush* since the water has changed (see *Pischei Teshuvah* 69:33. The twenty-four hour requirement applies to all liquids except salt brine (*Y.D.* 69:18, 105:1) and perhaps vinegar (ibid., *Shach* 105:2, however, contends that vinegar is no different than other liquids (see *D.T.* § 40). Foods soaked in salt brine are considered *kavush* after eighteen or perhaps even six minutes (see *D.T.* § 42).

Poskim disagree if kosher liquid that soaked in a non-kosher vessel is affected. The absorption takes place only at the end of twenty-four hours, however, the non-kosher taste that was previously absorbed in the vessel becomes stale (*pagum*) after a period of twenty-four hours and cannot impart its non-kosher taste. The point of contention is whether *kavush k'mevushal* causes the taste to be absorbed exactly at the end of the twenty-four-hour period, while the taste becomes stale only *after* twenty-four hours have passed. Thus, if the soaking started immediately after the vessel became non-kosher, it may impart its taste through *kavush k'mevushal*. Or perhaps, both the absorption and the spoiling of the taste take place simultaneously and thus a transfer of non-kosher taste of a vessel through *kavush k'mevushal* is impossible. See *B'er Heitev* 105:1 who contends that the liquid soaking in the vessel does not allow the absorbed taste to become stale. See also *D.T.* 105:14, for a discussion of the various opinions in this matter.

See *D.T.* (105:5) for a discussion as to whether *kavush k'mevushal* applies to a kosher taste. For example: does milk soaked in a vessel render it a dairy vessel?

One should note, however, that although *kavush* effects the equivalent of cooking, it is not considered an act of *bishul*. For example, one who soaks a food on *Shabbos* has not, in the opinion of *Chochmas Adam* 58:1, violated the Biblical prohibition of cooking. *Kreisi U'pleisi* 105:2, however, contends that in the opinion of *Rambam, kavush k'mevushal* applies to the prohibition of cooking on *Shabbos* as well. This interpretation of *Rambam* is shared by responsa *Nodah B'Yehudah* 2:60. One may also infer this from *Rashi: Pesachim* 44b. See also *Sidei Chemed (Ma'areches Chaf* no.43, vol. III, p. 119). *Chochmas Adam* does, however, concede that in the opinion of *Rambam, kavush* constitutes a Rabbinic prohibition of cooking. This question needs further study. See *M.B.* 318:37, who rules that one may prepare foods through soaking, without noting that the food should not be soaked for twenty-four hours. It is interesting to note that the opinion of *Kreisi U'pleisi* runs counter to a commonly accepted theory regarding *bishul* on *Shabbos:* Since *kavush* takes effect only after twenty-four hours, the *"bishul"* of *kavush* will always take place after *Shabbos* is over. Hence, it may be compared to someone that places a pot over a fire a moment before *Shabbos* is over. In the opinion of *Eglei Tal: Zoreiah* 2 (8), and *Minchas Chinuch* (32: *Zoreiah)* this is not a transgression of *Shabbos* since the pot will cook only after *Shabbos*. Perhaps *Kreisi U'pleisi* follows the opinion of *Reshash: Shabbos* 73a, and *Chelkas Yoav* 10 who compare the *melachah* of *bishul* to that of *zoreiah* (planting). In their opinion, just as one who plants a seed immediately violates *Shabbos* even though the seed germinates only after several days, so too one who places a pot over the fire immediately violates *Shabbos* (see complete discussion in *Eglei Tal, Chelkas Yoav* and *Afikei Yam* II 4:1). Perhaps *Kreisi U'pleisi* is referring to soaking in salt brine or vinegar which takes effect sooner that twenty-four hours. This too is not without problems since, in the opinion of *Shach* (105:2, although *Kreisi U'pleisi* disagrees with *Shach)* vinegar is no different than other liquids. He contends that the *"bishul"* effected by salt brine in a short period of time is rooted in the effect of the salt *(meliach k'roseiach)* not the soaking, thus it is of no help in resolving our problem which deals with *kavush k'mevushal*. In addition, one may question whether the quicker *kavush k'mevushal* effected by salt brine (and vinegar) is a quicker *"bishul"* or merely a quicker transfer of taste, while the actual *bishul* takes place only after twenty-four hours even in salt brine. Thus, the contention that *kavush k'mevushal* applies to *Shabbos* needs further study.

Similarly, one who soaks meat in milk has not transgressed the Biblical prohibition of cooking *basar b'chalav (Pesachim* 44b, *Rema* 105:1). The meat and milk, however are Rabbinically prohibited since they absorbed taste from one another *(Rashi: Pesachim* ibid., *Y.D.* 91:8).

See *M.Z.* (105,end of 1) that although cooked blood is only Rabbinically forbidden, blood that was absorbed into food through *kavush k'mevushal* is Biblically forbidden since it was not actually cooked. See also *D.T.* 105:16 and *Aruch HaShulchan* 105:15.

See Chapter Five, Section III,A for the practical applications of *kavush k'mevushal*.

◆§ *K'feilah,* קְפֵילָה — A chef:

There is a difference of opinion among *Rishonim* whether one may rely upon a Jewish or non-Jewish chef *(k'feilah)* to sample food to determine whether it tastes of any prohibited food. The primary opinions are discussed in *Minchas Kohen* II, 1:7.

a) In the opinion of *Rashi: Chullin* 97a, and *Rosh* (as cited in *Minchas Kohen)* the sampler, whether a Jew or a non-Jew, must be a professional chef. An amateur is incompetent to judge with certainty whether the taste is noticeable. In addition, a non-Jewish sampler must be unaware that his testimony has any relevance with regard to *halachah*.

b) In the opinion of *Ran: Chullin* ibid. (this appears to be the opinion of *Tosfos* as well), the requirement of a professional taster is based upon the need for his credibility, not his expertise. Even an amateur is able to detect a noticeable taste in food (a non-noticeable taste is of no concern). However, a non-Jewish amateur cannot be trusted to provide reliable information. A professional, however, would never compromise his professional integrity by providing inaccurate information. Thus, even (and especially) if the non-Jew is aware of the importance of his testimony, he is believed. Similarly, a Jew may sample the mixture (where permitted) even though he is an amateur. (Although an amateur may not notice a subtle taste, any taste not recognizable to the amateur is not *halachically* considered a noticeable taste — *Tur* 98). An amateur non-Jew, however, may not be relied upon.

c) In the opinion of *Rashba* (cited in *Beis Yosef* 98) even an amateur non-Jew is trusted if he is unaware of the importance of his testimony.

d) In the opinion of *Rambam* 15:30 (as noted in *Beis Yosef* 98 and explained in *Minchas Kohen*, see *S.D.* 98:2), any non-Jew may be trusted to sample the mixture. No one would provide false information where the deceit will become apparent as soon as the food is eaten and the non-kosher taste is noticed.

The practical *halachos* regarding sampling by a *k'feilah* are discussed in Chapter Four.

◆§ ***K'dei klipah,* כְּדֵי קְלִיפָּה — Literally, "(an amount) fit to be peeled":**

Under certain circumstances when kosher and non-kosher foods come in contact taste is transferred only minimally. In these cases a *k'dei klipah* of the area of contact must be removed and discarded. A *k'dei k'lipah* is defined as the thinnest surface that can be removed in one piece (see *Shach* 96:21).

◆§ ***K'dei netilah,* כְּדֵי נְטִילָה — Literally, "(an amount) fit to be taken":**

In certain cases taste is transferred beyond a mere *klipah* but not into the entire food. In these cases a *k'dei netilah* must be removed. A *k'dei netilah* the thickness of a thumb *(Y.D.* 105:4, see *Rambam: Shabbos* 17:36), which contemporary authorities define as approximately an inch or two and a half centimeters.

◆§ ***Kli rishon,* כְּלִי רִאשׁוֹן — Literally, "the first vessel":**

A *kli rishon* (the original vessel in which the boiling was done) can effect *bishul* as long as it is *yad soledes bo*. Similarly, any food cooked in a *kli rishon* has the ability to discharge or absorb taste *(Y.D.* 105:2) regardless of whether or not the food continues to cook *(Beis Yosef* 105) and regardless of whether the pot remains over the fire *(Rashi: Shabbos* 40b, *Chochmas Adam* 59:1). See, however, *Talmud Yerushalmi (Maasros* 1:4) which implies that *bishul* is effected only when the food is actually over the fire. Indeed, the *Rogachover Gaon (Tzofnas Pa'aneach: Rambam M.A.* 9:1) finds a basis for this view in *Talmud Bavli* as well. See also *Aruch HaShulchan* 68:24. Thus, according to this opinion, one who cooks in a *kli rishon* after removal from the fire has not Biblically violated *Shabbos*. Similarly, one who cooks meat and milk in this manner has not violated the prohibition of cooking *basar b'chalav* and has not produced Biblical *basar b'chalav*. See also, *R' Akiva Eger* in gloss to *Y.D.* (end of 91) who rules that beef (that requires intense cooking) cannot become *basar b'chalav* (in Biblical law) unless it is cooked over a flame. *Aruch HaShulchan* 105:18, notes that according to this opinion a *kli rishon* transfers taste even when it is no longer over the fire. In the opinion of *Maharshal (Yam Shel Shlomo: Chullin* 8:71, see also *Pischei Teshuvah* 105:6) a *kli rishon* over the fire is potent even if it is not *yad soledes bo;* others disagree *(Taz* 94:1). See *Matamei HaShulchan* 105:6, as to whether this question applies only to a *kli rishon* which had already attained the heat of *yad soledes bo* but subsequently cooled, or even to a *kli rishon* that, although sitting over the fire, has not yet attained *yad soledes bo*. However, it seems clear from *Aruch HaShulchan* (105:18) that according to those opinions this rule applies even in the latter case. See also *Taz* 94:1.

See also *"bishul"*.

See Chapter Five, Section II,C and Chapter Seven, Section II,A for the practical applications of these principles.

◆§ *Kli sheni,* כְּלִי שֵׁנִי — Literally, "the second vessel":

A liquid that is poured from the original pot used for cooking *(kli rishon)* into a second vessel *(kli sheni)* no longer has the ability to cause *"bishul."* This is true regardless of whether or not the liquid presently retains the heat of *yad soledes bo. Rishonim* explain that the cool body of the second vessel continuously cools the cooked liquid and prevents it from causing *bishul (Tosfos: Shabbos* 40b). See *Chavas Daas* (92:27) who discusses the question of whether the main criterion is the fact that the vessel of a *kli rishon* continues to warm the food or the primary consideration is the fact that the vessel of a *kli sheni* cools the food. Essentially, the question is: what is the status of food that is neither warmed nor cooled by the vessel. In the opinion of most *Rishonim* (see *Aruch HaShulchan* 105:19) heat of a *kli sheni* likewise cannot cause a discharge or absorption of taste. This is the first (and primary) opinion in *Shulchan Aruch* (105:2), the *Rema* (92:7, 105:3), *Rashbam, Rabbeinu Tam* and others cited in *Shach* 105:5. Others contend that although a *kli sheni* cannot cause *bishul,* it can induce an absorption of taste into a *klipah* of the food *(Rashba* cited as second opinion, ibid). In the opinion of *Maharshal: Chullin* 7:71 (cited in *Taz* 105:4, and *Shach* 105:5), a *kli sheni* can induce absorption into the entire food . This also seems to be the opinion of *Tur* 105 (see *Beis Yosef). Maharshal* concedes, however, that a *kli sheni* cannot cause two concurrent transfers of taste *(maflit u'mavliah k'echad"*, i.e., two cold foods placed in it do not transfer taste to one another (ibid.). If the liquid in the *kli sheni* is so hot as to scald a hand placed in it *(yad nichvas bo)* some authorities rule that it certainly must be treated as a *kli rishon (Taz* 105:4, *Chayei Adam* 20:4, *Chochmas Adam* 59:6, see *Matamei HaShulchan* 105:8, who cites a dissenting opinion).

See Chapter Five, Section II,C and Chapter Seven, Section II,A for the practical applications of these principles.

◆§ *Kli shlishi,* כְּלִי שְׁלִישִׁי — Literally, "the third vessel":

In the opinion of some *Poskim* even a *kli sh'lishi* (the third vessel into which the liquid from the *kli sheni* was poured) is equal in status to a *kli sheni.* In their opinion, as long as the liquid is *yad soledes bo* it may cause a transfer of taste (see *Pri Chadash* 68, *Chasam Sofer* cited in *Pischei Teshuvah* 94:7, *Chazon Ish (O.C.* 52:19). The *Shaar Hatziyun (O.C.* 451:10), however, implies that a *kli sh'lishi* certainly cannot bring about a transfer of taste. See also *Igros Moshe: O.C.* 4:74, *bishul* [15].

☙ *Lach b'lach,* לַח בְּלַח — Literally, "liquid (mixed) in liquid" (as opposed to *yavesh b'yavesh)*:

When two foods are mixed in a manner that taste is transferred from one to another, e.g., they are liquids or they are solids that are cooked together, *bitul b'shishim* is required. See also "*bitul b'shishim*".

☙ *Masiach l'fi tumo,* מֵסִיחַ לְפִי תוּמוֹ — Innocuous statement:

At times the testimony of someone normally unfit for testimony may be accepted regarding *halachic* matters if he is unaware of the fact that his testimony is of concern to us. The Talmud *Bava Kama* 114b rules that *masiach l'fi tumo* is only acceptable for *halachos* of Rabbinic origin or other special case. *Poskim* are therefore puzzled by the ruling in *Shulchan Aruch Y.D.* 98:1 that a non-Jew is relied upon to sample food to determine whether or not it contains non-kosher taste. See *Taz* §2 and *Shach* §2 who offer differing explanations. See "*k'feilah*".

☙ *Meliach k'roseiach,* מְלִיחַ כְּרוֹתֵחַ — Literally, "salting is the equivalent of heating":

Salting, in the proper amount, can effect a taste transfer similar to that of heat. This is known as *meliach k'roseiach* — salting is the equivalent of heat. Salting, however, differs from soaking in regard to the area affected by the taste transfer. Whereas soaking is compared to boiling and can impart taste throughout the food, salting lacks a liquid medium of transfer since the foods are not submerged into a liquid and is compared to roasting in that it can impart taste only to a *klipah* of the food. This is apparent from the terms used in the Talmud; *kavush k'mevushal* — soaking is like *cooking, meliach k'roseiach* — salting is like heating (see *Chullin* 97b). Salting is effective only if the salting was so potent that the food was inedible because of the salt upon it *(Pesachim* 76a, *Chullin* 112a). *Poskim* note three levels of salting: Meat salted for preserving purposes has the ability to impart its taste to a *klipah* of any food with which it comes in contact. The meat retains this power until the salt is removed by soaking the meat in water. Merely rinsing the meat of its salt, however, cannot eliminate the effect of the salt (*Y.D.* 91:5). Meat that was salted for boiling purposes (to remove the blood) has the ability to impart its taste on contact to the *klipah* of any food. However, once the meat is washed of the salt it cannot impart any taste. Meat that was salted for broiling is salted very lightly. This light salting is insufficient to effect a taste transfer. However, since we are not capable of differentiating between different levels of salting, *Ashkenazic* custom considers even this level of salting capable of imparting taste unless serious financial loss may be incurred (*Rema* 91:5). Although salting can transfer taste only to a *klipah* of the surface of contact, fatty foods provide the salt with the proper medium to carry the infusion of taste thoroughly (*Y.D.* 70:4, 91:6). Even if non-kosher lean food is salted with kosher fatty food the kosher fatty food imparts its fattiness to the non-kosher food which then imparts its taste to the kosher food (*Y.D.* 70:4). *Poskim* note that since it is difficult to judge which foods are fatty one should treat all foods as fatty foods (*Rema* 91:5, 105:9).

See Chapter Five, Section III,B for the practical application of these *halachos*.

◆§ *Min b'mino — Min b'sheaino mino,* מִין בְּמִינוֹ / מִין בְּשֶׁאֵינוֹ מִינוֹ — Literally, "a kind in its own kind — a kind in another kind":

Generally speaking, *min b'mino* is defined as similar tasting foods, not foods with similar names (*Shach* 98:6, as opposed to *Rema* 98:2, even though *Taz* in *Daf Acharon* offers a different interpretation of *Rema*, later *Poskim* follow *Shach*, see *S.D.* §6). Two foods dissimilar in taste are called "*min b'sheaino mino*" (lit., a kind in another kind). Pertaining to some other *halachos*, *min b'mino* is defined as foods with similar *names*.

◆§ *Nat-bar-nat,* נ״ט בַּר נ״ט — Acronym for "*nosen taam bar nosen taam*".

When food is cooked in a pot it infuses its taste into the pot. When another food is subsequently cooked in that pot (even after it has been scrubbed clean), the original taste is transmitted to the second food. This secondary transfer (i.e., food to pot to food) is known as "*nosen taam bar nosen taam* נוֹתֵן טַעַם בַּר נוֹתֵן טַעַם" (lit. infused taste, the son of infused taste) or *nat-bar-nat* for short. Presumably, the taste is weakened as it travels from matter to matter. When forbidden foods impart their taste, no distinction is made between primary and secondary transfers — *nat-bar-nat d'isurah*. Thus, if non-kosher food is cooked in a pot, the pot is *treif*. Any kosher food subsequently cooked in that pot becomes *treif* as well. If this food is then cooked in another pot, the taste is passed on to the second pot, which now also becomes *treif* (*Taz* 95:1). However, when taste of permitted food is infused into a vessel and subsequently imparted into other food, the secondary taste is no longer capable of producing a prohibited entity — *nat-bar-nat d'heteira*.

Poskim stipulate several important qualifications regarding *nat-bar-nat*.

- □ Two concurrent infusions:

  In the opinion of some authorities, a taste that is transferred twice while cooking and in contact with its original source cannot be considered *nat-bar-nat*. Thus, if milk splatters on the outside of a pot in which potatoes are cooking, the potatoes may not be eaten with meat. Although the milk taste was transferred twice (from milk to pot to potatoes), it is not considered *nat-bar-nat* since the two infusions were simultaneous (*Chavas Daas* §1b, 2c). In the event that the potatoes were subsequently cooked with meat, they are prohibited. Other authorities disagree (see *Yad Yehudah* §7a, *R' Akiva Eger: Drush V'chidush* responsa 7 at end of part one, *Pischei Teshuvah* 95:1, 97:5, *Kaf HaChaim* §12).

- □ Taste transfer from food to food:

  In the opinion of *Pri Migadim: M.Z.* 95:1, *nat-bar-nat* applies only to taste infused from the original food into a vessel and then into food, not from the original food into food and then into a vessel. For example, if hot vegetables were placed upon hot meat thereby absorbing its taste and subsequently cooked in a *parve* pot, the pot is considered a meat pot. Any milk boiled in the pot becomes *basar b'chalav*. *Pri Migadim* explains that the original transfer of taste from meat to vegetable, being a food to food infusion, is potent. Thus, the vegetables impart that primary taste to the pot. See, however, *Chavas Daas* §4, who disagrees. He contends that as long as one of the transfers is into a vessel, we apply the *nat-bar-nat* principle. He does concede (in §2) that if no vessel is involved, if the transfers are solely food to food, the taste is continually considered primary, not secondary (*Pri Migadim* ibid. see also *Aruch HaShulchan* §3 and *D.T.* §15,19).

- □ Food boiled in water:

  Based upon the two concepts cited above, *Poskim* never

consider the original taste transfer to the pot as *nat-bar-nat* (i.e., the meat to the water to the pot). The original infusions were concurrent (i.e., the meat was cooking in the pot while its taste was imparted into the pot). In addition, the taste transfer from meat to water is food to food and thus a more potent infusion (this is subject to the disagreement between *Pri Migadim* and *Chavas Daas* cited above).

- ☐ Taste transfer from vessel to vessel:
  We noted that a taste infusion from food to food is stronger than that from food to a vessel. Similarly, an infusion from vessel to vessel is still weaker. Thus, even *Rema*, who takes a more stringent position regarding *nat-bar-nat*, concedes that when only vessels are involved, *nat-bar-nat* be ignored *(M.Z.* 105:9).

The practical *halachah* regarding *nat-bar-nat* is discussed at length in Chapter Six.

◆§ *Ne'itzah,* נְעִיצָה — Literally, "thrusting":

Chazal mandated a specific method in which a knife (unlike other utensils), under certain circumstances, must be *kashered.* Generally, *ne'itzah* is required in situations where other utensils would not require *kashering* i.e., when there is no heat involved. *Ne'itzah* may be performed to permit the use of a knife on food for which it would otherwise be unsuitable. For example, one who wishes to cut bread for a dairy meal with a meat knife, or the reverse *(Shach* 89:22, *R' Akiva Eger* on *Shach* ibid.). *Ne'itzah* may be required as a means of *kashering* or cleaning a knife that was used inappropriately. For example, if a dairy knife was inadvertently used to cut cold meat and was not cleaned immediately after use, the residue dries onto the knife surface and is removable only with *ne'itzah (Yad Yehudah* cited in *D.T.* 94:102 based on *Rema* 69:20). See additional examples in Chapter Twelve, Section III. It should be noted that at no time may *ne'itzah* be substituted for another method of *kashering.* A knife requiring *libun* or *hagalah* cannot be *kashered* with *ne'itzah*. Popular misconception has it that any *treif* knife can be *kashered* with *ne'itzah;* this is erroneous. A non-kosher knife (whether a knife of a non-Jew or a knife of a Jew that became *treif)* may be used *temporarily* for *cold* foods after *ne'itzah*, never for hot foods (see Y.*D.* 121:7). In the opinion of most authorities, *ne'itzah* is essentially a cleaning process. The rubbing against the hard earth wipes the knife clean of all grease and residue of non-kosher food *(Darcei Moshe* 105:5 and *Toras Chatas* 23:7 and 61:13). See, however, *Shach* 10:6, who contends that *ne'itzah* removes the thin outer surface of the knife blade (although *S.D.* ibid. interprets the words of the *Shach* to imply that *ne'itzah* only causes the taste absorbed within the knife surface to be purged, *Yad Yehudah* 10:3a interprets the *Shach* that the *ne'itzah* removes a bit of the blade surface). See also *R' Akiva Eger* (gloss to *Shach* 96:9) who seems to assume that *ne'itzah* actually remove any taste absorbed in the surface of the knife blade (this is the opinion of *Yad Yehudah* (ibid.) as well. Another popular misconception has it that one can *kasher* a knife by merely letting it remain in the ground for twenty-four hours; this is erroneous.

See also *"davar charif", "duchka d'sakina".*

See Chapter Twelve, Section III as to the proper manner in which *ne'itzah* is to be done, as to which knives can be *kashered* with *ne'itzah* and as to whether another cleaning process may be substituted for *ne'itzah.*

⸎ *Nosen taam lifgam,* נוֹתֵן טַעַם לִפְגַם — Literally, "gives an unpleasant taste":

A taste that remained in a vessel for a period of twenty-four hours becomes *pagum* (stale) and affects any food cooked in that pot in a negative manner — *nosen taam lifgam*. A utensil in which the taste is not yet stale is called *"ben-yomo"* (see *"ben-yomo"* for a concise definition of this term). The question of *nosen taam lifgam* applies only to a clean vessel. An unwashed vessel retains non-kosher food residue and transmits the taste of that residue to any food cooked in the pot regardless of passage of time (see *Yad Yehudah* 103:24a, as to the status of a vessel that was washed but not scrubbed). Only absorbed taste becomes stale after twenty-four hours have passed. Actual food (or even the minute food residue on a vessel) is unaffected (the first opinion in *Y.D.* 103:5), unless the passage of time renders the foods completely inedible. Only taste absorbed into a *vessel* becomes *pagum.* Taste absorbed into *food* never loses its potency. Thus, potatoes boiled with non-kosher meat and subsequently warmed in a pot, even after twenty-four hours, renders that pot non-kosher *(D.T.* 103:75).

See also *"davar Charif".*

See Chapter Three, Section II,B.

⸎ *Reicha milsa,* רֵיחָא מִילְתָא — Literally, "aroma is something (significant)":

When two foods are baked simultaneously in an oven, there is a possibility of aroma being imparted from one to the other. This issue, is known as *"reicha milsa"* (aroma is significant). The consensus of opinion among *Rishonim* and the *halachic* conclusion as presented in *Shulchan Aruch* (*Y.D.* 108:1), is that *lechatchilah* — initially — one should avoid any possibility of aroma being imparted from non-kosher to kosher foods. However, *bidieved* (ex-post-facto) — in the event that kosher food did absorb aroma from non-kosher food, we assume *reicha lav milsa* (aroma is insignificant) and the food may be eaten (*Y.D.* 108:1). Not all foods impart aroma equally. *Chazal* were concerned with the aroma of fatty foods. Lean foods impart no significant aroma (see *Taz* §1 and *Shach* §1). However, since it is difficult to determine what constitutes lean meat, many authorities advise that one should not roast even two lean meats concurrently (*S.D.* 108:1, see also *Aruch HaShulchan* 108:9). One may, however, bake a kosher bread in the oven together with a non-kosher bread since breads have no fatty aroma (*S.D.* ibid). Sharp foods are especially prone to absorbing aroma. Thus, even in situations where *reicha* would not normally be problematic, sharp foods would be affected. The problem of *reicha* is also dependent upon the size of the oven in which the foods are baked. Foods baked in a confined area are more likely to absorb aroma than those baked in an open area which permits the aroma to dissipate. Thus, foods baked in a large, ventilated oven do not impart taste to one another, while foods baked in a small, confined oven will impart their taste. Household ovens are considered small ovens. An oven completely open at the top permits any aroma to thoroughly dissipate and therefore presents less of a *reicha* problem (*Shach* 108:3). A closed but vented oven that allows smoke to escape may nevertheless retain aroma and permit it to travel from food to food (*Rema* as cited in *Shach* ibid). An oven without any vent or outlet presents a more serious problem of *reicha* since the aroma is confined to the oven. Only uncovered foods are subject to *reicha*. Covered food cannot impart and will not absorb any aroma. Thus, even sharp foods baked in a small confined oven cannot impart aroma to one another if either of them are completely covered (*Y.D.* 108:1).

The issue of *reicha* is relevant to other situations besides baking in an oven. When warm bread is placed upon a barrel of non-kosher wine, it absorbs the aroma of the wine. This depends upon a) the warmth of the bread, b) whether the barrel is open or closed and c) whether the bread is of wheat or barley flour (barley is more absorbent) see *Y.D.* 108:4. The issue of *reicha* also relates to the question of whether one may enjoy prohibited fragrances. Fragrances from foods that are merely prohibited to eat, may be enjoyed (*Pri Chadash* 108:25.

See, however, *Biur Halachah* 216:2 s.v. *"hamusak")*. Fragrances of foods from which one may not derive benefit are prohibited (see *Y.D.* 108:5-7 and *Shach* §27).

The practical issues of *reicha* are discussed in Chapter Five.

◆§ *Taam k'ikar,* טַעַם כְּעִיקָר — Literally, "the taste of the (non-kosher) food is considered as its essence":

Kosher food imbued with a noticeable taste of non-kosher food is considered the equivalent of the non-kosher food itself.

Rishonim disagree as to whether the principle of *taam k'ikar* is Biblical or Rabbinic in origin. In the opinion of some *Rishonim,* this depends upon whether the actual substance of the non-kosher food or only its taste is present in the mixture. It further depends upon the ratio of kosher and non-kosher matter in the mixture and upon the amount of the mixture one eats. *Halachic* consensus assumes that *taam k'ikar* should usually be treated as a Biblical precept. A comprehensive discussion of the varying positions of the *Rishonim* can be found in *Minchas Kohen* II, 1:2-6. In short: i) In the opinion of *Rashi, taam k'ikar* is of Rabbinic nature whenever the non-kosher matter is a liquid or a solid that has dissolved. ii) In the opinion of *Ran,* whenever the non-kosher matter is present in the mixture (even if dissolved), the mixture is Biblically prohibited if the non-kosher taste is noticeable. If the non-kosher taste is not noticeable, *bitul b'shishim* is only Rabbinically required. iii) In the opinion of the *Rambam,* if the non-kosher matter is mixed into the food in a ratio of one *kizayis* to three *kibeizim* (egg volume), it is Biblically prohibited to eat three egg volumes of the mixture. According to the *Shulchan Aruch: O.C.* 486, a *kizayis* is one half an egg; thus, the ratio is one to six (or one to eight, see *M.B.* 208:43). Others *(Magen Avraham,* ibid.) contend that in the opinion of *Rambam,* a *kizayis* is one third of a *kibeitzah* and thus the ratio is one to nine (see *Chochmas Adam* 51:8). iv) In the opinion of *Rabbeinu Tam,* even if none of the non-kosher matter is present in the mixture, but the kosher food absorbed non-kosher taste, the food is Biblically forbidden. Furthermore, in his opinion, one who eats a *kizayis* of kosher food imbued with only the taste of non-kosher matter is liable for the punishment of *malkos* (forty lashes). This is the most stringent opinion regarding *taam k'ikar* found in the *Rishonim.* v) *Rashba, Raavad* and *Rabbeinu Chaim* agree in principle with *Rabbeinu Tam,* but disagree as to the precise conditions under which one who eats the affected food is liable for *malkos.* As noted above, *Minchas Kohen* offers an exhaustive analysis of each of these opinions and their sources in the Talmud. See also *Pri Chadash: O.C.* 442:1, 453:2.

See also *"bitul b'shishim"*.

The *halachic* ramifications of the *taam k'ikar* principle are discussed in Chapter Four.

◆§ ***Tatai gavar,* תַּתָּאִי גָּבַר — Literally, "the bottom overpowers":** When kosher and non-kosher foods are placed atop one another, one hot and one cold, the Talmud *(Pesachim* 76a) cites a difference of opinion whether *tatai gavar* ("the bottom overpowers" the top) or *elai gavar* "the top overpowers" the bottom). *Rashi* and *Tosfos: Pesachim* 76a, *Tur* 91. rule that one should follow the opinion of *tatai gavar*. Two reasons are given for the dominance of the lower food: a) The top food weighs upon the bottom and b) heat rises by nature *(Issur V'heter* 29:1. These reasons reflect the opinion of the *Issur V'heter* that *tatai gavar* applies only to two foods when placed atop one another, not when they are placed side by side). *Poskim* grapple with the obvious question: Why is no consideration given to the amount of the relative foods? Certainly, a large amount of hot food would warm a considerably smaller amount of cold food beneath it. Similarly, a large amount of cold food cannot be heated by a small amount of hot food beneath it (see *Yad Efraim*, beginning of *Y.D.* 76). Accordingly, *Aruch HaShulchan*, 91:11,12, rules that *tatai gavar* applies only to equal amounts of hot and cold matter. See also *Yad Yehudah* 105:21k,12a, who, in addition to the question above, poses the problem that an abundance of liquid poured over solid matter completely surrounds it. Thus, the liquid flows under the solid and becomes the *tatai*. Nevertheless, *Yad Yehudah* notes that it appears that *Poskim* make no distinction between the relative amounts of the foods.

The question of *tatai gavar* relates to a liquid poured over a solid food, or a solid food placed in a liquid. If, however, one liquid is poured into another, their respective tastes immediately blend into one another, regardless of their heat. Thus, the only remaining consideration is the respective amount of each liquid, i.e., whether the kosher food is sixty times the non-kosher food. Nevertheless, *Poskim* do discuss the effect of the heat on one another with regard to the prohibition of *bishul* on *Shabbos* and *basar b'chalav*. For example: if a larger amount of cold liquid is poured into a smaller amount of hot liquid, should we assume *tatai gavar* and *bishul* has occurred or should we assume that the greater amount of cold liquid immediately cools the hot liquid? See *Chavas Daas* 91:5, *D.T.* 91:15, *Taz O.C.* 318:18, *Magen Avraham* 318:35, *Machtzis Hashekel* and *P.M.* (ibid.).

Following the principle of *tatai gavar*, when cold food is placed on top of hot food, the bottom food warms the top food and enables it to impart or absorb taste throughout the top food (see *D.T.* 105:70, who cites a difference of opinion regarding a case when the top food clearly did not become thoroughly hot). Consequently, regardless of whether the non-kosher food is on top or underneath, if the bottom food is *yad soledes bo*, the kosher food is prohibited. If the top food is hot and the bottom food is cold, we assume that cold food overpowers and cools hot food placed above it. Thus, the taste is not transferred from one to another. Nevertheless, the Talmud explains that prior to its being cooled, the hot top food is able to absorb or impart taste to the thickness of a *klipah*. Therefore, regardless of whether the non-kosher food is on top or underneath, a *klipah* of the kosher food absorbs non-kosher taste and is prohibited *(Y.D.* 91:4).

The *halachos* of foods placed atop one another are found in Chapter Five.

⁂ *Te'imah,* טְעִימָה — Sampling:

The question of whether a Jew may sample food to determine whether or not any non-kosher taste is present. It is also questionable whether one may rely upon the sampling of a non-Jewish chef. See *"k'feilah"*.

See Chapter Four, Section I.

⁂ *Yad nichvas bo,* יָד נִכְוֵית בּוֹ — Literally, "a hand is scalded by it":

A food or liquid that is so hot as to scald a hand placed in it *(yad nichvas bo)* some authorities rule that even if it is in a *kli sheni*, it must be treated as a *kli rishon*. *Taz* 105:4, *Chayei Adam* 20:4, *Chochmas Adam* 59:6, see *Matamei HaShulchan* 105:8, who cites a dissenting opinion.

⁂ *Yad soledes bo,* יָד סוֹלֶדֶת בּוֹ — Literally, "a hand recoils from it":

The minimum degree of heat required to cause transfer of taste is defined as *"yad soledes bo"* — the degree of heat from which the hand recoils for fear of being burnt. According to some authorities, this connotes heat sufficient to cause immediate recoil even though it would not immediately scald the skin (see *Darcei Teshuvah* 105:51). Other authorities describe *yad soledes bo* as the degree of heat that would scald the hand after sustained contact (ibid). If, however, one is able to hold one's hand in the hot water for a short while, the water is not considered *yad soledes bo* (see *Yad Yehudah* 105:16k). Some

Poskim define *yad soledes bo* as the degree of heat that would scald the sensitive abdominal skin of a day-old child *(O.C.* 318:14. See *Issur V'heter* 34:20, who notes that these two definitions are synonymous). Common custom is to treat any food that one would eat without cooling beforehand as not *yad soledes bo* (see *D.T.* 105:51. and *Kaf HaChaim* 105:30). Contemporary authorities assume that any food cooler than 110° Fahrenheit, 43° Centigrade (in the opinion of *Igros Moshe: O.C.* 4:74 *(bishul* [3]) or 113° Fahrenheit, 45° Centigrade (in the opinion of Rav Shlomo Z. Auerbach *(Minchas Shlomo* 91:8) is certainly not *yad soledes bo*. See *Metzudas Tzion: Kitzur Shulchan Aruch* ch. 72 who contends that 104° should perhaps be considered *yad soledes bo. Igros Moshe* (ibid.) notes that 160° Fahrenheit, 71° Centigrade, is certainly *yad soledes bo*. See also *Matamei HaShulchan* 105:7.

◆§ ***Yavesh b'yavesh,* יָבֵשׁ בְּיָבֵשׁ — Literally, "dry (mixed) into dry"** (as opposed to *lach b'lach)*:

When dry non-kosher food mixes with dry kosher food it is *batel b'rov. Bitul b'shishim* is not required since the pieces are dry and were not cooked together, thus no transfer of taste occurred. See also "*bitul b'rov*".

◆§ ***Zeiah,* זֵיעָה — Steam:**

All liquids and many foods emit steam when cooked or baked. *Halachah* considers the steam of any liquid as having the status of that food. The source for this *halachah* is found in *Teshuvos HaRosh* 20:26, cited in *Tur* and *S.A.* 92:8. *Rosh,* in turn, bases this on the *Mishnah: Machshirin* 2:2, which rules that the steam of a *tameh* (spiritually unclean) bath transmits the *tumah* to the entire house. *Poskim* are uncertain whether *zeiah* is a Biblical or Rabbinical concept, see responsa *Minchas Yitzchok* 5:20;10. Thus, steam of non-kosher liquid is not harmless, non-matter vapor; it is actually *treif* and will impart its non-kosher taste and status to anything it penetrates. Similarly, steam of milk that condensed into water is nothing other than milk. It should not be considered pure water distilled from the milk. Accordingly, if this water subsequently mixes with meat, it is the equivalent of milk mixing with meat.

In the opinion of some authorities (see *Pischei Teshuvah* 92:6, citing *Pri Migadim* who in turn bases his opinion on *Rambam)* the principle that steam is the food itself applies to liquids only. They contend that steam emitted by foods (even when liquified, i.e., melted butter or chicken gravy) is *halachically* considered plain water and does not have the *halachic* status of the food. While most *Poskim* (see *Yad Yehudah* §53a and *D.T.* §164) reject this view, they concede that solid foods produce a negligible amount of steam (see *Rema: Toras Chatas* 35:6, and *Minchas Yaakov* 35:21). Thus, one must assume that the *zeiah* of all liquids, regardless of their source, carries their taste. However, one may assume that solids do not produce *zeiah* unless steam is actually detected (see *Igros Moshe, Y.D.* 1:40). The *halachic* problem posed by *zeiah* is the possibility that when foods cook in a confined area, steam condense onto a non-kosher surface while still hot. The condensed water vapor, having absorbed non-kosher taste, may fall into the kosher food rendering it *treif*. The ability of steam to impart taste or absorb taste from the surface above depends upon whether the steam is in an open area or a restricted area. Steam rising in an open area easily dissipates and is less likely to reach the upper surface in a volume and intensity of heat necessary to cause a transfer of taste. In addition, steam that dissipated sufficiently is less likely to condense on the upper surface and fall back into the cooking liquid.

The practical *halachos* regarding *zeiah* are discussed at length in Chapter Five, Section III,D and Chapter Nine, Section I,A and E.

Glossary

[Items followed by asterisk * are thoroughly explained in Chapter Fourteen.]

ach'shevei — one has accorded it the status of food.

*achilah** — eating.

achilah gassa — gluttony.

*ain m'vatlin issur lechatchilah** — one may not initially nullify non-kosher foods.

aino ben-yomo — not *ben-yomo*.

*aino ra'uy l'achilah** — unfit for consumption.

amah (pl. *amos)* — cubits (approximately two feet).

amirah l'Akum — telling a non-Jew to do a forbidden act.

Ashkenazic — (lit. from *Ashkenaz*-Germany) European Jews or their customs.

assur b'achilah — prohibited to be eaten.

assur b'hana'ah — prohibited to derive benefit thereof.

avodah zarah — idolatry.

b'dochek — with difficulty.

b'rachah achronah — an after-*b'rachah*.

b'rachah l'vatalah — a *b'rachah* recited in vain.

b'rachah rishonah — a *b'rachah* recited before partaking of food.

basar b'chalav — forbidden mixture of meat and milk.

batel b'rov — was nullified in a majority.

batel b'shishim — was nullified in a ratio of sixty to one.

beheimah temeiah — a non-kosher animal.

*ben-yomo** — lit. of the day (e.g., a pot used within the previous twenty-four hours).

*beriah** — a complete creation.

bidieved — *ex post facto*.

Bircas HaMazon — the blessings recited after eating a bread meal.

*bishul** — cooking.

bitul (was *batel)* — nullification (e.g., of prohibited foods).

*bitul b'rov** — nullification in a majority.

*bitul b'shishim** — nullification in a ratio of sixty to one.

blech — metal sheet placed over stove top to permit foods to be placed there for *Shabbos*.

chadash — new grain crop of any of the five species of grain, which may not be eaten until the sixteenth of *Nissan*.

challah (pl. *challos)* — a) colloquially, loaves of soft wheat-bread traditionally eaten at a *Shabbos* meal. b) portion separated from the dough and given to a *Kohen* (today it is burnt).

chametz — leavened bread prohibited during the Passover festival.

*chatichah ha'ruyah l'hischabed** — a piece of meat fit to serve to company.

*chatichah na'asis neveilah** — the piece (or mixture) becomes a non-kosher entity.

*chatzi shiur** — half the required amount (see "*shiur*").

chayah — non-domestic animal.

Chazal — acronym for, *chachameinu zichronom livrachah* - "Our sages of blessed memory".

cheilev — non-kosher fats.

chiddush (pl. *chiddushim)* — Talmudic or *halachic* novellae.

chinuch — Torah education (of minors).

chok — Biblical decree.

*chozer veniyur** — reawakening of non-kosher food that has been nullified.

chulent — a hot stew traditionally served at the *Shabbos* meal.

chumra (pl. *chumros)* — stringent application.

d'heteira — of permitted (foods).

d'issura — of forbidden (foods).

d'var issur — prohibited matter.

dag tameh — non-kosher fish.

dam — blood.

*davar charif** — sharp food.

*davar chashuv** — object of importance.

*davar gush** — solid food.

*davar hama'amid** — something that solidifies or jells food.

*davar she'biminyan** — object sold by unit.

*davar sheyesh lo matirim** — food that will, in time, become permitted.

dayan — *halachic* decisor or judge.

derech achilah — normal manner of eating.

dinim — laws.

*duchka d'sakina** — the pressure of a knife on the food it cuts.

*efshar l'sochto assur** — the non-kosher taste cannot be extracted from the mixture.

eiver min hachai — a limb from a living creature.

elai gavar — the top overpowers.

Eretz Yisrael — Land of Israel.

esrog — a citrus fruit used during the *Sukkos* festival.

g'reidah or *g'reirah* — scraping.

gadol — "great," term used for a person of great stature.

gid hanasheh — the sciatic nerve.

hagalah — *kashering* by means of scalding the object.

halachah (pl. *halachos)* — law; *(Halachah,* the body of Jewish Law).

hana'ah — deriving benefit of.

hefsed merubah — serious financial loss.

heter (heteira) — something permitted.

hilchos — the laws of.

*iruy** — pouring.

issur (issura) — prohibited matter.

issur achilah (pl. *issurei achilah)* — foods prohibited to be eaten.

issur d'rabbanon — something Rabbinically prohibited.

issur hana'ah (pl. *issurei hana'ah)* — matter that one may not derive benefit thereof.

k'dei achilas pras — the amount of time necessary to eat three (or four) *kizaysim* of wheat bread (approximately four minutes).

*k'dei klipah** — thinnest removable surface.

*k'dei netilah** — approximately an inch of the surface.

k'maachal ben drusai — lit. like the food of a bandit; food which has been cooked half or a third of full cooking.

kares — Excision: Divinely imposed premature death decreed by the Torah for certain classes of transgression.

kasher — to make proper, to purify.

kavush (k'vishah) — soaking.

*kavush k'mevushal** — soaking is the equivalent of cooking.

kehillah — community.

kilaei hakerem — vegetables or grain planted in a vineyard.

kilayim — different species grown together.

kizayis (pl. *kizaysim)* — the volume of an olive or half an egg (somewhat more than the volume of one fluid ounce).

*kli rishon** — first vessel; the original vessel in which the food was cooked.

*kli sheni** — second vessel; the utensil into which boiling liquid is poured from the *kli rishon*.

*kli shlishi** — third vessel; the utensil into which food is poured from the *kli sheni*.

klipah — thin removable surface.

Kohen (pl. *Kohanim)* — member of the priestly family descended in the male line from Aaron.

lechatchilah — initially.

libun — *kashering* by means of heating in fire until object becomes red-hot.

libun kal — *kashering* by means of heating in fire until object becomes hot enough to char a straw placed upon it.

lo nifsak ha'kiluach — the flow is not interrupted.

ma'achalos assuros — forbidden foods.

machmir — being stringent.

maikil — being lenient.

malkos — the thirty-nine lashes imposed as punishment for violation of Biblical prohibitions.

*masiach lefi tumo** — stating something innocuously.

*meliach k'roseiach** — salting is the equivalent of heat.

midas chasiddus — an act appropriate for the pious.

*min b'mino** — (mixture of) a kind in its own kind.

*min b'sheaino mino** — (mixture of) a kind in another kind.

Mishnah — writings of the early Talmudic sages (circa 200 B.C.E - 200 C.E.).

mitzvah (pl. *mitzvos)* — Biblical or Rabbinic commandment.

moreh hora'ah (pl. *morei hora'ah)* — *halachic* decisor.

muttar b'achilah — permitted to be eaten.

muttar b'hana'ah — permitted to derive benefit thereof.

nat (pl. *nats)* — acronym for *nosen taam*.

*nat bar nat** — acronym for *nosen taam bar nosen taam* — a secondary infusion of taste.

*ne'itzah** — thrusting a knife into the ground to cleanse it.

neveilah — carrion.

nifsak ha'kiluach — the flow is interrupted.

Nissan — first month of the Hebrew calendar.

nosen taam (nesinas taam) — infusion of taste.

*nosen taam lifgam** — imparting an unsatisfactory taste.

orlah — fruit of a tree during the first three years after planting.

pagum — stale (taste).

parve — food which is neither meat nor dairy.

Pesach — Passover.

Poskim — Authoritative Rabbinic decisors.

reicha — aroma.

reicha lav milsa — aroma is insignificant.

*reicha milsa** — aroma is significant.

Rishonim — Rabbinic authorities of the post-Geonic era (11th-16th century).

riviyis — a liquid measurement, the volume of an egg and a half (somewhat more than three fluid ounces).

rov tashmisho — the majority (usual) use of the utensil.
s'fek sfaika — a double doubt.
safek — doubt.
safek d'rabbanon — doubt pertaining to Rabbinical obligation.
se'udah — a meal.
se'udah shlishis — the third Sabbath meal.
Sefardic — (lit. from *Sefarad*-Spain) Middle Eastern Jews or their customs.
sefer — book on Jewish subjects.
Shabbos — the Sabbath.
shatnez — the prohibition of wearing garments mixed with wool and linen.
Shavuos — Pentecost; the festival that celebrates the giving of the Torah.
shechitah — the ritual manner in which an animal is slaughtered.
shelo k'darko — done in an unusual manner.
sheretz — swarming insects and rodents.
sheviyis — the Sabbatical year.
shiur — the required amount (e.g., of eating forbidden food to be considered a punishable act).
Shulchan Aruch — the Code of Jewish Law by R' Yosef Karo (16th century).
siman (pl. *simanim)* — sign, indication.
sukkah — the booths in which one sits on the festival of *Sukkos.*
Sukkos — the festival during which one dwells in a *sukkah.*
taam — taste.
*taam k'ikar** — the taste is like the essence (food that absorbed prohibited taste is, in itself, prohibited).
*tatai gavar** — the bottom overpowers.
tefach (pl. *tefachim)* — (a handbreadth) approx. four inches.
terumah — share given to a *Kohen* from most produce.
tevel — produce from which *terumah* and tithes were not designated.
treif — colloquial term for non-kosher.
treifah — mortally injured.
tumah — spiritual defilement.
tz'non — radish.
tzli — roasted.
*yad nichvas bo** — degree of heat which scalds the hand.
*yad soledes bo** — degree of heat from which the hand recoils.
yayin nesech — wine that was poured to *avodah zarah* in a sacrificial manner.
*zeiah** — steam.

Bibliography

Abarbanel — Classic commentary on the *Tanach* by (Don) R' Yitzchak Abarbanel, philosopher and finance minister to the King of Spain until the Spanish expulsion of 1492 (1437-1508).

Akeidas Yitzchok — Classical philosophical commentary on the Torah by R' Yitzchak Aramah (c. 1420-1494).

Aruch Ha'Shulchan — *Halachic* compendium following the order of the *Shulchan Aruch* by R' Yechiel Michel Epstein (1829-1908), Rav of Novardok, Russia.

Aishel Avraham — Commentary to *Magen Avraham* by R' Yosef Teomim, see *Pri Migadim.*

Atzei Ha'olah — Compendium on *Hilchos B'rachos* by R' Avraham Chaim Einhorn from Ober Visheve, Hungary (published by author in 1897).

Avudraham — A guide and commentary to the prayers by R' David ben Yosef Avudraham, 14th cent. *halachist* and liturgist.

Bach — Acronym for *Bayis Chadash*, a commentary on the *Tur* by R' Yoel Sirkis (c. 1561-1640), *Rav* of Belz, Brest-Litovsk (Brisk) and Cracow, Poland, father-in-law of the *Taz*.

Badei HaShulchan — Commentary to *Shulchan Aruch:Yoreh De'ah, Hilchos Basar B'chalav* and *Niddah* by Rav Feivel Cohen, contemporary Rav and *halachic* authority in Brooklyn, N.Y.

Bedek HaBayis — Critical notes on *Rashba's Toras Habayis* by R' Aharon HaLevy of Barcelona, see *"Re'ah"*.

Be'er Heiteiv — Commentary to *Shulchan Aruch: Yoreh De'ah* (basically abridged from *Taz* and *Shach)* by R' Zechariah Mendel (d. 1706), Rav of Belz, Poland (now Ukraine).

Be'er Moshe — Responsa of Rav Moshe Stern, *Rav* of Debreczin, Hungary, currently in Brooklyn, N.Y.

Beis Ha'otzar — Encyclopedic collection of original speculative *Chiddushim* on Talmudic topics by R' Yosef Engel (1859-1920), *Rav* of Cracow, Poland. Only the letter *Aleph* and part of *Beis* have been published.

Beis Meir — Commentary to *Shulchan Aruch* by R' Meir Posner (early 19th century).

Beis Shlomo — Responsa of R' Shlomo Rav of Skole, Poland, now Ukraine (mid 19th century).

Beis Yosef — Commentary by R' Yosef Caro to the *Tur*, see *Tur* and *Shulchan Aruch.*

Binas Adam — Notes to *Chochmas Adam* by the author, see *Chayei Adam*.

Bircei Yosef — Glosses to the *Shulchan Aruch* by "Chida," acronym for R' Chaim Yosef David Azulai (1724-1806).

Biur HaGra — Glosses to the *Shulchan Aruch* by the *Gra*, see *Gra.*

Biur Halacha — Part of *Mishnah B'rurah* encompasing more detailed explanations of the *halachah*, see *Mishnah B'rurah.*

Bnei Yisaschar — *Chassidic* discourses following the order of the calendar, by R' Tzvi Elimelech of Dinov, Galicia (1785-1841).

Chasam Sofer — The name of the responsa and principal works of R' Moshe Sofer (1763-1839). *Rav* of Pressburg and leader of Hungarian Jewry.

Chavas Daas — Commentary to *Shulchan Aruch Yoreh De'ah* by R' Yaakov Lorberbaum, *Rav* of Lissa, Poland (1760-1832), author of *Nesivos HaMishpat* on *Shulchan Aruch: Choshen Mishpat*.

Chavos Yair — Responsa of R' Yair Chaim Bachrach (1638-1702), *Rav* of Worms, Germany.

Chayei Adam — *Halachic* work comprising the laws contained in *Shulchan Aruch Orach Chaim*, by R' Avraham Danzig of Vilna (1748-1820).

Chazon Ish — *Halachic* work by R' Avraham Yeshayah Karelitz of Bnei Brak (1878-1953).

Chelkas Yaakov — Responsa of R' Mordechai Yaakov Breish, contemporary *halachic* authority, Rav of Zurich (d. 1977).

Chiddushei HaGrach — Talmudic *chiddushim* collected from the teachings of the *Grach* (acronym for *HaGaon* R' Chaim) Soleveichik, *Rosh Yeshivah* in Volozhin and later *Rav* of Brisk, Lithuania.

Chiddushei HaGershuni — Glosses to *Shulchan Aruch: Yoreh De'ah* by R' Gershon Ashkenazi, Rav of Nikolsburg and Metz, Germany (d. 1693), author of responsa *Avodas HaGershuni*.

Chinuch — Compendium on the philosophical and *halachic* aspects of the 613 *mitzvos* by an unknown Spanish author among the *Rishonim* of the 13th century.

Chochmas Adam — *Halachic* work comprising the laws contained in *Shulchan Aruch Yoreh De'ah*, by R' Avraham Danzig of Vilna (1748-1820).

Chok Yaakov — Commentary to *Shulchan Aruch Orach Chaim (Hilchos Pesach)* by R' Yaakov Reisher, Rav of Worms and Metz (c. 1670-1733).

Choshen Mishpat — One of the four sections of the *Tur* and *Shulchan Aruch*, dealing with monetary laws.

Daas Torah — Glosses on the *Shulchan Aruch* by R' Sholom Mordechai HaKohen Schwadron, renowned *halachic* authority, Rav of Brezan, Galicia (1835-1911).

Dagul Mervavah — Glosses on the *Shulchan Aruch* by R' Yechezkel Landau, author of the classic responsa *Noda B'Yehudah*, Rav of Prague (1713-1793).

Darchei Moshe — Glosses on the *Tur* by R' Moshe Isserles, see *Rema.*

Darcei Teshuvah — Encyclopedic commentary to *Shulchan Aruch Yoreh De'ah* by R' Tzvi Hirsh Shapira, *Rav* and *Rebbe* of Munkatch, Hungary, (1850-1913) the last volume was finished by his son and successor R' Chaim Elazar Shapira (1870-1937).

Divrei Chamudos — Comprehensive commentary to *Rosh* by R' Yom Tov Lipman Heller, the famed author of the *Tosfos Yom Tov,* commentary on the *Mishna* (1579-1654).

Drishah — Glosses on the *Tur* by R' Yehoshua Falk Katz, *Rosh Yeshivah* in Lemberg (d. 1614).

Eglei Tal — Compendium on the 39 primary prohibitions of *Shabbos* by R' Avraham Bornstein, *Rav* and *Rebbe* of Sochaczev, Poland (1839-1910).

Elia Rabah — Commentary to *Shulchan Aruch Orach Chaim* by R' Elia Shapira, *Rosh Yeshiva* in Prague (c.1660-1712).

Gilyon Maharsha — Glosses to *Shulchan Aruch: Yoreh De'ah* by R' Shlomo Eiger (1786-1852), son of and successor to R' Akiva Eiger as *Rav* of Posen, Poland.

Gra — Acronym for *HaGaon Rabbeinu Eliahu,* R' Eliahu ben Shlomo Zalman the famed and revered Gaon of Vilna (1720-1797).

Graz — Acronym for *HaGaon Rabbeinu Zalman,* R' Shneiur Zalman of Liadi, author of the *Shulchan Aruch HaRav* and the *Chasiddic* classic, the *Tanya, Rebbe* in Liozna and Liadi, Lithuania (1745-1813).

Hafla'ah — *Chiddushim* on tractate *Kesuvos* by R' Pinchas Horowitz (1730-1805), *Rav* of Frankfurt am Main. His gloss to *Shulchan Aruch,* called *Chiddushei Hafla'ah,* are printed in the back of many editions of *Shulchan Aruch.*

Hagahos Ashri — Notes and additions to *Rosh's halachic* compendium by R' Yisrael of Krems, Austria (early 14th century).

Hagahos Maimoni — Notes on *Rambam's Mishnah Torah* often citing opinions of the Tosafists, by R' Moshe *HaKohen*, a disciple of *Maharam* of Rottenburg. R' Moshe and his family perished in the massacres instigated by Rindfleish in 1298.

Horeb — An analysis of the fundamentals of Judaism and the philosophy of the *mitzvos* by R' Samson Raphael Hirsch (1808-1889), *Rav* of Frankfurt am Main and foremost leader of Orthodox German Jewry.

Ibn Ezra — R' Avraham b' Meir Ibn Ezra (1089-1164) poet, philosopher, grammarian and author of Biblical commentary by that name.

Igros Moshe — Responsa by R' Moshe Feinstein of New York, contemporary leading *halachic* authority (1895-1986).

Imrei Baruch — Gloss to *Shulchan Aruch* by R' Baruch Teomim Frankel, *Rav* of Leipnick, Moravia and author of *Sefer Baruch Taam* (late 18th — early 19th century).

Issur V'heter — *Halachic* compendium by R' Yonah b' Yisrael a disciple of *Terumas Ha'deshen* (late 15th century). Much of *Ashkenazic* tradition regarding dietary laws is based upon *Issur V'heter.*

Kaf HaChaim — Commentary to *Shulchan Aruch Orach Chaim* and part of *Yoreh De'ah* by R' Yaakov Chaim Soffer of Baghdad and later Jerusalem (1870-1939).

Kli Yakar — Commentary to the Torah by R' Shlomo Efraim Lunshitz of Prague (d. 1619).

Kreisi U'pleisi — Commentary to the first part of *Shulchan Aruch: Yoreh De'ah,* by R' Yonasan Eibshutz (1680-1764), renowned *Rav* of Prague.

Levush — *Halachic* codex closely following the style and order of the *Shulchan Aruch* by R' Mordechai Yafeh, Known by the name "*Levush*" after his many works whose names begin with that word (c.1535-1612).

Maadanei HaShulchan — Contemporary commentary to *Shulchan Aruch: Yoreh De'ah, Hilchos Basar B'chalav* and *Taarovos* by Rav Levi Rabinowitz (published in Jerusalem 1986).

Machtzis Hashekel — Comprehensive commentary to the *Magen Avraham* by R' Shmuel HaLevi Kelin (1724-1806).

Magen Avraham — The monumental commentary to *Shulchan Aruch Orach Chaim* by R' Avraham Gombiner (c.1634-1682).

Maharam Rotenburg — Acronym for *Moreinu Harav* R' Meir b' Baruch HaLevy of Rotenburg (1320-1390). One of the greatest *halachic* authorities of his time. *Rosh* and *Mordechai* were among his disciples.

Maharam Shick — Acronym for *Moreinu HaRav* Moshe Shick, author of responsa bearing that name, *Rav* of Chust, Hungary (1807-1879).

Maharshal — Acronym for *Moreinu HaRav* R' Shlomo Luria (1510-1573). Contemporary of *Rema.* Authored responsa and *sefer Yam Shel Shlomo,* a Talmudic commentary consisting of *halachic* essays on seven tractates.

Maharsham — Acronym for *Moreinu HaRav* Shalom Mordechai (Schwadron) noted for his responsa bearing that name, see *Daas Torah.*

Matamei HaShulchan — Additional notes to *Maadanei HaShulchan* see "*Maadanei HaShulchan.*"

Mateh Yonasan — Gloss to *Shulchan Aruch* by R' Yonasan Eibshutz, see "*Kreisi U'pleisi*".

Melamed L'hoil — Responsa of R' Dovid Tzvi Hoffmann Dean of the Rabbinical Seminary of Berlin (1843-1921).

Metzudas Tzion — Glosses on *Kitzur Shulchan Aruch* by R' Dovid Feldman, contemporary Rav in Manchester England.

Minchas Chinuch — *Chiddushim* on the 613 *mitzvos* by R' Yosef Babad (1800-1875), Rav of Tarnipol, Poland (now Ukraine), based upon *sefer Hachinuch* (Lemberg 1869). See "*Chinuch*".

Minchas Kohen — In depth analysis of the various opinions in the *Rishonim* regarding laws of *Taarovos* and *Shabbos* by R' Avraham HaKohen Pimental of Amsterdam, later *Rav* in Hamburg (mid 17th century). His opinions are cited by *Shach* and other *Poskim.*

Minchas Shlomo — Responsa by Rav Shlomo Zalman Auerbach, leading contemporary *halachic* authority and Rosh Yeshiva, Kol Torah, Jerusalem.

Minchas Yaakov — Commentary to *Toras Chatas* of *Rema* by R' Yaakov Reisher, see *"Chok Yaakov"*.

Minchas Yitzchok — Responsa of R' Yitzchak Yaakov Weiss Rav in Manchester, England and later *Rav* of the *Eidah HaChareidis* in Jerusalem (d. 1989).

Mishbetzos Zahav — see *Pri Migadim*

Mishnah B'rurah — Commentary to *Shulchan Aruch Orach Chaim* by R' Yisrael Meir *(HaKohen)* Kagan of Radun, Poland (1839-1933) known by the title of his classical compendium on the laws of *lashon ha'ra — Chafetz Chaim*.

Mishneh L'melech — *Chiddushim* on *Rambam's Mishneh Torah* by R' Yehudah Rosanes (1657-1727), *Rav* in Constantinople, Turkey.

Mordechai — *Halachic* compendium on most tractates of the Talmud by R' Mordechai ben Hillel (born c. 1240) R' Mordechai and his family perished in the massacres instigated by Rindfleish in 1298.

Nekudas Hakesef — Critical notes on *Taz* by R' Shabsai *HaKohen*, see *"Shach"*.

Nishmas Adam — Glosses on the *Chayei Adam* by the author, see *Chayei Adam.*

Noda B'Yehudah — Responsa by R' Yechezkel Landau, *Rav* of Prague (1713-1793), see *"Dagul Mervavah"*.

Ol'los Efrayim — *Halachic* rulings by R' Efrayim Zalman Margulies of Brodi (1762-1828).

Orach Chaim — One of the four sections of the *Tur* and *Shulchan Aruch*, dealing with laws of daily practice throughout the year.

Pischei Halachah — A short *halachic* work in Hebrew by the author on *halachos* of *Kashrus* (New York 1984).

Pischei Teshuvah — References to responsa works, following the order of *Shulchan Aruch* by R' Tzvi Hirsh Eisenstadt *Rav* of Utian, Lithuania (1812-1868).

Piskei Teshuvah — Short responsa and *halachic chiddushim* by R' Avraham Pietrokovski, *Dayan* in Lodz, Poland (published by author in 1933).

Pri Chadash — Commentary to the *Shulchan Aruch* by R' Chizkiyah de Silva (b. Leghorn, Italy, 1659, d. Jerusalem 1698).

Pri Migadim — A two part commentary to the *Shulchan Aruch,* on *Yoreh De'ah — Mishbetzos Zahav* on the *Turei Zahav (Taz)* and *Sifsei De'ah* on the *Sifsei Kohen (Shach)* — by R' Yosef Teomim, *maggid* of Lvov and later *Rav* of Frankfurt on the Oder (1727-1792).

Pri Toar — Commentary to the first part of *Shulchan Aruch: Yoreh De'ah* by R' Chaim b' Atar, author of the classical Biblical commentary *Ohr HaChaim*. Born in Sale, Morocco (1696) and died in Jerusalem (1743).

R' Akiva Eiger — Author of responsa *Teshuvos R' Akiva Eiger* (1761-1857) and many important *halachic* works, *Rav* of Posen (Prussia/Poland).

R' Tzadok HaKohen — (Rabinowitz) Lithuanian *gadol* who became a *chassid* of R' Mordechai Yosef Leiner of Izbica and eventually a leader of *Chassidim* in Lublin (1823-1900). Authored many works on *Chassidic* thought and responsa *Tiferes Tzvi.*

Raavad — Acronym of R' Avraham ben David of Posquieres, Talmudist and *Halachist* (c. 1120 — c. 1197)

Rabbeinu Bachaya — Disciple of *Rashba,* Torah commentator and kabbalist (d. c. 1340).

Rabbeinu Tam — R' Yaakov b' Meir (1100-1171), grandson of *Rashi* and one of the earliest and greatest of the Tosafists.

Rabbeinu Yerucham — R' Yerucham b' Meshulam (1280-1350). French Talmudist, author of *Toldos Adam V'Chavah,* a *halachic* compendium of all laws concerning a person throughout his lifetime.

Radvaz — Acronym for R' David ben Zimra author of an extensive responsa bearing that name, Chief Rabbi of Egypt (c. 1480-1573).

Rambam — Acronym for R' Moshe ben Maimon ["Maimonides"], author of the *Mishnah Torah — Yad HaChazakah* (1135-1204).

Ran — Acronym for R' Nissim, *Halachist* and Talmudic Commentator (c. 1290 — c. 1375).

Rashba — Acronym for R' Shlomo Ibn Aderes, Rav of Barcelona, known for his Talmudic Commentary and many responsa (1235-1310).

Rashi — Acronym for R' Shlomo Yitzchaki, leading Commentator on the Torah and the Talmud (1040-1105).

Rav Shlomo Z. Auerbach — see *Minchas Shlomo.*

Rav Y.S. Eliashiv — Leading contemporary *halachic* authority, *Dayan* in Jerusalem.

Rav Moshe Stern — See *"Be'er Moshe"*.

Rav Yosef Breuer — Grandson of R' Samson Raphael Hirsh, Rav and founder of the Frankfort *kehillah* in Washington Heights N.Y. (1882-1980).

Re'ah — Acronym for R' Aharon HaLevy (1230-1300). *Rav* of Barcelona, Spain (with *Rashba*). See *"Bedek HaBayis"*.

Rema — Acronym for R' Moshe Isserles, *Rav* and *Rosh Yeshiva* of Cracow. Author of *Sefer HaMapah* — annotations to R' Yosef Caro's *Shulchan Aruch* and *Darcei Moshe* to the *Tur;* ultimate *halachic* authority for all of *Ashkenazic* Jewry (1530-1572).

Reshash — Acronym for R' Shmuel Shtrashun of Vilna (1794-1872), author of supra commentary to Talmud, printed in the back of most editions of the Talmud.

Rif — Acronym for R' Yitzchak al-Fasi, Talmudist and Codifier (1013-1103).

Ritva — Acronym for R' Yom Tov Ibn Asevili, 14th century Talmudic commentator and *Halachist.*

Rivah — Acronym for R' Yitzchak b' Asher, 12th century Tosafist, headed a Yeshivah in Speyer, Germany.

Rosh — Acronym for R' Asher ben Yechiel, Talmudic Commentator and author of *Halachic* compendium arranged on the tractates of the Talmud, bearing his name (c. 1250-1327).

Salmas Chaim — Responsa of R' Yosef Chaim Sonnenfeld, *Rav* of the *Eidah HaChareidis* in Jerusalem (1848-1932).

Sefer Haterumos — *Halachic* compendium dealing with financial laws by R' Shmuel HaSardi, commonly referred to as the *Baal Sefer HaTerumos* (1190-1256) a Spanish *halachist*. His views on many subjects are quoted by *Tur.*

Shaagas Aryeh — *Chiddushim* on *halachic* subjects by R' Aryeh Leib Gunzberg (1695-1785).

Shaar Ha'tziyun — Footnotes containing source material for *Mishnah B'rurah* by the author, see *Mishnah B'rurah.*

Shaarei Teshuvah — References to responsa works arranged to the *Shulchan Aruch Orach Chaim* by R' Chaim Mordechai Margulies, Rav of Dubno, Russia, completed by his brother R' Efrayim Zalman Margulies, see *Ol'los Efrayim.*

Shaarei Yosher — A book of penetrating analysis of the Talmudic concepts of *safek, rov* and *chazakah,* by R' Shimon Shkop (1860-1940), *Rosh Yeshiva* of Grodno, Russia.

Shach — Acronym for *Sifsei Kohen,* classical commentary to *Shulchan Aruch Yoreh De'ah* by R' Shabsai HaKohen of Vilna (1622-1663).

Shoel U'meishiv — Responsa by R' Yosef Shaul Nathanson (1810-1875), *Rav* of Lemberg (Lvov, Poland, now Ukraine).

Shulchan Aruch — Universally accepted *Halachic* compendium encompassing all facets of practical *halachah,* by R' Yosef Caro (1488-1575).

Sidei Chemed — *Halachic* encyclopedia of many volumes covering a wide range of subjects by R' Chaim Chizkiyahu Medini, *Rav* of Karasubazar in Crimea, Russia (1832-1904). We have used the Freidman edition (New York 1962) and used those volume and page numbers for reference.

Smak — Acronym for *Sefer Mitzvos Kattan.* A compendium of all the *mitzvos* applicable today, by R' Yitzchak b' Yosef of Corbell (d. 1280).

Smag — Acronym for *Sefer Mitzvos Gadol.* A comprehensive compendium of the 613 *mitzvos*, by R' Moshe b' Yaakov of Coucy, an early 13th century Tosafist. Because this compendium is more extensive than that of R' Yitzchok of Corbell, they became known as *"Gadol"* and *"Kattan"* respectively.

S'ridei Eish — Responsa of R' Yechiel Yaakov Weinberg (1885-1966). Rector at the Hildesheimer Seminary in Berlin. Spent his last years in Montreux, Switzerland.

Taz — Acronym for *Turei Zahav*, classical commentary to all of the *Shulchan Aruch* especially *Orach Chaim* and *Yoreh De'ah* by R' David HaLevi *Rav* of Ostroh and later in Lemberg (1586-1667).

Teshuvos HaRosh — Responsa of *Rosh*, see *"Rosh"*.

Tiferes Yisrael — Commentary to the entire *Mishnah* by R' Yisrael Lipshitz (1782-1860), *Rav* in Danzig, Poland.

Toras Chaim — Commentary to *Chullin* and several other tractates, by R' Avraham Chaim Shor (d. 1632), served as Rav in Belz, Kremenitz, Satanov and Lemberg.

Toras Chatas — *Halachic* compendium of the *halachos* of *melichah, basar b'chalav* and *taarovos*, by *Rema*, see *"Rema"*.

Toras HaAsham — Commentary to *Rema's Toras Chatas* by R' Yom Tov Lipman Heller, see *"Divrei Chamudos"*.

Toras HaBayis — *Halachic* compendium of dietary laws, composed of the unabridged work *(Toras HaBayis Ha'aruch)* and a synopsis *(Toras HaBayis Hakatzer)*, by *Rashba*, see *"Rashba"*.

Tosfos — Talmudic commentaries of the Tosafists; the school of French and German Talmudic analysts of 12th and 13th centuries.

Terumas Ha'deshen — Responsa of R' Yisrael Isserlein, German *Halachist* (c.1390-1460).

Tur — *Halachic* compendium of R' Yaakov Baal HaTurim, son of the *Rosh*, upon which the *Shulchan Aruch* is based and patterned (c. 1275 — c. 1340).

Tzitz Eliezer — Contemporary responsa by R' Eliezer Yehudah Valdenberg, *halachic* authority and member of the *Beis Din* in Jerusalem.

Yabia Omer — Responsa by Rav Ovadiah Yossef, see *"Yechaveh Daas"*.

Yad Avraham — Gloss to Shulchan Aruch: Yoreh De'ah by R' Avraham *Maskil Le'aison* of Minsk, Russia (1788-1848).

Yad Efraim — Glosses on the *Magen Avraham* by R' Efrayim Zalman Margulies, see *Ol'los Efrayim.*

Yad Yehudah — A major commentary to the first part of *Shulchan Aruch: Yoreh De'ah* by R' Yehudah Leibush Landau, Rav of Sadigora (published by author in 1892).

Yoreh De'ah — One of the four sections of the *Tur* and *Shulchan Aruch,* dealing primarily with the laws of kashrus and purity.

Yechaveh Daas — Contemporary responsa by Rav Ovadiah Yossef, *halachic* authority and formerly *Rishon L'Tziyon* in Jerusalem.

Zeir HaShulchan — Contemporary commentary to *Shulchan Aruch: Yoreh De'ah, Hilchos Basar B'chalav* by Rav Moshe E. Traube (published in Jerusalem 1991).

Zeir Zahav — Commentary to *Issur V'heter* by R' Avraham Brown, Rav in vicinity of Ponevezh (published by author in 1891).

Zichron L'Moshe — A collection of eulogies, letters and stories about *Chasam Sofer,* collected and published by R' Yosef Stern, Rav of Grossverdein, Hungary, in 1938 commemorating the 100 anniversary of the death of *Chasam Sofer.*

TABLE OF ABBREVIATIONS

A.A. — Aishel Avraham
A.H. — Aruch Ha'Shulchan
B.H. — Biur Halachah
D.T. — Darcei Teshuvah
M.A. — Magen Avraham
M.B. — Mishnah B'rurah
M.Z. — Mishbetzos Zahav
O.C. — Orach Chaim
P.M. — Pri Migadim
P.T. — Pischei Teshuvah
S.A. — Shulchan Aruch
S.D. — Sifsei De'ah
Y.D. — Yoreh De'ah

Index

⁂ Index Of Primary Sources

This index will be most useful for someone studying these *halachos* from their primary sources. Any citation of *Issur V'heter, Shulchan Aruch: Yoreh De'ah, Rema, Taz* and *Shach* in this book will be found in this index. Thus, someone studying these texts will be able to easily relate their opinions to practical *halachos*.

TAZ	
87:4	188
87:5	186, 187
89:2	197
89:3	197
89:4	209
89:5	204
89:6	210, 307, 313, 337, 338
91:1	126
91:3	286
91:7	122, 123, 271
91:12	275
92:9	71, 380
92:11	72, 381
92:12	72
92:15	69
92:17	293
92:19	293, 294
92:20	294
92:22	294
92:25	398, 299
92:28	295, 296
92:30	114
93:2	131, 267, 272
94:1	113, 284, 393, 394
94:4	182, 286
94:5	284
94:13	304
94:14	116, 317, 383
95:1	156, 157, 397
95:3	157, 160, 241
95:4	160, 241
95:8	286
95:9	248
95:10	248
95:12	249, 250
95:13	278

TAZ	
95:14	251
95:15	251
96:3	319, 329, 332, 382
96:4	326
96:5	70, 172, 326, 328, 387
96:9	332, 383
96:10	321
96:12	313, 323, 383
96:13	314, 332
96:14	310
97:3	228
98:2	96-98, 395
98:7	102
98:8	104, 105
99:7	74, 75, 371, 372
99:10	75, 372
99:13	68
101:5	64, 380
102:8	65
102:10	62, 385
103:1	79, 85
103:2	81
103:3	83
103:9	89
105:1	267, 268
105:3	128
105:4	111, 115, 282, 298, 394, 403
105:5	124, 125
105:6	121, 279
105:13	70
108:1	139, 400
108:5	144
109:1	54, 55, 377
109:3	60
116:2	380
117:1	182